Christianity and Monasticism in Middle Egypt

Christianity and Monasticism in Middle Egypt

AL-MINYA AND ASYUT

Edited by
Gawdat Gabra
Hany N. Takla

A Saint Mark Foundation Book
The American University in Cairo Press
Cairo New York

113 Sharia Kasr el Aini, Cairo, Egypt
420 Fifth Avenue, New York, NY 10018
www.aucpress.com

Exclusive distribution outside Egypt and North America by I.B.Tauris & Co Ltd.,
6 Salem Road, London, W2 4BU

Dar el Kutub No. 23357/13
ISBN 978 977 416 663 1

Dar el Kutub Cataloging-in-Publication Data
Gabra, Gawdat
Christianity and Monasticism in Middle Egypt/Gawdat Gabra, Hany Takla.—Cairo: The American University in Cairo Press, 2015
p. cm.
ISBN: 978 977 416 663 1
1. Coptic Church—History
2. Coptic Monasticism and religious order—Egypt
I. Takla, Hany (jt. Author)
276.2301

1 2 3 4 5 19 18 17 16 15

Designed by Jon W. Stoy
Printed in Egypt

This volume is dedicated to Peter Grossmann in acknowledgment of his great efforts during the past half century in excavating, documenting, studying, and publishing the heritage of Egypt's Christian architecture

Contents

Illustrations

Contributors

Dominique Bénazeth is curator in the Coptic section of the Egyptian department of the Louvre Museum. She led the Louvre-IFAO excavations in Bawit from 2002 to 2007.

Renate Dekker studied Egyptology and Coptology at Leiden University and wrote her MPhil thesis on the "Encomium on Bishop Pesynthios of Koptos." She is currently working on her dissertation, on episcopal social networks ofTheban bishops (Abraham of Hermonthis, Pesynthios of Koptos) in late antique Egypt, at Leiden University.

Alain Delattre is assistant professor at the Université Libre de Bruxelles, working in Greek and Coptic papyrology. His dissertation (2004) was on papyri from the monastery of Bawit (Middle Egypt).

Frank Feder is a research associate at the Berlin-Brandenburg Academy of Sciences and Humanities. He holds a doctorate from the Martin-Luther-Universität Halle-Wittenberg, has taught at the Institut für Ägyptologie und Koptologie of the Westfälische Wilhelms-Universität in Münster, and has worked on dictionaries of ancient Egyptian and an edition of the Coptic Septuagint.

Cäcilia Fluck is a curator at the Skulpturensammlung und Museum für Byzantinische Kunst, Staatliche Museen zu Berlin, Stiftung Preußischer Kulturbesitz, where she is responsible for the artifacts of Late Antique and Early Christian Egypt. She has published books and articles on Egyptian epigraphy and archaeology, particularly textiles, of those periods.

Sherin Sadek El Gendi is associate professor of Coptic and Islamic art and archaeology in the Faculty of Arts, Ain Shams University. She is a member of the International Association for Coptic Studies, the Société d'Archéologie Copte in Cairo, and the Société archéologique d'Alexandrie.

James E. Goehring is professor of religion at the University of Mary Washington in Fredericksburg, Virginia. He has authored numerous works in the field of early Egyptian asceticism, including *Ascetics, Society and the Desert: Studies in Early Egyptian Monasticism* (1999) and *Politics, Monasticism, and Miracles in Sixth Century Upper Egypt* (2012).

Gisèle Hadji-Minaglou is an architect and archaeologist, and a researcher at the Institut français d'archéologie orientale (IFAO) in Cairo. She is in charge of the IFAO and Louvre Museum excavations at Bawit; chief excavator of the IFAO and Milan University mission in Tebtynis, Fayyum; and a member of the IFAO mission at Balat in Dakhla Oasis.

Karel Innemée is an affiliated fellow at the Faculty of Archaeology, Leiden University (Netherlands). He is the project director of the Leiden Wadi al-Natrun project, which includes excavation at Dayr al-Baramus, survey at the site of Dayr Abu Maqar, and conservation work at Dayr al-Surian.

Jochem Kahl is the chair of Egyptology at the Freie Universität Berlin. He received his PhD at the University of Tübingen in 1992. He is a visiting professor at the universities of Cologne and Vienna, project director and field director of the archaeological fieldwork at Asyut, and the author of several monographs and articles about Asyut.

Mary Kupelian is a lecturer in the Faculty of Tourism and Hotel Management, Helwan University. In June 2010, she was awarded a PhD in tourism guidance; her dissertation was on "Art and Archaeology in Egypt in the Byzantine Era" under the joint supervision of Helwan University and Leiden University (Netherlands). Her research interests include Coptic monastic wall paintings and the Armenian heritage in Egypt.

AnneMarie Luijendijk, professor of religion at Princeton University, is a scholar of early Christianity and a papyrologist. She holds degrees from Harvard Divinity School and the Vrije Universiteit Amsterdam. Her main publications are *Greetings in the Lord: Early Christians and the Oxyrhynchus Papyri* (2008) and *Forbidden Oracles: The Gospel of the Lots of Mary* (2014).

Bishop Martyros is General Bishop in the Coptic Orthodox Church in Cairo. He was formerly the hegumen of the Syrian Monastery in Wadi al-Natrun. He is a frequent contributor to international conferences of Coptology. He has authored multiple books on Coptic monasticism in Wadi al-Natrun.

Howard Middleton-Jones is an archaeologist with a special interest in the Coptic period in Egypt. He teaches Coptic Studies modules for the part-time humanities degree and the Department of Continuing Adult Education at Swansea University, Wales, UK. He is also the originator and author of the Coptic Multi-Media Database project.

Samuel Moawad is a researcher at the Institute for Egyptology and Coptology at the University of Münster (Germany), specializing in Coptic and Copto-Arabic literature.

Fr. Angelos al-Muharraqi is a monk, a specialist in studying and documenting the monastery's history, heritage, and antiques, and the editor of several books on these subjects.

Fr. Philoxenos al-Muharraqi is an active member of a group of monks studying the history, heritage, and antiques of the Monastery of the Holy Virgin Mary at al-Muharraq, Mount Qusqam. He is also responsible for foreign visitors and tour programs in the monastery.

Ashraf Nageh is a specialist conservator of wall paintings and building materials at the Supreme Council of Antiquities in Egypt. He is a member of the French mission in Bawit and the Dutch mission in Hammam Faroun. He holds a doctorate from Cairo University and participates in various restoration projects.

Adel F. Sadek is a lecturer at the Institute of Coptic Studies, Anba Ruways, Cairo. For many years he participated in the restoration of manuscripts of the Coptic Patriarchate and many monasteries. He has authored a number of books in Arabic about the history and heritage of several Coptic dioceses. He is currently a member of the editorial board of *Bulletin of Rakoti: Spotlight on Coptic Studies*, published in Arabic in Alexandria.

Ashraf Alexandre Sadek, professor of Egyptology, Coptology, and biblical archaeology at the University of Limoges (France), is the author of many books and articles of research in these fields and editor of the cultural collection *Le Monde Copte*. He also teaches in several faculties of theology in Europe and Egypt and gives lectures in many countries.

Sami Sabri Shaker has designed several cathedrals in the Coptic style. For many years he taught Coptic architecture and has published several articles. He is currently dean of the Institute of Coptic Studies, department head of Coptic architecture, professor of architecture at Cairo University, and affiliate professor at the American University in Cairo.

Mark Sheridan, originally from Washington, D.C., is a Benedictine monk of Dormition Abbey in Jerusalem and professor emeritus in the Faculty of Theology of the Pontificio Ateneo S. Anselmo, Rome, where he served as dean of the Faculty of Theology (1998–2005) and Rector Magnificus (2005–2009) of the Athenaeum. He continues his research in the areas of Coptology and ancient Christian literature.

Mark N. Swanson is the Harold S. Vogelaar Professor of Christian–Muslim Studies and Interfaith Relations at the Lutheran School of Theology at Chicago; previously he taught in St. Paul, Minnesota and in Cairo. He is the author of *The Coptic Papacy in Islamic Egypt (641–1517)* (2010), and was the Christian Arabic section editor for *Christian–Muslim Relations: A Bibliographical History,* vols. 1–5 (2009–13).

Hany N. Takla is founding president of the St. Shenouda the Archimandrite Coptic Society, director of the St. Shenouda Center of Coptic Studies, Coptic language instructor at the Pope Shenouda III Theological College in Los Angeles, and a member of the board of trustees for the St. Mark Coptic Cultural Center in Cairo. He is currently a Coptic-language lecturer at the University of California, Los Angeles (UCLA).

Asuka Tsuji is a postdoctoral research fellow of the Japan Society for the Promotion of Science at the Institute of Advanced Studies on Asia, University of Tokyo. She received her PhD from the University of Tokyo in 2014. Her current research interest is the history of the Coptic Church in the medieval period.

Jacques van der Vliet is professor of Egyptian religion at Radboud University, Nijmegen, and lecturer of Coptic at Leiden University, the Netherlands. His research covers most aspects of the literary culture of Egyptian and Nubian Christianity in late-antique and medieval times, with a particular focus on Gnostic and apocryphal scripture, magic, epigraphy, and papyrology.

Gertrud J.M. van Loon is a researcher at KU Leuven (Belgium). Her research interests include painting, iconography and iconology, and early monasticism. She is currently working in Middle Egypt, documenting monastic sites in pharaonic quarries and tombs.

Youhanna Nessim Youssef received his PhD from the University of Montpellier, France in 1996. He has worked in the Centre for Early Christian Studies, Australian Catholic University since 1999. He has published numerous journal articles and book chapters. He is now writing a book on the times and legacy of Severus of Antioch.

Ewa D. Zakrzewska holds an MA in Egyptology and a PhD in linguistics. She is an affiliated member of the Amsterdam Center for Language and Communication (ACLC) of the University of Amsterdam and a subject specialist in the university library. She seeks to apply insights from functional-typological linguistics, text linguistics, and contact linguistics to the study of Coptic, especially Bohairic.

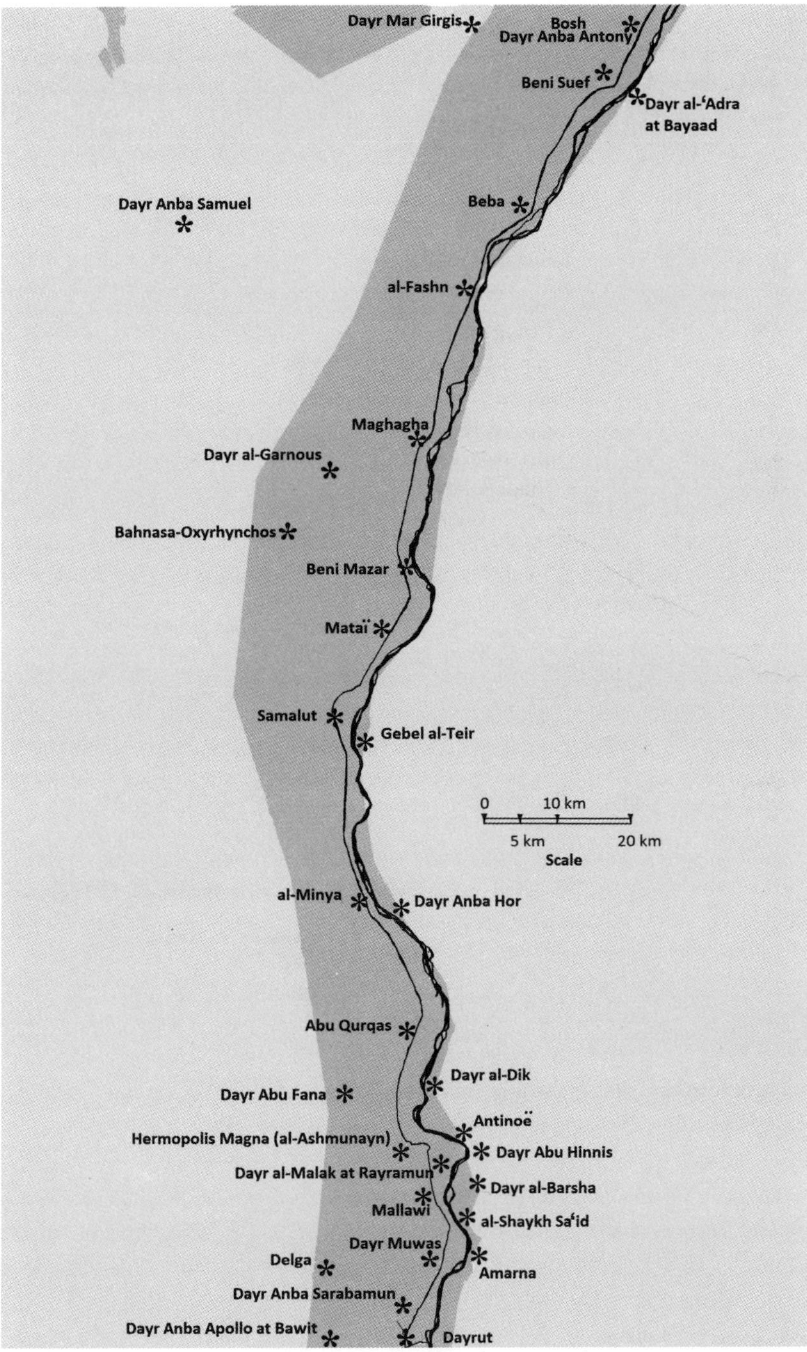

Map 1. Major Christian sites in the governorate of al-Minya

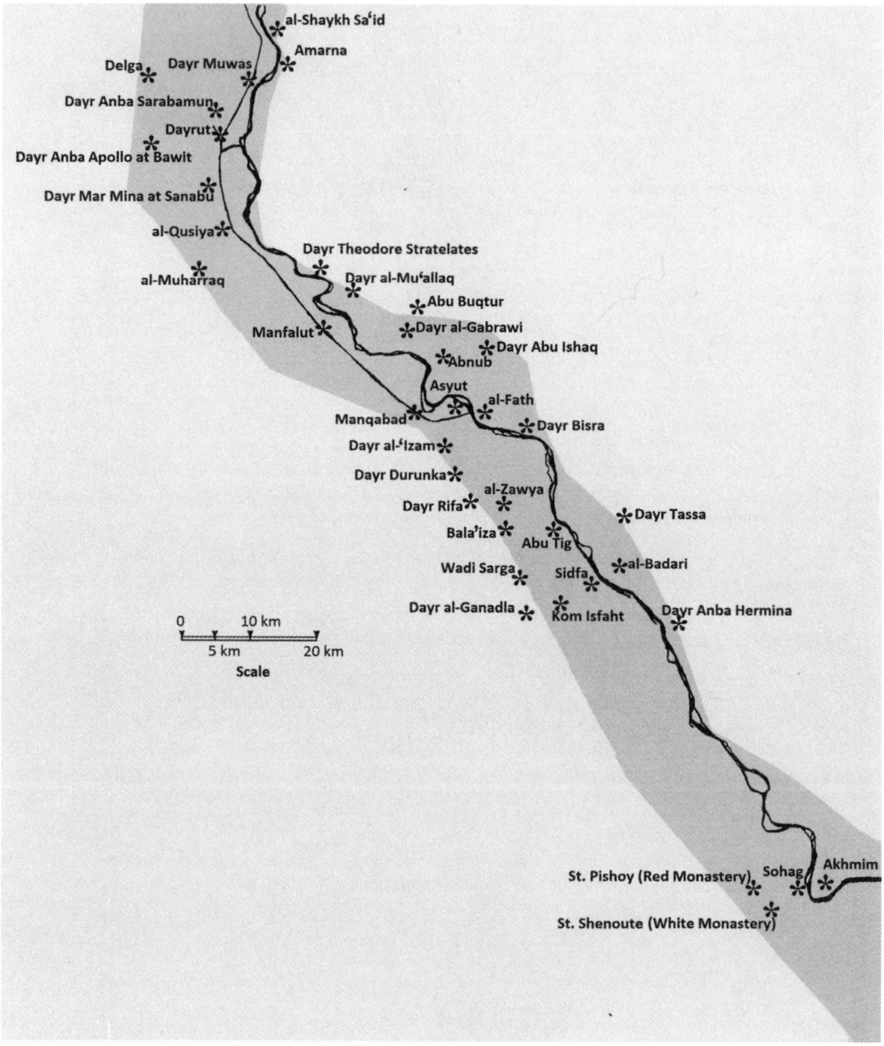

Map 2. Major Christian sites in the governorate of Asyut

Foreword

This is the sixth volume of the series *Christianity and Monasticism in Egypt*. It contains the essays presented at the sixth international symposium of the St. Mark Foundation for Coptic History Studies and the St. Shenouda the Archimandrite Coptic Society.

I am greatly blessed and honored by the invaluable support of His Holiness Pope Tawadros II, who personally inaugurated the symposium at al-Muharraq, received all its organizers and participants, and encouraged them to continue their research in the various aspects of Coptic monasticism. It was an unforgettable event that the first visit of His Holiness to a monastery after his enthronement as the 118th Pope of Alexandria and Patriarch of the See of St. Mark coincided with the occasion of our symposium.

The symposium was held on 4–8 February 2013 at the famous monastery of the Holy Virgin Mary, known as al-Muharraq. I am glad that the symposium was international and thus this volume brings together the contributions of scholars from Australia, Belgium, England, France, Germany, Japan, the Netherlands, Poland, and the United States in addition to a number of Egyptians. They represent Coptic studies and a variety of related fields, reflecting the multifaceted richness of Coptic civilization. I would like to thank each of the contributors for their valuable chapters, in particular those who traveled to Dayr al-Muharraq, deep in Upper Egypt, at that time. I look forward to the next symposium of the St. Mark

Foundation that will be held in the Monastery of St. Menas (Dayr Mari Mina) near Alexandria in February 2015.

I would like to give special thanks to Bishop Sawirus, Abbot of the Monastery of the Holy Virgin Mary (Dayr al-Muharraq), for hosting the symposium. I thank Father Beniamin al-Muharraqy for his great effort during the symposium.

My thanks are due to all the supporters of the symposium. My thanks go also to the symposium's organizing committee: Fahim Wassef, Dr. Mary Kupelian, and Dr. Ashraf Nageh. I would like to single out Hoda Garas, who finalized contacts with the contributors.

Finally, I extend my thanks to the American University in Cairo Press for their interest and dedication in publishing the proceedings of our symposia, especially to Nigel Fletcher-Jones, Neil Hewison, Nadia Naqib, and Johanna Baboukis.

Fawzy Estafanous, President
The St. Mark Foundation for
Coptic History Studies

Introduction

THIS VOLUME, *Christianity and Monasticism in Middle Egypt: Al-Minya and Asyut*, contains the papers that were presented in the sixth international symposium of the Saint Mark Foundation for Coptic History Studies and the St. Shenouda the Archimandrite Coptic Society. The symposium was held in the Monastery of the Holy Virgin Mary (Dayr al-Muharraq), 17–21 February 2013. A considerable number of scholars withdrew a few months, or even a few weeks, before the symposium, probably because of the uncertain political and security situation of Egypt at that time. Fortunately, some of those who were unable to participate in the symposium submitted their papers for publication. Thus the Christian heritage of each important site of that vast region, covering today the two governorates of al-Minya and Asyut, is represented by at least one chapter. Taken together, the contributors considered five main areas: Oxyrhynchos (al-Bahnasa); the sites of Antinoë, Hermopolis (al-Ashmunayn), and al-Shaykh Sa'id; Bawit; Dayr al-Muharraq; and Asyut.

The significant ancient city of Oxyrhynchos, which continued to grow in importance in late antiquity and became the capital of "Middle Egypt," yielded an enormous number of papyri. Only a few remains of Christian buildings have been encountered there, although literary and papyrological sources show that Christianity and monasticism flourished there for many centuries and the city was known as an episcopal see from the early centuries of Christianity and during medieval times. Bishops of al-Bahnasa (Oxyrhynchos) are attested also in the Ottoman period, even though they did not necessarily reside there. AnneMarie Luijendijk examines and intensively discusses the papyrological evidence and literary sources for female ascetics at Oxyrhynchos from the fourth and fifth centuries. She sheds light on the socioeconomic milieu and lifestyle of those ascetic women known as domestic virgins. Sherin Sadek El Gendi introduces Arabic sources that describe al-Bahnasa as a city and the situation of Christianity there during the centuries after the Arab conquest of Egypt. Bishop Martyros studies the sources related to Bishop Isaac, a remarkable and influential bishop of al-Bahnasa during the nineteenth century. Bishop Martyros touches on Egypt's political changes and the major developments in the history of the Coptic Church at that time. Frank Feder provides a list of all the published biblical, literary, and documentary texts that are written in the Mesokemic or Middle Egyptian Coptic dialect, known also as the dialect of Oxyrhynchos. He discusses its morphophonological characteristics and geographical situation.

Farther to the south, on the west bank of the Nile, lay the Monastery of Abu Fana and Hermopolis Magna (al-Ashmunayn); Antinoë occupies a large area on the east bank of the Nile opposite to them. The Monastery of Abu Fana was named after the fourth-century hermit Bane and it continued to be inhabited as late as the fourteenth century. An Austrian expedition carried out excavations there between 1987 and 1993 and discovered the remains of a fourth-century church with the tomb of St. Bane below the pavement of a sixth-century church. Hermopolis, a famous ancient Egyptian city, was the residence of a bishop beginning in the second half of the third century. It is mentioned in the *History of the Monks of Egypt* around the year 400 as a site of the Flight of the Holy Family into Egypt, and it has an imposing fifth-century cathedral. Antinoë, founded by Emperor Hadrian around AD 130, became one of Egypt's major cities in late antiquity. Beginning in the late nineteenth century, its monuments were excavated by a number of expeditions. Since 2000, an international team under the leadership of Rosario Pintaudi has been exploring the entire ancient town of Antinoë that is of great importance for the remains of its churches, monastic settlements, cemeteries, and enormous amount of textiles. The cliffs on the east bank of the Nile feature a number of ancient Egyptian necropolises of rock tombs that were inhabited by monks, such as those of al-Shaykh Sa'id and Tell al-Amarna.

Asuka Tsuji summarizes the Arabic *Life of Ibrahim al-Fani,* a Coptic saint of the fourteenth century. She tells the story of his early life, sufferings, discipleship under Marqus al-Antuni, and death. Tsuji discusses the date and purpose of the compilation of the life of that saint, and its literal, religious, and social implications as well. Samuel Moawad explores the tendency of praising and ennobling Egypt and the Copts in the writings of John of Shmoun on St. Antony and St. Mark. John was a contemporary of Patriarch Damianus (578–604). Moawad touches on the literary works of other Coptic writers concerning that issue. Căcilia Fluck publishes textiles from four children's burials that were discovered in 2007 in a peristyle complex at the eastern edge of the northern cemetery of Antinoë, in which coins and papyri that date from the third to the seventh centuries AD were found. She concludes that these children might have belonged to middle-class families, that the crosses found on some of their shrouds and on the shrouds of other burials witness to their Christian belief, and that the way in which their corpses were treated with textiles reflects a respected status. Gertrud van Loon introduces a significant project that aims to investigate the monastic heritage in the Old Kingdom tombs of the site of al-Shaykh Sa'id and of its surroundings and to document the building activities, decoration, and inscriptions there. Most modern archaeological methods of mapping and field surveys are applied.

The archaeological remains of the great Monastery of St. Apollo at Bawit are located between Hermopolis (al-Ashmunayn) and Dayr al-Muharraq on the west bank of the Nile at the foot of the cliffs on the edge of the desert. The monastery prospered from the sixth to the ninth century. This site suffered from illegal diggings in the late nineteenth century. At the beginning of the twentieth century Jean Clédat, Émile Chassinat, and Jean Maspero carried out soundings and excavations there. In 1976 excavations were again carried out by the Egyptian Organization of Antiquities. Beginning in 2002 new campaigns were undertaken by a team of the Institut français d'archéologie orientale (IFAO) and the Musée du Louvre, first under the direction of Dominique Bénazeth, later on under Gisèle Hadji-Minaglou. The Bawit carvings and wall paintings are of great significance for the history of Coptic art. Bawit yielded hundreds of ostraca and papyri that are mainly of documentary evidence. The last twenty years witnessed remarkable progress in investigating, reevaluating, and publishing the legacy of Bawit. Dominique Bénazeth provides a "Bawit Bibliography" that includes forthcoming publications. She enhances the value of this bibliography by classifying the data into nine categories: texts; artifacts in museums; topography; twentieth-century excavations; twenty-first-century excavations; monuments; sculpture; painting; and objects. It is known that only a small percentage of the vast archaeological site of Bawit has been examined. Gisèle Hadji-Minaglou introduces the results of the Bawit excavations that were accomplished there till the end of the 2012 season. She concludes that the South Church and the main basilica go back to the beginning of the seventh century; the latter features rebuilding until the beginning of the ninth century. The North Church was built at the end of the seventh century or the beginning of the eighth century. The pottery survey demonstrates that habitation of the site continued into the tenth and eleventh centuries. Karel Innemée explores the function of the Bawit buildings that have been called *chapelles* by Clédat and *salles* by Maspero. He concludes that these rooms most probably were the place for daily prayers and, in addition to this, made clear references to funerary architecture and its iconography. Alain Delattre studies the rare literary texts and other related material from Bawit that sheds light on the intellectual life at the monastery. He examines education and science there as well as the literary quotations on the walls of the monastery and the P. Cotsen schoolbook. Delattre rightly believes that more "museum archaeology" concerning the acquisition details could be helpful to determine which literary texts of unknown provenance once belonged to the monastery of Bawit.

Dayr al-Muharraq is probably the jewel of the area being studied because of its immense religious value, not only to the Copts, but for the Ethiopians also. Its claim to fame stems from its place in the Coptic tradition of the Holy Family's flight into Egypt, as one of the places that the Holy Family lived as they fled Herod's sinister aim to kill the child Jesus. Most important is the ancient church; Coptic tradition holds that its altar was consecrated by the Lord Jesus Christ himself following His resurrection, in honor of his mother, the Virgin Mary. Fr. Angelos al-Muharraqi shares the monks' reflections on the history of this great monastery, tracing all the documents that the monks were able to find about its origin and development. The work of the monks highlights the need for more research to fill in the many historical lacunas that still elude scholars about the monastery. Fr. Philoxenos's chapter provides a more detailed description of the monastery and its buildings. This includes information on both the old and new work done on the current structures existing in the monastery as well as those that are known only from literary sources or surviving remains. Howard

Middleton-Jones's chapter introduces us to a more scientific method of documenting every item found in this monastery in database form. This work is part of a larger project underwritten by a Belgian foundation related to documentation of monastic settlements on the east bank of the Nile in Middle Egypt. He describes the process of using modern technology to document ancient artifacts that our ancestors have left us.

In Ashraf Alexandre Sadek's chapter, we are introduced to the literary evidence of Qusqam. He investigates the mention of this place within the larger topic of the Holy Family's flight into Egypt. He utilizes texts from Coptic liturgical sources, literary sources, and hagiographic sources, all centering on the Holy Family and their stay in Qusqam. Mark Swanson sheds new light on an important manuscript, virtually unknown to scholars, that was made by a monk of the monastery. It is a rare edition of a work called *al-Hawi*, by al-Makin Jirjis ibn al-'Amid. Swanson highlights some aspects of this rare theological work of the fourteenth century. Youhanna Nessim Youssef describes the unique characteristics of the liturgical services performed in the monastery. Drawing from various traditions, both current ones and those known from manuscripts, he analyzes the characteristics of these services and how they reflect the long history of the region.

The region of Asyut is one of the most influential centers of Christianity and monasticism in all of Egypt from ancient times to the present day. The essays devoted to this region highlight this importance. It begins with the chapter by Fr. Mark Sheridan about the most famous monk from that area, John of Lykopolis. He has been described as the most famous among Egyptian monks, second only to St. Antony the Great. Sheridan surveys all the known sources about him, literary and documentary. Then he describes the roles that these sources portray, from miracle worker to spiritual leader. Jochem Kahl describes the new archaeological discoveries that found the famous three cells that the literary sources mention were used by St. John of Lykopolis. Jacques van der Vliet contrasts the plethora of Christian sites in the Asyut area with the little scholarly attention they have received. He cites the treasure hunting of documents and artifacts of the past as a contributing factor to the lack of real archeological discoveries and scholarly studies. He uses two examples of monastic ruins, Dayr al-Gabrawi and Dayr al-'Izam, to highlight the challenges facing scholars in establishing their history as result of the pseudo-archeological adventures of the past. Ewa Zakrzewska argues against the theory that differences between the literary Coptic dialects strictly reflect Egyptian regional speech; rather, they are a scribal choice. In particular she uses Dialect *L*★, a subdialect of the Coptic Lykopolitan dialect, used by the Manichaean community of Kellis, as an example of this community distinguishing themselves socially from the other groups in the area by means of their language.

James Goehring introduces yet another monastery that received little attention from its early excavators, the monastery of Apa Apollo in Bala'iza. Goehring introduces the latest findings about the site, its inhabitants, and in particular the rich manuscript fragments found there and now kept at the Oxford Bodleian Library. Renate Dekker discusses another monastery in the area that was also not excavated properly, the Monastery of Apa Thomas in Wadi Sarga. Using the literary material found there, now kept in the British Library, she proposes a new relative chronology of the monastery. Four more of the monasteries in Asyut are highlighted by Ashraf Nageh and Mary Kupelian. These are the rock-cut monasteries of Mar Mina on the eastern mountain of Asyut and the monasteries of Durunka, Rifa, and al-Ganadla on the western mountain. The authors discuss the history and archaeological description of these important sites, which are still frequented by pilgrims. Adel Sadek reviews the modern history of the region of Asyut over the past few centuries and the role it played in the overall modern history of Christianity in Egypt. He discusses the economic activities of the Copts there, the churches they pray in, their role in politics, and the extensive Protestant missionary work that started there in the middle of the nineteenth century.

The famous corpus of Nag' Hammadi, discovered in 1945, is written in either Asyutic Coptic (Dialect *L*) or in Sahidic with Asyutic influence. On the basis of this linguistic observation, Hany Takla postulates that Nag' Hammadi was the final resting place of this library, while the heterodox (Meletian) Asyut of the fourth and fifth century was its origin. The basis of his arguments includes both the dialect of the texts and the cartonnage found in the binding of these codices. Sami Sabri Shaker deals with the architectural typology of the historic churches from Oxyrhynchos in the north to Dayr al-Ganadla in the south, excluding the cave and rock-cut churches. He classifies them according to the formation of their naves and their roofing systems. A considerable number of floor plans enrich Shaker's contribution.

We would like to express our deep gratitude to His Holiness Pope Tawadros II, who inaugurated the symposium at al-Muharraq and personally encouraged its participants. We would also like to thank His Grace

Bishop Sawirus, abbot of the Monastery of the Holy Virgin Mary, Dayr al-Muharraq, for hosting the symposium.

Our heartfelt thanks are due to all the contributors for their valuable contributions to this volume. Our thanks go to Dr. Fawzy Estafanous, president of the St. Mark Foundation, for supporting the symposium and its proceedings, and to Mr. Ashraf W. Hanna for the design of the two maps included in this volume. We would like to express our thanks to the staff of the American University in Cairo Press for their interest and professionalism in publishing the proceedings of the symposia on Christianity and Monasticism in Egypt, and especially to Nigel Fletcher-Jones, Neil Hewison, Nadia Naqib, and Johanna Baboukis.

Finally, it is our pleasure and honor to dedicate this volume to Dr. Peter Grossmann in acknowledgment of his lifetime devotion to the Coptic heritage.

1 The Monastery of Apa Thomas at Wadi Sarga: Points of Departure for a Relative Chronology

Renate Dekker

THIS CHAPTER DISCUSSES the identification of the superiors of the Monastery of Apa Thomas at Wadi Sarga and presents some points of departure for reconstructing a relative chronology of this monastic community on the basis of Coptic epitaphs and documents.[1]

The Monastery of Apa Thomas, also called 'the Rock of Apa Thomas,' is situated on the west bank of the Nile, north of modern Kom Isfaht, at the mouth of Wadi Sarga. It was supposedly named after its founder, a certain Apa Thomas, and was inhabited until about the eighth century (Crum and Bell 1922: 6–9; cf. Timm 1984–92, vol. 3: 1400–1403; Wipszycka 2009: 90, 155–57).[2] The excavations by R.C. Thompson on behalf of the Byzantine Research Fund in 1913–14 yielded an abundance of textual and archaeological material, but as this has only partly been published, the history of the monastery is obscure (Thompson 1914: 187–88; Thompson in Crum and Bell 1922: 1–5).[3] Nevertheless, the published Coptic material provides sufficient information for setting some chronological parameters.[4]

In the first part of this chapter I will demonstrate that the monastic saints invoked in the epitaphs on stelae were in fact superiors of the Monastery of Apa Thomas, and that some of them are also attested in Coptic documents. The second part discusses a recent hypothesis proposed by Alain Delattre (forthcoming) that the monastery at Wadi Sarga was possibly dependent on the Monastery of Apa Apollo at Bawit. The last section presents the individuals who occur in several texts and can also be linked to one of the leaders. As a result, their appearance not only enables us to distinguish dossiers of contemporary texts, but also to refine the relative chronology of the superiors of the monastery.

The Superiors of the Monastery of Apa Thomas

According to W.E. Crum, Apa Thomas presumably was the founder of the monastery at Wadi Sarga and the first of a group of local saints invoked at the beginning of many Coptic epitaphs on stelae and ostraca from Wadi Sarga (Crum and Bell 1922: 7–8, 57–84). The persons listed in the invocation formula after Thomas include Peter, Joseph, Anoup, Pamoun, Germanus, Justus, and Enoch, some of whom also appear in Coptic documents. At first, Crum could not decide whether they formed a group of contemporaries or a sequence of successive officials (Crum and Bell 1922: 8). In a later publication, when writing about the *Topos* (Monastery) of Epiphanius, he remarked that "one imagines a series of names—such as that customary, for instance, at Wâdi Sarga—to indicate a chronological succession of abbots" (Winlock and Crum 1926: 214).

The gradual but consistent development of the invocation formula indeed confirms Crum's theory that the list of names refers to a sequence of monastic leaders (fig. 1.1). At the beginning, the formula only mentioned "Thomas and his brethren" (I.Sarga 29–30), but in the course of time it was expanded until it included the names of nine superiors, the latest being "Apa Am[...]," whom Crum did not identify (I.Sarga 54).[5] The name can be supplemented as "Apa Amoun," for P.Ryl.Copt. 294 shows that one of the fathers of "the Rock of Apa Thomas" was thus named (fig. 1.2).[6]

The invocation formula developed in seven phases, five of which are represented by a single inscription only. No fewer than eight epitaphs record the formula in phase 3, when it ended with Pamoun (I.Sarga 35, 37, 39–42, 50, 59). His inclusion in the list of the persons invoked implies that he had died and that these epitaphs date to the period when his successor, Germanus, was leader of the monastery. The list of names provides an excellent starting point for a relative chronology, but since none of the epitaphs bear an absolute date, clues for dating have to be derived from other textual sources.

Crum suggested that Thomas probably lived shortly before AD 600, on account of a list of names in a Syriac palimpsest that is presently kept at the British Library in London (Crum and Bell 1922: 8–9).[7] This parchment book contained biblical texts (Joshua, Judges, Ruth, Judith, and Esther) in Sahidic, which were overwritten with extracts from patristic writings in Syriac when the book was reused in Wadi al-Natrun in AD 913.[8] The dating of the Sahidic texts is problematic since they are "extremely difficult to read," as Crum had already observed (Crum 1905: 5). H. Thompson, the editor of the Sahidic texts, consulted H. Hyvernat, who proposed a dating "not later than AD 650, probably about 600" on the basis of the palaeography (Thompson 1911: vi), which Crum accepted (Crum and Bell 1922: 9). Nevertheless, the dating of a text on the basis of its script alone is hazardous.

The list of names, written at the end of the book of Esther, mentions Apa Thomas, Apa Peter, Apa Joseph, and Apa Mena.[9] The first three names correspond with those of the earliest superiors of the Monastery of Apa Thomas, but a leader called Mena is not attested. Perhaps he was the copyist of the manuscript, who wanted to commemorate the first superiors of his community (Crum and Bell 1922: 9),[10] or a monk who was himself commemorated together with the early superiors by the copyist. If the list was indeed intended for commemorative purposes, and if Thomas, Peter, and Joseph were dead when the Sahidic texts were copied, the copying should have taken place in the time of Anoup, Joseph's successor, and during the first phase of the invocation formula. When the dating proposed by Hyvernat for the Sahidic texts is accepted, Anoup's leadership and phase 1 can be tentatively dated to about 600–50.

When Anoup died, his name was added to the invocation formula (phase 2) and Pamoun succeeded him as leader of the monastery. He, in turn, was succeeded by Germanus, who was the superior when the above-mentioned epitaphs of phase 3 were carved. One of them dates to year 13 of the indiction cycle (I.Sarga 35). Germanus probably was the same person as the superior Apa Germane who appears in a tax receipt as the representative of the *dikaion*, or juridical body, of the Monastery of Apa Thomas in a first indiction year (O.Sarga 344).[11]

Judging from an acknowledgment of a debt, Apa Justus, the seventh superior listed in the invocation formula, represented the *dikaion* of the Monastery of Apa Thomas in year 13 of the indiction cycle (P.Ryl.Copt. 201). Either Justus succeeded Germanus in year 13, and so both the above-mentioned epitaph associated with Germanus (I.Sarga 35) and the document date to the same year and cycle, or the document is to be dated to a subsequent cycle, that is, fifteen years later. The reference to a *dux* in a letter addressed to Apa Justus (O.Sarga 102) indicates that this monastic leader must have headed the monastery well before AD 750 in view of the fact that the office of *dux* disappeared in the course of the first half of the eighth century (Sijpesteijn 2010: 111 and n. 23).

Apa Enoch appears once as the superior who represented the *dikaion* of the Monastery of Apa Thomas (Apa E[noch]; O.Sarga 164),[12] and as the sender of instructions to "my brother" Apa Enoch, the steward (O.Sarga 104). In addition, it was probably the superior Enoch, and not the homonymous steward, who sent an instruction to the steward Papnoute, since the sender referred to himself as "his father" (O.Sarga 95). It is likely, but not completely certain, that Papnoute was steward before Enoch, as I will discuss below.

When Enoch was superior of the monastery and his namesake was steward, the sailor of a *liburnus*-ship came to the former with a request for cables and ropes (O.Sarga 104). Crum suggested that the *liburnus* "should be a warship" (Crum and Bell 1922: 97 n. 1). According to P. Sijpesteijn, the ship belonged to the Muslim fleet (Sijpesteijn 2010: 111). Since the Muslim navy was founded during the caliphate of 'Uthman (644–56) by Mu'awya, the governor of Syria, any reference to the Muslim fleet postdates about 650.[13] If Sijpesteijn is right, the letter mentioning the ship is of a later date, and Enoch must have been superior of the monastery after AD 650.[14]

Apa Amoun, the "father of the Rock of Apa Thomas," features in a letter about the donation of a garden to the monastery (P.Ryl.Copt. 248). He was the ninth and last superior to be included in the invocation formula and appears on a single epitaph (I.Sarga 54).

One of the superiors of the Monastery of Apa Thomas and his second-in-authority, or steward, received a letter from his bishop, Eunomius of Sbeht (Apollinopolis Parva/Kom Isfaht; O.Sarga 375). Unfortunately, the name of the superior is lost.

The relative chronology should also include five monastic leaders who are attested in documents, but not on the epitaphs:

- Sarapamon, superior of the Rock of Apa Thomas, who sent a letter to the anonymous archimandrite of another monastery, requesting a deed of protection on behalf of certain youths who had fled from his (Sarapamon's) monastery (P.Ryl.Copt. 289);
- the anonymous archimandrite who received Sarapamon's letter (P.Ryl.Copt. 289);
- Apa George, the head and archimandrite, who represented the *dikaion* of the Rock of Apa Thomas when paying their taxes (P.Ryl.Copt. 124);

- Daniel, the archimandrite, who employed a carpenter in indiction year 12 to work at the monastery, presumably that of Apa Thomas (O.Sarga 161);
- Apa Victor, archimandrite of the "Holy Mountain," which probably does not refer to the Monastery of Apa Thomas, for the latter is never called "Mountain" (P.Sarga 96).

Judging from the documents, the leader of the Monastery of Apa Thomas was called "father" or "superior" *(proestos)* when he represented the *dikaion* of the monastery, and the archimandrites were associated with another monastery, which is once designated as the "Holy Mountain." At a later stage, archimandrites interfered with the administration of the Monastery of Apa Thomas: Apa George paid the taxes due from the monastery, and Daniel employed a carpenter. This observation also seems to apply to Dayr al-Bala'iza, or the Monastery of Apa Apollo, in the same district of Sbeht (Apollinopolis Parva/Kom Isfaht): five leaders were called "superiors," but two others were "archimandrites."[15] Interestingly, the title 'archimandrite' is particularly attested at the Monastery of Apa Apollo at Bawit (in the Hermopolite district), whereas only a few of its leaders were designated *proestos*.[16]

In the context of the Pachomian *koinonia* and the Shenoutian federation, the title 'archimandrite' designated the supreme leader of a group of monasteries, who resided at the main monastery.[17] It referred to a specific function and is likely to have been borne by a limited number of monastic leaders, but the documents from the monasteries at Wadi Sarga, al-Bala'iza, and Bawit provide various examples. In my opinion, it is unlikely that each of these monasteries housed *proestotes* as well as archimandrites. Since most archimandrites are associated with the Monastery of Apa Apollo at Bawit, I am inclined to think that this monastery was, or became, the center of a monastic congregation, which included at least the Monastery of Apa Thomas and Dayr al-Bala'iza.[18]

A Relationship with the Monastery of Apa Apollo at Bawit?

In a recent article, Delattre (forthcoming) observes that the monastery at Bawit was indeed involved with the administration of other monastic institutions, "peut-être dans le cadre d'une congrégation dont il aurait été l'élément central."[19] In addition, he proposes the hypothesis that the Monastery of Apa Thomas was administratively dependent on the Monastery of Apa Apollo at Bawit on the basis of P.Sarga 175 (P.Bawit.Clackson 60, seventh–eighth century(?), and P.Mich. XV 749, eighth century).

P.Sarga 175, which is only partly preserved, seems to be a Coptic "Our Father"–formula text, a type of document that is typical for the monastery at Bawit, but this example was discovered at Wadi Sarga.[20] It was issued by Daniel, whose title is not specified. P.Mich. XV 749, a Greek account relating to the corn tax, lists the Monastery of Apa Thomas (without mentioning a superior) as one of the suppliers of corn. According to Delattre (forthcoming), P.Mich. XV 749 is likely to have been issued by another institution, possibly the monastery at Bawit. He compares it with a tax account (P.Brux.Bawit 31) that refers to land holdings in the area of Kusai (al-Qusiya, between Mallawi and Asyut), but certainly originates from Bawit. It should be admitted that the texts referred to by Delattre do not mention the Monastery of Apa Apollo at Bawit, and that his hypothesis is mainly based on the discovery of an "Our Father"–formula text, supposedly originating from Bawit, at Wadi Sarga.

If Delattre's hypothesis is correct, at least with regard to the fiscal administration during the seventh/eighth centuries, it should be possible to identify the archimandrites attested in the documents relating to the Monastery of Apa Thomas (George, Daniel, and Victor) with namesakes at Bawit. At present, however, any suggestion is speculative. It appears that there were two archimandrites at Bawit called Daniel. On the basis of the script, Sarah Clackson (2008: 4, 94) distinguished the Daniel of P.Sarga 175 (P.Bawit.Clackson 60, seventh–eighth century?) from that of P.Sarga 174 (P.Bawit.Clackson 14, cf. 15–17, eighth century, indiction 8–9). We should also be cautious when attempting to equate Apa George, the archimandrite of P.Ryl.Copt. 124, with Apa George, the archimandrite of P.Mon.Apollo 26 (eighth century) and the signatory of three "Our Father"–formula texts (P.Bawit.Clackson 18–20, indiction 6–7).

Dossiers of Texts Relating to Well-attested Individuals

The relative chronology of the Monastery of Apa Thomas can be refined, not only by examining its ties with other monastic communities, but also by distinguishing groups of texts among the material from Wadi Sarga itself. The priests Victor and Phoibammon, the stewards Papnoute and Enoch, and Apa Hor and Apa Mena each appear in several texts and their individual dossiers can be linked directly or indirectly to a monastic leader (fig. 1.3).

The *papa* or priest Victor from Hage, "surnamed the less," is mentioned on no fewer than six epitaphs, after the invocation formula and the name and day of death of the deceased monk or priest (I.Sarga 35, 37, 42,

44–46).[21] These deceased individuals originated from various places (cf. nos. 35, 37, 42), and their relation to Victor remains unclear. The prominent appearance of his name on the funerary stelae suggests that he was either the dedicator or the sculptor (Crum and Bell 1922: 65 n. 2). In view of the fact that the invocation formula represents phase 3, the stelae and Victor's activities can be dated to the period of the superior Germanus. One of the stelae dates to a thirteenth indiction year.

Another dossier consists of the Coptic inscriptions that people from Iom (the Fayoum?) left during several visits. The priest Phoibammon was the first to have a commemorative slab carved with his prayer (I.Sarga 39). Judging from the invocation formula (phase 3), it dates to the period of Germanus. On another occasion, the priest Phoibammon returned together with a large group of people, including the priest Wenofer and the baker Anoup (I.Sarga 55). Part of this company returned and left another graffito (I.Sarga 56). One of the two persons called Hor, the one associated with Paul (and Hale), afterward died and was commemorated by an epitaph (I.Sarga 57). The dossier should also include the graffito by master Elias, the mason, and his apprentice Enoch, since Elias had also joined the company from Iom (I.Sarga 74, 55).

The dossiers of the steward Papnoute, the steward Enoch, Apa Hor, and Apa Mena at least partly date to the period when Apa Enoch was superior of the monastery (see above). Perhaps Papnoute was already present at the time of Apa Justus, but, if so, he was not yet called a steward (O.Sarga 113, 186). In his capacity as steward, Papnoute sent messages to Apa Hor, asking him to give wine or oil to certain individuals (O.Sarga 91, 177–78), and to Apa Mena, instructing him to give a priest called John a can of oil and a little meat (O.Sarga 181). Apa Hor and Apa Mena apparently were responsible for distributing supplies from the storeroom of the monastery. Apa Mena also received instructions from "Apa Enoch, his father," who was either the superior or the steward (O.Sarga 167–72). Crum attributed ten orders and receipts to "Enoch, doubtless the oft recurring steward" on account of his "clumsy hand" (O.Sarga 167–73, 176, 182, 183).[22]

Further study of the texts is likely to reveal more possible dossiers, which could contribute to the refinement of the relative chronology.[23]

Conclusion

As Crum already suggested, the group of individuals invoked in many of the epitaphs from Wadi Sarga can be identified as the earlier superiors of the Monastery of Apa Thomas in view of the gradual and consistent development of the invocation formula. The first leader to be commemorated was Apa Thomas, whereas Apa Amoun was the ninth and last leader whose name was added to the formula. Like his predecessors Germanus, Justus, and Enoch, Amoun is also attested in Coptic documents.

Some Coptic documents also record the activities of other monastic leaders, including Sarapamon, father of the Rock of Apa Thomas, and three archimandrites, who were perhaps associated with the Monastery of Apa Apollo in Bawit. Like Delattre, I am inclined to think that the monastery at Bawit formed the administrative center of a congregation consisting of various monasteries, including the Monastery of Apa Thomas and perhaps Dayr al-Bala'iza.

This contribution presents the first attempt to reconstruct a relative chronology of the Monastery of Apa Thomas by identifying its leaders, and isolates some dossiers relating to well-attested individuals in order to refine the chronology. However, before we can sketch the history of the site, it is essential that the unpublished material also be examined, and that the possible ties between this monastery and other monastic communities in Middle Egypt be clarified. It is, therefore, excellent news that the unpublished material in the British Museum and the British Library is now being prepared for publication.

Fig. 1.1. The superiors invoked in the Coptic epitaphs

Phase	Superiors	I.Sarga
1	Thomas "and his brethren"	29–30
2	Thomas, Peter, Joseph, Anoup	31
3	Thomas, Peter, Joseph, Anoup, Pamoun	35 (indiction 13), 37, 39–42, 50, 59
4	Thomas, Peter, Joseph, Anoup, Pamoun, Germanus	48
5	Thomas, Peter, Joseph, Anoup, Pamoun, Germanus, Justus	36
6	Thomas, Peter, Joseph, Anoup, Pamoun, Germanus, Justus, Enoch	51
7	Thomas, Peter, Joseph, Anoup, Pamoun, [Germanus], Justus, [Enoch], Am[oun]	54

Fig. 1.2. The superiors attested in the Coptic documents in chronological order

Superior	Coptic document
Apa Germane, "our father" superior representing the *dikaion* of the Mon(astery) of Apa Thomas	I.Sarga 84 (and 85: "saint"?) O.Sarga 344 (Tut 9, indiction 1)
Apa Justus (Jouste), father, superior representing the *dikaion* of the [Monastery] of Apa Th[omas]	O.Sarga 94, 102–103, 113, cf. 186 P.Ryl.Copt. 201 (indiction 13)
Apa Enoch, father, superior representing the *dikaion* of the Monastery of Apa Thomas (no title; giving instructions to his "brother," the steward Enoch) "his father" (giving instructions to the steward Papnoute)	O.Sarga 164 O.Sarga 104 O.Sarga 95
Apa Amoun, father of the Rock of Apa Thomas	P.Ryl.Copt. 294
[. . .], superior representing the Monastery of Apa Thomas, a contemporary of Bishop Eunomius of Sbeht/Kom Isfaht	O.Sarga 375
Sarapamon, (father) of the Rock of Apa Thomas, writing to [. . .], the archimandrite (of another monastery)	P.Ryl.Copt. 289
Apa George, father superior ("great man") archimandrite representing the *dikaion* of the Rock of Apa Thomas	P.Ryl.Copt. 124, I. ro. and II. ro. text I. ro. (indiction 14)
Daniel, the archimandrite, presumably the archimandrite	O.Sarga 87, O.Sarga 161 (Tut 26, indiction 12) P.Sarga 175 (= P.Bawit.Clackson 60)
Apa Victor, archimandrite of the "Holy Mountain" (probably *not* of the Rock of Apa Thomas)	P.Sarga 96

Fig. 1.3.
A relative chronology of the Monastery of Apa Thomas

Superior	Contemporary texts	Proposed dating
1. Apa Thomas		Shortly before AD 600?
2. Apa Peter		(ca. 600?)
3. Apa Joseph		
4. Apa Anoup	British Library, Add. MS 17183, fol. 147a I.Sarga 29–30 (fig. 1.1, phase 1)	ca. 600–50?
5. Apa Pamoun	I.Sarga 31 (phase 2)	
6. Apa Germanus	I.Sarga 35 (phase 3; indiction 13) Cf. I.Sarga 37, 39–42, 50, 59 O.Sarga 344 (Tut 9, indiction 1)	(Before AD 750, like Apa Justus) 6 September (657, 672, 687, 702, . . .)
papa Victor "the less" from Hage, who produced epitaphs *papa* Phoibammon *papa* Wenofer of Iom, Paul, Hor, Hale, etc.	I.Sarga 42 (Kiyahk 22), 37 (Amshir 7), 35 (Baramhat 4, indiction 13), 44–46 I.Sarga 39, 55 I.Sarga 55–56 I.Sarga 55–56 (alive); cf. 57 (Hor is dead)	18 December, 1 February, 28 February (655, 670, 685, . . .)
7. Apa Justus	O.Sarga 94, 103, 113, cf. 186 O.Sarga 103: reference to a *dux* P.Ryl.Copt. 201 (indiction 13) I.Sarga 48 (phase 4)	Before AD 750 (. . . , 669/70, 684/5, 699/700, 714/5, . . .)

8. Apa Enoch	O.Sarga 164, cf. 99, 104, 170–71, 183: I.Sarga 36 (phase 5)	
Steward Papnoute	O.Sarga 95, cf. 97–98, 110, 177–78, 181	
and Apa Hor	O.Sarga 91, 177–79	
and Apa Mena	O.Sarga 181	
Steward Enoch	O.Sarga 88, 104 ("*liburnus*-ship"), 378, cf. 173 (Thoth 1, indiction 12), 176 (Thoth 10, indiction 7), 182 (Pamenoth 11, indiction 12), 183	After AD 650? 29 August (668, 683, 698, . . .) 7 September (678, 693, 708, . . .) 7 March (684, 699, 714, . . .)
and Apa Mena	O.Sarga 168–69 (Misra 20), 170–71 (Thoth 1, indiction 3), cf. 167, 172	13 August 29 August (674, 689, 704, . . .)
9. Amoun	P.Ryl.Copt. 294 I.Sarga 51 (phase 6)	Seventh/eighth century
(?) Sarapamon	P.Ryl.Copt. 289	Seventh/eighth century
(?) George, the archimandrite	P.Ryl.Copt. 124: II. ro. (indiction 13) II. vo (Baba 26, indiction 14) I. ro. (Amshir 3, indiction 14) I. vo. (Misra 24, indiction 4)	Seventh/eighth century 23 October (685, 700, 725, . . .) 28 January (686, 701, 716, . . .) 17 August (691, 706, 721, . . .)
(?) Daniel, the archimandrite	O.Sarga 87, 161 (Tut 26, indiction 12) P.Sarga 175 (= P.Bawit. Clackson 60)	23 September (698, 713, 728 . . .) Seventh/eighth century
(?) Victor, the archimandrite	P.Sarga 96	

Notes

1 I would like to thank Dr. Gawdat Gabra for inviting me to write a contribution on Wadi Sarga. I am also much indebted to Jennifer Cromwell for sharing her views, for engaging in a stimulating discussion, and for correcting the English; to Elisabeth O'Connell for sending me the text of her 2012 Rome Coptic Congress paper and for her editorial comments; and to Alain Delattre for sending me three articles that are relevant to this topic, including one that is still in press.

2 Cf. Kahle 1954, vol 1: 26; Meinardus 1977: 398–99; Coquin and Martin 1991g: 2312; and Sijpesteijn 2010: 110, who incorrectly located the monastery at Wadi Sarga "close to Edfu"; Tudor 2011: 75, 414–15, cf. 204. For an elaborate description and photographs of the site, see Doresse 2000: 360–410, 532–33, figs. 26–41. Wadi Sarga is presently used by the military and inaccessible; cf. Klemm and Klemm 2008: 117, 144; Wipszycka 2009: 157.

3 During the Tenth International Congress of Coptic Studies in Rome (17–22 September 2012), Elisabeth O'Connell presented a paper on the unpublished excavation documentation and objects now in the British Museum. For information on the British Museum Research Project "Wadi Sarga at the British Museum" and scholars currently working on various corpora of objects, see British Museum, "Wadi Sarga at the British Museum," https://www.britishmuseum.org/research/research_projects/all_current_projects/wadi_sarga.aspx. Object records for Wadi Sarga are available via the British Museum Collections on-line database: British Museum, "Collection Online," http://www.britishmuseum.org/research/collection_online/search.aspx.

4 For the nonliterary texts relating to the Monastery of Apa Thomas/Wadi Sarga, see P.Sarga (also including ostraca) and I.Sarga 29–85: ed. Crum and Bell 1922; P.Ryl.Copt. 124, 201, 289, 294: ed. Crum 1909; National Museum of Antiquities, Leiden, F. 1946/4.6: ed. De Nie 1941: 615–18 (cf. Raven 1982: 80–81); P.Vat. Copt. Doresse 7: ed. Förster 2001: 195–97 (corrected reading by Lucchesi 2008: 203–206); P.Mich. XV 749: ed. Sijpesteijn 1982: 134. On the basis of the toponym 'Apollinopolis,' Sijpesteijn assumed that the last-mentioned papyrus came from Apollinopolis Megale/Edfu, but A. Delattre (forthcoming) argued that Apollinopolis Parva/Kom Isfaht is more likely. It probably dates to the eighth century (Delattre), rather than the seventh century (Sijpesteijn). Since Crum included P.Mich. Inv. 578 (= P.Sarga 174/P.Bawit.Clackson 14) in his edition, although it was not discovered at Wadi Sarga, E.M. Husselman (1951: 332–38) suggested that two similar texts, P.Mich. Inv. 1300 and 1520 (incorrectly "1524"), also came from Wadi Sarga. S. Clackson (2008: 4–5, 20), however, demonstrated that "Our Father"–formula texts like these are typical for the Monastery of Apa Apollo at Bawit. Cf. Delattre 2007: 147–51; Delattre 2010a. For a Coptic epistolary exercise from Wadi Sarga, see Cromwell 2013: 272–75.

5 This observation is contrary to Crum's remark (in Crum and Bell 1922: 7) that the names following that of Thomas were sometimes omitted.

6 Crum (in Crum and Bell 1922: 8 n. 3) assumed that the Pamoun mentioned in the invocation formula and the Apa Amoun of P.Ryl.Copt. 294 were one and the same, but I.Sarga 54 demonstrates that Pamoun and "Am[oun]" were two different individuals. The former is listed before Justus, the latter after Justus.

7 British Library, Add. MS 17183: ed. Thompson 1911; cf. Hyvernat 1888: pl. 7.1, 56.1; Crum 1905: 4–7, no. 12, when the manuscript was still in the British Museum.

8 Thompson 1911: v; cf. Crum and Bell 1922: 8.

9 British Library, Add. MS 17183, fol. 147a: ed. Thompson 1911: viii, 372; cf. Crum 1905: 7.

10 Previously, Crum (1905: 7) suggested that the names were "presumably those of the owners of the book."

11 On the term *dikaion*, see Kahle 1954, vol. 1: 31–32; Wipszycka 2009: 547–48, with further references.

12 Crum (Crum and Bell 1922: 135 and n. 2–3) read the abbreviated title as *pro(noetes)*, 'agent,' but it actually stands for *pro(estos)*, 'superior'; cf. Förster 2002: 679–80. In P.Ryl.Copt. 201, the *dikaion* of the Monastery of Apa Thomas is indeed represented by a '*proe(stos)*.'

13 On the foundation of the Muslim navy, see Fahmy 1966: 76–79. For 'Uthman, see Lapidus 2002: 45–47.

14 In a personal communication by e-mail on 6 October 2013, Jennifer Cromwell wrote to me that the text does not necessarily refer to the Muslim fleet. She observed that the monastery seems to have owned ships, and that ships were used for the transport of wine.

15 *Proestotes* during the seventh/eighth centuries: Abraham (P.Bal. 109), Ammone (P.Bal. 159, 100), Apa Kyre (P.Bal. 102), Apa Psha (P.Bal. 103–104), Isaak (P.Bal. 115). Archimandrites: Peter (P.Bal. 210), also called "father superior" (lit.: 'great man'; P.Bal. 291, 359), and John (P.Bal. 459): ed. Kahle 1954, vol. 1; cf. Wipszycka 2009: 330 n. 6, 450–51; Markiewicz 2009: 182–83, 201–202.

16 Archimandrites: Serenos (P.Amst. I 47–48; sixth century): ed. Salomons, Sijpesteijn, and Worp 1980; Daniel (P.Mon.Apollo 25; eighth century), George (P.Mon.Apollo 26; eighth century), Theodore (P.Mon.Apollo 38; eighth century), Zacharias (P.Mon. Apollo 59b; eighth century): ed. Clackson 2000; Delattre (forthcoming). *Proestotes*: Athanase (P.Mon.Apollo 24; eighth century): ed. Clackson 2000; Mena (Rome, Campo Santo, Inv. C 1 (Enß 3); eighth century): Delattre 2010b: 26–27. Delattre (2010b: 29–30) proposed identifying this Mena with the person depicted on the well-known icon of Christ and Abbot Mena in the Musée du Louvre (E 11565; eighth century).

17 For the title, see Wipszycka 2009: 329–31; cf. 335–40, on the superiors of the Pachomian and Shenoutian communities.

18 For the other monasteries in the neighborhood of Dayr al-Bala'iza, see Kahle 1954, vol. 1: 22–26.

19 Cf. Clackson 2000: 23, 32–33; Delattre 2007: 64–65.

20 For a reconstruction of the text, see Clackson 2008: 93–94. Jennifer Cromwell, however, observes that the text could also begin with "ⲡⲉⲛⲉⲓⲱ[ⲧ ⲉϥⲥϩⲁⲓ]" instead of "ⲡⲉⲛⲉⲓⲱ[ⲧ ⲡⲉⲧⲥϩⲁⲓ]," which is not a formula restricted to Bawit.

21 For the title *papa/papas*, see Derda and Wipszycka 1994: 54–56.

22 Crum and Bell 1922: 144 (O.Sarga 167, 176, 182), cf. 139–41 (O.Sarga 167 n. 3, 168 n. 3–4, 169 n. 2, 170 n. 2, 171 n. 2, 173 n. 3), 146 (O.Sarga 183 n. 3: "The same unskilled hand as in [O.Sarga] 167 etc.").

23 Jennifer Cromwell has photographed all the ostraca from Wadi Sarga, which are now available in the British Museum's online catalogue. See also her contribution "Wine and Monks in Christian Egypt" on the British Museum blog, http://blog.britishmuseum.org/2013/07/10/wine-and-monks-in-christian-egypt/.

2 Intellectual Life in Middle Egypt: The Case of the Monastery of Bawit (Sixth–Eighth Centuries)

Alain Delattre

The monastery of Bawit is located on the west bank of the Nile, on the edge of the desert. The site was excavated at the beginning of the twentieth century by a team from the Institut français d'archéologie orientale, led by the archaeologists Jean Clédat, Émile Chassinat, and Jean Maspero. A few campaigns were undertaken by the Supreme Council of Antiquities (SCA) in the 1970s and new excavations were undertaken in 2002 by a team from the IFAO and the Musée du Louvre, under the direction first of Dominique Bénazeth and later Gisèle Hadji-Minaglou.

The archaeological work and the discoveries in architecture, sculpture, and painting that were made on the site are fundamental to our knowledge of Coptic monasticism and art history. As for the texts, nearly fifteen hundred inscriptions were published by Clédat and Maspero. Ostraca and papyri were also found at the time, but only a few of these were published, most of them recently. On the other hand, Bawit has been plundered since the end of the nineteenth century and hundreds of ostraca and papyri have been sold on the antiquities market and come into collections worldwide (Clackson 2000: 9–14; Delattre 2007: 117–24). During the past twenty years, research on the formulae of the Bawit documents and the application of the principles of museum archaeology have allowed us to reconstruct to some extent the archives of the monastery. But what we have are mainly economic and administrative documents; as a result, the intellectual life of the monastery remains largely unknown. No library has yet been discovered in Bawit, nor is any book inventory preserved.

The contrast with other monasteries is striking. In Middle Egypt, the excavations of the Monastery of Wadi Sarga produced twenty-eight literary (biblical, theological, medical, and mathematical) fragments. In the Monastery of Dayr al-Bala'iza, sixty-two fragments were found (biblical, liturgical, and hagiographical texts; prayers; apothegms; martyrdoms; homilies; and even historical works and magical charms). In the Theban area, numerous sources show us the literary and educational environment: a few literary fragments, many letters asking for books, and even a few book catalogs, such as the one found in the Monastery of St. Elias, which mentions more than seventy books (Coquin 1975a). Despite the rarity of literary texts from Bawit, a few elements put together can give us a first glimpse into intellectual life in the monastery.

Literary Quotations and Echoes

As we do not have literary fragments or any trace of the library, the literary environment is difficult to define. Only a few quotations or echoes can be found in the documentation. Some literary compositions and biblical passages are written on the walls of the monastery, in the common areas such as the large reception room, as well as in individual cells. The genealogy of Christ (from Luke 3:23–38) is written in room 21 Maspero 1932–43: 130–31) and the Lord's Prayer in Greek is painted in chapel LII (Clédat 1999: 135). A psalmic composition is written in chapel XXXIII (Clédat 1999: 18; Delattre 2008: 75–76) and three unidentified narratives were found in room 5; one of them relates a miracle and maybe an apparition (Maspero 1932–43: 58–59). A copy of the letter of Jesus to Abgar is painted in a court (Coquin 1993a; Clédat 1999: 98–100). Finally, in the paintings of chapel XII, the biblical prophets hold a scroll in their hands, each with a quotation from his book (Clédat 1904–1906: 54–61).

No such literary quotation or echo is to be found in the papyrus and ostraca, except for one ostracon that preserves a short psalmic quotation (Calament 2008: 27–28), probably a pen trial.

Education in the Monastery

In Pachomian monasteries, the monks were supposed to learn to read (Rousseau 1985: 81). In the Theban hermitages we have evidence that literate monks did educate their disciples (Boud'hors and Heurtel 2010:

15). Information about education in Bawit is scarce. Some documents mention *kathêgêthai*, 'professors' or 'schoolmasters' (P.Clackson 36; Maspero 1932–43: 126; Delattre 2008: 77–78). We have some exercises on ostracon and papyrus (as O.Bawit 93), but most of them deal with learning or practicing administrative formulae, such as P.Mon.Apollo I 58–59 and P.Bawit. Clackson 76.

We find some steps of elementary teaching in the inscriptions. Firstly, alphabets were written on walls (Clédat 1904–1906: 142; Maspero 1932–43: 56 and 127); they can be interpreted as either exercises or models. Secondly, some lists of words starting with the same letter were also painted or scratched (words beginning with *bêta* or *gamma* in Clédat 1904–1906: 8 and 110). On the mountain in front of the site, in a room cut in the rock, some school inscriptions were painted on the walls, for example a list of two-syllable words beginning with *delta* and what looks like an exercise in conjugation (Clédat 1999: 190–91). Finally, some monks or visitors left letters or words on walls, which can also be interpreted as practice exercises (Maspero 1932–43: 51 and 126).

Room 18 was perhaps used as a school, since we find on the walls an inscription mentioning a professor, an alphabet, and some writing exercises (Maspero 1932–43: 126–27).

The P.Cotsen Schoolbook

P.Cotsen 1 is a beautiful schoolbook acquired on the antiquities market and now kept in Princeton; the document was described in 2006 and full photographic documentation was published in 2011 (Bucking 2006 and 2011). The context of the book is clearly monastic and the texts present some Middle Egyptian features. The colophon contains an invocation to "our father Apa Apollô," in all likelihood the founder of Bawit. These elements indicate that most probably this book comes from Bawit.

The contents are largely inspired by the Greek educational system; at some point, some exercises were probably translated and more or less adapted from a Greek schoolbook. The book begins at page 31 (the first page preserved) with simple syllables (*dap, dep, dêp, dip . . .; dar, der, dêr, dir,* etc.), then follow alphabetical lists of words of two syllables, and then of four. We next read the alphabet with the names of the letters, a list of *nomina sacra*, and a long enumeration of nonsensical words (used to develop the reading abilities of the learner). Other lists follow: the virtues of the Holy Spirit, the cities of Judah (from the book of Joshua), the peoples and kings defeated by the Hebrews (also from Joshua), and the chiefs of Edom (from Genesis). Then the book continues with biblical quotations, starting with the whole genealogy of Christ (from Luke), a text that is also to be found on a wall of the monastery (Maspero 1932–43: 130–31). After that, we read extracts from the Epistle to the Romans, the Epistle to the Philippians, and Psalm 1. The book was supposed to end there: a colophon is written on pages 155–56 after the psalmic quotation. But a new text starts from page 157, written by another hand. It was identified as a monastic narrative by Bucking, but it is a translation into Coptic of a homily of Basil of Caesarea on the duties of the monks (for the identification of Philippians 4:8, Psalms 1:3–6, and Basil's homily, see Delattre 2012b: 394). After this text, we find an apothegm; the end of the book is not preserved.

P.Cotsen 1 allows us to reconstruct a progression in teaching and learning. Once he had mastered the basics (alphabet, syllables, etc.), the student had to read and learn some lists of words. Then, he could progress to some biblical passages from the New and the Old Testaments. The schoolbook was later completed with a text of Basil, probably as a new step in the teaching program.

The schoolbook, probably from Bawit, gives us an idea of the literary context and the intellectual formation of the monks.

Science

We know that there was a hospital in Bawit, a common feature in monasteries. The library could have contained some medical books, as was the case at the St. Elias Monastery in the Theban area, according to the catalogue of the library there (Coquin 1975a). Otherwise, scientific activities are not attested in Egyptian monasteries. Nevertheless, an inscription from Bawit is of some interest in this respect.

The text is written on the north wall of chapel XIX. It is an unfinished table of twelve lines and five columns (Delattre 2010c), with the names of the months in the first column and numbers in the others. The second and fourth columns contain respectively the numbers 1 and 15, meaning the first and fifteenth day of the month. The numbers in the third and fifth columns increase by one unit until 27 December and decrease after this date. It appears that the numbers are linked in some way to the position of the sun. A more precise analysis shows that the table records the lengths in feet of a shadow at noon on the first and fifteenth of each month. A comparison with other shadow tables shows that the Bawit one is much more precise and is probably the result, at some point, of an actual experiment. The practical function of the text is unknown, but it could have been just an intellectual exercise.

In Search of the Library

As noted earlier, so far, excavations have failed to find the remains of a library in the monastery. If literary texts were found during illegal digging at the site, we are currently unable to assign them to Bawit, due to the lack not only of information but also of any comparison point.

An attempt could be made using the principles of museum archaeology, as has been done for the reconstruction of the economic and administrative archives of the monastery. If one text was sold with another known to come from Bawit, there is a good chance that the first one is also from the monastery. An analysis of the acquisition details could be helpful to determine which literary texts were sold with documentary texts from Bawit, and then to build a general idea of what could have been in the library of the monastery.

For example, Yale University acquired in 1964 a group of two hundred papyri. It is possible to say positively that at least twenty or so of these come from Bawit, and there is no obvious reason to reject such a provenance for any of them. There are a few literary texts in this group: for example, Psalms; Joel; Joshua; a Christian monastic narrative concerning Ammon (?), Poimen, and a woman whose name is not preserved; and scenes from a narrative of the Dormition of Mary (Inv. 1779, 1782, 1786, 1788, 1789). All these fragments could therefore be tentatively attributed to the monastery.

Once a possible corpus of literary texts from Bawit has been constituted, we would need to find some codicological or paleographical similarities among the selected fragments, to be used as possible criteria to help assign further literary fragments to the monastery. That is the challenge for the future.

3 Christianity and Monasticism in al-Bahnasa according to Arabic Sources

Sherin Sadek El Gendi

LOCATED ABOUT two hundred kilometers south of Cairo on the western bank of Bahr Yusuf (literally, the Sea of Joseph, but actually a canal running off from the Nile), in Minya governorate, about sixteen kilometers northwest of the district of Bani Mazar, al-Bahnasa (Oxyrhynchos, or the Oxyrhynchite province) has been one of the most important cities in Egypt throughout history. In fact, the early history of al-Bahnasa is obscure. The situation of al-Bahnasa was given in *Claudius Ptolemaus*, and this is one of the earliest references to it (Vogt 1920, vol. 5: 29). In the *Itinerarium Antonini Augusti*, it was placed on the military road running along the west of the Nile (Parthey and Pinder 1848). The river and the desert formed the western and eastern boundaries of the Oxyrhynchite province. The name of al-Bahnasa is mentioned in the *Scaloe coptes-arabes*, in the *Chronicle of John of Nikiou* (John of Nikiou 1916: 555), in the *History of the Patriarchs* (Sawirus Ibn al-Muqaffa' 1959),[1] and in several other Coptic texts and Arabic translations and sources, which identify it as one of the most prosperous cities during the Byzantine period.

Al-Bahnasa's Name

In ancient times, the importance of al-Bahnasa was due to the ancient tombs built on its outskirts, and to the ruins of ancient Egyptian temples like those of Theoris, the local hippopotamus goddess, and the sacred sharp-nosed fish that gave the town its name. The city is mentioned in the records of the Kushite king Piye (the more usual name for Piankhy), who captured it during his reign (ca. 741–ca. 712 BC).

The town itself was the nome capital in the seventh century BC (Bagnall and Rathbone 2008: 158–59). Speaking about the oasis of al-Bahnasa, Abu al-Makarim,[2] who lived during the Fatimid period (AH 351–555/AD 952–1160), cited the Little Oasis or the Oasis Parva.[3] Its Coptic name was ⲟⲩⲁϩ ⲡⲉⲙϫⲉ· which is directly translated into Arabic as 'Wah al-Bahnasa.' It was also named 'Wah al-Bahariya' because it is located to the north of Kharga and Dakhla oases. Abu al-Makarim recorded the meaning of al-Bahnasa's Coptic name as 'marriage' or 'place of marriage' (ⲙⲁⲛϣⲉⲗⲉⲧ). He mentioned that this town was built for the maidens who were the virgin daughters of the kings, or for those married to the sons of kings who originated from this place. The place in which Joseph the Truthful worshiped was near al-Bahnasa (Abu al-Makarim 1895: fol.75 a, 215).

In their books, Ibn Khirdadhabah (AH 205–80/AD 820–93) and Yaqut al-Hamawi (AH 626/AD 1228) mention the name of al-Bahnasi (Ibn Khirdadhabah 1955: 247; Yaqut al-Hamawi 1955, vol. 1: 771). Al-Bakri (d. AH 487/AD 1094) also mentions it as al-Bahnas or Bahnasat al-Wahat (1992: vol. 2: 145/2, 147 note 2, 187, 286).

Ibn Mammati (AH 544–606/AD 1149–1209) also mentions its Arabic names, al-Bahnasa and al-Bahnasawiya (1943: 81, 345–46). Al-Qalqashandi (AH 756–821/AD 1355–1418) wrote of al-Bahnasi and al-Bahnasawiya on the western bank of the Nile (1963, vol. 3: 377, 390, 393). In the *Description de l'Égypte*, the city is mentioned with the name "Bahnasa" (182, vol. 4: 391; vol. 18: 115).

Amélineau and Muhammad Ramzi give the ancient Egyptian name of al-Bahnasa as Pamâdjat or Pamazet (Amélineau 1893: 91–93; Ramzi 1960, vol. 3: 212). The name of al-Bahnasa is mentioned by Isambert (1881, vol. 2: 467); Boinet (1899: 105); Maspero (1912: 40, 140); Maspero and Wiet (1919, vol. 39: 51, 173–91); Combe, Sauvaget, and Wiet (1932: vol. 3, no. 939); and Wiet (1960: 926). Timm also wrote of it as "al-Bahnasa" and "Pemèe" (1984, vol. 1: 111). According to Muhammad Ramzi, al-Bahnasa is one of the ancient Egyptian villages previously mentioned by Gauthier (1925) under the religious name Permaza or Permazd. Its civic name was Mert. Its Roman name was Oxyrhynchos (Ramzi 1960, vol. 3: 211). Al-Bahnasa's name in Greek is ξεριχου or εξερίου (Timm 1984–92, vol. 1: 111–28, 283–300), and in Coptic it is ⲡⲉⲙϫⲉ or ⲡⲉⲙϫⲏ ('Ali Mubarak 1881, vol. 11: 3; Timm 1984–92, vol. 1: 111–28, 283–300). According to Grenfell and Hunt, the ancient al-Bahnasa received the official Greek name of Νεα τοὐοτινου πόλις during the sixth century AD (1898, vol. 1: 51–52, 126, 33).

MacLennan writes concerning the name of al-Bahnasa: "It took its outlandish name from a certain species of fish which in antique times was adopted as a sort of genius loci. This fish-cult dated back to remote pharaohs and during Roman times had apparently lost most of its importance" (MacLennan 1968: 11–12; Meinardus 1969: 259). Mary Magdi added that al-Bahnasa was the capital of the nineteenth province in Upper Egypt, in which the locals worshiped a type of fish called *Mormyrus* that was common in this city (Milad 2000: 59–60; Magdi 2011: 306).

After the Arab conquest of Egypt by 'Amr ibn al-'As in AH 21/AD 641–42, al-Bahnasa received other names, such as 'Izbat al-'Abadiya and Bahnasat Ahmad (Magdi 2011: 306).

Muhammad Ramzi adds that al-Bahnasa was mentioned in AD 1820 with the name of al-Bahnasa al-Gharbiya, a name that is still used by the Ministry of Interior, perhaps because the town is located west of the Nile in front of Sandfa, which is called by the locals 'al-Bahnasa al-Sharqiya.' When Muhammad Pasha al-Nashangi became the prefect of Egypt for the first time in AD 1720, he ordered the removal of the 'prefectus diwan' from al-Bahnasa to al-Fashn, to be near the main road between Cairo and Upper Egypt. In AD 1830, under Muhammad 'Ali Pasha, al-Bahnasa became the main town of Middle Egypt, and perhaps also its center of government, after all the towns in the districts of Minya and Abu Qurqas were added to it. Since that time, al-Bahnasa has been considered a part of the district of Bani Mazar (Ramzi 1960: 212).

Al-Bahnasa in Arabic Sources

Under the rule of the Roman emperors, al-Bahnasa was the most important municipal center in the area; it was the main capital or metropolis of its district and also of the Oxyrhynchite province (Bowman et al. 2007: v–vi). In AD 200, when Septimus Severus visited Egypt, he held his assizes first at Pelusium and then at al-Bahnasa. It may have become a regular seat for the prefect's *conventus* in the late third century AD (Turner 1952; Meinardus 1969: 256). In 1912, Maspero mentioned Futuh al-Bahnasa, a historical reference without any real documentary value for the purposes of this chapter (1912: 40). He described only the towers and the military architecture of Roman Bahnasa without giving any information about its Christian religious buildings.

Narrating the details of the Arab conquest of Egypt and the battle of Heliopolis, Butler said, "They advanced in this way to a town called

Bahnasa which they took by storm, and slaughtered all before them—men, women and children" (1902: 223). He mentioned also how the city of al-Bahnasa resisted the Arab conquest.

Al-Bahnasa was also one of the most important sources for the wood used for the Egyptian fleet under the rule of the Fatimids and the Ayyubids (AH 567–647/AD 1171–1249). It is known that the famous historian al-Musabihi (AH 366–420/AD 977–1029) was the prefect of al-Bahnasa during the time of the Fatimid caliph al-Hakim Bi Amr Allah (AH 386–411/AD 996–1021) (Anan 1999: 49–50). The well-known historian and geographer Ibn Hawqal (d. AH 367/AD 977) described al-Bahnasa as a town in Upper Egypt (1938, vol. 2: 155; 1965, vol. 1, 2nd ed.: 105, 159).

Many are the other Arabic sources in which al-Bahnasa is mentioned, such as the work of al-Quda'i (d. AH 454/AD 1062), who was born during the time of the Fatimid caliph al-Hakim Bi Amr Allah (Anan 1999: 57–58), and who mentioned al-Bahnasa simply as one of the cities of Egypt. Other Arabic sources describing al-Bahnasa include the books of Ibn Qudama (d. AH 486/AD 1093), Ibn al-Hamadhani (d. AH 759/AD 1357), and al-Ya'bubi (AH 1313–85/AD 1895–1965).

Al-Muqaddasi (AH 819–88/AD 1416–83) wrote about the luxury linen textiles produced in Oxyrhynchos, which was a big city inhabited by a large population (al-Muqaddasi 1980). For Ibn al-Ji'an (d. AH 930/AD 1524), this town declined to the point where it existed in name alone (1898: 159).

After visiting Egypt, several foreign travelers, such as Nasir-i Khusraw 'Ulwi (fifth century AH/eleventh century AD), 'Abd al-Latif al-Baghdadi (AH 557–629/AD 1162–1231), and Ibn Batutta (AH 703–79/AD 1304–77), described al-Bahnasa as a big city surrounded by several gardens (Nasir-i Khusraw 'Ulwi 1993; 'Abd al-Latif al-Baghdadi 1810: 685; Defremery and Sanguinetti 1969, vol. 1).

Christianity in al-Bahnasa in Arabic Sources

In Arabic sources, al-Bahnasa is mentioned as flourishing, due to its ancient Egyptian temples, its Coptic monasteries, and its churches. John of Nikiou mentions the city while writing about the Arab conquest of Egypt (John of Nikiou 1916: 555).

Abu al-Makarim also writes that the churches of this city and the neighborhood are several and he specifically mentions the church of St. Ammon (Abamun). He mentions the existence of about 360 churches in the area of al-Bahnasa. Among them are the church of Mary[4] and the church of St.

John or Abu Hanna the martyr, constructed perhaps in Najaj, to the north of Rifa[5] and Udrunkah (Evetts and Butler 1895: fol. 75 a, 215; Hyvernat 1886: 174; Amélineau 1890: 141). Abu al-Makarim also speaks about the churches of the martyred saints George and Bartholomew.[6] The latter suffered martyrdom on 1 Tut/29 August, either in the oasis of al-Bahnasa or on the Egyptian or Nubian seacoast; his body was in a church in al-Bahnasa named the church of Karbil. Abu Salih the Armenian says about this martyr:

> On this day is commemorated the death of the holy disciple Bartholomew, one of the Twelve. To this apostle it was allotted that he should go to the Oases. So he and Peter travelled thither, and he preached the gospel to the inhabitants of the Oases, and called them to the Knowledge of God, after wonderful signs and astounding miracles had been shown to them. After converting the people in the Oases, then he went to the country on the sea-coast, to those who knew not God; and he preached among them and turned them to the Knowledge of God and to faith in the Lord Christ. But Agharbus, the king, heard of him and was wroth with him, and commanded that they should put him in a sack of hair-cloth and fill it with sand and cast him into the sea. (Evetts and Butler 1895: 215–16)

In addition, Abu al-Makarim reports the existence of the churches of saints Mark, Stephen, and Theodore in al-Saqya, also called Saqyat Mahfuz (Evetts and Butler 1895: 215; Ibn Duqmaq 1893, vol. 5: 8). There were also the churches of St. Abadir, of the archangels Michael and Gabriel, renovated by a certain official, the churches of the disciples and the apostles, and the church of the Holy Virgin Mary. He adds to his list the church of the martyr Istafura, that is, St. Christopher or Christianos, named the Dog's Face.[7] This martyr, whose church was on the canal outside the city, was one of those who were usually associated with the pure disciples and the fathers. For each of the two saints George and Mercurius, there were two churches on the borders of the lake in al-Bahnasa and in Idfak,[8] in addition to churches bearing the names of saints Paul and Thomas. Most probably the historian means here St. Paul the first hermit or St. Paul of Tamwuh, known for his austerity, who is commemorated on 7 Baba/4 October (Evetts and Butler 1895: 217). Concerning the church of St. George, built in the oasis of al-Bahnasa, according to Abu al-Makarim it is said that it contained only his body without the head (Evetts and Butler 1895: 258–59). In Ashrubah in the district of Bani Mazar, there were also two churches of the Cross.[9] At Saft Rashin, to the north of al-Bahnasa and to the south of Beni Suef, there was the church of St. Theodore the Oriental, which was wrecked by the Ghuzz and the Kurds. Later, this church was transformed into a mosque (Evetts and Butler 1895: 214).

Al-Maqrizi (d. AH 845/AD 1441) mentions that the city of al-Bahnasa was built by a Copt named Minawish ibn Minqawish (1835, vol. 1: 237). He also writes about the Monastery of the Holy Virgin Mary, outside Tanbda, a small village away from the main road. At that time, only one monk was living in this monastery. The same historian adds that in al-Bahnasa many monasteries and churches were built but had lately been destroyed (al-Maqrizi 1835, vol 1: 237; al-Maqrizi 1998: 164, 217 n. 3; 'Ali Mubarak 1887, vol. 11: 3). According to Gabra, perhaps some of these monasteries and churches declined or were abandoned after the heavy tax imposed on the monks for the first time in AD 705 (2008: 204). Al-Bakri confirms the arrival of the Savior and his Mother in al-Bahnasa, where palms flourished (1992: vol. 2, 147 n. 2). Yaqut al-Hamawi mentions that there was also a chapel in al-Bahnasa where the Holy Family stayed for about seven years before they returned to Jerusalem.[10] In fact the duration of the stay of the Holy Family in Egypt has long been a matter of controversy, perhaps because the duration is not mentioned in the Holy Book, in the historical sources, or in the homilies. But it is known that the Savior and his Mother stayed in Egypt for about three years and eleven months according to the Coptic Orthodox tradition and also to the contents of a Coptic papyrus published at Cologne University in May 1998 by Gesa Schenke (2004: 151–55). Mary Magdi mentions that the news of this papyrus, dating from the fourth–fifth century AD, was published in the second edition of *al-Ahram* under the title "Bardiya qibtiya al-masih 'asha fi misr arba' sanawat" (Magdi 2011: 42–43).[11] According to Mikha'il Maksi Iskandar and Abba Demetrius, from this papyrus,[12] written in Fayoumic Coptic, we learn that the arrival of the Savior was in the Coptic month of Pashons, as follows: "ⲈⲔⲈϢⲰⲠⲒ ⲚϨⲨⲠⲞⲠⲀⲆⲒⲞⲚ ⲚⲎⲒ ϨⲘ ⲠⲈϨⲀⲞⲨ Ⲛ̄ⲦⲈⲔ̄ ⲔⲖⲎⲢⲞⲚⲞⲘⲒⲀ Ⲙ̄ⲠⲀϢⲀⲤ" ('You shall be the homeland for my feet in the day of your inheritance in Pashons'). Gesa Schenke published this text as follows: "Du wirst mir zum Fußschemel werden, am Tage deines Erbes im (Monat) Paschons" (Schenke 2004: 154). In the same papyrus, the following is written: "ⲦⲘⲈⲦⲔⲞⲨⲒ Ⲙ̄ⲠⲀϢⲎⲖⲒ ⲈⲤⲈϢⲰⲠⲒ ⲚϨⲎⲦⲔ ⲚⲄ̄ ⲚⲖⲀⲘⲠⲒ ⲘⲚ ⲒⲀ̄ ⲚⲀⲂⲀⲦ" ('The childhood of my son will be in you three years and eleven months when the enemies shall follow him') (Iskandar 1999:

75; Adli 1999: 130; Abba Demetrius 2000: 55; Abba Demetrius 2007: 13, 37–46; Athanasiyus al-Maqqari 2007: 11; Magdi 2011: 42–43).

Following Abu al-Makarim, al-Maqrizi also mentions that there were about 360 churches in Bahnasa province, all of which were damaged except for the Church of the Virgin, which still existed in al-Maqrizi's time (al-Maqrizi 1835, vol. 1: 237; al-Maqrizi 1998: 164, 217 n. 3; 'Ali Mubarak 1887, vol. 11: 3).

Al-Bahnasa was well known for its fine textiles made out of linen, wool, cotton, and silk. These rich fabrics were exported to the Mediterranean area and to the Arab countries. At the end of Mamluk rule (AH 648–923/ AD 1250–1517), many historians spoke about al-Bahnasa as a glorious and considerable city, and they mentioned that all kinds of textiles produced in it were decorated with its name. The woolen fabrics produced in this city impressed several historians and travelers, such as Ibn Mammati and Ibn Battuta (Ibn Mammati 1943: 81, 344–45; Ramzi 1960, vol. 3: 212; Defremery and Sanguinetti 1969, vol. 1: 96). Some examples are displayed in the Coptic and Islamic Art museums in Cairo, as well as in other internationally known archaeological museums in Europe and America.

Describing al-Bahnasa, 'Ali Mubarak confirmed that there were two cities bearing this name: one in the Wah oasis and the other in Middle Egypt between Minyat Khasib and Beni Suef. According to 'Ali Mubarak, the large city of al-Bahnasa in Middle Egypt was well known before the Arab conquest of Egypt. Its area was about one thousand feddans. During the conquest, al-Bahnasa was a distinguished city with high walls, towers, and gates. It had four gates oriented to the four cardinal points: Bab al-Ghabal, Bab Qandas, Bab al-'Izabi, and Bab Tuma. Each gate consisted of three towers. Between each pair of towers, there were several windows. Al-Bahnasa contained the largest number of Coptic monasteries and churches in Egypt. The inhabitants used to pray in the twelve main churches ('Ali Mubarak 1887, vol. 11: 1–3). Its gates and suburbs were protected by guards who used to receive foreign visitors. The city was also inhabited by a great number of monks and priests. They outnumbered the craftsmen and the workers of the city. Relying on what the historian Palladius wrote after his visit to Egypt in AD 407 (Lucot 1912, vol. 34), 'Ali Mubarak wrote that there were perhaps two thousand nuns and five thousand monks and hegumens who lived in the monasteries and inside the city walls of al-Bahnasa. These figures may be compared with what Maspero wrote in 1923 when he said that, in a period previous to his own, the number of the religious in this city was equivalent to the number of unbelievers (Maspero 1923: 55). In the *Historia Monachorum in Aegypto,* the author reports that, in the fourth century AD, about ten thousand monks and twenty thousand nuns were subject to the bishop of the diocese of Bahnasa (Meinardus 1969: 256; Stewart 1991). Mary Magdi confirms that during these two centuries, al-Bahnasa was one of the well-known Coptic bishoprics, containing the same number of monks but only twelve thousand nuns (Magdi 2011: 307). Meinardus mentions that these numbers were "enough to turn the town into a kind of holy city, where monks congested the streets and the town was so full of monasteries that monkish songs were heard in every quarter." He added that the town had its own hospital and became a considerable episcopal see during the sixth century AD (Meinardus 1969: 256). Also according to Meinardus, the monastic population of Egypt exceeded half a million souls.

These exaggerated numbers show that during the fifth century AD the towns and villages of the province of al-Bahnasa were full of Christians, monasteries, and churches. It is evident that al-Bahnasa was the seat of the bishops and it became the capital of the province of Arcadia in Middle Egypt (Bagnall and Rathbone 2008: 158–59). Mary Magdi mentions the names of Elia the Eunuch, Isaac, and Apios, who suffered martyrdom under the rule of the Roman emperor Diocletian (AD 284–305) (Iskandar 1999: 51–52; Magdi 2011: 307). She also mentions the name of Abba Butros as one of the famous bishops of al-Bahnasa who attended the Council of Ephesus in AD 431, in addition to other bishops such as Theodosios, Blagios, Dionisios, Theodoros, Apollonios, and Cyril, who wrote and explained the Gospels of saints Luke and John (Magdi 2011: 307). After AD 1821, the locality went into severe decline.

Al-Bahnasa in Recent References

At the turn of the twentieth century in al-Bahnasa, Grenfell, Hunt, and their successors discovered the biggest collection of papyri at that time, the most important pieces of which Edgar Lobel conserved at Queen's College, Oxford. In the winter of 1896–97 and from 1903 to 1907, these scholars discovered many Greek, Hebrew, Syriac, and Coptic texts dating from the time of Augustus until the eighth century AD (Turner 1952; Poethke 1991; Bowman et al. 2007: v–vi). These included possible works of Ephorus, the *Life of Euripides* written by Satyrus in the form of a dialogue, and a popular biography, as well as a literary find in an example of a Latin text (Meinardus 1969: 257). Since 1890, remains of granite columns, fragments of capitals, and other stonework, as well as pottery objects, have been discovered. Recently, scholars have written much about al-Bahnasa, which came to international fame because of its long and important Christian history, its monuments, and its papyri, but little or no mention has been made of Christianity itself in this locale.

About eighteen kilometers to the west of Bani Mazar, the church of St. Theodore was built on the eastern bank of the Sea of Joseph in the al-Bahnasa region. The existing building dates back to the eighteenth–nineteenth century AD. The translation of the relics of St. Theodore to Shutb, located in the south of Asyut, is annually celebrated here on 20 Abib/27 July (Meinardus 2003: 78).

Flinders Petrie discovered the Roman and the Byzantine necropolis, as did the members of the Italian scientific archaeological missions (Bagnall and Rathbone 2008: 160). In 1923, the church of Saint George the Roman was built in al-Bahnasa by Ibrahim Ghattas and Father Butros Ishaq in the same place as the ancient archaeological church of the Holy Virgin Mary. In 1955, remains of an archaeological church were discovered inside the Islamic tombs of al-Bahnasa.[13] From 1985 until 1987, the members of the Kuwaiti archaeological mission worked on the Islamic remains at al-Bahnasa. In 1992, Catalan–Egyptian excavations took place in the northwestern necropolis of al-Bahnasa, and a Coptic oratory and access to three crypts were discovered (Bagnall and Rathbone 2008: 161). Nowadays, anyone can visit the only ancient archaeological site existing, which includes the tree of Mary and a well that is inside the recent Islamic cemetery about ten kilometers from the Garanus monastery.

In conclusion, al-Bahnasa was blessed by the visit of the Savior, according to the Coptic Orthodox tradition. Immediately after the introduction of Christianity in al-Bahnasa, according to several Arabic sources, the number of Christians increased in this town. The Arab historians affirms that during medieval times, al-Bahnasa was a prosperous city known for its rich Christian tradition. It was the birthplace of many saints and martyrs. Several ancient temples of al-Bahnasa were transformed into monasteries and churches. Other monasteries and churches were built throughout the city. Later, Islamic buildings were constructed there. In al-Bahnasa, there was also the largest archaeological discovery of Greek papyri in the nineteenth and the twentieth centuries. For a long recent period the entire city was covered by sand, and today the appearance of al-Bahnasa has totally changed from the large and vibrant city described by various Arab historians and travelers. Nowadays, the bishop of Beni Suef is the bishop of al-Bahnasa and Beni Suef.

Notes

1 This source, most probably written by the ecclesiastical historian Mawhub ibn Mansur ibn Mufarrig, was later wrongly attributed to Sawirus Ibn al-Muqaffa', who was bishop of al-Ashmunayn. See Swanson 2010: 61.

2 This book, written by Abu al-Makarim, was wrongly attributed to Abu Salih the Armenian.

3 Abu al-Makarim wrote the following: "The oasis of al-Bahnas, to which there is a road from the town after which it is named, is reckoned a part of the province of the Fayoum, and consists of four districts: That of Buwiti with 1,675 inhabitants; that of al-Kasr, the chief town with 1,387 inhabitants; that of Mundishsh with 1,506 inhabitants; and that of az-Zabu with 808 inhabitants; the total being 5,436 inhabitants" (Abu al-Makarim 1895: 258–59 n. 2; Amélineau 1893: 290 f.).

4 This is the name of two different martyrs who lived during the rule of Diocletian (AD 284–305). Their death is commemorated on 13 Abib/17 July. See Evetts and Butler 1895: 210, 214–15, fol. 73b, no. 3.

5 Rifa is a small and poor village in the neighborhood of Asyut on the west bank of the Nile. Its name in Coptic is ⲉⲣⲏⲃⲉ. Remains of an ancient Coptic monastery still exist there. See Evetts and Butler 1895: 214.

6 The church of this saint was in al-Turfah village in the province of Bahnasa; it was later included in the district of Qalusana in Minya. In 1885, its inhabitants numbered about 435. Mawhub saw the relics of Bartholomew in the Saint Shenute Monastery in Sohag. Some of his relics were also preserved in Karbil church in the Bahnasa Oasis. See Meinardus 1969: 155; Abu al-Makarim 1895: 215.

7 In Alwah in Nubia, the Copts commemorate St. Christopher on 2 Baramuda/28 May. Zoega 1810: 235; Evetts and Butler 1895: 216; Basset 1922: 408–409.

8 Name given to an unknown place. Evetts and Butler 1895: 215–17.

9 This place is described by Ibn Duqmaq as a place of no importance. It belonged to al-Bahnasa in the fourteenth century AD and it was mentioned in the revenue list of the year 1375. Evetts and Butler 1895: 217; 'Abd al-Latif al-Baghdadi 1910: 685.

10 Qur'an (Sura "The Believers," 50); Yaqut al-Hamawi 1955, vol. 1: 516–17; al-Maqrizi 1835, vol. 1: 237; al-Maqrizi 1998: 164, 217 n. 3; 'Ali Mubarak 1887, vol. 11: 3; Meinardus 1969: 256.

11 In 1998, the news of the Coptic papyrus of Cologne University was announced in *al-Ahram* as follow: "Bardiya qibtiya al-masih 'asha fi misr arba' sanawat" [Coptic Papyrus: Christ Lived in Egypt Four Years], *al-Ahram*, no. 40724, 2nd ed. (6 June 1998), p. 1. The same text was also published with the same title in *Magalat rabitat al-Quds*: "Bardiya qibtiya al-masih 'asha fi misr arba' sanawat" [Coptic Papyrus: Christ Lived in Egypt Four Years]," *Magalat rabitat al-Quds*, no. 210 (July 1998).

12 Unknown provenance. Dimensions: 31.8 x 8.7—31.5 x 8.4 cm. Preserved at first in the library of Cologne University (Magdi 2011: 42–43).

13 Samah 'Abd al-'Atti, "Athar al-'a'ila al-muqadasa fi Alminya: bi'ran wa shagara wa arba' kana'is, Rihlat al-'a'ila al-muqadasa, al-halaqa al-rabi'a," *Al-Masry Al-Youm*, 10 January 2010; Magdi 2011: 42–43.

4 Mesokemic or 'Middle Egyptian'—the Coptic Dialect of Oxyrhynchos (?)

Frank Feder

Zum Gedenken an Hans-Martin Schenke

Mesokemic (siglum: *M*) is a dialect of Coptic that was discovered relatively late. It was Paul E. Kahle (Kahle 1954: 196, 220–27) who first described its characteristics and distinguished *M* clearly from the other dialects of Upper Egypt and the Fayoum. The corpus of texts in Mesokemic then known to Kahle was very small, but comprised very early documents that shed light on the early development and usage of different dialectal varieties of Coptic for literary texts in the third and fourth centuries. The corpus has grown substantially since then, and we possess today quite a comprehensive idea of Mesokemic's lexical and morphological features. Hans-Martin Schenke's description in *The Coptic Encyclopedia* gives a concise and appropriate evaluation of *M*: "It [Mesokemic] is one of the relatively minor Coptic idioms and probably flourished only briefly in the early period of the Coptic language (fourth and fifth centuries), but nevertheless developed in this period into a highly standardized written dialect" (Schenke 1991).

Morphophonological Characteristics of *M*[1]

Among the Coptic dialects, *M* shares most characteristics with Fayoumic *(F)*, except, however, for the lambdacism of the central variety of *F* (*F4* and *F5*). In this respect the sub-varieties of *F* (*V* and *W*) are even closer to *M*. The consonants are the same as in Sahidic, but *M* does not show the graphic vocalic germination (representation of aleph /'/), here conforming to *F4*, *V4*, *F7*, *W*, and *B*. A simple example may show the characteristics of *M* in comparison especially with the *F*-Group and the other major dialects of Coptic (cf. Kasser 1990; Kasser 2004: 105–10):

B	**ⲫⲣⲱⲙⲉ ⲉⲧⲟⲛϧ ⲟⲩⲟϩ ⲫⲏ ⲉⲧϣⲟⲡ ⲛⲁⲱ**
S	**ⲡⲣⲱⲙⲉ ⲉⲧⲟⲛϩ ⲁⲩⲱ ⲡⲉⲧϣⲟⲟⲡ ⲛⲁⲱ**
F5	**ⲡⲗⲱⲙⲓ ⲉⲧⲁⲛ(ⲁ)ϩ ⲁⲩⲱ (ⲁϩⲁ) ⲡⲉⲧϣⲁⲁⲡ ⲛⲏⲱ**
F4	**ⲡⲗⲱⲙⲓ ⲉⲧⲁⲛϩ ⲁⲩⲱ ⲡⲉⲧϣⲁⲡ ⲛⲉⲱ**
V	**ⲡⲣⲱⲙⲓ ⲉⲧⲁⲛϩ ⲁⲩⲱ ⲡⲉⲧϣⲁⲡ ⲛⲉⲱ**
W	**ⲡⲣⲱⲙⲓ ⲉⲧⲁⲛϩ ⲁⲩⲱ ⲡⲉⲧϣⲁⲡ ⲛⲉⲱ**
M	**ⲡⲣⲟⲙⲉ ⲉⲧⲁⲛϩ ⲁⲩⲱ ⲡⲉⲧϣⲁⲡ ⲛⲉⲱ**
L	**ⲡⲣⲱⲙⲉ ⲉⲧⲁ(ⲁ)ⲛϩ ⲁⲩⲱ ⲡⲉⲧϣⲟⲟⲡ ⲛⲉⲱ**
A	**ⲡⲣⲱⲙⲉ ⲉⲧⲁⲛϩ ⲁⲟⲩ ⲡⲉⲧϩⲟⲟⲡ ⲛⲉⲱ**

At a first glance it becomes obvious that the most peculiar characteristic making *M*-texts almost immediately recognizable is the vowel **ⲟ** in the stressed syllable instead of ϥ in all other dialects. Moreover, the use of **ϩⲁ-**, **ϩⲁϥ-** as conjugation morpheme of the affirmative perfect makes the differentiation between the circumstantial and the focalizing conversion ("second tense")—consequently also for the present in the durative conjugation—clearer than in the other dialects (Funk 1981; Schenke 1991). Table 4.1 illustrates this in comparison to Sahidic.

There can be no doubt that *M* was a comparatively highly standardized variety of Coptic. But since new witnesses of Mesokemic texts keep appearing, it is clear that, at least in the fourth century, the process of standardization was still underway. This led to the differentiation of two sub-varieties, *M4* and *M5* (Kasser 2004: 105–11; Kasser 2006: 420–21) and, in the case of the earliest biblical Mesokemic papyrus, the Gospel of Matthew (Ms Schøyen 2650), which differs in several respects from the *M4*/*M5*-Group, even the designation *C (Catamésokémique)* (Kasser 2004: 99; Kasser 2006: 408) was chosen, although this has remained a matter of discussion (cf. Bosson 2006). The influx of new manuscripts until recently makes it probable that further Mesokemic documents will appear. We might, therefore, soon be forced to revise our overall picture of Mesokemic and its text corpus.

Table 4.1. Comparison of Mesokemic and Sahidic conjugations

Mesokemic

Conjugation *M*	preterite	circumstantial	relative	focalizing
ϥ	ⲛⲁϥ	ⲉϥ	ⲉⲧϥ	ⲁϥ
ⲥⲉ	ⲛⲁⲩ	ⲉⲩ	ⲉⲧⲥⲉ (ⲉⲧⲟⲩ)	ⲁⲩ
Nominal	ⲛⲁⲣⲉ	ⲉⲣⲉ	ⲉⲧⲉ	ⲁⲣⲉ
ϩⲁϥ	ⲛⲉϩⲁϥ	ⲉϩⲁϥ	ⲉⲑⲁϥ	ⲉϩⲁϥ, ⲁϩⲁϥ
ⲙⲡϥ	ⲛⲉⲙⲡϥ	ⲉⲙⲡϥ	ⲉⲧⲉ ⲙⲡϥ	
ⲙⲡⲁⲧϥ	ⲛⲉⲙⲡⲁⲧϥ	ⲉⲙⲡⲁⲧϥ		
ϣⲁ(ⲣⲉ)ϥ	ⲛⲉϣⲁϥ	ⲉϣⲁ(ⲣⲉ)ϥ	ⲉⲧϣⲁ(ⲣⲉ)ϥ	ⲉϣⲁϥ
ⲙⲉϥ		ⲉⲙⲉϥ	ⲉⲧⲉ ⲙⲉϥ	
ⲉϥⲉ			ⲉⲧⲉϥⲉ	
ⲛⲛⲉϥ		ⲉⲛⲛⲉϥ	ⲉⲧⲉ ⲛⲛⲉϥ	

Sahidic

Conjugation *S*	preterite	circumstantial	relative	focalizing
ϥ	ⲛⲉϥ	ⲉϥ	ⲉⲧϥ	ⲉϥ
ⲥⲉ	ⲛⲉⲩ	ⲉⲩ	ⲉⲧⲟⲩ	ⲉⲩ
Nominal	ⲛⲉ(ⲣⲉ)	ⲉⲣⲉ, ⲉ	ⲉⲧⲉⲣⲉ, ⲉⲧⲉ	ⲉⲣⲉ
ⲁϥ	ⲛⲉⲁϥ	ⲉⲁϥ	ⲉⲛⲧⲁϥ	ⲛⲧⲁϥ
ⲙⲡϥ	ⲛⲉⲙⲡϥ	ⲉⲙⲡϥ	ⲉⲧⲉ ⲙⲡϥ	ⲉⲧⲉ ⲙⲡϥ
ⲙⲡⲁⲧϥ	ⲛⲉⲙⲡⲁⲧϥ	ⲉⲙⲡⲁⲧϥ	ⲉⲧⲉ ⲙⲡⲁⲧϥ	
ϣⲁϥ	ⲛⲉϣⲁϥ	ⲉϣⲁϥ	ⲉⲧⲉ ϣⲁϥ, ⲉϣⲁϥ	ⲉϣⲁϥ
ⲙⲉϥ	ⲛⲉⲙⲉϥ	ⲉⲙⲉϥ	ⲉⲧⲉ ⲙⲉϥ	
ⲉϥⲉ		(ⲉϥⲉ)		
ⲛⲛⲉϥ		ⲉⲛⲛⲉϥ	ⲉⲧⲉ (ⲛ)ⲛⲉϥ	

Extant Manuscripts in Mesokemic (and Its Varieties)

Biblical Texts (in Chronological Order)

Greek–Coptic glossary to Hosea and Amos (London, British Museum EA 10825 (Trismegistos database: 61982)), papyrus, late 3rd century

Provenance: unknown

Publication: Bell, H.I., and H. Thompson. 1925. "A Greek–Coptic Glossary to Hosea and Amos." *Journal of Egyptian Archaeology* 11: 241–46.

Codex Schøyen (Oslo, collection Martin Schøyen: MS 2650), papyrus, first half of 4th century

Content: Gospel of Matthew

Provenance: unknown

Publication: Schenke, H.-M. 2001. *Coptic Papyri in the Schøyen Collection, vol. 1: Das Matthäus-Evangelium im mittelägyptischen Dialekt des Koptischen (Codex Schøyen).* Manuscripts in the Schøyen Collection 2. Oslo: Hermes Publishing.

On the website of the Schøyen Collection we can read among the notes on the context of the Gospel of Matthew papyrus that MSS 2648 (Joshua 9:27–11:3; 6 leaves, Greek, 2nd century), 2649 (fragments (8 leaves) of Leviticus, Greek, 2nd century), 2651, and 14 ff. of Isaiah (in Mesokemic, ca. 300) were found tipped in among the leaves of MS 2650. Probably from the same hoard as the Chester Beatty papyri, now in Dublin: Chester Beatty Library.[2]

Dialect: *C* (new proposal of Kasser)

Codex Mudil (Cairo, Coptic Museum: inv. no. 12488), parchment, 4th–5th century

Content: Psalter

Provenance: al-Mudil (eastern shore of the Nile, about 45 km northeast of Oxyrhynchos, 7 km north of al-Hiba)

Publication: Gabra, G. 1995. *Der Psalter im oxyrhynchitischen (mesokemischen/mittelägyptischen) Dialekt mit Beiträgen von N. Iskander, G. Mink und L. Sharp.* Abhandlungen des Deutschen Archäologischen Instituts Kairo, Koptische Reihe 4. Cairo: ADAIK.

Bosson, N., and Rodolphe Kasser. 1997. *Wörterverzeichnis zu Gawdat Gabras Ausgabe des Psalters im mesokemischen (oxyrhynchitischen/mittelägyptischen) Dialekt des Koptischen (Mudil Kodex).* CSCO 568, Subsidia 96. Louvain: Peeters.

Dialect: *M4*

Fig. 4.2. The Psalter (al-Mudil Codex). Coptic Museum, inv. no. 12488. Photograph by Gawdat Gabra

Codex Milan (Milano, Istituto di Papyrologia dell'Università degli Studi di Milano, P.Mil.Vogl Copt. 1 inv. no. 15) papyrus, 4–5th cent.
Content: Letters of St. Peter
Provenance: unknown
Publication: Orlandi, T. 1974. *Papiri della Università degli Studi di Milano (P. Mil. Copti), vol. 5, Lettere di San Paolo in copto-ossirinchita. Edizione, commento e indici di Tito Orlandi, Contributo linguistico di Hans Quecke*. Milan: La Goliardica. [New edition by N. Bosson in preparation].
Dialect: *M4*

pOxford (Sackler Library, Papyrology Rooms number unknown; Trismegistos database: 107980, parchment, 4th–5th century (?)
Content: Epistle to the Romans
Provenance: Oxyrhynchus.
Publication: Crum, W.E. 1927. "Some Further Meletian Documents." *Journal of Egyptian Archaeology* 13: 25–26.
Dialect: *M5*

Codex Scheide (Princeton, University Library: M 144), parchment, 5th century
Content: Gospel of Matthew
Provenance: unknown
Publication: Schenke, H.-M. 1981. *Das Matthäusevangelium im mittelägyptischen Dialekt des Koptischen (Codex Scheide).* Texte und Untersuchungen zur Geschichte der altchristlichen Literatur 127. Berlin: Akademie-Verlag.
Dialect: *M5*

Codex Glazier (New York, Pierpont Morgan Library: G 67), parchment, 5th century
Content: Acts
Provenance: unknown
Publication: Schenke, H.-M. 1991. *Apostelgeschichte 1,1–15,3 im mittelägyptischen Dialekt des Koptischen (Codex Glazier).* Texte und Untersuchungen zur Geschichte der altchristlichen Literatur 137. Berlin: Akademie-Verlag.[4]
Dialect: *M5*

Genesis Fragment (formerly British Museum Or. 9035, now British Library Or. 9035 (45) (46) (49)), parchment, 5th century
Content: Genesis (6:7–19)
Provenance: Wadi Sarga, Monastery of Apa Thomas[3]
Publication: Barns, J.W.B., and R. Kasser. 1971. "Le manuscrit moyen-égyptien B.M. Or. 9035." *Le Muséon* 84: 395–401.

Job Fragment (formerly British Museum Or. 9035, now British Library Or. 9035 (41)), parchment, 5th century
Content: Job (30:8–9, 17–18)
Provenance: Wadi Sarga, Monastery of Apa Thomas
Publication: Crum, W.E., and H.I. Bell. 1922. *Wadi Sarga: Coptic and Greek Texts from the Excavations Undertaken by the Byzantine Research Account.* Coptica 3, 29–30. Copenhagen: Gyldendalske Boghandel–Nordisk Forlag.

Literary Texts

Cyriacus Fragments (University of Michigan Collection P. Mich 1291; Selly Oak College, Central Library, Birmingham, P. Harris 16), papyrus, 5th century
Content: Martyrdom of Cyriacus and Julitta

Provenance: unknown
Publication: Husselman, E.M. 1965. "The Martyrdom of Cyriacus and Julitta in Coptic." *Journal of the American Research Center in Egypt* 4, pp. 79–86 (PMich 1291, re-edited in Schenke, H.-M. 1991. *Apostelgeschichte*, pp. 245–48 (see above).
Schenke, H.-M. 1999. "Mittelägyptische Nachlese III. Neue Fragmente zum Martyrium des Cyri(a)cus und seiner Mutter Julitta im mittelägyptischen Dialekt des Koptischen." *Zeitschrift für Ägyptische Sprache und Altertumskunde* 126, pp. 149–72.
Dialect: *M5*

P. Oxyrhynchus 4 1B 74/K(a), Oxford, Sackler Library, papyrus, 4th century (?)
Content: Martyrdom (?)
Provenance: Oxyrhynchos
Publication: Alcock, A. 1982. "Persecution under Septimius Severus." *Enchoria* 11, pp. 1–5; cf. also: Schenke, H.-M. 1991. "Bemerkungen zum P. Hamb. Bil. 1 und zum altfayumischen Dialekt der koptischen Sprache." *Enchoria* 18, pp. 86–88.
Dialect: between *M4* and *M5*

Documentary Texts

P. Michigan Inv. 525, papyrus, 4th–5th century
Provenance: unknown
Publication: Schenke, H.-M. 1990. "Ein Brief als Textzeuge für den mittelägyptischen Dialekt des Koptischen (P Mich. Inv. 525)." *Journal of Coptic Studies* 1, pp. 59–72.
Dialect: *M5*

P. British Library Or.11173(2), papyrus, 4th–5th century
Provenance: unknown
Publication: Schenke, H.-M. 1992. "Mittelägyptische Nachlese II. Ein Privatbrief im mittelägyptischen Dialekt des Koptischen [P. British Library Or.11173(2)]." *Zeitschrift für Ägyptische Sprache und Altertumskunde* 119, pp. 43–60.
Dialect: *M5*

The Geographical Situation of *M* and Some Conclusions

Since Paul E. Kahle's first evaluation of Mesokemic,[5] it has been assumed that the original area and center of this dialect was the city of Oxyrhynchos and its surroundings. However, if we take into account the few localized documents mentioned above we would have to span an area possibly covered by Mesokemic reaching from al-Mudil, northeast of Oxyrhynchos, to Wadi Sarga, southwest of Asyut, a space of roughly 250 kilometers from north to south. Moreover, this region includes the areas generally regarded as the 'home' of two other dialects, Akhmimic (center Panopolis/Akhmim) and Lykopolitan (center Lykopolis/Asyut)—dialects that share only a few characteristics with *M*.

The reason for the southernmost documentation of *M* at Wadi Sarga may well have been an 'exile' of a persecuted heterodox Melitian community (coming from a region farther north) in the Monastery of Apa Thomas, as the Melitian background of these documents suggests.[6] As we have seen, there is only one document (P. Oxyrhynchus 4 1B 74/K(a)) that can be safely located in Oxyrhynchos. But this is much too little to prove the origin of *M* in Oxyrhynchos.

As early as 1978, before many of the documents known today came to light, Jürgen Osing expressed doubts about the localization of *M* at Oxyrhynchos (Osing 1978). He based his argumentation on a morphophonological comparison of the *M*-witnesses with an Old Coptic (magical) papyrus clearly from Oxyrhynchos (P. British Museum 10808; about AD 150) whose language tried to be older (classical) Egyptian, but its vowels and consonants, as well as its word and syllable structures, show the same stage of historical development as the Coptic dialects. His conclusion was:

> To sum up: the dialect of the Oxyrhynchos text agrees with Middle Egyptian in the very significant distribution of **ⲟ** and **ⲱ** and in some other features, where it agrees also with Fayyumic and mostly also with Achmimic and Subachmimic. On the other hand it also shows some important differences in comparison to Middle Egyptian and Fayyumic, agreeing in these features with Achmimic and Subachmimic. As most of the differences cannot have developed between AD 150 and AD 300 we have to conclude that the dialect found in the Oxyrhynchos text is not the same as, though closely related to, the Coptic dialect Middle Egyptian.[7]

Given the above-mentioned proximity of *M* to the sub-varieties of Fayoumic, localization farther north seems more likely. Reconsidering the difficulties in classifying the dialect of the Schøyen Papyrus (MS 2650), Nathalie Bosson proposed for this witness a (probable) localization at Herakleopolis Magna (Bosson 2006). This would result in a geographical situation with the dialect of the Schøyen Papyrus (*C* according to Kasser, or *H* as suggested by Bosson) in close proximity to *F7* and *W*, followed southward by *M4* and *M5*, which would in this model, again, also cover the area of Oxyrhynchos (Bosson 2006: 70–73). All in all, without more documents with a secured localization, it will remain extremely difficult to fix the geographical location for *M* or any other dialect.

As far as we know, the use of Mesokemic, at least in written documentation, expired around 500. One of the reasons for this extinction may have been that it was an idiom used by heterodox Christians. The texts from a Melitian community found in the Monastery of Apa Thomas in Wadi Sarga and the Cyriacus fragments (P. Mich 1291 and Birmingham, P. Harris 16), which obviously contain material difficult to accept as orthodox, point in this direction.

Another very interesting feature, particularly of the biblical texts of *M*, is the sometimes unique version they offer in comparison to the mainstream of Coptic translations of the Old and New Testaments. Above all, the Schøyen Papyrus (MS 2650) has attracted specialists in textual criticism of the New Testament due to its hitherto unknown version of the Gospel of Matthew (cf. Boismard 2003a and b; Schenke 2004a and b; Ten Kate 2007; Emmenegger 2007).

Notes

1 Cf. Kasser 1990; Schenke 1991; Kasser 2006.

2 Schøyen Collection, http://www.schoyencollection.com/bibleCoptic.html; cf. also Schenke 2004b.

3 There is hope that the new project of the British Museum under the direction of Elisabeth O'Connell will be able to locate and also (re)publish the Mesokemic manuscripts that were found in the remains of the Monastery of Apa Thomas in Wadi Sarga: British Museum, "Wadi Sarga at the British Museum," http://www.britishmuseum.org/research/research_projects/all_current_projects/wadi_sarga.aspx

4 On p. 3 of this edition, H.-M. Schenke mentions, "on the visible side of the pastedown," a fragment with the text of 4 Kings 1:2–3 in Mesokemic!

5 Kahle 1954: 196, 220–27; he preferred the designation 'Middle Egyptian.'

6 In the same way the (Lykopolitan) Manichaean texts found at Medinet Maadi in the Fayoum seem to witness to an 'exiled' Manichaean community.

7 Osing 1978: 35* (81). Osing therefore uses 'Middle Egyptian' instead of Oxyrhynchite; Subakhmimic is now referred to as Lykopolitan.

5 The Monastery of Apollo at Bala'iza and Its Literary Texts

James E. Goehring

Dayr al-Bala'iza, situated at the edge of the desert on the west bank of the Nile some eighteen to nineteen kilometers south of Asyut, gained initial recognition among Coptic scholars through the large cache of manuscripts, both literary and documentary, discovered at the site during the British excavations conducted by Flinders Petrie in 1907[1] and subsequently published by Paul Kahle in 1954.[2] Petrie's archeological efforts and subsequent published accounts focused as usual on the pharaonic period. The Coptic sites that were explored as part of the larger program, including Dayr al-Bala'iza, receive limited and incomplete treatment at best. The peripheral attention given to this material led, in fact, to questionable and seemingly contradictory theories as well as occasional confusion of materials from various sites.[3] In the introduction to the published account of the work at Giza and Rifa, for example, the Coptic sites or *dayrs* situated south of Asyut are described as

> all of one type; in each case a quarry-cave of Roman age has served as a refuge for the Egyptian at the Arab invasion; walls were built in the great rock caverns to divide them into houses; as peace became established the buildings extended out over the foot-hill in front of the quarry-cave; lastly, at any time during the past eight centuries, one or another of the old strongholds has been abandoned, and the Copts

> have settled in villages on the edge of the cultivation, leaving their old refuges with little or no regard. (Petrie 1907: 2; Grossmann 1993: 172)

While such a view, as Peter Grossmann rightly observes, "fully calls into question the meaning [of the site] as a monastery in the sense of a settlement and abode for monks," elsewhere in the same volume Crum takes the monastic nature of the site for granted, and the *Archeological Report 1906–1907* reports that Petrie "explored the ruins of two Coptic monasteries at Balaizah and Ganadlah."[4] It is difficult to reconcile the two statements. The monastic nature of the site was confirmed by Kahle's 1954 edition and discussion of the Bala'iza texts, many of which leave little doubt as to their monastic provenance (Kahle 1954, vol. 1: 1–45). Clarity with respect to the significant physical remains of the site, however, had to await surveys conducted by Peter Grossmann between 1982 and 1985, accounts of which appeared in print initially in 1984 and fully in 1993 (Grossmann 1986; Grossmann 1993: pl. 12–16; Grossmann 1991; see also Coquin and Martin 1991a). His careful analysis of the evidence greatly improved on the earlier accounts, supplying detailed and fascinating information on the monastery's site plan, its various buildings, its organizational structure, and its history, in so far as they can be reconstructed.[5]

The Physical Monastery and Its History

The monks of Bala'iza constructed their monastery outward from within the bowl-shaped space and caves cut into the face of the western cliff by one of the earlier Roman-era quarrying operations common to this region of Egypt (Grossmann 1986: 35). The existence of a functioning deep well constructed in connection with the quarrying operation surely drew the initial monastic inhabitants to the site and facilitated its later expansion (Grossmann 1993: 175). The evidence suggests that the ascetic community began within the quarry face and caves, improved by the monks for their own use through the construction of additional mud-brick walls (Grossmann 1993: 176; Grossmann 1986: 35–36). Subsequent expansion moved outward from the inner recesses of the quarry with additional buildings constructed in tiers down the slope of the escarpment toward the valley below. The whole complex was eventually encircled by a long wall that connected to the cliff faces on either side of the quarry.[6]

Specifics with respect to the initial use of the site by Christian ascetics, however, remain obscure. Dated documents uncovered among the texts found at Bala'iza range from AD 685 to 740, indicating primary occupation and use of the site as a monastery from the late seventh to the middle of the eighth century (Kahle 1954, vol. 1: 16; Grossmann 1986: 35; Grossmann 1993: 203). Initial use of the site by monks could, of course, have begun somewhat earlier, prior to the period when its size and prestige led to the production of the vast majority of documentary texts.[7] Kahle suggests that "the rather considerable number of early literary texts found at Bala'izah [the majority date before AD 685, with some reaching back to the fourth and fifth centuries] makes it probable that the settlement existed long before the eighth century" (Kahle 1954, vol. 1: 20). Grossmann, however, advises caution in the use of the literary texts to date the occupation of the site, pointing out that such texts may well have come to the monastery after its later founding, either as possessions of individual monks or as gifts (Grossmann 1993: 205; Kahle 1954, vol. 1: 16–17). The fact that the scribal hand of one fourth-century manuscript from Bala'iza closely resembles the hand of the scribe who copied *Pistis Sophia* in the Askew Codex appears to support this contention (Kahle 1954, vol. 1: 7; vol. 2: 322–27 (Ms. 7 = 4 Kings); Grossmann 1993: 205). More reliable evidence of earlier monastic occupation comes from the structure of the small lower church near the gate, which Grossmann dates to the middle of the seventh century (Grossmann 1993: 205). Claims of earlier occupation remain speculative. As for the end of the site's monastic usage, Kahle holds that "there seems little doubt that the monastery was either deserted or destroyed shortly after AD 750, a time when most of the lesser Coptic monasteries disappeared" (Kahle 1954, vol. 1: 19). Grossmann, while noting limited evidence that suggests some form of continuing occupation at least until the beginning of the ninth century, agrees that the end of Bala'iza as a significant monastic community must correspond with the end of the papyrological record, which occurs in the mid-eighth century.[8] It thus seems best to identify Dayr al-Bala'iza as a significant early-Arabic-era Coptic monastery of the mid-seventh to the mid-eighth century.

In its heyday, the Bala'iza monastery would have made a strong visual impression on those who looked up from the valley below toward the cliffs against which it had been built. Impressive architectural structures formed a sizable community or 'city in the desert' shut off from behind by the cliffs of the quarry and from the front and sides by a newly constructed wall.[9] Entrance would have been gained through a gate that opened midway along the eastern wall facing down into the valley. Visitors were housed in a guesthouse located outside of the wall adjacent to the gate, and a gate-keeper regulated entrance from a small room inside the wall beside the gate (Grossmann 1993: 194–96). Having gained entrance through the wall, one would have noticed first the community's well to the right, followed by a small three-aisled church further up the escarpment on the left.[10]

Above the church ranged the majority of the buildings, constructed on natural tiers in the escarpment leading up into the basin of the quarry. As one ascended to this portion of the monastic 'city,' one would have been struck first by the two sizable three-aisled refectories that sat side by side in the center of the first tier of buildings. These were surrounded on both sides and above by a series of single- and multi-story buildings built along narrow streets, each with long narrow rooms that served to accommodate the monks. Narrow windows that allowed for the circulation of air but minimal light suggest that these buildings functioned as monastic sleeping quarters or dormitories.[11] The buildings above the two refectories would have accommodated some four hundred monks, which, when considered alongside the monastery's significantly greater overall surface area, suggests that Dayr al-Bala'iza might well have housed over one thousand ascetics during its peak period of operation (Grossmann 1993: 202). Moving above the monks' quarters, one would have come to a series of buildings, including one to the north with a series of niches in its walls that suggest its use for the community's archive and library.[12] Beyond these, one enters into the quarry itself, where one finds a second, sizable church, constructed around and out from a cave that formed part of the remains of the bowl of the quarry (Grossmann 1993: 181–85). South of this cave church along the west side of the quarry's rock face lies an installation with a series of basins, perhaps used to full or felt cloth, followed in turn by a series of small rooms built into the southwest corner of the quarry's cliff face, the purpose of which remains unknown.[13]

The extensive monastic campus with its impressive physical structures, the evidence of expansion over the more than one hundred years of its existence, and the numerous documents to which we will soon turn all suggest that the Monastery of Apollo at Bala'iza played an integral role in the Upper Egyptian cultural landscape of the seventh–eighth centuries. The gated, walled-in community, with guesthouse, gatehouse, two churches, two refectories, library, and numerous dormitories establishes the monastery's general cenobitic nature. Early efforts sought naturally to link the monastery to the Pachomian movement through its apparent ancient designation as the Monastery of Apollo, mentioned in no fewer than twenty-six documents uncovered at the site (Crum 1907b: 39; Kahle 1954, vol. 1: 15). Assuming that the monastery was named after its founder, Kahle suggested the possible identification of this Apollo with the Pachomian monk of the same name who left the Monastery of Pbow during the sixth-century conflict over Chalcedon that shattered the federation.[14] The panegyric on this Apollo mentions his subsequent founding of two ascetic communities.[15] While the linkage fits nicely into the traditional view of Egyptian cenobitic monasticism as fundamentally Pachomian in origin, Grossmann rightly dismisses the suggestion (Grossmann 1993: 171, n. 3). Among other problems, he notes the infrequent mention of Pachomius in the Bala'iza texts and the fact that little evidence exists of the community's existence prior to the middle of the seventh century, much too late to be the result of the Pachomian Apollo's mid-sixth-century efforts. Even more significant, again as Grossmann makes clear, the dormitories at Bala'iza were constructed as sleeping quarters for multiple monks, a structural format at odds with the Pachomian practice of housing each monk in his own cell or the later Shenoutian development that placed two or three monks in the same room (Grossmann 1993: 201–202). While one might view the dormitories at Bala'iza as a further development along this same path, it seems clear that the end result represents a distinctly different cenobitic structure. While the Monastery of Apollo at Bala'iza may have been influenced in a general way by earlier efforts, such as those of Pachomius and Shenoute, the evidence supports its independent development. Its distinctive cenobitic structure, including its numerous dormitories, sets it apart from other known ascetic communities, serving once again to underscore the diversity of monastic practice in Egypt.[16]

The Manuscripts

The new-found clarity with respect to the structural campus of the Monastery of Apollo at Bala'iza allows one to better situate the better-known Bala'iza manuscripts within their proper historical context. While it is unfortunate that those who explored the site in 1907 kept no record of where the manuscripts were found, it seems evident that they represent, in Crum's words, "the debris of the monastic library and charterhouse" (Crum 1907b: 39; cf. Kahle 1954, vol. 1: 3). The find included over three thousand fragments, including both literary and documentary texts (Kahle 1954, vol. 1: 5). While most were naturally written in Coptic (85 percent), a lesser number of Greek (9 percent) and Arabic (6 percent) texts also occur (Kahle 1954, vol. 1: 8). The Coptic texts are principally Sahidic, though the collection does include two items in the Fayoumic dialect and three in Bohairic.[17] The Greek texts include four literary pieces and a number of documentary texts dealing with tax issues, including two letters from the Arab governor.[18] The Arabic documents again deal mainly with tax and administrative issues (Kahle 1954, vol. 1: 9). Of the Coptic and Greek material, Kahle deemed 375 fragments worth publishing, including 63 literary and 312 documentary texts.[19] The non-literary texts, on which Kahle based his important analysis of Coptic dialect variations,[20] supply a fascinating view into the workings of a late Byzantine-era Coptic monastery. Kahle's introduction includes chapters on the various monasteries mentioned in the texts (chs. 3–4), the community's organization as evidenced in the use of various technical terms (ch. 5), issues of taxation (ch. 6), and the use of an unusual oath formula (ch. 7). The texts, as one has come to expect, portray an ascetic community that, while spatially separate, remained fully integrated into the broader cultural and economic environment. Legal documents record appointments within the monastery, repayment of debts, deeds of sale for land and movable property, receipts of various sorts, tax assessments, and tax receipts. One finds lists and accounts related to taxes, monastic expenses, food, wine, wheat, skins, and church (?) property, all of which serve to detail the inner workings of the community. The cache of texts supplies valuable information on the taxes paid by monastic communities in the Arab period, including a land tax, poll tax, expenses tax, and what appears to be a special artisan's tax. The tax documents include texts in Coptic, Greek, and Arabic, all of which indicate a heavy communal burden that frequently required the monastery to borrow money or appoint as superior a wealthy individual who could effectively shoulder the burden (Kahle 1954, vol. 1: 41–45 (Chapter 6: Taxation at Bala'izah)).

The fragments of over one hundred letters include documents from the Arab governor, letters to and from the bishop, and various letters relating to government service, monastic issues, legal matters, and taxation. Once again, the monastery's involvement with the civil and ecclesiastical world beyond its walls is clear. While spatially isolated, the web of governmental, ecclesiastical, and societal engagement reached into and absorbed the monastic community into a broader cultural framework. Four letters written by a monk named Shenoute (nos. 188–91) underscore the interactive relationship between the monastery and the outside world. Having been expelled earlier for some infraction of the rules, Shenoute wishes to return, but has been warned by those with whom he is currently living that if he returns to the monastery he will be singled out for some extra duties (?). He writes expressing his desire to return, but also wanting assurance that he would be treated like all the other monks (Kahle 1954, vol. 2: 602–22). Clearly the affairs of the monastery were the subject of discussion outside its walls. So, too, a rare Coptic marriage contract (no. 152) found among the documents illustrates familial ties that reached across the monastic wall.[21] Victor, the groom and hence probably not a member of the community, is the son of Makare the priest, who most likely represents the connecting link to the monastery. Kahle speculates that he had left a wife and two sons behind when he embarked on the monastic life, and that the family had later assembled at the monastery on the occasion of Victor's marriage to receive the father's blessing.[22] Why the contract remained in the monastery, however, is not explained.

The non-literary documents from Dayr al-Bala'iza, together with the impressive physical remains visible from the fertile valley below, establish the Monastery of Apollo at Bala'iza as both a visible symbol of the other-worldliness of the ascetic calling and, at the same time, an integrated player in the political, social, and ecclesiastical realities that formed Upper Egyptian culture and society in the seventh and eighth centuries. While Kahle's 1954 analysis of these texts certainly goes a long way in reconstructing the world of the monastery, one suspects that a new, detailed examination of this material that connects it more fully with Grossmann's reconstruction of the physical campus, drawing at the same time on the ever increasing corpus of documentary texts from other sites, would fashion an intriguing picture of a single early Arab-period Coptic cenobitic community. My interest in the following few pages, however, turns to the monastery's literary texts, which, while published in Kahle's edition, played only a minor role in his analysis.

The Collection of Literary Texts

Kahle's list of literary manuscripts includes some sixty-three separate texts.[23] Of these, the first twenty-five are biblical, including ten texts from the Old Testament and fifteen from the New Testament. As expected, though always interesting, the New Testament manuscripts include copies of Matthew (3), Luke (1), and John (2), but no Mark. Kahle associates a further fragment that appears to be biblical or apocryphal and an apocryphal gospel with the biblical texts insofar as he places them immediately after the biblical texts in his list (nos. 26–27). The following twenty-five fragments (nos. 28–51), while not separated out by Kahle as a group, represent primarily patristic and ascetical texts. These include copies of the liturgy and the canons of Basil, lives of various ascetics (Apa Jacob the Anchorite, Apa Hamoi, and two copies of Paul the Anchorite), two encomiums (one for an archpriest and one for a bishop), two martyrdoms, including one of St. Theodore the Oriental, two prayers (one in Greek), seven or eight homilies, including one attributed to Athanasius and one against Nestorius, a copy of Eustathius of Thrace on the Archangel Michael, and four ascetical texts, including a collection of apothegms, an introduction to a series of rules,[24] a story about Athanasius and Antony, and a page containing advice to a monk. The final eleven fragments in Kahle's list include a gnostic treatise (no. 52), two unidentified fragments, and nine miscellaneous items listed together as varia. These include a historical chart, a list of canonical books, an epitaph, a prayer, an amulet (?), a horoscope (?) in Bohairic, and three magical texts—a very interesting hodgepodge of items for a seventh–eighth century monastic library. It is interesting to note that nothing from Shenoute appears among the surviving manuscripts.[25]

I do not have space here to analyze the collection of literary texts in detail, but want rather to focus on their dates as supplied by Kahle and speculate a bit on what the evidence suggests with respect to the monastery's acquisition and preservation of manuscripts. A table containing Kahle's list of literary texts together with the dates he ascribes to them appears at the end of this chapter (fig. 5.3).[26] I have further divided his nine date categories (centuries 4, 4–5, 5, etc.) into three (centuries 4 to 5, 5–6 to 6–7, and 7 to 8), separated by narrow black dividing lines. The last category, centuries 7 to 8, which corresponds to the main occupation of the monastery, is shaded gray. In the following list and corresponding graph (figs. 5.1 and 5.2), I have added up the number of manuscripts assigned by Kahle to each of the nine century markers that he used (4, 4–5, 5, etc.)

I have altered Kahle's list in only one respect: I have moved the so-called Gnostic Treatise, Kahle's ms. 52, up so as to include it with the other biblical and apocryphal texts. The treatise, which contains a dialogue between Jesus and John, and is replete with typical 'gnostic' revelatory language, properly belongs with the accounts of Jesus, biblical and apocryphal.[27] Kahle's separation and relegation of it to the end of his list, just before the odd collection of varia, speaks more to nineteenth-century attitudes toward such material than to those of the era of their production and continuing use.

Fig. 5.1. Number of texts from Bala'iza by subject and century: table

Century	4	4–5	5	5–6	6	6–7	7	7–8	8
Biblical/apocryphal/ so-called 'gnostic'	5	4	3	6	3	2	4	0	1
Patristic/ascetic	0	0	0	1	2	2	6	9	4
Charts/lists/epitaphs/ amulets/horoscopes/magic	0	0	0	0	0	2	1	1	5

Fig. 5.2. Number of texts from Bala'iza by subject and century: graph

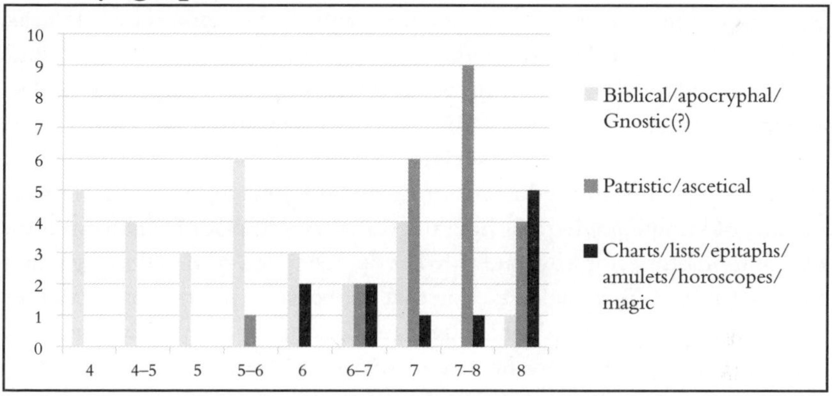

What becomes immediately clear in this list is the division between the biblical/apocryphal texts, the majority of which predate the monastery's existence, and the remaining patristic/ascetic/other texts, which mostly derive from the era of the monastery itself, perhaps copied in its own scriptorium. In fact, with the movement of the so-called Gnostic Treatise to its proper location, all twelve manuscripts dating from the fourth to the fifth century, 100 percent of those surviving in the monastery, belong to the biblical/apocryphal category. Between the fourth and the sixth to seventh centuries, twenty-three of the twenty-eight manuscripts, over 80 percent, derive from the same category. When one moves to the seventh to eighth centuries, the era of the monastery's existence, however, only five of the thirty-one manuscripts, some 16 percent, represent biblical/apocryphal texts, while nineteen (over 61 percent) preserve patristic or ascetic material.

If the Monastery of Apollo had its origins in the middle of the seventh century, it means that most of its biblical texts, including the so-called Gnostic Treatise, came from pre-existing sources outside of the community. Whether brought by individuals who joined the monastery, donated by outside supporters, or acquired by the monks themselves, biblical texts were not the primary focus of manuscript production during the period of the monastery's existence. Perhaps enabled by the survival of sufficient biblical manuscripts from earlier centuries, interest had shifted to the production and/or collection of patristic and ascetic texts, including such pieces as the Canons of Basil and Eustathius of Thrace on the Archangel Michael, whose authorship lay outside of Egypt. The existence of the so-called Gnostic Treatise among the community's holdings raises interesting questions with respect to its origin, its preservation prior to its acquisition, its acquisition by the community, and its preservation within the community. If peak interest in so-called 'gnostic traditions' occurred in the second and third centuries, followed by vociferous ecclesiastical opposition and more or less successful suppression in the fourth and fifth centuries, the existence of this text at Bala'iza betrays the survival of interest in such material, to some degree, much later in the history of Egyptian Christianity. While we have no way of knowing where or how the text survived prior to its acquisition by the monastery, nor how and to what degree it was read and used within the community, it is at least clear that it did survive and that, whether actively acquired, donated, or brought to the monastery by a new member, those in charge either saw no reason or lacked the power to reject it or remove it from the monastery. While the text's earlier survival might have depended on mere chance and its preservation in the monastery on the fact that the struggle against gnostic traditions belonged to the past, the fact of its continued presence in the library suggests a later degree of openness to such traditions within at least certain elements of Coptic Christianity. Gnostic-oriented traditions never represented a majority position in Egypt, and the text clearly occupies a minority position in the Bala'iza collection.

It is interesting in this regard that the other suspect documents among the community's literary holdings—the amulet (no. 59), the horoscope (no. 60), and at least one of the three magical charms (nos. 61–63)—date to the opposite extreme, namely the seventh–eighth century, the most active period of Bala'iza's existence.[28] One can only wonder about the presence of such common extra-ecclesiastical traditions within the community. Did they arrive and survive by chance, or were they produced in the monastery?

Were they treasured by certain elements within the community or were they seen as meaningless scraps? Might their existence reflect an openness to the same diversity that allowed the preservation of the so-called Gnostic Treatise? Whatever the explanation, it suggests that the boundaries that defined appropriate literature were more pervious than the received tradition suggests. In the end, of course, we will never know which exigencies of history resulted in the existence of such texts within the monastery. Their production and/or preservation nonetheless raise intriguing questions with respect to the nature of the community. At the same time, one has to remember their clearly limited role within the monastery. The overwhelming majority of its texts, biblical, patristic, and ascetical, illustrate the community's fundamental alignment with Coptic ecclesiastical orthodoxy. The Gnostic Treatise, amulet, horoscope, and magical charms account for but a small portion of the library, six out of sixty-three texts, less than 10 percent of its holdings.[29]

What conclusions can one draw from this evidence? One has to assert, first and foremost, not much with any degree of certainty. On the other hand, while the great tradition of the Church certainly shaped and controlled the broader culture of Coptic Christianity in the seventh- to eighth-century period of Bala'iza's existence, other traditions, little traditions if you will, persisted among the people who identified themselves as Christian. By the seventh–eighth century, all indications suggest that the great tradition in its dominant role accounted for the vast majority of textual production in Egypt. The evidence from the Monastery of Apollo supports this pattern. At the same time, however, the continued preservation of so-called 'gnostic' and other apocryphal texts, and the ongoing production of extra-ecclesiastical amulets and charms, represent a continuing, if limited, interest in such things among certain segments of the Coptic Christian population. In this regard, the ascetic inhabitants of the Monastery of Apollo appear to reflect the Coptic community as a whole. Predominantly aligned with the great tradition, elements that ran counter to it continued to find a limited place within the community. Based on the physical evidence of the manuscripts found at Bala'iza, the monastery proves to be more similar to the Coptic community as a whole than the literary accounts of Coptic monasticism produced by those representing the great tradition suggest. While the monastery and its inhabitants may have served as an imaginative icon of the angelic life, in reality they as often as not, in many ways, mirrored the world left behind.

Fig. 5.3. The literary texts from Dayr al-Bala'iza and their dates[30]

Manuscripts		**Centuries**						**Bala'iza occupied**		
Number	Title	4	4–5	5	5–6	6	6–7	7	7–8	8
Biblical										
1	Genesis					X				
2	Exodus		X							
3	Deuteronomy				X					
4	I Samuel							X		
5	I Samuel				X					
6	I (III) Kings				X					
7	II (IV) Kings	X								
8	Psalms							X		
9	Psalms				X					
10	Isaiah			X						
11	Matthew						X			
12	Gospels							X		
13	Matthew									X
14	Luke				X					
15	John			X						
16	John				X					
17	Pauline Epistles			X						
18	Pauline Epistles		X							
19	Philippians		X							
20	Pauline Epistles						X			
21	Pauline Epistles		X							
22	Pauline and Catholic Epistles	X								
23	Catholic Epistles	X								
24	Apocalypse					X				
25	Greek–Coptic Lectionary	X								
26	Biblical?							X		
27	Apocryphal Gospel					X				

Patristic and ascetical texts										
28	Liturgy of St. Basil							X		
29	Prayers								X	
30	Prayers							X		
31	Canons of St. Basil								X	
32	*Apophthegmata*							X		
33	Sermon against Nestorius							X		
34	Life of Proclus?								X	
35	Athanasius and Antony								X	
36	Life of Apa Jacob/ Rules								X	
37	Life of Apa Hamoi							X		
38	Life of Paul the Anchorite?						X			
39	Life of Paul the Anchorite?								X	
40	Encomium on an Archpriest							X		
41	Encomium on a Bishop									X
42	Martyrdom of Theodore								X	
43	Martyrdom of Theodore						X			
44	Sermon by Athanasius								X	
45	Eustathius of Thrace									X
46	Homily on the Virgin								X	
47	Homily on the Devil				X					
48	Homily on Fasting					X				
49	Two homilies									X
50	Hortatory Sermon					X				
51	Advice to a Monk									X

Other										
52	Gnostic Treatise	X								
53	Fragment						X			
54	Fragment							X		
55	Historical chart									X
56	List of canonical books									X
57	Epitaph									X
58	Prayers									X
59	Amulet									X
60	Horoscope (Bohairic)						X			
61	Magical charm								X	
62	Magical?	No date given								
63	Magical?	No date given								

Notes

1 Petrie 1907: 1–2, 30; Crum 1907b; Petrie 1909: 21, pl. 51–54; Griffith 1907: 29, 75. For a general review of the site, see Timm 1984, vol. 2: 686–91.

2 Kahle 1954. The manuscripts are first mentioned in Griffith 1907: 29 and Crum 1907b.

3 Kahle (1954, vol. 1: 2), in referring to the depositing of the manuscripts from Dayr al-Bala'iza and Dayr al-Ganadla, reports that "unfortunately no attempt was made to keep the two finds separate."

4 Grossmann 1993: 172 n. 7 (my translation); Crum 1907b; Griffith 1907: 75. It would appear that in spite of the theory proffered in the *Gizeh and Rifeh* volume, Petrie and crew did treat the sites as monasteries.

5 The following account draws heavily from Grossmann's two articles.

6 Grossmann 1986: 36, Ab. 1; Grossmann 1993: pl. 1 between pp. 180 and 181; Grossmann 1991: 787. Coquin and Martin (1991a: 786) note that the wall exceeds a mile in length.

7 Grossmann 1993: 204–205; Kahle notes that "the absence of documents from any site during any particular period is not sufficient reason to assume that the locality did not exist then" (1954, vol. 1: 20).

8 Grossmann 1993: 203–204; Coquin and Martin indicate that the "strong encircling wall would argue for a date of abandonment later than 750" (1991a: 786).

9 The most detailed account of the site remains that of Grossmann 1993, on which this account depends.

10 Grossmann 1993: 175 for the well, and 176–80 for the lower church.

11 Grossmann 1993: 190–94. He sees an analogy for such construction in as yet unpublished evidence from the monastic complex of Ober-Ansina; cf. Wypszycka 2007: 119–20.
12 Grossmann 1993: 185–89; he remains characteristically cautious with respect to the identification of the building as a library (188–89).
13 Grossmann 1993: 199–201. He rejects the basins' use for wine or oil production on the basis of their structure, and notes in support of this interpretation the presence of tax receipts for "weaving-garments-tax" found among the Bala'iza texts; cf. Kahle 1954, vol. 1: 44; vol. 2: 545–48.
14 Kahle 1954, vol. 1: 18–19; cf. van Cauwenbergh 1914: 158–59. On the sixth-century crisis that shattered the Pachomian federation, see Goehring 2006; Goehring 2012: 32–67.
15 Kuhn 1978, vol. 394: 34, 5–6 = vol. 395: 26, 4. One of the monasteries appears to have been named the Monastery of Isaac (vol. 394: 1, 5–6 = vol. 395: 1, 4–5).
16 Grossmann (1986: 35) also notes the radically different nature of Bala'iza's solution to monastic accommodation from that found at Kellia.
17 Kahle 1954, vol. 1: 9–10. The Fayoumic texts include a Life of Paul the Anchorite (no. 38) and a letter (258); the Bohairic include a copy of Philippians (19), an apparent horoscope (60), and a legal document (151).
18 Kahle 1954, vol. 1: 8–9. The literary texts include "a fragment of Exodus (no. 2), a liturgical text, a fragment of prayers (29), and a literary work containing some curious aphorisms."
19 Kahle 1954, vol. 1: 5; the table of contents supplies a list of the texts (xiii–xvii). Kahle numbered the literary texts (1–63) first, and then began the documentary texts with number 100; hence, numbers 64–99 do not exist. Kahle regretted that he could not include the Arabic texts in his edition (vol. 1: 9 n. 3).
20 Kahle's work is perhaps best known in terms of this analysis, which occupies some 220 of the 290 pages (chapters 8–9) of his introductory first volume.
21 Kahle 1954, vol. 2: 566–71. Mentioned in Griffith 1907: 29; a first translation appeared in Crum 1907b: 42.
22 Kahle 1954, vol. 2: 570–71; cf. ms. no. 187 (Kahle 1954, vol. 2: 599–602), a text that deals with government service, with its reference to "Apa Abraham and [his] wife and his children."
23 Kahle 1954, vol. 1: xiii–xv supplies the list. The edited texts appear in volume 2. For the initial review, see Crum 1907b.
24 Crum (1907b: 40) suggests the possibility of this being from the rules of Pachomius, though there is no parallel from a known text of the rules. Kahle (1954, vol. 2: 430–33) follows Crum's suggestion, and while acknowledging the uncertainty of the attribution, fills in the lacuna that held the name of the apa to whom the rules were attributed with the name Pachom.
25 Noted by Crum 1907b: 40.
26 Dating Coptic manuscripts is notoriously difficult. I have for the purposes of this exercise simply used the dates assigned by Kahle, fully aware of the problems inherent in that decision.
27 Kahle 1954, vol. 2: 473–77; an earlier, less complete edition was published by Crum 1943.

28 Kahle (1954, vol. 2: 486–87) only supplies a date for the first magical charm (61). The other two (62–63) are so small that he lists them only as "Obscure fragment, probably magical."

29 Furthermore, the extent to which the pattern of the surviving manuscripts represents that of the actual holdings of the monastery remains unknown.

30 Kahle 1954, vol. 1: xiii–xv for the list; dates found in the introductions to the individual texts in volume 2.

6 "Twenty Thousand Nuns": The Domestic Virgins of Oxyrhynchos

AnneMarie Luijendijk

Historia Monachorum in Oxyrhynchos

The *Historia Monachorum in Aegypto* contains a literary testimony of Christians in the city of Oxyrhynchos.[1] Its anonymous author, an eyewitness from Palestine writing at the turn of the fifth century, boasts that this city in Middle Egypt abounds with monasteries, both within its walls and outside. He even notes that the bishop claimed to have under his jurisdiction a stunning "ten thousand monks and twenty thousand nuns." Also, the *Libellus Precum* by Marcellinus and Faustinus (c. 383), a document preserved in the Collectio Avellana, mentions, during the episcopate of Theodorus in Oxyrhynchos, "sacred virgins, whose monasteries the citizenship itself venerated for their being worthy of sanctity."[2]

As most scholars have recognized, the number of ascetics mentioned in the *Historia Monachorum*—"ten thousand monks and twenty thousand nuns"—is too marvelous to be taken literally (see also Luijendijk 2008: 3–6). Yet the prominence of this passage in scholarly discussions on Oxyrhynchos and Egyptian monasticism, combined with the fact that many papyri from this city feature monastics, makes it remarkable that no one has researched monasticism in Oxyrhynchos as a microcosm to be studied for its own sake. To be sure, although no specific studies on monks and nuns at Oxyrhynchos exist as of yet, the topic of the papyrological evidence for Egyptian monasticism is not—please excuse the pun—virgin scholarly territory: two recent books by Ewa Wipszycka and María Jesús Albarrán Martínez have addressed the topic thoroughly.[3] In this chapter I am particularly interested in the earliest documentary evidence of female ascetics at Oxyrhynchos. One phrase in the *Historia Monachorum* draws my special interest: the bishop's estimation of "ten thousand monks and twenty thousand nuns," with twice the number of nuns compared to monks. Since most other sources for monasticism suggest that monks outnumbered nuns in Egypt (Wipszycka 1996: 316), the double dose of nuns mentioned in this passage in the *Historia Monachorum* is especially striking. So, how does the papyrological evidence compare with this statement and what can we learn from the papyri about Oxyrhynchite nuns?

As we will see, the earliest evidence for female ascetics in papyri from Oxyrhynchos confronts us not with cenobitism, but with a different kind of asceticism. The nuns we will encounter in Oxyrhynchite papyri that are roughly contemporary with the *Historia Monachorum*—the neighbor Annis, the apotactic sisters Theodora and Thauris, and a man's sister Athonis—are so-called 'domestic virgins.' These women practice a form of monasticism known also from literary sources. They live not in a nunnery, but at home, either with their family, alone, or in a small group, and renounce marriage. Furthermore, they abstain from leisure, including food and wine. A mid- to late-fourth-century text, the *Gnomes of the Council of Nicaea*, is quite specific in stipulating the behavior and daily activities of such domestic virgins: they should dress modestly and spend their days fasting and studying. Furthermore, they should lead socially restricted lives (especially from men).[4] Another fourth-century text, the *Canons of Pseudo-Athanasius* (in Arabic translation), exhorts every family to set aside one of their daughters for this lifestyle, upon whose asceticism the salvation of the entire household depends: "In every house of Christians it is needful that there be a virgin, for the salvation of the whole house is this one virgin" (canon 98).[5] The *Gnomes of the Council of Nicaea* assert similar family coverage from a domestic virgin: "If your daughter desires (ἐπιθυμεῖν) a state of virginity (παρθένος) you obtain a mighty grace, for on her account you are remembered by the Lord." According to these prescriptive texts, there is a lot at stake in the decision to become a domestic virgin, not just for the women themselves, but also for their families. But we should remember that these sources, of course, indicate how we should imagine the ideal domestic virgin from the perspective of their authors. The papyri from Oxyrhynchos that feature nuns both complement and complicate the picture evoked by the *Historia*

Monachorum and other literary sources. So, after this brief literary tour, we now turn to our papyri from Oxyrhynchos to take a closer look.

Didyme and the Sisters

The earliest evidence of female monastics at Oxyrhynchos is difficult to ascertain.[6] It hinges on the interpretation of two letters written around the year 340 by a certain "Didyme and the sisters" (Διδύμη καὶ αἱ ἀδελφαὶ, P.Oxy. XIV 1774[7] and SB VIII 9746).[8] The letters are each addressed to a woman, Atienatia and Sophias respectively. In their letter to Atienatia, for example, Didyme and the sisters write:

> To my lady sister Atienatia, Didyme and the sisters [send] greetings in the Lord. First of all it is necessary to greet you, praying that you are well. Write to us, my lady, concerning your health and whatever orders you need, with full liberty. Let us know if you received your orders. There is a balance with us from the money of your orders, I believe, of 1,300 denarii. Canopic cakes received for you from them will be dispatched. Greet my blessed lady sister Asous and her mother and . . . ([Address]: To my lady sister Atienatia, Didyme with the sisters. Trans. Bagnall and Cribiore 2006: 194)

Both letters contain the customary well-wishes followed by communications about exchanges of goods. Whereas the letter to Atienatia features an all-female cast of characters, the one addressed to Sophias complicates the picture, presenting both women and men. None of the men mentioned, however, appear to reside with Didyme and the sisters.

So how should we interpret the reference to "the sisters" here and the fact that we have a group of women writing? At stake is whether "Didyme and the sisters" represent a group of ascetic women or whether they are just family members or even friends. The analysis of these letters proves to be highly significant, for if they indeed involve female monastics, then they constitute the earliest evidence for such women at Oxyrhynchos. For this reason these documents have received ample scholarly scrutiny. Their inclusion in or exclusion from the dossier of female ascetics considerably affects the prosopography of Oxyrhynchite nuns—involving three women (Didyme, Atienatia, and Sophias) and the group of monastics. Moreover, it would significantly alter our view of the lives and activities of domestic ascetics, as these documents show them with a bustling social circle and lively exchange of goods. Wipszycka contends that one can understand this correspondence without having to resort to the "monastic hypothesis."[9] Elsewhere, she observes that scholars easily succumb to their desire to push the evidence for monastics back in time.[10] While Wipszycka has a point there, the letters are intriguing enough that they cannot be easily set aside as irrelevant to the discussion of female monasticism. Indeed, a host of scholars, most recently María Albarrán, has argued that these "sisters" are probably religious sisters, nuns.[11] In her assessment of this correspondence, Alanna Emmett observes: "Didyme and the sisters have not withdrawn from the world but are aware of and catering for worldly and practical items."[12] And Susanna Elm concludes: "While caution is advisable, the evidence favours a community of women and men who are not relatives and are united by other than business interests alone: at the very least by their shared Christianity, but perhaps by ascetic principles as well" (Elm 1994: 243–44). Elm's observation that these people do not appear to be relatives is especially relevant. It is possible to interpret the letter to Atienatia as referring to business transactions, for mention is made of a balance of money, but not necessarily so; it is equally possible that they are purchasing on Atienatia's behalf.[13] The phraseology of the greeting with "Didyme and the sisters" as senders is unusual.[14]

If Didyme and the sisters are ascetic sisters, this would be the earliest evidence for any monastics, male or female, at Oxyrhynchos. We would then observe a group of female ascetics who are actively engaged in sending and producing goods and who have a lively social circle comprising women and men. While this case in the end will have to remain undecided, one may wonder how this picture compares to other ascetics from Oxyrhynchos. So what (other) ascetics do we encounter in Oxyrhynchos?

Nuns as Neighbors: Annis

The first unambiguous female monastic from Oxyrhynchos is Annis. She appears in a document from 25 January of the year 392 that details the division of a property among a group of people (PSI VI 698).[15] The boundaries of the house are described as follows: it borders on the south (?) a public street, to the east the property of "the nun Annis" (l. 7 ἀπηλιώτου Ἄννιτος μοναχῆς), and to the southwest that of the "heirs of Apion from the *primipilarii*." What additional information can we glean about Annis besides the fact that she was a monastic? First, she is a neighbor important enough to mention by name and profession. Just as Apion, the neighbor to the southwest, is identified by his social (namely military) rank as "from the *primipilarii*," so is Annis, as *monache*.[16] Furthermore, the property seems to be her own.[17]

If the property in question borders a public street on the south and Annis's property on the east, then it follows that Annis's property is located on that same street. Thus Annis the nun did not seek the desert's isolation or lived tucked away in a dark alley. Rather, she resides in a house located on a public street. But whether her neighbors or those strolling the street actually had small talk or deep theological conversations with her, or whether they even laid eyes on her, remains to be seen. Our literary sources do not imagine such women to appear in public by themselves, if at all. In his *Historia Lausiaca*, Palladius recounts that at Antinoë he had a domestic virgin as neighbor, who, in fact, was so domestic that he had never seen her: "There was another neighbor of mine whose face I never beheld, for she never went out, so they say, from the time when she left the world. She had completed sixty years in ascetic practices along with her mother" (Palladius 1991: 141). Just like Palladius at Antinoë, at Oxyrhynchos the neighbors know that Annis is a nun, but whether they spotted her or conversed with her on the public street remains unknown. The papyrus contains no clues that either confirm or shatter this image.

According to María Albarrán Martínez, the fact that only Annis is mentioned in the papyrus indicates that she lives by herself (Albarrán Martínez 2011: 128). While that is plausible, she may also have lived with her relatives (recall that Palladius's neighbor lived with her mother and so did other domestic virgins) or other people. In Annis's case, the other houses mentioned in the document were inhabited by multiple people and thus must have been relatively spacious.[18] It is therefore even possible that Annis rented out rooms to others, as we witness two other domestic ascetics doing in a lease made up a few years later. So we pay them a visit next.

Apotactic Sisters Theodora and Tauris

This lease dates from June–July 400, thus around the time that the *Historia Monachorum* was also composed (P.Oxy. XLIV 3203). It is a contract for the lease of "one ground-floor room, namely a hall, together with the one cellar in the basement, with all appurtenances." Two women, "Aurelia Theodora and Aurelia Tauris, daughters of Silvanus, of the illustrious and most illustrious city of Oxyrhynchos, apotactic nuns," rent out these rooms to "Aurelius Jose son of Judas, Jew, of the same city" (see also Albarrán

Martínez 2011: 111, 153). While the *Gnomes of the Council of Nicaea* declare that "a wise virgin does not speak to men at all,"[19] this document forces us to nuance that statement as it presents us with interactions between the nuns and Jose (and his family). Furthermore, we can glean from this text that the nuns Theodora and Tauris supported themselves financially by renting out part of their property.[20] This gives us important information about their social class, namely, they were wealthy enough to own a house, but not independently wealthy, and had to supplement their income by rent. As a result, they shared their living quarters with a family, which must have affected their monastic lifestyle. Moreover, their housemates, Jews, were a family with different religious practices, and it is interesting to imagine how, if at all, their lifestyles would have impacted on each other.[21]

The meticulous language of the lease addresses Theodora and Tauris as "apotactic nuns" (μοναχαῖς ἀποτακτικαῖς). A note on this status is due. The term 'apotactic' (ἀποτακτική, -ός) appears in eight papyri, but only in this case applies to women.[22] In Pachomian literature, it indicates a follower of Jesus (and Pachomius), who radically renounced (ἀποτάσσομαι) the world, including family and possessions, according to a passage in the Gospel of Luke (Luke 14:26–33). Therefore, the use of this word in the papyri for monastics who clearly own possessions (e.g., Theodora and Tauris as landlords)[23] generated surprise among scholars of monasticism. Wipszycka proposes a convincing interpretation of the term: instead of thinking of one specific form of renunciation as applied in the Pachomian writings, she argues that we should understand the term more generally, namely as applying to people who have renounced marriage and in addition perhaps other pleasures of life, such as family, food, wine, wealth, and leisure (Wipszycka 2009: 315–16).

The nuns Theodora and Tauris apparently renounced marriage, but kept property. Moreover, they also did not fully reject their family, since they lived together as biological sisters (they have the same father, Silvanus).[24] In a private letter that we will read next, we encounter another nun, Athonis, who also did not renounce her family and remained living with them.

Athonis

This personal letter, palaeographically dated to the fourth or fifth century, is from a man called Philoxenus to his family (Grenfell and Hunt 1898: P.Oxy. LVI 3862). It contains an enumeration of goods received or still needed and an extensive section with greetings. I reproduce here the part of Philoxenus's greetings back home relevant for our inquiry: "Greetings from me to my lady and to my lady Maria and the nun Athonis (l. 19, τὴν μοναχὴν Ἀθῶνιν) and my most sweet brother Heraclammon and my sister Herais and to Joseph and John and Paragorius and Theon the carpet-maker" (Grenfell and Hunt 1898: P.Oxy. LVI 3862, 135). In his lengthy section with greetings to an abundance of relatives and acquaintances, Philoxenus mentions Athonis the nun between his mother and siblings. In contrast to the other nuns from Oxyrhynchos we have encountered thus far and who lived by themselves, this nun lives with her parents at home.

Our correspondent supplies no further information for us about his sister, unsurprisingly, for he is writing home. Literary accounts allow us to imagine what Athonis's life may have looked like. As we glean from the *Canons of Pseudo-Athanasius*, when the rest of the family enjoys their meals, ascetic daughters fast during the day and abstain from meat and wine, even on holidays—at least, that is what the text prescribes: "Eat ye and drink nothing doubting; but the virgin shall maintain her fast each day until even and nought shall she eat whence blood cometh forth at any of the feasts, nay not at the great feast of the Lord. Nor shall she drink wine, lest the lamp of her virginity be extinguished" (Pseudo-Athanasius 1904: 62, trans. Riedel and Crum). Palladius in his *Historia Lausiaca* 31 tells of a certain Piamoun, "a virgin who lived with her mother spinning flax and eating only every other day at evening" (Palladius 1991: 90–91). Apparently, it was tempting to treat these humble domestic ascetics, who guaranteed the salvation of the entire household, as domestic assistants, for the *Canons of Pseudo-Athanasius* warn against such abuse (canon 103).[25]

Thus, while remaining with her family may have provided for a female ascetic many of the comforts of home, it also brought its own special temptations and challenges. Some of those were alleviated for women choosing to live in a nunnery with like-minded women. I wonder if that is the reason that in our later sources (both Oxyrhynchite and literary) domestic virgins disappear from view?

In Conclusion

This chapter was inspired by the *Historia Monachorum*'s passage about the profusion of nuns at Oxyrhynchos. By examining Oxyrhynchite papyri from the fourth and fifth centuries we encounter multiple ascetic women. At least four of them we know by name: Annis, Athonis, Tauris, and Theodora. They were all so-called domestic virgins. The papyri we have examined indicate that these women were recognized as ascetics by their families and by outsiders, and that their status was an important enough to be mentioned in official documents (instead of patronymics) and in private letters. The monastic choice must have radically influenced these women's lives, a fact that those around them acknowledged. It seems to have given the nuns a certain level of respect in their communities, even functioned as an important marker of identity.

While such ascetic women are familiar to us from literary sources, the papyri allow us to add to and also complicate their stature. The papyri offer noteworthy moments and introduce us to a side of the lives of these women that is less known or even unknown from the literature. There, we observe domestic virgins spending time inside fasting, praying, and reading; here, we encounter them in business transactions, or simply as sister, neighbor, or housemate. Whether these nuns lived independently or remained with their family, in any case these ascetics spent their lives in close proximity to others, non-monastics, male and female.

Apart from recording rent collection, the sources remain tight-lipped with regard to the daily activities of these women. The literary evidence for domestic asceticism gives the impression that these women were relatively well off. This matches the lean information in the texts we have reviewed here: in two documents we encountered women as property owners. To be sure, papyrological evidence mostly favors the wealthy, since they had more occasions necessitating written documentation (see especially Bagnall 1995: 13–16). The papyri have brought us in touch with nuns who owned a house big enough that they could rent out a room and a basement. While they had their own home, they were apparently not independently wealthy and needed the income. This gives us an indication of the class of these two women.

In none of the texts securely relating to Oxyrhynchite nuns do we hear these women in their own voices. Instead, in all instances, others (all males) point out and name nuns to us. The nuns appear in documents from, for, and about men: brother, father, neighbor, renter. That is, unless we count Didyme and the sisters among the female ascetics. Thus, as it turns out, whether Didyme and the women around her count as monastics or not has huge implications for the reconstruction of the life of nuns at Oxyrhynchos. So let us revisit Didyme and the sisters.

The letter from Didyme to Sophias betrays a wide social network. If these women are nuns, then these letters introduce us to socially very well connected nuns—perhaps surprisingly so. But if we imagine the circumstances of the apotactic monastic sisters Theodora and Tauris, who rented part of their house to Jose and his family, or Athonis and the many others in and around Philoxenus's parental house, other ascetics belonging to lively households come into view. However, the fact that we cannot tell assuredly whether Didyme and the sisters are monastics or laywomen is still interesting from a methodological point of view. This correspondence shows us that we can understand certain markers of identity only within a larger context and confronts us with the fact that some of them, such as 'sister,' remain ambiguous without other markers (see also Wipszycka 2009: 292 and 292 n. 12).

Literary sources pertaining to Oxyrhynchos insist on the presence of nunneries in the city in the late fourth century.[26] Attested elsewhere in Egypt since the end of the third decade of the fourth century,[27] women's convents appear on the Oxyrhynchite papyrological horizon only toward the end of the fifth and early sixth centuries.[28] It remains an intriguing question why we see no nunneries at Oxyrhynchos this early in our papyri (at least, those published so far). Part of the answer may be that papyrus documents favor certain kinds of ascetics—namely propertied women such as Annis, Theodora, and Tauris, who owned a house. Furthermore, depending on how we interpret Didyme's correspondence, she and the sisters could be nuns residing in a nunnery. Here, again, we have an indication of how difficult it is to understand and contextualize what at first sight appear to be simple letters.

The papyri from Oxyrhynchos thus differ from other sources on monasticism in regard to the early and relatively frequent references to domestic ascetics and, probably, the late appearance of female convents. In this early period, women who chose a monastic lifestyle had several options. It appears that a popular one at Oxyrhynchos was not to retreat into the desert, but rather to practice an ascetic lifestyle at home and renounce food, wine, and leisure not in the loneliness of the wilderness but among the temptations of the household or while living in a small group with other ascetics in the city. Indeed, according to Wipszycka, it would be exceedingly hard for women to live in the desert (Wipszycka 1996: 291–92, 316). Since the Oxyrhynchos papyri derive from an urban environment, this explains in part the bias toward nuns.

Like Palladius, we only barely catch glimpses of these women who chose to lead humble, ascetic lives and preferred to stay out of the public eye. It seems that they succeeded for the most part. They were noted and appreciated by the author of the *Historia Monachorum* (although he exaggerates);

they were recognized and respected as neighbors, sisters, housemates. They showed up in public to take care of business and to provide for their livelihood, and in so doing they were caught on record, which then accidentally made it into history.

Notes

1 This chapter forms part of a larger research project I am conducting on the monastics at Oxyrhynchos. I am grateful to Gawdat Gabra and Hany Takla for inviting me to contribute and to Bryan Kraemer, PhD candidate at the University of Chicago, for his excellent help researching this topic. I presented a different version of this paper in the Papyrology and Early Christian Background Section of the 2013 SBL Annual Meeting in Baltimore and thank the audience for its questions and feedback.

2 "Sacrarum uirginum . . . , quarum monasteria pro merito sanctimoniae earum ciuitas ipsa ueneratur." Edition: CSEL 35/1, 99, p. 35. I thank Lincoln Blumell for this reference.

3 Wipszycka 2009. See also Wipszycka 1996: 281–336; on Oxyrhynchos, Wipszycka 1996: 314–17 and Wypszycka 2002b; Albarrán Martínez 2011. See also Wipszycka 2013a: 337–52. An English study incorporating papyrological materials is Elm 1994.

4 English translation by Alistair Stewart, "The 'Gnomes' of the Council of Nicaea," http://suciualin.files.wordpress.com/2013/06/gnomesofnicaea_18thjune2013.pdf (at footnote 192, no page number). Regarding the date of the text, Stewart remarks: "We would probably not be way out if we placed the production . . . between 360 and 400."

5 Pseudo-Athanasius 1904: 62. This passage comes at the very end of the text and is only preserved in Arabic translation; the Coptic manuscript lacks this stipulation. The canons date to the fourth century; see Wipszycka 2009: 591.

6 The first male monastic appearing in a papyrus from Oxyrhynchos is a certain *apotaktikos* named Ammonius, who is involved in a dispute about an inheritance. The papyrus dates to AD 373–74 (P.Oxy. XLVI 3311.7 and 9–10, Ἀμμώνιος … ἀποτακτικός).

7 The Oxyrynchus papyri can be found in Grenfell and Hunt 1898.

8 In the *editio princeps* (P.Oxy. XIV 1777, 187), this letter is dated to the "early fourth century." Wipszycka dates it to ca. 340 (Wipszycka 2002a: 469–73, especially 470).

9 Wipszycka 2002a: 473. "La situazione attestata da *SB* III, 7243 e da *P.Oxy.* XVI, 1774 si può, alla luce dei testi analoghi, riconstruire senza ricorrere all'ipotesi 'monastica.'"

10 Wipszycka 2009: 292 n. 12: "On cède facilement au désir d'augmenter le dossier monastique concernant les premières décennies de l'existence du monachisme."

11 Albarrán Martínez 2011: 226. She notes that the redating of the letters to the year 340 by Wipszycka makes it more plausible that this could be a domestic monastic community. Albarrán Martínez concludes that "the group of women led by Didyme probably formed an ascetic community" in Oxyrhynchos: "Así pues, el grupo de mujeres liderado por Didyme probablemente formó una comunidad ascética situada en la ciudad de Oxirrinco" (2011: 227).

12 Emmett 1984: 83. According to Emmett, such a community is a precursor to later monasticism.

13 See Bagnall and Cribiore 2006: 194. They deny that these letters are business letters for, as they rightly state, the exchange of goods in them is completely in line with other private letters.

14 See also Bagnall and Cribiore 2006: 193: "The plural forms in the opening are not paralleled elsewhere in family letters."

15 PSI VI 698 (1920). The text itself specifies that the properties discussed are in Oxyrhynchos (reconstructed in l. 3, certain in l. 5: ἐν τῇ αὐτῇ Ὀξυρυγχι[τῶν πόλει]).

16 In this period, the term *monache* securely indicates that she is a nun, an ascetic; see Albarrán Martínez 2011: 105–106.

17 See Albarrán Martínez 2011: 136–37 about the legal background of monastics owning property.

18 The document (evidently) does not specify the size of Annis's house. Albarrán Martínez (2011: 139) assumes that the neighborhood is rather homogenous and that therefore Annis's house is of similar dimensions to that of the others mentioned in the contract.

19 Translation by Stewart, at http://suciualin.files.wordpress.com/2013/06/gnomesofnicaea_18thjune2013.pdf.

20 For the amount of the lease: Haslam (P.Oxy. XLIV 3203, 184, note to line 19) mentions: "The same amount is paid in AD 444 for the lease of two dining rooms (VIII 1129)."

21 On Jews at Oxyrhynchos, see Epp 2006 and Kasher 1981.

22 On this term, see Albarrán Martínez 2011: 110–13, with the papyri listed at 111 n. 117. On its meaning, see especially Wipszycka 2009: 308–15 (this text discussed at 312).

23 See also footnote 5 above.

24 Even though these apotactics have renounced worldly life and their families, they are still referred to and indicated in familial relationships in these letters. This is, according to Albarrán Martínez (2011: 149–50), because these are official contracts.

25 Pseudo-Athanasius 1904: 66, trans. Riedel and Crum: "Rich women shall not keep by them virgin nuns in the part of servants, as (do those) that send them unto places of gold workers or of dyers, so that their σχῆμα is despised and they serve in worldly affairs."

26 The *Historia Monachorum* and the *Libellus Precum*.

27 The first Pachomian nunnery was founded in 329 near the male monastery at Tabennesi (Wipszycka 2009: 568). Also at Antinoë, Palladius knew of multiple nunneries early on.

28 P.Oxy. LXVII 4620 (ca. 475–550) mentions monasteries of Ama Juliana and Ama Maria. See also P.Oxy. XXIV 2419 (sixth century) and P.Oxy. XLIII 3150 (sixth century).

7 Anba Isaac, Bishop of the Fayoum, al-Bahnasa, and Giza, 1834–81

Bishop Martyros

ANBA ISAAC, THE BISHOP of the Fayoum, holds a unique place in the history of the Coptic Church during the mid-nineteenth century. This standing is due, in part, to his massive diocese, which included three Egyptian governorates: Giza, the Fayoum, and Beni Suef. It is also recognition of what he achieved in both ecclesiastical life and the monastic life in Wadi al-Natrun during his time as bishop of a diocese, which lasted for almost forty-seven years. No article about him, however, was included in *The Coptic Encyclopedia* edited in 1991.

Anba Isaac was among sixteen monks living in the Monastery of the Holy Virgin al-Suryan in the early nineteenth century. It is known that he was greatly loved by his brother monks (al-Suriani 1968: 166). When the diocese of the Fayoum, al-Bahnasa, and Giza lost its bishop due to the death of Anba Yussab, who had shepherded this diocese from 1820 to 1833, the monks of the Monastery of the Holy Virgin al-Suryan asked Pope Peter VII of Alexandria (Boutros al-Gawly), who used to select his bishops from among the monks of the Monastery of St. Antony on the Red Sea, to ordain their brother monk Isaac as bishop of the vacant diocese. The patriarch agreed, and the consecration took place in the papal residence in the Cathedral of St. Mark in Azbakiya, the old cathedral in downtown Cairo, which was built by the famous archon Ibrahim al-Gohary (al-Masry 1992: 267).

The Geographical Boundaries of the Diocese of Anba Isaac

The diocese of Anba Isaac included three entire governorates (or states), namely the Fayoum, al-Bahnasa (Beni Suef), and Giza, and also a part of al-Minya governorate as far as the town of Bani Mazar. Anba Isaac was consecrated a bishop in 1834 at a time when Prince Hussein Agha was the governor of the province of the Fayoum (which was formerly divided into two parts). Prince Hussein was a member of the dynasty of Muhammad ʻAli, who was the ruler of Egypt from 1805 to 1849. Later, in 1868, Khedive Ismaʻil, the ruler of Egypt, issued a decree combining the Fayoum and Beni Suef into one entity. In 1870, another decree was issued turning the Fayoum into an independent governorate. It is noteworthy that these administrative divisions did not have any impact on the pastoral mission of the bishop who was consecrated for these provinces according to the tradition at the time of his enthronement to the bishopric (al-Masry 1992: 267).

Anba Isaac remained in his diocese until 1858, and later, at an unknown date, he was ordained a metropolitan, which is a very high-ranking bishop. He lived until 1881; unfortunately, it is unknown exactly when he died or where he was buried.

Anba Isaac's Achievements as Bishop

The following are the bishop's known achievements in his diocese:

1. In 1856, he built the first church, which had the name of the Holy Virgin, in the town of Beni Suef in an area called Darb al-ʻAbd. In 1869, he built a church named for St. George in an area called Abu Seir al-Malak in the province of al-Wassty. A third church also bearing the name of the Holy Virgin was built by him in al-Fashn in 1861 (Daoud and Fakhry 2011: 252).
2. He restored a number of churches and monasteries in the Fayoum governorate, among which were the Church of the Holy Virgin, the Monastery of al-Amir Tadros (Prince Theodore) in an area called Dessia, and the church of Abu Sayfayn (Abraam 2004: 309).
3. In 1862, he built a church in the name of the Holy Virgin in the village of Atris, which was affiliated with the province of Awssim, Giza governorate. This church belonged to—and still belongs to—the monks of the Monastery of the Holy Virgin al-Suryan. In 1872, he built a church in the same village in the name of St. Macarius, which still belongs to the monks of the Monastery of St. Macarius in Wadi

al-Natrun. In 1881, he started the construction of St. Mark's Church in Giza (Daoud and Fakhry 2011: 279).

4. He ordained several priests in the three governorates.
5. He participated in the recommendation made for Hegumen (chief priest) Daoud of the Monastery of St. Antony to be ordained a general metropolitan in 1853, and later he participated in consecrating him as patriarch under the name Pope Cyril IV in 1854. Years later, Anba Isaac also participated in recommending the monk Mikhail of the Monastery of St. Macarius in Wadi al-Natrun to be consecrated as patriarch, taking the name Pope Demetrius II in 1862 (al-Masry 1992: 311).
6. He played a major role in bringing about the enthronement of the monk Youhanna the Scribe as patriarch of the See of St. Mark under the name Cyril V in 1874. An interesting story may be mentioned here: Archon Wahba al-Gizawi (a senior government official) was opposed to the nomination of Youhanna the Scribe to the patriarchate. Al-Gizawi instead supported the nomination of Anba Morcos, the metropolitan of al-Beheira (al-Masry 1992: 381). Anba Isaac went to al-Gizawi in the company of a number of bishops to reason with him on the necessity of consecrating Youhanna the Scribe as patriarch as soon as possible, as the dioceses of Qusqam, Manfalut, Asyut, Qena, Esna, and Khartoum (in present-day Sudan) were without leadership because of the deaths of their bishops, and it was known that there was, at least for the time being, the legally required number of bishops necessary for the consecration of a new patriarch. The archon told them he would reply to them after three days. Anba Isaac shouted at him, saying, "Why this delay, my son? And what are we to do if we do not find you alive when we come to you after three days?" Then Anba Isaac stood up and declared angrily that the Church had a Lord to look after it. And it came to pass that Archon al-Gizawi died on the third day, and Youhanna the Scribe was consecrated as patriarch on 1 November 1874 (Abraam 2004: 309).

Anba Isaac's Achievements in the Monasteries of Wadi al-Natrun

Anba Isaac took great care of the four monasteries of Wadi al-Natrun, especially al-Suryan Monastery, to the extent that he used to spend half the year caring for his diocese and the other half in the monasteries of Wadi al-Natrun. As soon as he took over the diocese, he ordained so many priests and monks that he was called the "Chief of the Monasteries of Wadi al-Natrun, and the Caretaker of the Monastery of the Holy Virgin al-Suryan." It is noteworthy that there is preserved in this monastery a vestment of his, ornamented with silver wire, embroidered with depictions of the twelve disciples, Melchizedek, and Aaron the priest. On it is written, "He who loves this reverend father—Anba Isaac, bishop of al-Bahnasa and al-Fayoum—in the Monastery of the Holy Virgin al-Suryan—AM 1555—AH 1245 (AD 1839)" (Daoud and Fakhry 2011: 276).

Anba Isaac's achievements can be summarized as follows:

1. He restored the Church of the Holy Virgin al-Suryan in Wadi al-Natrun, sometimes called "the Cave" (Evelyn-White 1933: 212) because it was built about 1.5 meters below ground level. This unique church was inaugurated on 23 April AD 1853, corresponding to the Coptic date of 17 Barmuda AM 1569. This was recorded in the manuscript of the four Gospels given by him as a gift to the monastery, mentioned below. This manuscript is still at the monastery.
2 Together with his sister Hanona, he presented to the Monastery of the Holy Virgin al-Suryan a manuscript of the four Gospels in both Coptic and Arabic, dated to the year AD 1852. It was transcribed by a monk called Shenouda from al-Suryan Monastery. It was stamped by the bishop's round seal, "Isaac the bishop 58." He bought this manuscript for 350 Roman piasters. He also presented to the same monastery another manuscript of "The Consecration of Churches" in both Coptic and Arabic in AD 1834 (AM 1550). He inscribed in this manuscript, "The vile person Isaac, Bishop of al-Bahnasa—in the name of God the merciful and compassionate and glory be to God in the highest heaven—a perpetual and everlasting endowment to the Church of the Holy Virgin al-Suryan in the wilderness of St. Macarius . . . AM 1550." He signed it in Coptic, "The vile person Isaac the bishop." This manuscript is now kept in the patriarchal library in Abbasiya, Cairo (Daoud and Fakhry 2011: 251).
3. He always accompanied the patriarchs in their visits to the monasteries of Wadi al-Natrun. This was mentioned in a manuscript describing the visit of the Coptic patriarch Pope Peter VII in AD 1835, stating that Pope Peter "was accompanied by the reverend bishop Anba Isaac, of al-Bahnasa and Fayoum and the caretaker of the Monastery of the Holy Virgin al-Surian" (Daoud and Fakhry 2011: 251).

4. He played a major role in increasing the number of monks in the monasteries of Wadi al-Natrun, who numbered 150 in 1890. The number of monks had been only around seventy-five in 1833 (Tosson 1935: 46). The number of monks in the Monastery of the Holy Virgin al-Suryan was forty in 1896 (Meinardus 1988: 140).

The Influence of Different Circumstances in the Nineteenth Century on the Diocese of Anba Isaac

No doubt the diocese of the Fayoum and al-Bahnasa was affected by the economical, political, and scientific changes that took place in the nineteenth century at the hands of the ruler of Egypt Muhammad ʻAli and his successors. These changes can be observed in the following:

1. The prevalence of foreign missionaries in Egypt, especially the Catholic ones who came from Rome and the Protestant ones who came from the United States and England. These missionaries spread their faith among the Orthodox Egyptians by offering social and educational services to the people and establishing scientific schools, institutes, and civil societies (al-Masry 1984: 44).
2. The Coptic archons (who were high-level government officials) played a major role in mediation between the Church and the rulers. These archons held senior positions in government departments, owned large estates, and established charities. Examples of such notable archons are Moallams Ghali and his brother Francis, Boktor, Youhanna, Mansour, Yacoub, and Beshara (al-Masry 1992: 380).
3. The remarkable role played by the Coptic patriarchs of the nineteenth century in confirming the Orthodox faith among Egyptians. One example of these popes was Pope Peter VII or, as the Egyptians knew him, Boutros al-Gawly (al-Gawly is the name of a village in Upper Egypt). This patriarch was keen on sending pastoral letters to the different dioceses for the sake of confirming the Orthodox doctrine, in the face of encroaching European churches. Another example was Pope Cyril IV, who built a printing house for publishing the books of the teachings of the Orthodox Church. He also established Coptic schools. A third example was Pope Demetrius II, who intensified his pastoral visits to his congregation, especially in Upper Egypt, for the sake of confirming their faith. He did this under the auspices of Khedive Isma'il, the ruler of Egypt at that time. We can say that the spiritual renaissance of the Coptic Church went

hand in hand with the late nineteenth-century scientific and economic renaissance in Egypt.

Anba Isaac Strays from Church Teachings on the Subject of Divorce

For reasons unclear to us in the present day, Anba Isaac went against Church teachings and allowed divorce, permitting those who got divorced for trivial reasons (both men and women) to remarry. This prompted Pope Demetrius II to send a letter to the people and the priests of al-Bahnasa, the Fayoum, and Giza warning against and objecting to this matter.

It seems that the issue of divorce was raised at this time as a result of the weakness of the pastoral role of the Coptic Church in the previous period, which witnessed a state of political strife between the Mamluks and the Ottomans. This lasted for more than two centuries until Muhammad 'Ali ended the Mamluks' power completely in the famous massacre at the citadel in Cairo.

In AD 1822, an important yet most unfortunate series of events related to the subject of divorce took place. The most respectable Archon Ghali had a younger brother named Francis, who was also an archon. In an audacious act with deadly consequences, Francis forged a letter in the ruler Muhammad 'Ali's name and, with his forged signature, requested the Roman pontiff to ordain a friend of his who was a pupil in the Roman Propaganda (the Roman Catholic office of missionary activities) as archbishop of Memphis, promising to coerce the Copts into submission to Rome. Previously, Archon Ghali and Archon Francis had converted to Catholicism by the command of Muhammad 'Ali. Archon Francis sent this forged letter because of a dispute between him and the Catholic bishop Maximus related to the issue of divorce. When the forgery was brought to light, in accordance with the oriental concept that the head of the family is responsible for the actions of its members, Muhammad 'Ali ordered the execution of Archon Ghali, who was innocent, but yet was held responsible for his younger brother's illegal actions. These events came as quite a shocking blow to the Christian community in Egypt (Sourial 1984: 134–35).

It seems that the phenomenon of divorce was trying to raise its head, but the popes of the church were keen on restricting it to the circumstances mentioned in the Bible, meaning divorce was allowed in case of adultery only. It seems that pressure was being put on the bishops by rich people and the nobles to be lenient in this matter. Some of these bishops acquiesced to this pressure, and it seems Anba Isaac was among them.

Consequently, Pope Demetrius II (AD 1862–70) sent a letter to the people and priests of the diocese of the Fayoum and al-Bahnasa gently blaming Anba Isaac and excommunicating a priest called Awad:

> May the entire blessing and comprehensive grace be bestowed upon the ears of all the blessed sons and the trustworthy priests of the diocese of al-Bahnasa and the Fayoum. May the Lord bestow on them the best spiritual blessings and the greatest heavenly bounties, Amen. We inform you that we received news from many people and objections from some of our Christian Orthodox sons around the diocese. From this news and these objections, we know that our brother, Bishop Isaac, is acting against the Christian religion, such as breaking the ecclesiastical law by allowing some women to obtain a divorce from their husbands, and then giving them documents permitting them to get married again. As we all know that what God has joined together, man must not separate, as said in the Holy Bible, we find it a must to send you this letter asking you not to accept any of these documents from anyone, but instead try to reconcile the husband and wife who want to divorce, as the Lord says, "How blessed are the peacemakers; God shall call them his sons." Whoever of you divorces a husband from his wife, or accepts documents from the bishop allowing remarriage, let him be excommunicated by the power of the word of God, the bishops of the Holy Synod, and me, Demetrius the vile servant of the See of St. Mark.
>
> As for the priest Awad, who writes these documents with his own hand, we have stripped him of the priesthood and we ask you not to deal with him. My beloved sons, we ask whoever reads this letter to act according to its content and keep a copy of it for use if necessary. We ask every priest who reads this letter to pass it on to other priests all over the diocese. May God's blessing be bestowed on obedient children. (Abraam 2004: 620)

Conclusion

We have briefly studied the life of a very influential bishop of the Coptic Church during the nineteenth century, who not only greatly influenced the renaissance of the Coptic Church by his interest in building churches and repairing monasteries, and by increasing the numbers of monks and priests in his diocese, but was also influential in the enthronement of at least three patriarchs. In the swirl of social changes and challenges in Egypt during his time as bishop, it seems that Anba Isaac's judgment strayed from the dogma of the church. And while the patriarch gently rebuked him, it seems he continued to hold his high position, perhaps in deference to all his previous achievements for the Church.

It is strange indeed for such an influential figure as Anba Isaac, who was a bishop, then metropolitan, for almost fifty years, that when he died the exact date of his death was seemingly lost to history, as was the location of his grave. Still, we honor him for the many positive effects he had on the Coptic Church during the nineteenth century, and hope that someday more of his story emerges.

8 The Monastery of the Holy Virgin Mary at al-Muharraq, Mount Qusqam: History and Heritage (Reflections of Its Monks)

Fr. Angelos al-Muharraqi
and a group of the monastery's monks

Introduction[1]

THE HISTORY of the Coptic Orthodox Church makes no mention of any information about the monastic community or the Holy Virgin Church in the Qusqam region until the fourteenth century AD. The name Qusqam (al-Muharraq Monastery) is mentioned for the first time in the *History of the Patriarchs*, when the Lord selected a monk from the monastery to be the eighty-sixth patriarch of the Coptic Church, Pope Gabriel IV (AD 1370–78) (Burmester and Khater 1970: 234). However, manuscripts and documentation preserved in the monastery prove that there were both activity and continuity of life in the Church of the Holy Virgin Mary in Qusqam before this. Accordingly, a group of the monastery monks was formed in 1986 to study the history, archeology, and monastic life in the Qusqam region from the time of the dwelling of the Holy Family there to the present day.

The Name[2]

'Qusqam' is an ancient Egyptian name, referring to the entire desert region where the monastery is located. Its root is a combination of two Coptic words:

1. Qos (ⲕⲱⲥ or ⲕⲟⲥ): 'to bury' (Crum 1939: 120; Vycichl 1983: 88b)
2. Qam (ⲕⲁⲙ): 'reed, rush' (Crum 1939: 108a; Vycichl 1983: 80b).

The popular name is 'esparto grass' (alpha grass), which is used in making burial shrouds. In religious terms it signified 'infinity' or 'forever.' The origin of the name of al-Muharraq Monastery lies in the fact that it was near to an area where harmful plants and weeds were burned, and so the whole region was known as the 'burnt' area.

However, the Church of Our Lady the Virgin Mary at Mount Qusqam, together with its monastic community, originally had the name of Our Lady Church at Mount Qusqam, and this was used in preference to referring to it as a 'monastery' at that time. But, with the spread of the Arabic language, the monastery's name changed gradually from Abu Mahruqa to al-Maharraqa Monastery (which means 'burnt area'), and finally it became known as al-Muharraq. The other titles continued to be used for a period of time in the Middle Ages until the name al-Muharraq became used exclusively.

Historical Background

Initially, the history of the monastery's location goes back to shortly after the birth of Christ when the area of al-Muharraq Monastery, which is located at Mount Qusqam, was a barren desert except for an abandoned house and an adjacent water well. The Holy Family, the Child Jesus and His mother St. Mary, St. Joseph the carpenter, and Salome, who was their helper, settled in that modest house, which St. Joseph renovated. They remained in Qusqam for a period of over six months or about 185 days.

It was here, at this very spot, that the angel of the Lord appeared to St. Joseph in a dream, saying, "Arise, take the young Child and His mother, and go to the land of Israel, for those who sought the young Child's life are dead" (Matthew 2:20–21). As Christianity spread in Egypt, through the preaching of St. Mark the Apostle and Evangelist, churches were built throughout the land. Among these was the church built on the site of the house where the Holy Family had lived, as recorded in Coptic tradition. It later became a church dedicated to the name of the Holy Virgin Mary. It is believed to have been the first church in Upper Egypt; so hallowed are its associations that many named it 'The Second Jerusalem.'

The Church of the Holy Virgin Mary at Mount Qusqam became an attraction to visitors through the ages. For the needy and the sick, it was their shelter and comfort in times of distress through the intercessions of the Mother of God, St. Mary the Virgin. Each year, multitudes of pilgrims from every district flocked to visit the monastery, as the site was well known for its signs, wonders, and healing of many diseases.

It is worth mentioning the prophecy of Isaiah that said: "In that day there will be an altar to the Lord in the midst of the land of Egypt, and a pillar to the Lord at its border" (Isaiah 19:19). Despite some biblical scholars' attempts to interpret this prophecy either allegorically or symbolically, the handed-down monastery tradition interprets this verse literally and refers to the altar of the Holy Virgin Mary's church in the monastery as the altar to the Lord in the midst of the land of Egypt. This is considered a historical fact and a prophecy for all generations.

Early Christianity and Monastic Life in Qusqam

The site of the Holy Virgin Mary's church in the wilderness of Qusqam played an important role in attracting people to dwell and to worship God nearby due to its simplicity and humble conditions. The site had a unique privilege: it was a safe and a fairly comfortable shelter for the Holy Family, away from urbanization, where they led a humble life; and they blessed the place by their presence. So it is said that those who come to lead a life of purity and sanctity to worship God, as the Holy Family did, will enjoy the same blessings the Lord of Glory has bestowed on the place. They will also earn the crown of eternal life.

According to René-Georges Coquin and Maurice Martin, "nothing is known for certain about the date of the foundation of this monastery" (Coquin and Martin 1991d). It is, however, widely believed by the monks in the monastery that it follows the Pachomian cenobitic system. The monastery is known for welcoming all visitors seeking the water of the

Fig. 8.1. Qusqam, general view inside the monastery. Photograph by Fr. Maximous al-Muharraqi.

well, blessed by the Lord Jesus, for healing. They also come to ask for the prayers and intercession of the Lord's Mother, the Holy Virgin Mary.

In the late fourth century, the twenty-third pope of Alexandria, Theophilus (AD 385–412), visited the monastic community of about three hundred monks at the time at Qusqam church, and he took care of them and provided funds for the establishment of some necessary facilities and to help the poor and the sick. During this visit, the Blessed Virgin Mary appeared to him in a vision and told him that she had come with her beloved Son, Joseph, and Salome to the abandoned house in the Mount Qusqam wilderness. The Ethiopian manuscripts indicate many miracles that came to light at the time of the reconstruction of the monastery during the visit of Pope Theophilus. There is a clear reference to the presence of Ethiopian monks at Qusqam, in *The Paradise of the Holy Fathers*: *The Triumph of the Blessed Apollo and Ammon*. It states: "And we saw also there Ethiopians who lived with the monks, and they excelled to such a degree in the ascetic life that in them were fulfilled the words which are said in the Book, 'Kush [Ethiopia] shall deliver the hand unto God'" (Psalm 68:31) (Budge 1907: 347). The Blessed Apollo was in the Bawit area, nearly twenty kilometers north of Qusqam.

Documentary Evidence and Historical Events (Sixth–Twelfth Centuries AD)

There are several confirmed pieces of evidence to show that there was life and activity in the Church of the Holy Virgin in Qusqam during the sixth to twelfth centuries. The most notable are as follows:

1. Coptic tradition of the biography of St. John of Heraclia, attributed to Constantine (Constantinios), bishop of Asyut (sixth–seventh century AD). It states that he visited the Church of Our Lady at Qusqam for three days, a few days after his ordination.[3]
2. Coptic tradition of the martyrdom of St. Theodore Stratelates (the General), attributed to Pope Benjamin, thirty-eighth patriarch of Alexandria (AD 623–62). It states that Pope Benjamin took refuge in the Church of the Lady, the pure Virgin Mary, on Qusqam Mountain for a period of time. Subsequently, he moved to other churches. This occurred during his thirteen-year flight from Alexandria due to the installation of Cyrus, the imperially ordained patriarch by decree of the Byzantine emperor, Heraclius. Cyrus ordained many new bishops for Egyptian provinces and persecuted the people who adhered to the non-Chalcedonian faith.[4]

3. During the twelfth to thirteenth centuries AD, Abu al-Makarim wrote an Arabic manuscript, titled by its publisher *The Churches and Monasteries of Egypt and Some Neighbouring Countries*.[5] The information found in the manuscript about Qusqam Monastery at that time is of great value.[6] Some of this is as follows:
   a. "Pilgrimages have been made by many multitudes from all districts to this church from ancient times, because it has been celebrated on account of signs and wonders and the healing of various diseases; and the time of pilgrimage is at Easter, every year" (Evetts and Butler 1893–95: 227).
   b. "Adjacent to this church there is a large and ancient keep,[7] which had fallen into decay, but was renewed and restored to its original condition by the Shaikh Abu Zakarî ibn Bû Nasr, the administrator of Al-Ushmûnain; may God have mercy on him and grant rest to his soul! This was in the caliphate of al-Hafiz (AD 1130–49)" (Evetts and Butler 1893–95: 227).
4. On the surface of the altar of the ancient Church of the Holy Virgin Mary, there is a piece of marble with a semicircular edge where there is engraved a Greek inscription. It reads, "O Lord, give rest to the blessed Colluthos," dated 15 Kiyahk AM 463 (11 December AD 746). The semicircle of marble is considered a peculiarity that distinguishes ancient Coptic altars in Egypt. The idea of the semicircular shape is an ancient Coptic convention and appears in ancient icons of the Last Supper, where the table is a semicircle. The Greek inscription was published by Gustave Lefebvre (Lefebvre 1915: 138–39).[8]
5. In the *History of the Patriarchs*, the biography of Pope Cyril II (sixty-seventh patriarch, AD 1078–92) mentions the presence of the tomb of the martyr St. Elias (Helias) at Qusqam (Atiya and 'Abd al-Masih 1959: 228 [text], 362 [trans.]).[9]

The Age of Revival (Thirteenth–Fifteenth Centuries AD)

When viewed on a map, it can clearly be seen that the Nile Valley in Upper Egypt is very narrow in the area where the monastery is located, right on the boundary between agricultural land and the desert. The distance between the Nile and the monastery does not exceed ten kilometers when measured perpendicularly. Due to the proximity of the monastery to the agricultural and populated areas (especially in the Middle Ages), the monastery was affected by the situation of the country and the people's standard of

Fig. 8.2. Qusqam, part of the southern wall during the restoration. Photograph by Fr. Maximous al-Muharraqi.

Fig. 8.3. Qusqam, the ancient Church of the Holy Virgin Mary, southwestern side. Photograph by Fr. Maximous al-Muharraqi.

Fig. 8.4. Qusqam, the ancient keep. Photograph by Fr. Maximous al-Muharraqi.

Fig. 8.5. Qusqam, part of the ground floor of the ancient keep, mid-twentieth century. Photograph by Fr. Maximous al-Muharraqi.

Fig. 8.6. Qusqam, the sanctuary of the ancient Church of the Holy Virgin Mary. Photograph by Fr. Maximous al-Muharraqi.

living. During those days, active monasticism ceased to exist in many monasteries all over the country due to monks abandoning them. Despite these hard times, one finds our monastery, by the grace of the Lord of Glory, kept from destruction, epidemics, and famines. The monastery was always full of visitors who came to pray to the Lord for help during these difficult times, and to ask for the intercession of the Holy Virgin Mary to help them and their children. It is also worth mentioning that the fourteenth-century manuscripts in the monastery and in some libraries abroad confirm these ongoing visits to the monastery. In addition, the Ethiopian manuscripts record many miracles performed by the Holy Virgin Mary for people who asked for her intercession. The importance of the monastery at that time is confirmed by the testimonies written by the following Arab historians:

1. The historian 'Abdallah Yaqut ibn 'Abdallah al-Rumi al-Hamawi, who resided in Hamah and Baghdad and is also known as Shihab al-Din (AH 575–626, AD 1179/80–1228/29), says in his book *Kitab mu'jam al-buldan* (The Dictionary of Countries) that the monastery had magnificent architecture and one could not miss the beauty of these buildings. He states that the Christians magnified it, and it is alleged that Jesus Christ settled there during His visit to Egypt.
2. Al-Maqrizi (AD 1364–1441) mentions that the Christians alleged that Christ had settled in this place (al-Muharraq Monastery) for six months and many days, and that many people gathered there for "a great feast known as the feast of al-Zaytuna and the feast of Pentecost and a great multitude gather in it" (Wüstenfeld: 41 [text], 101 [translation]).

The patriarch fathers

The Lord of Glory granted His grace to the monastery by choosing some of its monks to be popes of Alexandria and the See of St. Mark:

1. Pope Gabriel IV (eighty-sixth patriarch, AD 1370–78)
2. Pope Matthew (the Great) I (eighty-seventh patriarch, AD 1378–1409)
3. Pope Matthew II (ninetieth patriarch, AD 1452–65)
4. Pope John XII (ninety-third patriarch, AD 1479–82)

Sixteenth–Eighteenth Centuries AD

These were gloomy times for the Christians in Egypt, following the Ottoman conquest. But the Lord wished to preserve the monastery through the prayers of the saints living there; then a ray of hope appeared on the horizon.[10]

Nineteenth–Twentieth Centuries AD

These times are considered to be reflected in the words of the Psalm: "The Lord renews your youth like the eagle's" (Psalm 103:5).[11]

Tradition and Heritage

The Coptic Language and Manuscript Production in the Monastery

The monks cared greatly for the Coptic language, especially when it began to fade away in the Middle Ages, as some of the monks had command of both the Coptic and the Arabic languages. They maintained the Coptic language, but they did not neglect Arabic. Manuscripts show that works such as lectionaries for liturgical readings and biblical books used for their private readings were produced in Coptic only. Other manuscripts had both Coptic and Arabic versions in parallel. Many of these were transcribed in a most perfect script.

Interest in using the Coptic language at the monastery continued tirelessly, as is evident from the manuscripts produced in subsequent centuries. It seems that interest in producing manuscripts in Arabic only began in the nineteenth century when manuscripts, including Acts, St. Paul's Epistles, and Ecclesiastes, and some other liturgical manuals, were copied for the public to understand the service. There is an indication that the Arabic language was first used around the middle of the eighteenth century AD in church readings for events such as Paskha (Passover) Week, Lakan (Blessing of the Water), and Genuflection services.

It seems that the monastery's reputation for Coptic language proficiency attracted Michael El-Sabbagh to learn the Coptic language there. He stayed in the monastery, as a visiting scholar, at the end of the eighteenth century until he had command of the language. He was introduced to Mr. Elias Buqtur of Asyut, who was a translator and personal secretary to Napoleon. Michael went to Paris in AD 1801 and worked there as a consultant for various orientalists, including Baron Silvestre de Sacy. He then became the librarian of the National Library at Paris (Graf 1944–53, vol. 3: 249).

Several manuscripts of the lectionary, *Psalmody*, and the *Euchologion* were scribed in Coptic only. This provides an indication that Coptic was revived and flourished in the monastery at the time of their production. This is true in the nineteenth century and especially during the tenure of Hegomen 'Abd al-Malak al-Hory, the monastery abbot, and later. In fact, the liturgical prayers in church were and still are recited in Coptic only. This Coptic revival continued to such a degree that many of the monks of the monastery at the end of the nineteenth century mastered the primary skills of the Coptic language: speaking, reading, and writing.

With regard to the manuscripts, the monastery has assisted multiple scholars and researchers in their academic studies, as they have been granted special permission to discuss and/or inspect a specific manuscript.[12]

Some of the most notable scribes among the monastery's monks are:

1. Hegomen Quzman, fourteenth century AD, who was responsible for the copying of some books of the Holy Bible.
2. Hegomen Eqlouda (Pope Gabriel IV's brother), fourteenth century AD, who copied some of the Coptic lectionaries.
3. Hegomen Yohanna, nineteenth century AD, from Etleedem, who copied sixty-four manuscripts in forty-eight years. He was deserving of the title 'Father of Scribing.'

Some of the monastery manuscripts published from 1908 to the present are as follows:

1. "Commentary on the Gospels by al-Meshreqy," edited by Youssef Manqarious, 1908.
2. "al-Sheikh al-Rohani (St. John Saba)," edited by Fr. Boulos (Fouad) Basili. First published in 1947.
3. "Commentary on the Psalms," in three volumes, 1988.
4. "al-Hawi (The Theological Encyclopedia) of al-Makin Girgis Ibn al 'Amid," volumes 1 and 2 in 1999, and volumes 3 and 4 in 2001.
5. "Miamer (Homilies) of St. Gregory the Theologian," two volumes, 2003.

The Heritage of Church Ritual and Religious Ceremonies at the Monastery

There is a long history of Coptic liturgical tradition at the monastery, such as for daily liturgies and Psalmody prayers, glorification of the saints, and hymns of the feasts. More notably, and unique, is the water prayers tradition during the feast of the Cross on 17 Tut of the Coptic year (11 September). This was observed during the Nile flood period prior to the construction of the High Dam in the 1960s.[13]

Final Word

It is our sincerest hope that the reader has now gained a better understanding of the long history and tradition of al-Muharraq Monastery or, more correctly, the Monastery of the Virgin Mary at Gebel Qusqam. It is a history that stretches from the time the Holy Family stayed there while the Lord Jesus was a child, and the tradition of His consecration of the ancient church, all the way to our present time. It endured centuries of neglect in the Middle Ages, but because of its divine foundation it emerged better than ever out of these dark years. It is regarded by its monks and pilgrims as the Second Jerusalem.

Notes

1 For more information on the monastery, consult Timm 1984–92, vol. 2: 751–56.
2 The names 'Qusqam/Qosqam' and 'al-Muharraq' are discussed in detail in Dayr al-Muharraq 1996: 184–94.
3 For the bishop's biography, refer to Coquin 1981: 154–55.
4 Refer to Girgis 1988.
5 The manuscript was bought by the traveler J.M. Vansleb in Egypt in the seventeenth century and is deposited at the Bibliothèque Nationale de France (Arabe 307). It was published by Evetts and Butler, but falsely attributed to Abu Salih al-Armani.
6 For the Arabic text, refer to Evetts and Butler 1893–95: ms folios 78a, 78b, 79a, and 79b; and for the English translation, pp. 224–27.
7 For more information on the keep of the monastery, refer to Fr. Philoxenos' chapter in this volume.
8 For further information, refer to Meinardus 1985.
9 St. Elias the martyr was a bishop of al-Qusiya and the Church of Our Lady at Qusqam. He was martyred during the reign of Emperor Diocletian (early fourth century AD), and, after a period of time, his body was transferred from al-Qusiya to Qusqam (Basset 1907: 491–94). There is in the possession of the monastery today a tombstone engraved in the Coptic language that includes the name Elias, dated AM 807 (AD 1090/1091).
10 For more details about this period, refer to Dayr al-Muharraq 1992: 98–111.
11 For more details about this period, refer to Dayr al-Muharraq 1992: 112–62.
12 There is a valuable manuscripts index, prepared in 1932.
13 For more details on these services, refer to Dayr al-Muharraq 1992: 185–99.

9 John of Shmoun and Coptic Identity

Samuel Moawad

After the Council of Chalcedon in AD 451 and in particular after the Arab conquest of Egypt in AD 641, the need to demonstrate Coptic self-identification became more important than before.[1] Usually, there is the need to stress one's identity and define or form its features when one feels that one's cultural or ethnic existence is threatened and association with other groups of different ethnic or religious origin leads to the loss or distortion of one's identity. Such feelings are to be found in particular among persecuted or ignored minorities.

Coptic literature preferred to deal with the theme of identity in an indirect way. In Coptic and Copto-Arabic writings, we find some hints and allusions that emphasize the superiority of Egypt and its Church. These hints are not limited to post-Chalcedonian Coptic literature but are also found in pre-Chalcedonian texts that were reworked or re-edited by interpolating passages to demonstrate Coptic identity, as we can see in the *Life of Patriarch Peter* (300–11).

John of Shmoun (Hermopolis Magna), now al-Ashmunayn in Middle Egypt, is a special case regarding this theme.[2] Very little is known about him. He was contemporary with Patriarch Damianus (578–604), as John himself mentioned in his *Panegyric on Saint Antony*.[3] Before his consecration as bishop of Shmoun, he lived as a hermit monk and priest in the same region. The *Arabic History of the Patriarchs* mentions John among the prominent bishops in the time of Damianus (the blessed John the Hermit) without saying anything about his person.[4] In addition, there is a papyrus found in Hermopolis Magna (P.Rainer Cent. 79) and dated to the sixth century (Maehler 1983). It contains a private letter in Greek signed by Bishop John, who could be the same John under discussion. However, it does not provide any further information concerning him.[5] It is not known when and by whom John was consecrated as bishop, but it was probably by Patriarch Damianus. From his literary writings, it can be concluded that John received a good education and was familiar with the writings of the Church Fathers in Greek and Coptic as well.[6]

From the literary writings of John of Shmoun, we have only two works in Sahidic Coptic: one panegyric on the Apostle Mark and another on St. Antony the Great.[7] Both were written when John was still a monk, before his consecration as a bishop, as the prologue of his panegyrics reveals. It is not clear whether John wrote other works besides these two panegyrics. However, his choice of these two famous saints, Mark and Antony, shows his tendency to emphasize the superiority of the Coptic Church. This tendency remains limited to John of Shmoun and cannot be generalized to describe Coptic literature in that period in general, since there are no other Coptic writings entirely dedicated to this purpose (Mikhail 2004: 135–38 n. 366).

Unfortunately, the panegyric on Mark is fragmentary. However, the remaining text suffices to suggest how John of Shmoun dealt with his theme. First of all, John demonstrates how Egypt before Mark lived in the darkness of paganism. He speaks very clearly about "our worshipers of the vain idols in that time."[8] He identifies the beginning of the real history of Egypt with the coming of Mark when he says, "Before Mark came, there was in Egypt no morning at all, but a continuous night. But when Mark, the light, came, the morning began."[9] After that, John mentions the famous Egyptian monks, such as Pachomius, Pijoul, Shenoute of Atripe, and others.[10]

These short citations from the *Panegyric on Mark* draw our attention to two important points, which will be discussed in the following pages in some detail: the Coptic view of the pre-Christian history of Egypt and the role of St. Mark in the formation of the Coptic identity.

Copts and the View Back to the Pre-Christian Past

Although Copts descend from the ancient Egyptians and in modern times are often considered their successors,[11] we do not find any trace of this blood relationship in their Christian-oriented writings. The historical works of Copts in Coptic as well as in Arabic do not mention the pharaohs in the lists of the rulers of Egypt. Despite some chapters in the *Chronicle* of John of Nikiou in which he mentions some data concerning the history of Egypt, he does not mention the ancient Egyptians as his own ancestors. He sees Egypt before Christianity as a pagan land that worshiped idols and demons.[12] The first time that John relates himself to 'Egyptians' is when he speaks about "the prayers of our Egyptian Fathers."[13] He shows respect and pride for Egyptians when he speaks about "the holy fathers, the Egyptian monks, who were clothed with God."[14] He relates himself only to Christian Egypt, the Egypt of martyrs, saints, and monks.

The same attitude is also to be found in an undated homily preserved in Arabic and attributed to Theophilus of Alexandria (385–412). The anonymous author of this homily sees in Egypt before Christianity nothing but sinners and pagans. According to his view, the land of Egypt was full of impurity and a dwelling place for Satan, but after its Christianization it became the place of God and his angels.[15]

Coptic historians were not interested in their own ancient Egyptian history, not only because they wanted to distance themselves from paganism, which ancient Egypt embodied, but also because they lacked the necessary information to write about this era. It was a coincidence that Egypt changed its religion and its written script at the same time. In the fourth century, Christianity became the religion of the majority of Egyptians, and about the same period or a little bit earlier, Coptic developed into a standard language with a markedly different grammar and orthography from its past. This fact was enough to cut off any connection with the past. Coptic historians were not able to read and understand the ancient Egyptian script and considered ancient Egyptian religion to be satanic worship.[16] The new situation led the Copts to see themselves as spiritual descendants of the holy men of the Old Testament more than as successors of the heathen pharaohs. They adopted the view of the early Christian generations, who were predominantly of Jewish origin, and saw in the pharaohs a symbol of evil and an embodiment of Satan himself, as, for example, in the first canticle in the Coptic psalmody book. In his commentary on the Gospel of John, Origen (185–254) considered the Christians to be the spiritual Israel.[17] In Coptic literature and particularly in the monastic tradition, the word 'Israelite' became a positive description for saintly monks.[18] Egyptian Christians considered Jerusalem a symbol of spirituality, in contrast to Egypt and Pharaoh, both of which symbolized evil and earthly life (Frend 1982: 24).

A fragmentary homily, which Shenoute of Atripe (ca. 347–465) preached at an ancient Egyptian temple converted to a church, makes Shenoute's opinion of pharaonic temples clear. For him, it was a place for unclean spirits where the people sacrificed to and worshiped Satan. To clean and purify it, it had to be transformed into a church.[19] For Shenoute, the temple symbolized heathenism and aberrance, which everyone must leave to come to the knowledge of Christ. The temple that had been transformed into a church became an example of repentance.[20] Shenoute's depiction and explanation of the hieroglyphic script on the temple's wall show his ignorance of the ancient Egyptian language and religion and his disgust with everything related to this pagan Egyptian past.[21] This is in contrast to Clement of Alexandria (d. 220), who shows a good understanding of the Egyptian script and how it functions.[22]

It is true that some pre-Christian funerary customs and habits, such as mummification and caring for the body of the dead, survived in Christian Egypt, even in monastic and clerical circles (Baumeister 1972: 58–63, 73–86). However, we cannot consider this continuity to reflect a survival of the belief upon which ancient Egyptians established their funerary rituals. The continuity of these practices was due to the perfect compatibility of Christian dogmas with ancient Egyptian religion concerning the resurrection of the body. Some customs and habits were practiced not only in Egypt, but also elsewhere in the Byzantine world. Thus, it is not correct always to prefer an Egyptian explanation when other factors could play a role (Papaconstantinou 2006: 66–67, 73–75).

Coptic identity was based primarily on Christian fundamentals. In Coptic identity there are no traces of ancient Egypt. Coptic Christians rejected the glories of pre-Christian Egypt and did not seek national identity. Coptic Christians did not understand Christianity as a national movement, but rather as a way of life and thinking. Thanks to Christianity, Copts gained a new cultural awareness and a sense of identity. They became adherents and members of a culture that could challenge Greek (pagan) philosophy (Frend 1982: 23–24). With the passage of time, this feeling of cultural superiority increased, particularly after the Arab conquest, as Copts believed that the Muslim conquerors had no culture to offer and that their Arabic language was not worthy to be spoken. As we can see in the *Apocalypse of Pseudo-Samuel of Qalamun*, Copts found no point of resemblance between the Coptic language of the saints and the Arabic language of the Bedouin (Papaconstantinou 2007: 292).

Despite the disappearance of any positive connection between Christian and ancient Egypt in literary sources and particularly in historiographical writings, Coptic art offers enough evidence for such a connection. Copts adopted some ancient Egyptian elements into their art after Christianizing them. Some ancient Egyptian elements and motifs survived in Coptic art and show the continuity of ancient Egyptian art in the early Coptic period. The scene of the raising of Lazarus is a good example to demonstrate how Coptic art was influenced, technically, ideologically, and religiously, by the pre-Christian art of Egypt. This scene was painted on various materials and in different ways. Among the variants is one where Lazarus is coiled like a mummy in an aedicula while Jesus stands before him and holds his rod upon the head of Lazarus. The Coptic version of Lazarus's scene is reminiscent of an old Egyptian ritual, namely the Ritual of Opening the Mouth, which derives from the legend of the Egyptian god Osiris. The parallels between the two illustrations demonstrate how Coptic artists were influenced by ancient Egyptian art (Hermann, 1962; Meurer 1971; Galal 1986: 201–203).

John of Shmoun and Praising Egypt

In his *Panegyric on Saint Antony,* John of Shmoun used the opportunity to praise Egypt as a holy land that bore saints and where prophets lived or were buried. He says: "Antony, said Athanasius, was Egyptian by origin. Where will the sun rise except in the east? And where do you wish Antony to shine forth except in Egypt? . . . For most of the saints who have lived have been from Egypt or Egypt has attracted them from other places."[23] After that, John mentions some prophets of the Old Testament who visited Egypt or were buried there, such as Abraham, Jacob, and Moses. Then he turns to reminding his audience that the famous monastic leaders were Egyptian.

> In the same way, the leaders of all the monks practiced ascetic discipline in Egypt. . . . The land of Egypt is fertile not only for growing fruits that perish but also for people who bear fruit according to God. . . . Other lands bring different kinds of fruit to us, and we find enjoyment in them, but our pride is in our own (fruit), in particular, in what belongs to us and in what existed here, the likes of which are not elsewhere. For it is said concerning papyrus or paper that it is made only in Egypt and does not grow in other countries. In the same way, Antony lived in this country, and there is no other Antony like him.[24]

Here, it is clear how proud of Egypt John was. Other literary sources tell us the same about Antony and ennoble him over all other monks, since he symbolizes Egyptian monasticism. Shenoute of Atripe believes that "even if all the monks of this time came [together] in a single place, they would not make a single Antony!"[25] This and other writings are quoted by John of Shmoun in his panegyric.[26]

Also, the *Life of Dioscorus* attests that only the bishops of Egypt can endure pains and punishment for their belief. The author of this Life says to the Chalcedonian bishop of Gangra: "Who but he could endure what you do against my father.... I attest before you that there is no other bishop equal to him except only in Egypt."[27]

St. Mark and the Coptic Identity

When John of Shmoun decided to write a panegyric on St. Mark he did it not only because Mark was the preacher of Christianity in Alexandria and the first martyr in Egypt, but also because he became a symbol of legitimacy for every Coptic patriarch who is, first of all, considered the successor of St. Mark. It is true that the struggle for primacy among the great patriarchates, that is, Rome, Alexandria, and Constantinople, began in the fourth century. However, after the Council of Chalcedon in 451, and the establishing of the Melchite (Chalcedonian) Church in Egypt, the need to stress the relationship between the Coptic patriarchs and the memory of St. Mark became more important than before to confront those who put the legitimacy of the Coptic patriarchs in question. From that time on, the Coptic Church not only had to prove the correctness of its faith before the Christian world, but also had to defend the legitimacy of its patriarchs and hence its existence. During this struggle, the memory of St. Mark played a considerable role. Coptic and Copto-Arabic sources offer some hints that refer to the interest of Coptic historians in demonstrating the role of St. Mark in the process of establishing and forming the Coptic collective identity.

The martyrdom of Patriarch Peter I (300–11) offers an interesting passage in which Peter prays at the tomb of St. Mark before his martyr's death.[28] In his prayer, Peter follows the succession of the Alexandrian patriarchate in order to assert the apostolic origin of the Alexandrian Church and the legitimacy of its patriarchs. The prayer of Peter of Alexandria at the tomb of Mark thus serves to demonstrate the unbroken continuity between Mark and Peter of Alexandria, and to assert the foundation of the Coptic Church by Mark.[29]

Although this visit of Peter to the tomb of St. Mark may not have a historical basis (Davis 2004: 41 n. 87), it later found high popularity among the Copts by its inclusion in the Arabic *History of the Patriarchs* and the Arabic *Synaxarion* under 29 Hatur. In his prayer, Peter demonstrates the apostolicity of the Coptic Church that was founded not only by Mark but also by God himself, since God chose Mark to preach the gospel in Egypt. For Peter—or, more precisely, for the author of the martyrdom—it was important to mention the late patriarchs of Alexandria by name to demonstrate the apostolic succession in the see of Alexandria and thus to legitimize them and their successors as well. Although it is not clear when exactly the *Martyrdom of Peter* was expanded, it can be assumed that the additional parts had been interpolated after 451 since other post-Chalcedonian Coptic sources have the same tendency, as we will see.

A very similar passage is to be found in the so-called *Life of Dioscorus*.[30] On the ship from Alexandria to Constantinople to attend the Council of Chalcedon, Dioscorus prays to God and mentions his predecessors from Mark to Cyril.[31] The *Life of Dioscorus* never ceases to accent and highlight this close relationship between St. Mark and Dioscorus as his legal successor (Moawad 2011: 165–75).

The *Panegyric on Macarius of Tkôw*, another anti-Chalcedonian Coptic text, uses the memory of St. Mark to prove the correctness of the Alexandrian faith. After the Council of Chalcedon, a troop of soldiers tried to force the monks of Apa Longinus to sign the decisions of the council. When Apa Longinus found out that Dioscorus did not sign, he also refused to sign it. He told the commander that one of his monks saw a vision in which the Apostle Peter was weeping because the things he planted through the whole world had been plucked out, but the things which Mark planted (in Egypt) took root.[32] The *Panegyric on Macarius* does not discuss any theological details to support the correctness of the Alexandrian faith. It lets St. Peter himself confess this truth and praise St. Mark and his successors for keeping the Christian faith intact. This scene is a clever attempt by the anonymous author to grant the Egyptian Church infallibility.

The usage of the memory and the figure of St. Mark in the formation of the Coptic identity is not limited to Coptic literature but extends also to Coptic art. In an early seventh-century ivory relief, we see St. Mark seated on a throne and holding his Gospel. He is surrounded by his thirty-five immediate successors, the patriarchs of Alexandria, from Anianus (d. 85) to Anastasius (605–19). In the background, we see the city of Alexandria. This relief comes from Alexandria and is now preserved in the Musée du Louvre in Paris (Davis 2004: 1–2). Here, the stress on the apostolic origins of the Coptic Church and the legitimacy of its patriarchs is explicit, and not implicit as in the written texts. In the period from the second half of the fifth century to the seventh century, the need to present collective self-identification among Copts increased to face the power and the authority of the Melchite Church, which enjoyed the financial and military support of the Byzantine state.

Literature and art were instruments to keep the memory of St. Mark alive among Coptic believers. However, there was another more important way to keep his memory immortal, namely the relics of St. Mark himself. With the passage of time, the veneration of the head of St. Mark became an important part in the consecration of a new patriarch. On the day after his consecration, according to Ibn Sabba', the patriarch should visit the head of the apostle where it is preserved and bow before it. After that, he prayed with incense and read the beginning of the Gospel of St. Mark. After the prayer, he exchanged the old covering of the head with a new one, took it in his arms, and let the assembled people kiss it. Ibn Sabba' ends his chapter with the following phrase: "With this ceremony his consecration as a patriarch is completed because he is the one who sits on the throne of the apostle Mark."[33] The *History of the Patriarchs* by pseudo-Yusab of Fuwwa mentions two patriarchs by name who practiced this ceremony, namely Mark III (1167–89) and Cyril III (1235–43).[34]

As we see, John of Shmoun is not the only Coptic author who is interested in praising and ennobling his land, Egypt, but he may be the only known author who expresses this tendency explicitly in his works. Other Coptic authors preferred to refer to their pride in their homeland and in their Coptic Church implicitly, using key figures. However, the figure of St. Mark remains by far the most often used and the most effective figure.

Notes

1 I am deeply indebted to my colleague Dr. Christian Askeland (Münster) and to Connie Sletto (Elgin, IL) for correcting the first draft of the English version.

2 For Shmoun/al-Ashmunayn, see Timm 1984–92: 1:198–220.

3 John of Shmoun, *Panegyric on Antony* §35, ed., with French translation, Garitte 1943: 344–45; Italian translation, Orlandi 1981: 262; English translation, Vivian, Athanassakis, and Greer 2003: 31; modern Arabic translation, Moawad 2013: 367.

4 *The History of the Patriarchs*, ed. Seybold 1912: 92. Later manuscripts of the *History of the Patriarchs*, the so-called vulgate recension, omit "the blessed John" and mention only "the Hermit (εγκλειστος)" as a proper name. Cf. *The History of the Patriarchs*, ed. Evetts 1904: 477.

5 In Sahidic Coptic with Bohairic influences there is a private letter by a certain Bishop John of Shmoun. Because the letter is written on paper, it cannot be dated before the ninth century and hence it deals with another John. See Steindorff 1892: 38.
6 John of Shmoun, *Panegyric on Antony* §34, Garitte 1943: 344–45; Orlandi 1981: 261–62; Vivian, Athanassakis, and Greer 2003: 30; Moawad 2013: 365–66.
7 *Panegyric on Mark*, ed., with Latin translation, Orlandi 1968: 7–52; modern Arabic translation, Moawad 2013: 371–78. *Panegyric on Antony*, Garitte 1943; Orlandi 1981: 249–64; Vivian, Athanassakis, and Greer 2003: 1–35; Moawad 2013: 341–70. For a literary analysis of both writings, see Sheridan 2011: 448–53.
8 Orlandi 1968: 16a.
9 Orlandi 1968: 16a.
10 Orlandi 1968: 16b.
11 For a detailed discussion, see van der Vliet 2009.
12 John of Nikiou, *Chronicle* 19, 2; 31, 1; 30, 6–11; English translation, Charles 1916: 21, 28–29.
13 John of Nikiou, *Chronicle* 89, 1; English translation, Charles 1916: 121.
14 John of Nikiou, *Chronicle* 56, 24; English translation, Charles 1916: 46.
15 Pseudo-Theophilus, *A Homily on the Honor of Saint Peter and Saint Paul*, ed., with French translation, Fleisch 1935–36: 381, 383.
16 The *Bohairic Life of Pesynthios* (ed., with French translation, Amélineau 1887: 141–44; English translation, Budge 1913: 326–27) tells that Bishop Pesynthios of Coptos (598–632) was in a cave full of mummies. He found a scroll including the names of the dead. He unrolled it and could read it. It is unclear in what language the scroll was written. While Amélineau and Müller believe that it was written in Demotic, Lee refutes this opinion and is "sure that it was in Coptic." See Müller 1964: 298; Lee 1982: 40.
17 Origen, *Commentary on the Gospel of John* I. 1.1–5, ed., with French translation, Blanc 1966: 56–59; English translation, Menzies 1912: 297.
18 Antonius, *Ep.* V. 1; VI. 2, 78, 93; VII. 5, 58[b]; English translation, Rubenson 1995: 212, 216, 221, 223, 225, 229; *The Life of Pachomius* 133, ed. Lefort 1952: 183–84; English translation, Veilleux 1980–82, vol. 1: 190–91.
19 Shenoute of Atripe, *Acephalous Work A6*, ed. Young 1981: 349a, English translation: 353.
20 Young 1981: 350, English translation: 354.
21 Young 1981: 349b, English translation: 354.
22 Clement of Alexandria, *Stromata* V. 4, ed. Stählin 1960: 339; English translation, Roberts and Donaldson 1885: 449.
23 John of Shmoun, *Panegyric on Antony* §6, ed., with French translation, Garitte 1943: 118–19; Italian translation, Orlandi 1981: 252–53; English translation, Vivian, Athanassakis, and Greer 2003: 12; modern Arabic translation, Moawad 2013: 350–51.
24 Garitte 1943: 120–23; Orlandi 1981: 253–54; Vivian, Athanassakis, and Greer 2003: 14; Moawad 2013: 352.
25 *Life of Shenoute* §69, ed. Leipoldt 1906: 35; English translation, Bell 1983: 62.
26 John of Shmoun, *Panegyric on Antony* §34, Garitte 1943: 344–45; Orlandi 1981: 261–62; Vivian et al. 2003: 30; Moawad 2013: 365–66.
27 *Vita Dioscori*, Arabic version, ed. Moawad 2013: 303. The Syriac version varies; cf.

Nau 1903: 84, French translation 292.

28 The martyrdom of Peter is preserved in three versions, different in length, in various languages. See Vivian 1988: 64–68; Davis 2004: 41–42.

29 *The Martyrdom of Saint Peter* 12, ed. Devos 1965: 171–72; English translation, Vivian 1988: 75. See also the Coptic version in Hyvernat 1977: 274–75; the Arabic version in Seybold 1912: 54, and Evetts 1904: 397–98.

30 For more details on this source and its versions, see Moawad 2011.

31 *Vita Dioscori*, Arabic version, ed. Moawad 2013: 280–81; Syriac version, ed. Nau 1903: 37–39, French translation: 255–57.

32 *The Panegyric on Macarius of Tkōou* IX.1–3, Sahidic version, ed. Johnson 1980, vol. 1: 72–73, English translation 2: 56; modern Arabic translation, Moawad 2013: 239; Arabic version, ed. Moawad 2010: 87–88, German translation 129–30. A similar episode in the Pseudo-Theophilus, *A Homily on the Honor of St. Peter and St. Paul*, ed. Fleisch 1935–36: 391, 393.

33 Ibn Sabba', *al-Jawhara al-nafisa* 86, ed. Mistrih 1966: 284, 287; Latin translation 541, 543.

34 Pseudo-Yusab of Fuwwa, *The History of the Patriarchs*, fols. 148r, 152v, ed. al-Suriany and Daoud 1987: 158, 163.

10 Christianity in Asyut in Modern History

Adel F. Sadek

A Historical Introduction

By the second half of the eighteenth century Asyut had taken Girga's place as the capital of Upper Egypt. With Muhammad 'Ali's interest in administratively organizing Egypt's governorates, the construction of the governorate building in Asyut began in 1811. In 1822, Asyut's population was around seventeen thousand inhabitants. By 1846 it had reached twenty thousand. In 1850, Asyut was the largest city in Upper Egypt and the sixth largest in Egypt. In 1843, one traveler estimated the Copts' population there to be no more than a thousand inhabitants, while in 1849 the estimation by Asyut's bishop pointed to six thousand inhabitants (Walz 1978: 113). It was a wealthy town: its cultivated land had increased from 134,422 to 164,843 feddans between AD 1298 and AD 1315 (Russell 1966: 77). Asyut had always been known as the Copts' 'capital,' due to either its large population of Copts—estimated, in the mid-nineteenth century, to be as high as 50 percent of Asyut's entire population—or their economic power and wealth.[1]

The construction activities of Muhammad 'Ali and his family had a great impact on the governorate's revival. These included the al-Magzoub Barrage in 1835 and the 1872 extension of the railway there by Khedive Isma'il. Khedive Tewfik also visited Asyut and its famous Caesarian market (known as the Kaysariat) in 1879, and he was received by Wissa and Wassef

Khayyat, two senior Coptic merchants, who rolled out precious carpets on the ground before the khedive's carriage (Fayd Allah 1940: 53–54).

At the turn of the twentieth century, Asyut's wealth was displayed in the orchards and gardens that surrounded its oldest districts, such as al-Alwah, with its large concentration of Copts, and Kom Abbas, which later became a high-income district. Asyut's markets were characterized by their abundant supplies from Cairo, Hijaz, and Sudan (Walz 1978: 114). Historians mention that wealthy families of Copts built themselves palaces with gardens by the river bank (Leeder 1918: 336).

For a long time Asyut remained the seat of two governors: the governor-general of all of Upper Egypt and the provincial or local governor. Until the beginning of the twentieth century the administrative divisions of Asyut consisted of four units, each of which was headed by a mayor, *omdah*, or *sheikh al-balad*. A provincial governor was entrusted with assisting tax collection, the organization of individuals to work on projects requiring corvée labor, and the conscription of young men. By the end of the nineteenth century a special 'omdaship' (or local mayorship) was created for the Coptic community. In modern times, Asyut knew three prominent guilds: brokers for ordinary goods (wholesalers), the slave merchants' guild (those who brought slaves from Sudan), and the Cameleers Association (camel owners, camels being the main means of transportation back then) (Walz 1978: 114 nn. 8 and 9).

Studies of Asyut's social structure suggest that the ruling class was composed of a number of large influential families, most of which were traders and landowners, known as 'the notables.' A few of these were of Turkish descent. These families formed a strong social network through the intermarriage of their sons and daughters. One study has monitored nearly sixty-four families, of which more than sixteen were Coptic (Fayd Allah 1940: 172–200). It was out of these households that the holders of the most important administrative positions in the governorate generally came in the mid-nineteenth century, such as the mayor and the senior clergymen.

Economic Activities of the Copts

The accepted measures of wealth included owning no less than fifty feddans of agricultural land, or owning orchards, palm trees, other trees, or a trade agency, and also took into account the number of slaves owned by the family (Fayd Allah 1940: 54). Of the large Coptic families, one can mention al-Gohari, Shenouda, Wissa, Khayyat, Maqar, Hanna, Daghesh, al-Meqaddes Girgis, and others. Some of these donated property to churches as endowments, and restored or built churches and schools on a portion of their property, such as the Shenouda family, which restored the church of St. Abadir the Martyr (Fayd Allah 1940: 172–200).

The main reasons for the strong economy of the city of Asyut were excellence in agricultural production and the fact that it was the capital of Upper Egypt, as well as its central location through which tourists passed during their Nile cruise between Luxor and Aswan in the winter. Asyut was a four-day journey by steamer from Cairo, and it was necessary to stop there to reprovision the boats. This afforded an opportunity for tourists to visit the city's attractions and the nearby ancient Egyptian monuments, as well as to buy handicrafts at the bazaars (Hunter 2004: 43). As for its agricultural production, it was abundant and diverse. Asyut produced corn, barley, wheat, and fava beans. In the mid-nineteenth century, it was one of the largest governorates in area of cultivated land and its productivity. The foreign grain trade was one of the trades monitored by the state. Taxes in Upper Egypt used to be paid in kind rather than monetarily until 1880. Grains were collected in silos and shipped to Cairo and Alexandria where auctions were held by traders, especially European exporting companies. Those traders, some of them being Copts such as the al-Gohari family, played the role of mediator or agent. Foreign events, such as the Crimean War, also contributed to a rise in grain prices, which was in the interests of Asyut's traders and their trade. Since the turn of the twentieth century, Asyut has been fortunate in having a fairly good industrial base with the expansion of its cotton, wool, and silk textile factories. It was famous for its fine silk and cotton sheets. Asyut's wool was of such high quality that it was often described as being smooth as silk. Copts have largely dominated the dyeing industry in Asyut, performing most of the dyeing for Egypt's and Europe's textile factories, especially for fabrics exported to Sudan (Walz 1978: 117–18).

Trade with Sudan played an important role in the growth of Asyut's economy. Asyut's distinguished medial location between the markets of Europe, Sudan, and Darfur led to the flourishing of convoy-based trade. The main commodities were textiles, dyeing materials, ostrich feathers, natron (natural salt), ivory, gum, and slaves. Copts, such as the al-Gohari and Shenouda families, took part in these trades, with the latter being able to pay a sum of twenty-five thousand piastres as a tribute or *jizya* on behalf of the Copts of Asyut in the days of Muhammad 'Ali (Walz 1978: 119). This was due to the fact that at that time the town was treated as a fiscal unit; that is, its inhabitants were collectively responsible for the payment of taxes (Baer 1959: 56).

The Shenouda family also acted as a commercial representative for the interests of the sultan of Darfur for some time. Other well-known Copts in the convoy trade were the families of Maqar, Khayyat, Wissa, Elias, and al-Meqaddes Girgis, as well as many Muslim families, to such an extent that almost half of Asyut's senior families took part in the convoy trade until the 1952 revolution. Some of the Coptic traders partnered with foreign agencies to bolster their position and for fear of exploitation. During the last quarter of the nineteenth century, some of them acted as consuls or representatives of foreign countries, which would in turn confer their protection. 'Abd al-Massih Shenouda al-Gohari of the al-Gohari family became consul of France in Asyut to assist in French tourism in the region. Maqar Demian of the Maqar family succeeded him in that position. In 1861 Wassef Girgis Khayyat became consul of the United States in Asyut, and in 1868 Wissa Boctor became consul of Spain (Walz 1978: 122).

There were three major trade routes connecting Egypt with sub-Saharan Africa, and the size of the trade coming along these routes fluctuated according to political conditions prevailing in both Egypt and the interior of the continent. The first route from Cairo to Sudan via the Libyan Fazzan oases was unsafe. The *darb al-arbain*,[2] a second route, leading from the middle Egyptian Nile Valley to the west of Sudan, may have begun to flourish toward the end of the seventeenth century with the rise of the new and powerful state of Darfur, which depended on external trade. A third route led into the kingdom of Funj at Sennar[3] from trade centers in Upper Egypt (Walz 1972: 263).

The flourishing trade that developed between Egypt and Darfur, Fazara, and eastern Sudan along the *darb al-arbain* in Sudan (Powell 1999: 401) seems not to have started much before the turn of the eighteenth century, although the route was well known before this time. Merchants traveling to these regions and to the Funj capital via the desert route would have assembled in Upper Egypt at Girga in Sohag, before Asyut replaced it, with the caravan progressing to Kharga Oasis before it joined the *darb al-arbain* (Walz 1979: 213–14). Of the cities of Egypt, Asyut at the end of the eighteenth century was the chief entrepôt for merchants coming from and going to the interior of Africa. The area of Upper Egypt, from Asyut in the north to Aswan in the south, was ruled by a Bedouin tribe, the Hawwara. Originally from Tunisia, the Hawwara,[4] who had settled in Egypt in the sixteenth century, were tributaries of the Turks, to whom they provided grain. But they enjoyed considerable independence and were frequently dissatisfied with their overlords. The tribal chiefs were served by a bureaucracy consisting almost entirely of Copts (Hamilton 2006: 48). The trade with Sudan included textiles of various sorts, cotton stuff, printed cotton, slaves, and eunuchs,[5] as slavery was an important part of the economy. In eastern Africa, important African castration centers were in Ethiopia, at Aswan on the Egyptian border, and near Asyut in Upper Egypt (Toledano 1984: 383). Late in the eunuch trade, the stretch of the Nile between Girga and Asyut drew considerable notice from travelers, with activity reported at or near Girga itself, at the monastery of Dayr al-Ganadla near Abu Tig, and the town of Tahta, both south of Asyut. This was especially true at Zawiyat al-Dayr, a predominantly Coptic village that some authorities describe as the center with the largest output.[6] A large shipment of slaves arrived in the Asyut area twice a year (Hogendorn 1999: 142; Baer 1967: 419). Castration was prohibited by law in Egypt in 1841 (Walz 1985: 159). Slavery in general was addressed by the state, and, in one incident, troops from Cairo reached Asyut on 25 April 1880 when Khedive Muhammad Tewfiq was informed about the arrival of a large caravan of 1,200 slaves at Asyut (La Rue 2002: 81–82). This incident became a cause célèbre in diplomatic and British anti-slavery circles. It helped to shape British public opinion toward the Egyptian regime of Khedive Tewfiq and was a factor in the decision to send back to the Sudan Charles Gordon, who had gained considerable public acclaim for his anti-slavery work there. Shortly after his arrival, he became a British martyr as the most famous victim of the Sudanese Mahdiyya (La Rue 2002: 83).

Churches and Monasteries

The wealth of the Church arose from its *waqfs*, or endowments, which were divided into two main branches: endowments to monasteries and endowments to specific churches in the form of lands and houses. Church authorities were secretive about these *waqfs*, and consequently suppressed information relating to them. From other sources it is possible to form some picture of Church possessions. A study has estimated that in 1906 monasteries and churches controlled about 15,000 feddans; Jirjis Hunayn, a Copt in the service of the Ministry of Finance, reckoned the *waqfs* of monasteries as amounting to 4,044 feddans, based on his own investigations in 1906 (Seikaly 1970: 261). A Coptic writer affirmed that thirteen Coptic families owned between 2,000 and 30,000 feddans each. Another hundred families owned between 100 and 2,000 feddans separately. Altogether, the

Copts possessed about 1,500,000 feddans. To this must be added wealth arising from other sources, with the result that the Copts controlled one-fifth of the wealth of Egypt (Seikaly 1970: 268).

As one would expect in a place with a long and rich tradition of Christianity, there are a number of churches and monasteries in and around Asyut. *The Coptic Encyclopedia* refers to about seventeen monasteries and churches. A recent census study registered about sixty-eight sites.[7] For the Catholic Church, there are about thirty-nine churches in Asyut. It was part of the Thebes diocese, founded in 1898. It became the Diocese of Lykopolis fifty years later in 1947.[8] Asyut was the target of missions more than any other governorate, and there were thirty-seven Evangelical churches there by 1947.[9]

Missionaries' Activities

American missionaries, who started coming in the middle of the nineteenth century, formed the largest group of missionaries working in Egypt. By 1917, their number ranged between two hundred and three hundred. They spent a total of over LE800,000 and established several schools. They educated many Coptic notables, particularly in Asyut. While Muslims did sometimes attend American missionary schools, they did not do so in large numbers. Catholic missionaries, notably Franciscans, made their first Coptic converts to Catholicism in Upper Egypt in the eighteenth century. They were more tactful in their methods and also more tolerant of Coptic religious custom than were the Protestants. Prime Minister Isma'il Sidqi once pointed out that the Egyptian government had never had any problem with Catholic missionaries and he praised, in particular, the Jesuits for their subtlety and skill. Missionaries formed a visible and very vocal interest group that the Residency (i.e., the patriarchate) was hard pressed to resist and the Egyptian government to ignore. By 1930, there were 450 foreign missionaries in Egypt with a native staff of 1,500 and an annual expenditure of $700,000 (Carter 1984: 19–20).

John Hogg, a Protestant missionary in Egypt from the United Presbyterian Mission, reached Asyut in February 1865. A school was opened by Mr. Hogg on 5 March 1865 and six boys and two girls joined it. By 13 March they had increased to eighteen boys and thirteen girls; by 12 June the number of boys enrolled was thirty-five (Sedra 2007). Through the intrigues of the Coptic clergy and the connivance of government officials, the number was reduced during the following two years, but afterward it rallied and grew apace. Consequently, the missionaries felt that a high school should be established where young men might pursue studies of a higher grade than were to be found in the existing boys' school. Therefore, an academy was established in Asyut for more advanced literary training of candidates for the theological path. The academy was under the direction of Dr. Johnston starting on 15 October 1874, when the theological classes began for the winter. On 8 February 1875, Dr. Johnston was elected president, and the institution was called the Asyut Training College. The number of pupils in 1875 was 96, 100 in 1876, 96 in 1877, 165 in 1878, and in 1879 it reached 199 (Watson 1904: 451–52; McNaugher 1930: 56–61). The need to provide a place for girls from the surrounding towns and villages produced a boarding school. It was opened in 1866, and at the end of the year there were seven girls in it. During 1867 the number increased to nine, but at the end of the year there were only six. At the close of 1879, there were twenty-four girls in the school. The pupils were from Asyut, Jawili, Mallawi, Banub, Azziya, Muti'a, Mas'udi, Nakheila, Tima, and even from Alexandria. Its name was changed to the Pressly Memorial Institute after a donation from Mr. William Pressly, of Monmouth, in the United States (Watson 1904: 446).

The conflict between the native Church of Egypt, the See of St. Mark, and the missionaries during the reign of Khedive Isma'il was inevitable. The American missionaries started their campaign in Upper Egypt to convert Copts to Protestantism. They succeeded in annexing two well-known families from Asyut. The Copts had the full support of the khedive, who sponsored a tour for Pope Demetrius (1862–70) in Upper Egypt to confront the missionary activity there (Hamed 1991: 1692). In 1867, the year that saw the establishment of the first Protestant church by the missionaries in Asyut, he made a tour of Upper Egypt to rally the Coptic flock around the mother Church (Shoucri 1991). On 11 March, the Coptic patriarch, accompanied by clergymen, left Cairo in a government steamer lent to him by the viceroy, ostensibly to visit his people in Upper Egypt, but really, and as all his attendants averred, to stamp out the Protestant heresy. Letters were sent to the governors of the provinces to supply the patriarch with an escort of soldiers.

Nothing of special importance to the mission occurred during the patriarch's tour until he reached the towns of Abnub and al-Hammam, about thirteen kilometers south of Asyut. There he summoned before him the leading Copts and addressed them, saying he had been recently informed that some of the agents of the American mission were in the habit of visiting their towns in order to disseminate their abominable heresies, and, as this was not only prejudicial to the interests of the Coptic Church but was also displeasing to the viceroy, he hereby gave them warning not to bring injury or pain upon themselves. Watson reported that "as the Patriarch is regarded by all devout Copts as the Vicar of Christ upon earth, and is called by them 'the earthly Christ,' or 'present' Christ, or the living Christ, so on reaching Asyut, where there is a large Coptic population, the procession from the steamer to the town was arranged in imitation of our Lord's triumphal entry into Jerusalem" (Watson 1904: 200–201). The American Presbyterian Synod of the Nile was formed in 1899, and in 1926 it was recognized as the Evangelical Coptic Church (Hamilton 2006: 278).

Asyut is also linked to the name of Lillian Trasher, a Christian missionary who arrived in Asyut in October 1910 and opened her shelter in February 1911. At the beginning of her service she visited many villages using animals, as they were the prevalent means of transport in those days, and sailboats during the flood. By the mid-twentieth century her establishment became home to 650 children and widows. The twelve-acre campus had thirteen major buildings. In her lifetime, Trasher served more than ten thousand orphans and widows (Howell 1960: 59, 76, 104, 150).

Cultural Activities of the Coptic Community

Copts began publishing religious, intellectual, and political periodicals in the second half of the nineteenth century. Some journals and newspapers were written to appeal to Muslims as well as Christians, while others focused more narrowly on communal and church affairs. The newspapers with the widest circulation in Asyut were *al-Nuzhah*, published bi-monthly at Asyut by George Khayyat from 1886 to 1890; *Asyut Weekly*, published by Amin Khayr al-Asyuti from 1930 to 1954; and the monthly *Buq al-Qadasah*, first published in Asyut in 1902, and then relocated to Cairo. *Buq al-Qadasah* is still being published (Ghali 1991: 2012; Baron 1994: 217–40).

The spread of education due to the missionaries' activities led the affluent Coptic women of Asyut to adopt modernism. They entirely discarded the veil and moved about as freely as if they were in England, except for some necessary compromises (Leeder 1918: 21). This atmosphere of relative liberty led to the appearance of prominent female figures such as Ester Akhnoukh Fanous or Esther Fanous, also known as Esther Wissa (19 February 1895–August 1990), who was an Egyptian Christian feminist born in Asyut. In March 1923 Esther Fanous established, along with other women, the Egyptian Feminist Union to improve women's stature in literature and social aspects, and to promote equal treatment with men in rights and obligations. She was involved in other associations, such as the Young Women's Christian Association (YWCA) and the Labour Association of Egypt, as well as other charitable associations (Wissa 1994: 144).

Political Activities in Asyut

The positions and financial skills of the Coptic bureaucrats enabled them to wield a certain administrative influence. However, by virtue of their religious affiliation, they were not permitted to play a commensurate role in public life until late in the nineteenth century. As compensation, they desired to play that role within and on behalf of the Coptic community: their proximity to the rulers would enable them to influence decision-making by the state toward the Church. Coptic sources would apply to these bureaucrats the historical term *al-arakhina* (singular *arkhon*, meaning 'influential layman in church affairs') (Afifi 1999: 277–97).

Muslim–Christian tensions in Egypt, exacerbated by the assassination of the Coptic prime minister Butros Ghali in 1910, along with a lack of unity within the Egyptian Coptic community, were the catalysts for the Coptic Congress of Asyut. It was convened on 6–8 March 1911 with reluctant permission from Patriarch Cyril V and the Egyptian government. Issues raised at this conference included a call for an end to religious discrimination in state employment and education, and proportionate representation for Copts in parliament (Bahr 1991). National unity has been the hallmark of Egypt since the formation of the Wafd Party in 1919. The party upheld a firm policy of cooperation between Muslims and Christians. When George Khayyat asked Saad Zaghlul, the founder of the Wafd Party, what the future of the Copts would be after independence, the answer was, "Their status will be our status, they will have the same rights and the same duties, with no difference between any of us" (Ghali 1991: 950).

When the Muslim Brotherhood began to expand its organization in the 1930s, after its founder, Hasan al-Banna, had moved from Ismailiya to Cairo, new branches and sub-branches were located primarily in the Delta while Asyut was the only new branch in Upper Egypt (Lia 1998: 121–22). The rise of al-Gama'a al-Islamiya, or Islamic Group, in the Upper Egypt governorates of Qena, Asyut, Sohag, Minya, and Aswan must be examined in relation to the social fabric and spatial organization of their cities and towns. The complexity of social organization based on tribe and family, and the hierarchies characterizing social, economic, and political positions in the various provinces, have yet to be studied in a comprehensive manner (Ismail 2000: 363 n. 2).

A modus vivendi was established between the Islamists and some official figures, among them governors, university deans, intermediate cadres in the government party, and high-level functionaries. Asyut in particular and Middle Egypt in general provided the 'laboratory' where this modus vivendi was tested: de facto prohibition of the distribution and consumption of alcohol in the governorate started in April 1986 with the cancellation of all distribution licenses, although Asyut had one of the highest percentages of Copts in the country; de facto sexual segregation in university halls; an Islamist takeover of sporting and youth clubs (Daly 2008: 386).

Omar 'Abd al-Rahman[10] was chosen as spiritual leader of the young Islamists of the Jihad and al-Gama'a al-Islamiya. His ideas were influenced in part by the thinking of the Muslim Brotherhood, and particularly by reading Sayyid Qutb.[11] He offered religious legitimacy and expertise to the group's activities, as reported later in some of the testimony at his first trial in Egypt in the early 1980s. Indeed, he was arrested after President Anwar Sadat's assassination and sat among the defendants during the trial against the murderers of the Egyptian president (Zeghal 1999: 393). His main duty was to issue edicts, *fatwa*s, to legitimize the activities of the Tanzim, a secret organization. They committed several crimes, from ransacking jewelry stores in Nag' Hammadi in the deep south and in Shubra al-Khayma, north of Cairo, to committing acts of violence against Christian places of worship, such as bomb explosions in churches. The person who led the attack on jewelry stores in Nag' Hammadi confessed that his thinking was influenced by the sermons of the group leader in Asyut (Ansari 1984: 125–29).

All through the late 1970s and in 1980, house-to-house searches for hidden weapons were conducted in parts of Asyut and Minya, thus increasing tension. This culminated in the bloodiest clashes ever with the security forces in Asyut, two days after Sadat's assassination. The militants' doctrine further sanctioned collecting *jizya* or poll tax from non-Muslims. Among the consequences of this doctrine were assaults on the security forces, which cost the state more than one hundred lives in Asyut alone, and the robbing of Christian jewelry stores in different parts of the country (Ansari 1984: 131–38).

The sectarian tension and violence greatly affected the income of Asyut in general and the Coptic Church in particular.[12] One of the most important sources of income is the *mulid*s, or annual festivals of the Virgin and saints (Girgis 2002). Nearly three and a half million pilgrims a year converge on the village of Durunka, ten kilometers southwest of Asyut, and half of that number visit during the annual *mulid* in honor of the Holy Virgin (Kamil 2002: 12). The history of the foundation of the Monastery of the Blessed Virgin Mary (Dayr al-Muharraq) is closely interwoven with the tradition of the Holy Family's journey to Egypt. Copts who live near Dayr al-Muharraq refer to the place as the 'Second Jerusalem' or the 'Second Mount of Olives.' The Holy Family's visit to the area has endowed it with great spiritual importance. Every year, from 21 to 28 June, a hundred thousand pilgrims journey to the monastery to commemorate the consecration of the Church of the Blessed Virgin Mary (Watson 2000: 12).

Asyut represented and still represents an obsession in the minds of many politicians because it was the headquarters of the first Coptic Legion. It was founded by Mu'allem Ya'qub (1745–1803), finance commissioner, then military leader in the French expedition of Egypt by Bonaparte. He formed the Coptic Legion of nine hundred men in the region of Manqabad near Asyut. He was promoted to the rank of brigadier general and headed an Egyptian delegation that left for Europe with the French forces on 10 August 1801. His plan was to create an Egyptian army and seek the assistance of European powers. His plan came to be known as the "project for the independence of Egypt," as it is referred to in the Public Record Office of London, in two documents (Foreign Office Records 78 Turkey vol. 33). A historian described this project as "perhaps the first official project and plea for Egyptian independence in modern times" (Meinardus 2002: 67; see also Haddad 1970 and Louca 1991). The same obsession appeared in an article published in 2012 about the division of Egypt by the Middle East Media Research Institute (MEMRI).[13] In 1980, President Anwar Sadat (25 December 1918–6 October 1981) accused Pope Shenouda III (3 August 1923–17 March 2012) of plotting to become the political as well as the religious leader of the Copts and to "set up a separatist Coptic state with Asyut as its capital" (Heikal 1984: 228).

The features of present-day Asyut have been shaped by different factors, among which are its Coptic heritage, social, political, and economic aspects, and its geographical location in the middle of Egypt.

Notes

1 On population, see Baer 1969: 134–35, table 2.

2 The 'Forty Days' Road,' from Asyut in Egypt to Darfur. For a discussion of trade and caravans in this region through the history of one of the caravan leaders, see La Rue 1984.

3 The Funj are a line of kings who ruled in the Nilotic Sudan of eastern Africa from the sixteenth to the nineteenth century. The Funj capital was the city of Sennar, on the left bank of the Blue Nile above its confluence with the White Nile.

4 A faction from the Hawwara had been moved from Buheira province in the Delta by Barquq (when not yet sultan) in the fourteenth century to counterbalance the power of other tribes in Upper Egypt and Nubia (Walz 1979: 217).

5 The major demand for slave eunuchs was as supervisors of women, especially in the harems of rulers, nobility, and the wealthy in the Ottoman Empire and its Muslim precursors and neighbors.

6 Although in general high mortality characterized the 'manufacture' of eunuchs, travelers in the early nineteenth century reported that the castration center near Asyut on the Upper Nile was registering significant reductions in deaths from the operation. Burckhardt, a traveler who visited the area in 1813–14, drew special attention to the Coptic village and monastery of Zawiyat al-Dayr. He claimed that the monk-surgeons at this location had managed to reduce the death rate to a spectacularly low figure.

7 Nine in al-Qusiya, seven in Manfalut, nine in Abnub and al-Fath, twenty-three in Asyut, five in Dayrut, four in Sanabu, and seven in Abu Tig (Gabra, forthcoming).

8 Catholic Church in Egypt, http://www.catholicchurch-eg.com/catholicchurch/contactsf.php/2010/04/21/200-2.html

9 http://coptcatholic.net/p7058/

10 Commonly known in the United States as the Blind Sheikh, he is a blind Egyptian Muslim leader who is currently serving a life sentence at the Butner Medical Center, which is part of the Butner Federal Correctional Institution in Butner, North Carolina, in the United States. Formerly a resident of New York City, Abd al-Rahman, with nine others, was convicted of seditious conspiracy, which requires only that a crime be planned, not that it necessarily be attempted. His prosecution grew out of investigations of the 1993 World Trade Center bombings. Abd al-Rahman was accused of being the leader of al-Gama'a al-Islamiya (also known as the Islamic Group), a militant Islamist movement in Egypt that is considered a terrorist organization by the United States and Egyptian governments. The group is responsible for many acts of violence, including the November 1997 Luxor massacre, in which fifty-eight foreign tourists and four Egyptians were killed. Middle East Media Research Institute, "Egyptian Government Daily: U.S. Striving to Divide Egypt into Four Countries," 17 February 2012, http://www.memri.org/report/en/0/0/0/0/0/0/6104.htm#_edn1.

11 An Egyptian author, educator, Islamic theorist, poet, creative thinker, and the leading member of the Egyptian Muslim Brotherhood in the 1950s and 1960s. Although he joined the Brotherhood at a much later date, Sayyid Qutb, whose writings would in due course become a catalyst in fundamentalist thinking, was born in Musha near Asyut in 1906. He even wrote his memoirs about the village while still in the

literary, pre-fundamentalist stage of his life. In 1966 he was convicted of plotting the assassination of Egyptian president Gamal Abdel Nasser and was executed by hanging. Another prominent figure in the 1970s, Mustafa Shukri, the leader of the Takfir wa-l-Hijra (Anathema and Exile) group, was born in the village of Abu Khurus near Asyut in 1942. He first joined the Muslim Brotherhood in the early 1960s and later participated in the assassination of President Sadat (Kupferschmidt 1987: 407–408).

12 After the ousting of President Muhammad Morsi on 4 July 2013, the mosque of Rabaa al-Adawiya, in the Nasr City district of eastern Cairo, turned into a sit-in camp for the supporters of Morsi. The security forces raided it to end the six-week sit-in, with the result of a violent backlash on 15–17 August of which Copts bore the brunt with more than sixty churches, schools, businesses, shops, and vehicles burned or ruined. The fiercest attacks were in Minya, Asyut, Sohag, Beni Suef, and the Fayoum in Upper Egypt. National targets such as the Mallawi Museum and the governorate building of Giza also came in for a fair share of the brutal attacks. In Asyut, two churches were burned and thirty homes and businesses belonging to Christians were plundered, while in Minya the number reached nineteen churches and more than 250 properties (Makaryous 2013: 73–96).

13 "The Real Plot to Partition Egypt, 20 February 2012," http://copticliterature.wordpress.com/2012/02/20/the-plot-to-partition-egypt/

11 The Place of Qusqam in the Textual Data on the Flight into Egypt

Ashraf Alexandre Sadek

DAYR AL-MUHARRAQ is for Christian Egyptians a very blessed place—maybe the most blessed place in Egypt. Tens of thousands of people come here every year on special feasts and occasions: not only for the feast of the Assumption of the Virgin Mary on 22 August, but throughout the year on many occasions. I visited Dayr al-Muharraq once with a group on Sham al-Nessim; it was so crowded that our bus could hardly enter the yard, and it took ages to reach the place where it was supposed to park. The Europeans who were with me had never experienced such a crowd. They could not believe it, and it remains one of their strongest memories.

The fame of Dayr al-Muharraq is linked to its history, and this history is very much dependent on the traditions of the Holy Family's sojourn on the spot, Qusqam, where the monastery now stands. On what grounds did such traditions develop? We shall focus, in this chapter, on the textual data; our scope is to give a comparative view of the available documents and of the place occupied by Qusqam in this documentation.

Our study is recapitulated in the "Table of the Sources and Events Concerning Qusqam," at the end of this chapter, which comes as a complement to the tables we established and published in the first part of our *Trilogy* on the Flight into Egypt: *Le Monde Copte* no. 34, *Un fleuve d'eau vive, Vol. 1, Les sources* (Sadek and Sadek 2011). In this study, we listed fifty texts that may, in our view, be considered as the textual 'sources' of the traditions on the coming of the Holy Family to Egypt. These texts have only two points in common: they mention at least one aspect of the legend of the Flight into Egypt, and they all have their origin before the eighth century. Apart from that, they are extremely different and belong to four main categories: the apocryphal infancy gospels; reports of pilgrims and travelers during antiquity and the early Middle Ages; Church Fathers in early anti-Christian literature; and Coptic textual evidence. Among these fifty texts listed, ten mention Qusqam; the first point to mention is that all of these belong to the group of Coptic textual evidence.

The first part of this chapter will be dedicated to the presentation of these texts; the second part will deal with the events or facts they mention.

Presentation of the Coptic Textual Evidence Mentioning Qusqam

Coptic textual evidence is the most developed category of documents in the corpus of texts on the Flight into Egypt. It comprises four types of documents: homilies; liturgical texts; hagiographical stories; and a prophetical text.

Homilies

The homilies are the most important group of documents. They are written either in Coptic or Arabic and include:

- The *History of Joseph the Carpenter*, fourth–sixth centuries (in Coptic), in which Jesus tells his disciples the life of his stepfather, Joseph, including the Flight into Egypt. Some of the stories told in this Coptic apocryphon also appear in the infancy gospels.
- The *Vision of Theophilus* was composed in the fourth century by Anba Theophilus, twenty-third Pope of Alexandria, and written down in Coptic by his successor, St. Cyril the Great. It is probably the earliest text that reports an itinerary of the Holy Family in Egypt. This text was transmitted orally and in several written variants throughout the ages down to today. It played a very important part in the history of the Copts by showing the link between Christian Egyptians and the land of Egypt. It is still a constant reference in Egypt. It stresses the importance of Qusqam (Dayr al-Muharraq). Although the antiquity of this text was for a long time refused by western scholars, a recent academic study on the *Vision of Theophilus* has enabled scholars to understand the historical grounds of this story, concerning

both its dating and the traditions to which it refers. The author of this research, Dr. Fatin Guirguis, after a close study of the manuscripts, reached two important conclusions. First she showed how all manuscripts, in spite of their differences, converge in transmitting the same basic story; then she proved that this variety itself is in fact a testimony to the fact that these traditions had been transmitted orally since the fourth century. "Although oral tradition, like language, is dynamic and in constant dialogue with cultural conditions, *The Vision*'s core message and values remain stable" (Guirguis 2010: 271). She goes on to say, "From the above, one has to conclude that the Coptic original version of *The Vision* was in wide circulation before the sixth century, which brings it very close to the time of its recording by Pope Cyril, patriarch of Alexandria, from a fourth-century oral narration by Pope Theophilus, patriarch of Alexandria (AD 385–412), who is said to have visited Al-Muharraq Monastery sometime between AD 393–5" (Guirguis 2010: 287).

- The *Homily of Zacharia of Sakha* dates back to the seventh century. It develops the *Vision of Theophilus* and adds many comments on the Incarnation and on the various sites visited by the Holy Family.
- Two *Homilies* by Cyriacus of al-Bahnasa, which were probably written in the early eighth century. They develop the veneration of the sites of Dayr al-Garnous and Qusqam.
- The *Homily of Anba Timotheos Aelure*, or *Homily on the Church of the Rock*, was first written in Coptic, in the fifth century. It praises the site of Gebel al-Teir, east of Samalut. It is a very important text, full of interesting theological elements that help in understanding the meaning of the Flight into Egypt.

All these homilies mention the sojourn of the Holy Family in Qusqam, except for the first, the *History of Joseph the Carpenter*. The *Vision of Theophilus* is the most developed on the subject, as we shall see later.

Liturgical Texts

It is difficult to date these, but they were certainly in use during the Middle Ages. They include:

- The *Synaxarion*, on 24 and 25 Bashans (1 June, entry of the Lord into Egypt), 8 Ba'una (Mahamma), 6 Hatur (consecration of the church of Qusqam). As we can see in the table, the texts of 6 Hatur and 8 Ba'una mention the passage of the Holy Family to Qusqam.

- *Doxology* and *Psalmody* of 24 Bashans: the *Psalmody* mentions Qusqam.
- *Difnar* of 24 Bashans, 8 Ba'una (arrival of the Holy Family in Qusqam), 6 Hatur (consecration of the church of Qusqam): the last two texts mention Qusqam.

The other two texts—an anaphora of Cyriacus of Bahnasa, still in use in Ethiopic liturgy, and the Fraction prayer for 24 Bashans—deal with the Holy Family in Egypt without mentioning Qusqam.

Lives of Martyrs and Saints

Several *Lives* of saints mention the Flight into Egypt: *Paese and Thecla* (martyrs, fourth century); *Apater and Irai* (martyrs, fourth century); *Victor the General* (son of Romanos, Roman martyr, fourth century); *Olympios* (from Nicomedia, martyr, fourth century); *St. Shenoute*; *Wadamon of Armant;* and, lastly, *St. Dilagui* (a martyr of Esna, fourth century). St. Dilagui's passion is the only one that mentions Qusqam; we are told in this text that St. Dilagui was a mother of four boys, all of them killed during the Diocletian persecution. The author of the text (Paul, Bishop of Asyut) compares her sons to the sons of Joseph, one of whom ran from Israel to Qusqam in Egypt in order to tell the Holy Family that Herod had sent his soldiers to capture them in Upper Egypt.

The Prophetical Text of the Fayoum

To this list of Coptic documents should be added "The Prophetical Text of the Fayoum," often called the Fayoum papyrus. This famous Coptic manuscript, kept in Cologne in Germany, is from the fourth century. It was translated into German and published in 1997 by the papyrologist Gesa Schenke. We published a French translation of this text in our book *Un fleuve d'eau vive.* It hints at the coming of Christ to Egypt in several ways: it mentions a stay of three years and eleven months, and His coming during the month of Bashans; it hints at the fact that Egypt, which was the symbol of 'nations,' (pagan countries) will become a 'Holy Land.' Qusqam is not mentioned explicitly in this text, so we have not listed it among the ten texts chosen for their information about this site; however, this 'prophecy' mentions that Jesus blesses Egypt by saying "My twelve sons will visit you." This may be a hint at the event of the consecration of the church on Mount Qusqam after Christ's ascension, one of the events reported by several texts, as we shall see in the next section.

Facts and Events in Connection with Qusqam Related in the Textual Data

We shall now sum up the various elements contained in these texts concerning the site of Qusqam and what happened there. In this respect, the elements developed by these sources deal with five main themes:

1. The arrival and the stay of the Holy Family in Qusqam
2. Herod's attempt to reach Jesus in Qusqam, and how the Holy Family was protected
3. The departure from Qusqam
4. The consecration of the church of Qusqam by Jesus after his Ascension
5. The special blessings linked to the site of Qusqam

For each of these themes, we shall see which texts mention the event (summarized in the Table of the Sources and Events Concerning Qusqam) and what is said by each document.

The Arrival and Sojourn of the Holy Family in Qusqam

The vision of Theophilus takes place "on the mountain of Qusqam" itself; according to this text, the Holy Virgin herself told Theophilus that they stayed there for six months: "We arrived in this holy place on the seventh of the month of Baramouda and left on the sixth of Baba, on the day when the angel of the Lord appeared to Joseph and said, 'Come take the boy and his mother and return to the land of Israel.'"

Zacharia from Sakha, in his *Homily*, says only that the Holy Family, after leaving Ashmunayn, "walked to the mountain of the West. They arrived at the mountain of Qusqam, known in our days as the Dayr al-Muharraq. There, they built a small shelter, where they lived for six months." According to the scholar Gabriele Giamberardini, the reason why Zacharia does not further emphasize the sojourn of the Holy Family in Qusqam is that "he knew that this place was already famous enough" (Giamberardini 1975: 53).

In his *Homily on Qusiya*, Cyriac of Bahnasa describes Qusqam, on the arrival of the Holy Family, as "a desert of ruins and misery," which, according to Cyriac, Jesus "turned into a place which can be compared to the heavenly Jerusalem" (Giamberardini 1975: 67). Then Cyriac finds a box containing a text written by Joseph the Carpenter, which says, "I, Joseph the Carpenter from Nazareth, called the Father of the Lord Jesus according to the flesh, and servant of this great mystery, I declare that myself, my wife the Virgin, Salome and the Lord of Glory, we lived for some time on this pure mountain."

Timotheos, in the *Homily on the Church of the Rock*, mentions a six-month sojourn in Qusqam with few details, his focus being mainly on Gebel al-Teir.

The *Synaxarion* of 8 Ba'una mentions Muharraq without any comment, while the *Psalmody* of 24 Bashans says that, after leaving Ashmunayn, "they walked in joy to the mountain of Qusqam, where they stayed for several months" and "God manifested himself among us on the Mountain of Qusqam." The *Difnar*, on 8 Ba'una, mentions, "They went south and reached Qusqam, where they stayed until the death of Herod."

Herod's Attempt to Reach Jesus in Qusqam, and How the Holy Family Was Protected

Three texts, the *Vision of Theophilus*, the *Homily on the Church of the Rock*, and the *Life of St. Dilagui, Martyr of Esna*, mention that Herod was told of the place where the Holy Family had found a shelter, in Qusqam, and consequently sent his soldiers to kill them.

According to the *Vision*, it was the devil himself who informed Herod, who sent ten soldiers to Egypt. However, "a prophet named Youssa, a relative of Joseph the Carpenter," having heard of the plan, hurried to Qusqam, where he arrived before the soldiers, in spite of the devil who tried to discourage him. Having informed Joseph and Mary, he died there and Jesus consoled his parents, while the soldiers died before reaching Qusqam.

In some versions of the *Homily on the Church of the Rock*, the messenger is called Moussa. More interesting is the version given by the *Life of St. Dilagui*, which develops the story through a comparison, saying that the messenger is one of the four sons whom Joseph had from a previous marriage.

All three documents mention that the body of the messenger was buried by Joseph on the mountain of Qusqam.

The Departure from Qusqam

Most texts situate the angel's second message to Joseph in Qusqam. As in Matthew's gospel, the angel tells Joseph that Herod is dead, and that he must take the child and his mother and go back to the land of Israel. In the *Vision of Theophilus*, the angel adds that all the soldiers Herod had sent died on their way to Qusqam; the news that the Holy Family can return to "the house of holiness" (Jerusalem) makes them rejoice; and after Jesus says a long benediction for the place where they have spent the longest time during their flight, the Holy Family leaves and goes to Ashmunayn. In the *Homily on the Church of the Rock*, it is said that the angel was Gabriel, after whose coming "they returned to their country till the Crucifixion."

The Consecration of the Church of Qusqam after the Resurrection

According to the *Vision of Theophilus*, on 6 Hatur, some time after Christ's Resurrection and Ascension, Mary, Salome, Mary Magdalene, and all the disciples (dead as well as alive) were brought on a cloud to the house of Qusqam, which Jesus consecrated and where he celebrated the first liturgy with his own hands: "The hands that created Adam and his offspring and that were nailed to the cross sanctify and bless this great house."

The *Homily of Cyriac* places the mass on 7 Barmuda. It provides the nicety that, as the first mass was celebrated here, so also would be the last mass. The *Synaxarion* on 6 Hatur and the *Difnar* on the same date also mention the consecration of this church by Jesus.

This is a very important tradition for the place of Qusqam: the altar of the old church of Dayr al-Muharraq is thus considered as having been consecrated by Jesus himself in the place where the Holy Family lived for six months.

It should be noted that the same kind of event is described in the *Homily on the Church of the Rock* as happening in Gebel al-Teir instead of Qusqam, which shows that the two sites were rivals.

The Blessings Attached to This Holy Place, Qusqam

Again, it is the *Vision of Theophilus* that develops this theme:

> When it was time to leave this mountain, the Lord (to him be the glory), said: "The blessings of my good father and the Holy Spirit be upon this house where a good altar will be consecrated and pure offerings will be made. The angel of peace will come and bless all those who come to it and kneel down in faith, and I will forgive all their sins. Should they repent and refrain from sinning again, they will be counted among the saints. All those who are sick or in tribulation or in pain or in grief or in fear and come to this place and ask faithfully, their prayers will be answered in honor of your name, my dear mother. It will become a refuge for strangers and a house for monks and all those who come with gifts, vows, tithes, and first offerings. My blessing and peace will be upon those who reside in it as long as no one there is against me. And as long as it stays as it is

and doesn't change from what it is today and doesn't miss any of its parts, it will last till the end of times." (Sarkis 1936: 90)

The *Vision* ends with another blessing:

What can we say about the honor of this holy house? It is a house of forgiveness, a house of healing, and a house of angels, saints and struggling anchorites. Blessed is he who comes here and makes an offering or fulfills a vow. The Virgin Mary will intercede on his behalf and offer it as an acceptable offering to her only son, whom we ask to forgive your sins, your errors and weaknesses, repose your deceased on good faith, raise your children, strengthen your aged, elevate your homes and grant you the flooding of the Nile, a fruitful harvest, a fair sovereign, deliver you from the trials of the devil and make you winners of good deeds before the end of time. (Sarkis 1936: 95)

Cyriac also prophesies that this church will never be destroyed, and emphasizes the forgiveness of sins for all the pilgrims, through the intercession of the Holy Virgin. He foretells the development of monasticism in this place.

Conclusion

All the traditions concerning Qusqam/Muharraq tend to point to this place as the center of Christian Egypt, because of the very special blessing bestowed on it by the long presence of the Holy Family. The situation of this place in Upper Egypt, in the middle of the Nile Valley, is also a factor of unity and strength for the Christian community. Both the written texts and the oral transmission contribute to the importance of Dayr al-Muharraq.

The main feasts celebrating the Holy Family in Dayr al-Muharraq are as follows:

6 Baba (16–17 October): departure from Qusqam for Israel
6 Hatur (15–16 November): consecration of the old church to the Virgin Mary
8 Ba'una (15 April): arrival of the Holy family in Qusqam
24 Bashans (1 June): entry of the Holy Family into Egypt.

Appendix: A Description of the Icon of the Holy Family of al-Muharraq

This large icon is a unique representation of the return of the Holy Family from Egypt to the land of Israel. Jesus is a three- or four-year-old child, pulling his mother's hand and showing her, with his right hand, the way back to their homeland. His left hand holds an apple, which symbolizes the fruit of obedience to the Father—as opposed to the disobedience of Adam. The Virgin Mary follows her son with obvious willingness, and raises her left hand in submission. Joseph is now at the back, leaving the leadership to his son, and holding the old and faithful donkey, a symbol of the whole creation. While Jesus and Mary have a nimbus, Joseph does not, which shows his status as the last prophet of the Old Testament, while Jesus and Mary are heralds of the New Testament.

The composition of the icon is remarkably balanced: in the back stand three trees while the upper left corner is occupied by a kneeling angel, full of solicitude and awe in front of the Holy Family. The style, especially the trees, is characteristic of the paintings of Ibrahim al-Nasikh, who worked from 1745 to 1783 with Yuhanna the Armenian. They painted thousands of icons, in a Byzantine-Coptic style of their own that heavily influenced eighteenth-century Egyptian iconography.

The message of the icon is clear: the observer is called to imitate the Virgin Mary in taking Jesus' hand and following him with confidence and obedience toward the heavenly Jerusalem, the Kingdom where the Father will welcome him or her. The 'Return from Egypt' is indeed the sign of the redemption of humanity realized by the sacrifice of the Son, which opened again for man the Paradise of Joy.

Fig. 11.1. Table of the sources and events concerning Qusqam

	Events / Texts	Arrival and sojourn in Qusqam	Herod's attempt to reach Jesus in Qusqam	Departure from Qusqam	Consecration of the church	Blessings attached to the place
1	*Vision of Theophilus* 4th century?	Six-month sojourn from 7 Barmuda to 6 Baba	Long narration	Angel's message, benediction of the place and departure for Ashmunayn	Detailed description	Many blessings and forgiveness of sins for pilgrims
2	*Homily of Zacharia of Sakha* 7th century?	Arrival after Ashmunayn, building of a shelter, sojourn of six months		Angel's message; departure		
3	*Homily of Cyriac of Bahnasa on Qusiya* 6–7th century?	Arrival "in a desert place" on 7 Barmuda Text by Joseph saying that they lived there "for some time"			7 Barmuda The first liturgy was celebrated there, and so the last one will be	Many blessings and forgiveness of sins for pilgrims
4	*Homily of Timotheos on the Church of the Rock* 6th century?	Six months	Long narration	The angel Gabriel comes and they "return to their country"	In this text, it is Gebel al-Teir which is consecrated by Jesus, instead of Qusqam	
5	*Egyptian Synaxarion* 8 Ba'una	Mention of the passage				
6	*Egyptian Synaxarion* 6 Hatur				Developed comment	
7	*Psalmody* 24 Bashans	Mentions a few months' sojourn in Qusqam				
8	*Difnar* 8 Ba'una	Mentions a sojourn "until the death of Herod"		Angel's message on Herod's death		
9	*Difnar* 6 Hatur	Mentions a stay of three and a half years			Mentions the celebration with details	
10	*Life of St. Dilagui* 4th century?		Gives an original version			

12 John of Lykopolis

Mark Sheridan

As Sebastien Lenain de Tillemont observed over three centuries ago, among all the solitary saints in Egypt "there is after St. Antony no one whose renown is greater than that of St. John of Lycopolis" (Tillemont 1732, vol. 10: 9). Tillemont also observed that, besides the principal accounts of John of Lykopolis found in the *Historia Monachorum (HM)* and in Palladius's *Historia Lausiaca (HL)*, information regarding him or knowledge of him was to be found in the works of Sulpicius Severus, Augustine of Hippo, Jerome, John Cassian, and the *Apophthegmata*. On the basis of these sources he attempted to give an integrated account of the life of John. Since the time of Tillemont, much progress has been made in sorting out these various sources and their interconnection with one another.

The Sources

The longest, most detailed account of John is to be found in the *HM*, where it occupies the first place and constitutes about one-fifth of the entire work. The *HM* is the account of a journey to Egypt undertaken by a group of seven monks from the Mount of Olives in Jerusalem. The anonymous author, who was one of this group, explains that he has written the account at the insistence of the community on the Mount of Olives.[1] The Greek text of this work was for a long time confused with the text of the *HL* by Palladius in both the manuscript tradition and printed editions.

It was the great merit of Cuthbert Butler to have shown that the Greek text of the *HM* was the original and not the Latin translation by Rufinus, which had been identified by Jerome as an original work of Rufinus, an identification that misled even Tillemont.[2] Tillemont, although assuming that the Latin text was an original work by Rufinus and using a Greek text of the *HL* interpolated with the Greek text of the *HM*, arrived at the conclusion that the party of seven was not the same as the party of Evagrius which, according to Palladius, visited John two months after Palladius himself (*HL* 35,11). Doresse, on the other hand, assumes that these two groups were the same (see Doresse 2000, 139). Tillemont's arguments are more convincing (Tillemont 1732, vol. 10: 719 n. 4; see also Butler 1898–1904).

Although Tillemont thought the Latin text of the *HM* to be an original work of Rufinus,[3] he was aware that Greek texts corresponding to it could not be part of the *HL* (Tillemont 1732, vol. 10: 719 n. 4). The only contact between these groups was literary and later, due to the fact that Palladius, as will be explained below, knew the Greek text of *HM*. A brief notice about Evagrius is found in the chapter on Nitria of the *HM*, which could hardly have been written by someone who had traveled all the way to Lykopolis with him. It states rather, "We also visited Evagrius, a wise and learned man who was skilled in the discernment of thoughts, an ability he had acquired by experience" (Russell 1981: 107). Evagrius had in fact written several works on the discernment of thoughts *(logismoi)*.

The *HM* is structured as a travelogue or account of a journey to investigate first-hand the wonders of Egyptian monasticism by visiting and interviewing well-known monks. Egyptian monasticism had long since acquired fame well beyond the borders of Egypt through literary accounts such as the *Life of Antony* and the accounts of travelers such as Melania, Rufinus, and Egeria. There is no reason to doubt that the *HM* describes a real journey that began with a visit to John at Lykopolis and proceeded down the Nile to Scetis, Nitria, and the Delta.[4]

From a literary point of view the account of the visit to John is well structured, with an inclusion formed at the beginning and end by a reference to John's predictions regarding the emperor Theodosius. It begins with several stories illustrating his gift of clairvoyance, his refusal to meet women, and cures that he worked indirectly (1–12). The narrator explains that John had spent forty years "in the cave, neither going out himself nor allowing a woman to come into his sight. . . . As a matter of fact not even male visitors ever entered into his cave. He merely gave his blessing through the window and in this way greeted those who came and spoke with each of them about his personal affairs" (*HM* 1,4). There follows the account of the visit proper, beginning with John's rebuke of the brother who tried to conceal the fact that he was a deacon and then a lengthy discourse by John on the spiritual life. This discourse is followed in turn by several stories told by John of various monks to illustrate problems of the spiritual life. The Latin translation by Rufinus is substantially the same, although Rufinus at times offers a paraphrastic and expanded version (see Russell 1981: 141–55).

The date of the visit by the seven to John must have been fairly late in 394. According to *HM* 1,64, John told his visitors just before they left that "today the victory proclamation of the pious Emperor Theodosius has arrived in Alexandria announcing the destruction of the tyrant Eugenius." This refers to the battle of the River Frigidus on 5–6 September 394 (Devos 1991). John also predicted a natural death for Theodosius, which occurred in 395. The epilogue mentions that the party was in the Delta at the time of Epiphany. The chapter on John also concludes with the notice that the group learned of the death of John while they were visiting "other fathers." Thus the visit must have begun in the latter part of 394 and concluded in 395. The work itself would have been written perhaps later in 395 or 396. The Latin translation by Rufinus must have been made in 404, for it refers to his translation of Eusebius' *Ecclesiastical History*, which was made in 401–403 (see Butler 1898, vol. 1: 13; Tillemont 1732, vol. 12: 656; de Vogüé 1996, vol. 1: 301, 317).

The *Lausiac History*

In the work known since the seventeenth century as the *Lausiac History* by Palladius (Katos 2011: 99), chapter 35 is dedicated to "a certain John" in Lykopolis. Palladius first offers details regarding John's pre-monastic life, that he had learned the art of carpentry and that his brother had learned that of a dyer. At the age of about twenty-five John renounced the world, spent five years in different monasteries, and then withdrew to the mountain of Lyko, where he built three domed cells and walled himself inside. After spending thirty years in this way, he was given the gift of clairvoyance. He predicted various things regarding Emperor Theodosius, in particular that he would return from Gaul after having vanquished Maximus. Then Palladius relates that, because Evagrius wanted to know about John, he (Palladius) undertook the arduous journey of eighteen days to visit him.

After waiting until Saturday, he finds John seated at his window. Upon questioning by John (through an interpreter named Theodore), Palladius admits to being from the "circle" of Evagrius (*HL* 35,5). This implies John already knew about Evagrius. Then suddenly the governor, Alypius, arrives and John devotes his entire attention to him for a long time. Because of this, Palladius suffers negative thoughts, and after the departure of Alypius, John reprimands him for his impatience. There follow predictions on the part of John, including that Palladius will be become a bishop. This introduces an exchange in which Palladius plays on the word 'bishop' and claims that he is already a bishop in the kitchen. John predicts his sufferings as bishop.

After the interview with John, Palladius returns to the desert (of Nitria) and recounts all "to the blessed fathers" (*HL* 35,10). Then he mentions that because of poor health he had to leave the desert, and that he went first to Palestine and from there to Bithynia, where he was consecrated bishop. After that, an allusion is made to the whole affair of the deposition of John Chrysostom and Palladius' own exile spent in Upper Egypt.[5]

According to his own indications, Palladius wrote his account around the year 419–20, that is, twenty-five years after the events it purports to relate (Katos 2011: 99). Palladius's visit to John would have had to be in the late summer of 394, if his mention of another visit by "the blessed fathers" took place two months later and before the death of John. Palladius's account of his visit to John has been subjected to a devastating analysis by P. Peeters, who notes that, according to Palladius, the goal of his expedition to Lykopolis was to report to Evagrius his observations concerning John.[6] But, in the presence of the saint, he speaks only of himself, and then uses the occasion to recount his own story to the reader, forgetting completely to give the final judgment of Evagrius, and so the story of his journey is left without a conclusion. Peeters suggests that the reference to the second group of visitors to visit John two months later is in fact inspired by the account in the first chapter of the *HM*. Likewise, behind the exchange between Palladius and John over his connection with Evagrius (not spontaneously admitted by Palladius), Peeters sees the story of the deacon in the *HM* who did not admit his identity. Peeters concludes that Palladius made use of the *HM*, written twenty-five years earlier, to construct his own narrative and that the idea that he had visited John of Lykopolis before the group of the seven is a fabrication.[7] If Peeters is correct in suspecting the historical veracity of Palladius's whole account of his visit to John, then the prior knowledge of John about Evagrius may be doubted. On the other hand, several references to the "seer of the

Thebaide" in Evagrius's *Antirrhetikos*[8] show that John's fame had reached the monastic settlements of Lower Egypt and may reflect a visit to John.

The Latin Sources

In the works of John Cassian, written about the same time as Palladius's *Lausiac History*, we also find traditions concerning John of Lykopolis, which, however, Cassian may have heard much earlier during his lengthy stay in Egypt in the desert of Scetis. In the *Institutes* 4.23, John is cited as an example of the most perfect obedience to his elder, which resulted in his receiving the gift of prophecy so that "he was sought after even by the kings of this world," Theodosius in particular. Among the incidents cited to demonstrate his obedience is the story of watering the dry stick for a whole year at the command of his elder. In Cassian's version of the story, the fruit is only the virtue of obedience, not a miraculous flowering as in other versions. At the end of the *Conferences* (24,16–17) Cassian again cites John as an example of those who have received a hundredfold, which includes being honored by mighty rulers. This is perhaps testimony to the fame of John in Lower Egypt in the years between 395 and 400, when Cassian left Egypt, but it may also have been derived from the *HM*. It does not really add to our knowledge of John himself.

The same must be said for another version of the story about the dry stick related by the traveler Postumian in the *Dialogues* of Sulpicius Severus (*Dial.* 1,19). In this version "a certain man," seeking admission to a monastery of severe observance, is commanded by the Abbot to water a stick of storax daily for three years, which meant carrying water from the Nile, a distance of two miles. At the end of the third year, "the twig began to show signs of life." Sulpicius died in about 420. The date of his *Dialogues* is uncertain, but obviously earlier. Later on, this story was also attributed to St. John Colobos, the founder of a monastery in Scetis. After examining the various versions and other evidence of confusion between John of Lykopolis and John Colobos, Doresse came to the conclusion that the story of the dry stick belonged to the beginning of the career of the recluse and should be situated in the Wadi Natrun, where he would have gone, like so many others, for his monastic initiation before returning to his native Thebaide (Doresse 2000: 153–56).

Augustine had also heard of John of Lykopolis and mentions him in two works: *De Civitate Dei* 5,26, where he cites the prediction of victory for Theodosius, and *De cura gerenda pro mortuis* 17,21, where he regrets being unable to ask John about certain problems, since he (John) had shown himself "in a dream" to the wife of a tribune. In both cases his source appears to be Rufinus's translation of the *HM*.[9]

In the *Apophthegmata* only two sayings are attributed to John of Lykopolis and both have a literary origin in the instruction he gives in the *HM* (Devos 1991).

Coptic Sources

The surviving Coptic literary material relating to John of Lykopolis, found in several Sahidic codices from the White Monastery, is testimony not to the historical figure but to the development of his fame after his death (see Till 1935: 138–54; Peeters 1936; Devos 1969a; Devos 1970; Devos 1976; Devos 1995: 76–86). The point of departure is a translation of some of the material found in the *HL*, which is then developed and extended so as to make John a contemporary of the emperor Marcian and opponent of the Council of Chalcedon more than fifty years after his death. One story, not found in the Greco-Latin material, concerning John's intervention on behalf of Lykopolis when it was under threat by Theodosius, may be historical (Devos 1991: 1365). The later attribution of writings to John of Lykopolis has been shown to be erroneous (Doresse 2000: 155; Guy 1974).

Documentary Sources

Some documentary sources exist that may throw light on the activity of the historical John. Constantine Zuckerman has argued that both Greek and Coptic papyri preserved separately in the John Rylands Library belong to the same archive of an Apa John and has carefully reconstructed the path by which they arrived in Manchester from the monastery of Dayr al-'Izam.[10] Doresse had earlier identified this site as the most likely location of the monastery founded by John of Lykopolis (Doresse 2000: 417–23). The existence of this monastery would also explain how it was possible for John to have lived as a recluse for so long; his disciples from the monastery would have provided the necessary support structure. The Greek and Coptic papyri brought together by Zuckerman, datable paleographically to the end of the fourth century, fit together quite well with what is reported in the *HM*. The Apa John of the papyri is presented with requests for prayers, and is asked to resolve troubles and to intervene with the authorities. One letter tells of a *dux* who was delighted to receive John's blessing. As Zuckerman notes, "His renown went much farther than the monastic milieu. Simple people, who claim no previous acquaintance with him, entreat his protection and expect his intervention to carry weight with the highest authorities of the province."[11] Of particular interest is the bilingual composition of the archive, which shows that John's petitioners were both Greek- and Coptic-speaking. One letter from John (evidently never sent) is written in Greek, but contains Apa John's personal greeting at the end in Coptic.

The Historical John of Lykopolis

The fame illustrated by these documentary sources might explain why the party of seven from the Mount of Olives would have begun their visits to the Egyptian monks with John of Lykopolis. However, although the account of the *HM* mentions John's fame for clairvoyance and his healings, the main attention is focused on John as a spiritual teacher. This fits well also with the citations in Evagrius's *Antirrhetikos*. John tells his visitors that their laborious pilgrimage is a good undertaking, but more important is imitating the virtues of the monks they visit. He emphasizes the importance of purity of mind and resisting inappropriate thoughts. They must not let themselves be disturbed by passions or by honor, glory, or self-love. "Otherwise," he says, "the entire undertaking becomes pointless when, in conversing with the Lord, one is seduced by opposing thoughts" (*HM* 1,25). Without genuine renunciation of the world, one is absorbed with preoccupations and must struggle with the passions, which interfere with the vision of God (*HM* 1,26). Slow and steady spiritual progress should be sought. The discourse concludes in the Greek version with a statement that is particularly significant:

> The will, then, of those who seek God must be free from all other concerns. For Scripture says, "Be still and know that I am God" (Psalm 46:10). Therefore, he who has been granted a partial knowledge of God—for it is not possible for the whole of such knowledge to be received by anyone—also attains to the knowledge of all other things. He sees mysteries, for God shows him them; he foresees what belongs to the future; he contemplates revelations like the saints did; he performs mighty works; he becomes a friend of God, and obtains from God everything he asks.[12]

The concept of "friend of God" is especially important, for this is the basis for John's gift of clairvoyance and his ability to read hearts. John commends those who engage in active works of charity as being "exceedingly good." But such a person is still occupied with earthly things. "Better and greater than he is the contemplative, who has risen from active works to the spiritual sphere and has left it to others to be anxious about earthly things.... He stands unimpeded in the presence of God, without any anxiety holding him back. For such a man spends his life with God; he is occupied with God, and praises him with ceaseless hymnody" (*HM* 21,62–63). Here we have the same terminology and the same concept of the spiritual life that is found also in the writings of Evagrius of Pontus and many others of the same period.

It is legitimate to ask to what extent this well-crafted discourse by John reflects his own teaching or the ideas of the narrator, who might have found them elsewhere. There is no way of answering this question with certainty. However, it is possible to investigate the use of the same terminology in the *HM*. The key term *apatheia* is found in the chapter on John and in chapter 8 on Apollo. Noting that the "saint taught us much else about ascesis," the author says that John taught that one should "try through ascesis to free the appetites from passion" (*HM* 1,29). In chapter 8, Apollo teaches: "'Let it be a sign to you of progress in the virtues,' he said, 'when you have acquired mastery over the passions and the appetites'" (*HM* 8,15). The terminology is remarkably close. Apollo also teaches the necessity of striving against evil thoughts *(logismoi)*.

Summary and Conclusion

The various sources for the figure of John of Lykopolis mention three aspects of his activity: his role as clairvoyant, counselor, and intercessor (whether with the authorities of this world or the next); his role as miracle worker and healer; and his role as spiritual teacher. Doresse has analyzed his role as clairvoyant–oracle by noting that the references in the *Historia Monachorum* to his prophecies regarding Theodosius, Eugenius, and Theodosius's natural death were probably redacted under the influence of the real events (Doresse 2000: 149). The original responses to questions were probably more vague.[13] Such is the case with the story of the prediction of victory for a general over the Ethiopians: "If you march against them, you will take them by surprise and defeat them and subdue them, and you will find favor with the emperors" (*HM* 1,2). The author is content to state that that is what happened without adding further details (Doresse 2000: 145).

John's role as miracle worker is actually played down by the *HM*, which states that "the blessed John did not perform cures publicly." He gave out oil to be used in effecting cures and offered prayers for those who requested his intercession.

His most important role, at least from the point of view of the anonymous author of the *HM,* was that of spiritual teacher. Although the author is giving a plausible account of a journey, he is also seeking to edify and instruct, as he himself indicates in the prologue. He uses language and ideas found elsewhere in early Egyptian monasticism, but that does not mean that he is wrong in attributing them to John. Since John's discourse conforms to the common teaching, it is entirely plausible.

Notes

1 For the Greek text, see Festugière 1961 and Festugière 1964, vol. 4, pt. 1. On the basis of a notice by Sozomen, *Historia Ecclesiastica* VI, 29,2, it has been suggested that the author was named Timotheus. See Butler 1898–1904, vol. 1: 276–77; Chitty 1977: 51, 62 n. 42.

2 Jerome's misleading identification is found in Letter 133 to Ctesiphon, §3 (CSEL 56: 246); see Butler 1898–1904, vol. 1: 11 n. 1. For his demonstration of the Greek text as original, see pages 12–51. Butler's identification was in fact a by-product of his investigation of the Greek text of the *HL*. Jerome had in fact exempted John of Lykopolis from his censure, although many others in the book are dismissed as Origenists.

3 The Latin text of Rufinus is found in *PL* 21: 387–462 and Schulz-Fluegel 1990. See de Vogüé 1996, vol. 1, pt. 3: 317–42.

4 Russell 1981: 4–5; Butler had come to the same conclusion in 1898. See Butler 1898, vol. 1: 198–203. See also Doresse 2000: 143. Rufinus mentions John of Lykopolis also in his continuation of Eusebius's *Ecclesiastical History* II, 19 and 32, which he translated and wrote in 401–403. His source appears to have been the *HM*, which he translated shortly thereafter in 404. See de Vogüé 1996, vol. 1: 301. The notices regarding Theodosius consulting John and John's predictions appear to reflect *HM* 1,1–2, and 1,4.

5 Palladius had already written a work in defense of John Chrysostom and his own role in the whole affair in late 407 or early 408: *Dialogue on the Life of John Chrysostom*. See Katos 2011: 26–27.

6 Peeters 1936. Doresse, while not denying a personal visit on the part of Palladius, notes that details may have been borrowed from the account in the *HM* as well as from traditions that he may have heard during his long exile in Antinoë. Doresse was well aware of Peeters' critique of Palladius's chapter on John and appears to agree in general. See Doresse 2000: 140–41.

7 Peeters offers multiple reasons for this conclusion. The critique of Palladius's reliability voiced by Peeters has been strongly underlined by Telfer 1937, who shows that the Coptic author knew both the *HL* and the *HM*, correcting the former with the latter.

8 Evagrius of Pontus, *Antirrhetikos*: Fornication 36, Anger 6, Acedia 16, Vanity 19. Cassian's notices concerning John show the same. See below. However, see Devos 1991: 1364, who assumes that the references to John in the *Antirrhetikos* are due to his visit to John.

9 Mention is made of John also by Eucherius of Lyons (*De laude heremi* 27), and Prosper of Aquitaine records the prediction of the victory on the Frigidus on the exact date in his *Chronicon*. Among the Greeks, the *Historia Ecclesiastica* of Sozomen (6.28, 1; 7.22, 6–8) gives more information than that of Theodoret (5.24, 1–2). See Devos 1991.

10 Zuckerman 1995. Choat has expressed reservations regarding this thesis. See Choat 2007 and Wipszycka 2009: 83–85.

11 Zuckerman 1995: 190. Zuckerman says that John stands at the beginning of the phenomenon of the imperial court's consultation of famous ascetics, but, according to the *Life of Antony* by Athanasius, it is necessary to date the beginning at least fifty years earlier (1995: 194).

12 The English translation is from Russell 1981: 56, §§27–28.

13 Doresse 2000: 144: "L'art de rendre de tels oracles réside, en pareil cas, plus dans ce qui n'est pas dit que dans ce qui s'y trouve précisé."

13 Discerning the True Religion in Late Fourteenth-Century Egypt: Pages from the Dayr al-Muharraq Edition of *al-Hawi* by al-Makin Jirjis ibn al-'Amid

Mark Swanson

Introduction

In recent years, Dayr al-Muharraq has shared some of its riches with the wider world through the publication of transcriptions of manuscripts from the monastery's library. As examples, I can point to the monastery's publication in two volumes of an Arabic-language collection of thirty homilies by St. Gregory Nazianzen (Dayr al-Muharraq 2003), as well as a single-volume copy of the Copto-Arabic Christological florilegium known as "The Confession of the Fathers" (Dayr al-Muharraq 2002).[1] Both of these texts are important for understanding the patristic heritage available to medieval Arabic-speaking Copts; "The Confession of the Fathers," in fact, is an eleventh-century landmark in the history of the arabization of the Coptic heritage (Rubenson 1996: 8–10). As far as I know, until today it is only the Muharraq editions of these important collections that provide complete printed copies of them, which can then be fruitfully used alongside other scholarly studies.[2]

Yet more ambitious than these projects, and probably of even greater usefulness to the scholarly world, was the publication between 1999 and

2001, in four volumes, of *al-Mawsu'ah al-lahutiyyah al-shahirah bi-l-Hawi l-Ibn al-Makin* (The Theological Encyclopedia known as *al-Hawi* by Ibn al-Makin) (Dayr al-Muharraq 2009–11, henceforth abbreviated *Hawi*). The publication of *al-Hawi* was a major accomplishment. In the first place, with the Muharraq edition we have, for the first time in print, the *entire* text of a major work entitled (according to one important manuscript) *al-Hawi al-mustafad min badihat al-ijtihad*, which I have attempted to render as "The Profitable Compilation, from the Faculty of Ratiocination."[3] The 'compilation' consists of two major parts, each divided into six (Part One: an introduction and five chapters; Part Two: six chapters), with each chapter *(bab)* subdivided into three subsections *(fusul)*. Before the Muharraq edition, only the introduction and the first three chapters had been published—and that in a rare volume published in Cairo in 1906 (Butrus 'Abd al-Malik 1906); a later publication in Cairo (Tawadrus Shahhat and Fu'ad Basili n.d.) includes only the introduction and chapter one. The Muharraq edition makes the *entire* text readily available—and, slowly but surely, students of Copto-Arabic literature and Coptic Church history have been picking it up and making use of it (Mikhail 2004: 365–67; Faltas 2010; Faltas 2011; Faltas 2012–13; Sidarus and Swanson 2013; Swanson 2014). There is even a one-volume condensation of the work now available in Cairo (Iskandar 2003), although this is perhaps best used as an extended table of contents that quickly leads the student back into the Muharraq edition.

Furthermore, my 'soundings' to date in the Muharraq edition suggest to me that it is a fairly close and faithful transcription of the manuscript,[4] without obvious signs of simplification or rewriting. What may strike the modern reader as infelicities in orthography or punctuation may, in fact, faithfully reproduce what is found in the manuscript.[5] This impression of faithfulness should, of course, be tested; when Bishop Sawirus (Severus) states in his preface (*Hawi* 1: 7) that the text should come to light "with the same expressions in which the manuscript is written, with slight changes to clarify the meaning," the scholar who hopes for a careful transcription is given grounds for both a certain confidence ("the same expressions") and some concern ("with slight changes").[6] These changes include conforming biblical quotations to the Arabic "Smith–Bustani–Van Dyck" Version commonly used in the Coptic Orthodox Church today, and adding chapter and verse references.

Next, it is necessary to point out that the Muharraq edition participates in a long-standing confusion between two Coptic authors who shared the name al-Makin Jirjis ibn al-'Amid: a thirteenth-century historian, conventionally referred to as "al-Makin"; and the late fourteenth-century monk and author of *al-Hawi*, to whom one can refer as "al-Makin 'the younger'" or, as I shall do here, "Ibn al-'Amid." The Muharraq edition of *al-Hawi* has an introductory chapter on "The Life of Jirjis ibn al-'Amid, known as Ibn al-Makin" (*Hawi* 1: 13–24) which draws on a variety of standard sources for Coptic Church history[7] in order to tell—mostly—the story of the *thirteenth*-century historian, into which a few notices about the *fourteenth*-century monk are then mixed. The confusion between the two authors, while understandable, was cleared up by Georg Graf in 1947 (Graf 1947: 450–53), and the distinction between the two authors is made plain in a variety of recent studies, both in English (Moawad 2012; Sidarus and Swanson 2013; Sidarus 2013: 199–201) and Arabic (Wadi 1996–97: 457–58; Athanasiyus al-Maqqari 2012: 778–86). Let us therefore be clear: the author of *al-Hawi* was a late fourteenth-century priest, civil servant, and practical physician who withdrew from life in the world to become a hermit near the Monastery of St. Arsenius (or Dayr al-Quseir) at Tura to the south of Old Cairo. He had composed *al-Hawi* by 1398/9, the date of an autograph copy. While he was undoubtedly from the same family as al-Makin "the elder," several generations had passed between the two, and their precise relationship is not known.

It is worth pointing out that distinguishing the thirteenth-century historian al-Makin from the late fourteenth-century hermit Ibn al-'Amid yields a very interesting result: *al-Hawi* does *not* come from the intensely fruitful period of the 'renaissance' or 'golden age' of Copto-Arabic literature in the thirteenth century, where, as a theological encyclopedia, *al-Hawi* would invite comparisons (perhaps not in its favor) with al-Mu'taman ibn al-'Assal's monumental *Majmu' usul al-din* (Wadi 1997; Wadi 1998–99), among other works. Rather, *al-Hawi* comes at the end of the fourteenth century, a period in the Coptic Orthodox Church better known for the remarkable saints who strove to shore up the community in difficult times (for example, Murqus al-Antuni, Ibrahim al-Fani, Anba Ruways, and Patriarch Matthew I; see Swanson 2010b: 107–17; Tsuji in this volume) than for its theological sophistication. Precisely so, *al-Hawi* is an important witness to the ongoing theological life of the Coptic Orthodox Church beyond the thirteenth-century 'renaissance,' well into what has sometimes been seen as a period of intellectual stagnation.

The ongoing theological life to which *al-Hawi* contributed was not limited to that of Egypt. Perhaps in the late fifteenth century it was translated into Ge'ez and circulated among Ethiopian Orthodox Christians under the title *Tälmid* (Colin 1985; Colin 2010). We do not know where or by whom this translation was made. The *fact* of this translation, however, points to the importance of *al-Hawi* in the intellectual history of the Christianities (plural!) of the Nile Valley. It must be left to others to comment on the role of Dayr al-Muharraq, which was well known to medieval Ethiopian Christians (Bausi 2010), in the transmission of literature from the Egyptian to the Ethiopian church, and whether the translation of *al-Hawi* might have been part of that story.

Al-Hawi on Discerning the True Religion

One could choose any number of topics with which to illustrate the way in which *al-Hawi* fits into the heritage of theological writing in Arabic. Here I would like to turn to a few pages in which Ibn al-'Amid makes a contribution to one of the earliest apologetic topics in the history of Christian–Muslim controversy, that of how to discern the true religion from among the various religions on offer. Already at the beginning of the ninth century AD, the Melkite bishop and theologian Theodore Abu Qurrah had developed at least two separate apologetic approaches to the issue. One approach, which takes up a good part of his *Maymar fi wujud al-Khaliq wa-l-din al-qawim* (ed. Dick 1982: 199–258; trans. Lamoreaux 2005: 1–25 under the title "Theologus Autodidactus"), built on the conviction that human minds are capable of outlining the parameters of acceptable doctrines with respect to God, morality, and the afterlife, and can then discern which of the various doctrines offered by the religions conforms most closely to what reason demands (see also Griffith 1994). But in an appendix to the same work (ed. Dick 1982: 259–70; trans. Lamoreaux 2005: 41–47 under the title "That Christianity is from God"), Theodore *also* pioneered a very different approach to the same topic. This time, he began with an analysis of the humanly comprehensible reasons for adopting a religion: coercion; gain in wealth, power, or status; license with respect to the passions; and the familiarity or attractiveness of the religion's teachings. He then proceeded to a step-by-step argument that the primitive Christian faith spread for *none* of these reasons; notably, its teachings were *not* familiar or attractive but novel, strange, and unappealing to natural human reason. But, the demonstration continues, Christian faith indisputably *did* spread—and so, therefore, must have done so not because of humanly comprehensible reasons, but because of *divine* power made manifest in evidentiary miracles.

And, thus, Christianity is the divinely-willed religion, QED! We note the somewhat different evaluations of human reason found in these two apologetic approaches. While both claim to be rational, in the first approach human reason plays a positive role in discerning religious truth, while in the second, the revulsion of natural human reason toward core Christian doctrines is made, paradoxically, into an argument for those doctrines' truth. Whoever would have believed in the crucifixion of the incarnate Son of God for the redemption of the world had it not been for divine power made manifest in miracles?

It was the *second* approach—providing an analysis of worldly, humanly comprehensible reasons for accepting a religion that, on close inspection, turns out to be incapable of explaining the spread of the Christian faith—that caught on among the early Arabic-speaking apologists. We find versions of it in the works of other ninth-century arabophone Christian thinkers such as Habib Abu Ra'itah, 'Ammar al-Basri, and Hunayn ibn Ishaq (see, for example, Griffith 1979; Swanson 2010a; Swanson 2013b)—and furthermore, their versions of the apology were known to thirteenth-century Copts. We note, for example, that chapter 12 of al-Mu'taman ibn al-'Assal's *Majmu' usul al-din* consists of an extract from Hunayn's apology followed by a brief quotation from that of Habib (Wadi 1998–99: 1 [text]: 278–84).

It is against this background that we may read *al-Hawi* and inquire about Ibn al-'Amid's approach to the question of how the true religion is to be discerned. One chapter where the question arises is part one, chapter 2, subsection 3, on the relationship between the Mosaic *shari'ah* and the Messianic *shari'ah (Hawi 1:277–302)*. This word *shari'ah* is probably best translated 'way' rather than 'law': Ibn al-'Amid points out that the word is derived from *shari'*, the one who leads people to *al-tariq ila-llah*, 'the way to God' (277). Ibn al-'Amid affirms that God's ultimate purpose for humankind is constant: "the refinement of souls and their elevation to the world of light and eternity" (280). But God works in a wisely calibrated, step-by-step manner in order to achieve God's purposes. Thus God first revealed, through the willing receptivity of the prophet Moses, the Way of Justice *(al-'adl)*, which was appropriate to the weakness and limited understanding of those to whom it was revealed (280–81). In the Incarnation through the willing receptivity of the Virgin Mary, however, God revealed the Messianic *shari'ah* or Way of Grace *(al-fadl)*: it is through Christ that one obtains the fullness of the blessing promised to all through Abraham (Genesis 12:3), "inexhaustible, imperishable good things" (288). I have repeated the phrase "through the willing receptivity of . . ." in order to emphasize a point important to Ibn al-'Amid: that free human actors—the prophet Moses and the Virgin Mary—are critically important in the history of revelation. Questions such as "Why did God reveal at this particular time, and not earlier?" can be answered in terms of the mysterious but temporally located meeting of the divine will to reveal with the human being who was prepared and willing to receive the revelation (291–94).

Toward the beginning of the chapter, Ibn al-'Amid had made the passing comment that God's "scripturally revealed ways" *(al-shara'i' al-naqliyya)* could be comprehensively categorized as establishing justice *(al-'adl), or* grace *(al-fadl), or* their combination *(al-majmu')* (280).[8] Near the end of the chapter, this comment opens the way to an objection:

> You have said that the comprehensive categorization of *shara'i'* [includes those that] establish justice, or grace, or the combination. You have claimed that the Mosaic *shari'ah* brought justice, and that the Messianic *shari'ah* brought grace. It is inevitable, then, that a third category appear, one that combines justice and grace, since no aspect of incompleteness whatsoever may befall the deeds of God (may he be exalted!). (294)

Although Ibn al-'Amid does not say so, what appears to be coming to word here is a specifically Islamic argument; a frequently-heard modern form of it claims that Islam brings the divinely willed 'middle way' between a Judaism that (allegedly) stresses unbending justice and a Christianity that (allegedly) stresses impractical grace.[9] Ibn al-'Amid makes several points in response. The Messianic *shari'ah* with its evangelical teachings *already* incorporates the Mosaic *shari'ah*: the Golden Rule *is* "the Law and the prophets" (Matthew 7:12) (295); but the Messianic *shari'ah* goes on to teach the love of enemies (Matthew 5:44, 46–47), which is the "way of grace and perfection" (296). There is no third way beyond the Messianic program *(minhaj)* that comprehends both. Anyone who calls to justice and grace beyond this Messianic program is not saying anything original, so that even if what that person says is true, that one is better categorized among the *chroniclers* of the past *(al-mu'arrikhin)* than among the *prophets* (296–97). Or, if there were in fact a third way, it could only represent a decline *(inhitat)* from that which is perfect to that which is lesser and lacking *(akhass wa-anqas)* (298)—and it is impossible to imagine God withdrawing his grace and leading his servants from that which is perfect to that which is inferior (298–99).

So far, there is nothing particularly surprising in this. Already in the eighth-century conversation between the Abbasid caliph al-Mahdi and Timothy the Great, catholicos of the Church of the East, a Christian theologian had insisted that, with the coming of the heavenly in Christ, there was no reason to accept any subsequent revelation (Mingana 1928: 39). A bit more surprising is Ibn al-'Amid's statement that the veracity of the claim that the Messianic *shari'ah* represents the pinnacle of generosity *(nihayat al-jud)* may be witnessed in practice: "The conditions of those who put it into effect and cling to its principles and ramifications bear witness to the veracity of the claim" (*Hawi* 1: 299); concretely, this has to do with the realization of the commandment to love all people, even one's enemies. Ibn al-'Amid records the obvious objection: "One does *not* find this commandment [being observed] in any of the Christians!" (300) He responds that if close examination shows the prescription to be noble, then "even if the practice of what is prescribed turns out to be difficult, that does not detract from the perfection of the way." In any event, there is the example of Christ, who not only gave and taught the commandment to love all people but also enacted it when "he voluntarily gave his body to death on the cross" (300).

This is followed by another objection—which leads us to what might be the most interesting and original point in the entire chapter. Ibn al-'Amid has his interlocutor say:

> Another *shari'ah has* appeared since the "*shari'ah* of perfection" [that is, Christianity], and has grown, and many from the nations have entered into it. It is present in many regions of the earth; its sword is victorious, its tower[10] is lofty, and many people have believed in it. (300)

This objection brings to word another standard argument: that *worldly success is evidence for a religion's truth*. In the present context this argument is understood to be one made by *Muslims*, since this new, successful *shari'ah* can only refer to Islam. However, Christians were by no means immune to the argument from worldly success, which had been a temptation since the time of the emperor Constantine, and would be a temptation whenever Christian armies were winning battles. And perhaps we can even see an echo of the argument from success in the popular argument for the truth of Christianity described above: Christianity can be seen to be true because of its extraordinary spread throughout the world, *despite* the absence of humanly comprehensible reasons that explain that spread.

Against this background, Ibn al-'Amid's response is significant: the argument from worldly success does not work! After all, *both* the Christian and the Muslim communities have experienced success, in different times and different places.

> If you believe that the truth is present in any *shari'ah* whose word stands, whose sword is victorious, and whose laws are manifest—in one place but not another, and among one people but not another—then the affirmation is necessary that the Messianic [Christian] *shari'ah* is *also* the truth wherever you find that its word stands, its sword is victorious, and its tower lofty. (300)

Ibn al-'Amid goes as far as to claim that *most* of the people of the earth were in fact Christian—a dubious claim, but perhaps one that was tempting for a member of a community that had likely long since lost its numerical majority in Egypt, but which could still look north to Christian Europe or south to Christian Ethiopia. Ibn al-'Amid's point, however, is not to attempt to establish truth by a head count. Rather, he wants to make the point that worldly success provides no positive evidence for religious truth; otherwise different religions would have to be considered simultaneously true in different places, or consecutively true in a single place. And thus:

> The scholars and estimable leaders of the Christian community were not content at all with such an inference to verify the reliability of the Christian call and the establishment of its principles. . . . For them, the continued existence of religious claims was not, on its own, sufficient evidence for the verification of a religious claim. There have been numerous religious claims, varied sets of customary practice, and many beliefs that have manifestly been in existence—their word standing, their sword effective—before the appearance of the Mosaic *shari'ah*, whose laws did not encompass all the nations, and before the appearance of a *shari'ah* that did spread in all directions, by land and by sea. (301)

The various pre-Christian and even pre-Mosaic religious claims, customary practices, and particular beliefs extended to differences in who or what was worshiped, and thus, for Muslims as well as Christians, a variety of unwholesome doctrines. And thus:

> The opponent affirms that these forms of worship are not the true way or the truthful opinions; rather they are depraved and reprehensible, not pleasing to God. Despite this, they continued in existence for extended periods and ages of time. And so it is apparent that not every call that continues in existence for a period of time—and whose word stands, whose laws are manifest, whose sword is conquering, whose command is victorious—is something in which one must acknowledge the presence of the truth, nor must one rely upon and have recourse to it. (301–302)

Ibn al-'Amid may have been thinking of ancient Egyptian religion, or of Greek or Roman religion: these were powerful systems that sustained mighty empires—and yet no Christian or Muslim would acknowledge them to be religiously *true*.

> Therefore, the inference [of the truth of a religion] from the aspect of its continuing existence, victory, and exaltedness of its word in a particular place and a particular time amounts to nothing: the argument based on it is flimsy and its bases failing and empty. (302)

If this is so, however, then anyone who sincerely desires to examine the truth of a religion must look with all one's rational capacities into its *content*—its actual commands and prohibitions—and do so "without stopping at names, or being hindered by customs or fettered by familiarity, traditions, and what comes naturally" (302) but with the sincere purpose of finding everlasting life, victory over the demons of nature, and the greatest possible godliness both for this life and for the life to come.

Conclusion: Discerning the True Religion in Late Fourteenth-century Egypt

What is striking in Ibn al-'Amid's chapter is the vigor with which he rejects the idea of worldly success—whether in terms of continued existence, military victory, or cultural accomplishment and prestige—as in any way an indicator of a religion's truth. In doing so, he may well have been countering forms of argumentation that he had heard from Muslims; but he also cut off at the root a Christian form of argumentation that had been a temptation from the time that Christianity achieved imperial approval under the emperor Constantine.

The assertion of Christianity's remarkable spread had played a key role in the apology for the true religion that had become so popular among arabophone Christians of all Christian communities: the fact that Christianity spread *despite* the lack of humanly comprehensible reasons for its spread was itself an indicator of the not human but, rather, divine power in it. While Ibn al-'Amid still clearly believed (and perhaps took comfort in) the remarkable spread of Christianity throughout the world, at least in this chapter it plays no probative role in his argument.

Ibn al-'Amid's prescription for discerning the true religion, then, is closer to Abu Qurrah's *first* approach to the issue, in which he had affirmed the capacity of human reason to arrive at some basic truths with respect to God, the moral life, and the life to come. Ibn al-'Amid's confidence in the capacity of human reason may be seen from the vocabulary he uses to describe how one should think about the content of religious proposals: these require study and examination (*al-bahth, al-istiqra'*; *Hawi* 1:299), as well as careful consideration and probing by the rule of syllogistic reasoning (*al-nazar fiha, sabruha bi-l-qanun al-qiyasi*; 302), while discerning and discarding tendencies merely to follow custom, tradition, or the lead of people of reputation (302). So equipped, Ibn al-'Amid is convinced that rational people may see in the teachings of the Gospel the *shari'ah* of perfection that cannot be surpassed.

It is tempting to see in Ibn al-'Amid's approach to the question of discerning the true religion an approach particularly suited to his time at the end of the fourteenth century, during which the Coptic community had suffered and had lost many prominent members through conversion to Islam (see, for example, Little 1976). It was no time for any sort of triumphalistic argument—such as an argument based on Christianity's successful spread through the world, or one based on public shows of divine power. Indeed, the 1380s and 1390s were not remembered for any public demonstration of Christian truth such as the Muqattam miracle of early Fatimid times (see den Heijer 1994), but rather for the public 'performances' of voluntary martyrs, both apostates from Islam who made public confession of their Christian faith and Christians who joined them by means of anti-Islamic preaching (see el-Leithy 2005: 101–39; Swanson 2010b: 114–17). Any 'power' possessed by the forty-nine martyrs of the time was demonstrated in extreme vulnerability, not in dazzling demonstration.

However, a Christian teacher such as Ibn al-'Amid could still appeal to reason—as he could also point to those who, with respect to the commandment to love all people, "put it into effect and adhere to its principles and ramifications" and who thereby "bear witness to the veracity" of Christian teachings (*Hawi* 1:299). Is it possible that Ibn al-'Amid was thinking of some of the remarkable saints of his own days? Murqus al-Antuni and Patriarch Matthew I are remembered for practical service and deeds of mercy that, while focused on the welfare of the Coptic community, were often extended to Muslims as well as Christians (Swanson 2010b; Swanson 2013b). And if the martyrs did not extend themselves in similar service, in their own way they attempted to follow the Christ who "voluntarily gave his body to death" (*Hawi* 1:300).

This chapter has presented just a tiny sample from *al-Hawi*, but this sample is perhaps enough to suggest that the work is important in a variety of ways, not least as an artifact of a significant period in the history of the Coptic community—one not usually known for its theological production. We owe a debt of gratitude to the monk of Dayr al-Muharraq who has done such a careful work of transcription, and to the monastery as a whole and to Bishop Sawirus for the publication of this remarkable text.

Notes

1 Note that the published volume carries the title *I'tirafat al-aba'*, "The Confessions of the Fathers" (in the plural), rather than the correct *I'tiraf al-aba'* (in the singular), "The Confession"—that is, the creed or the faith—"of the Fathers."

2 Thus, the Muharraq edition of *I'tiraf al-aba'* can be used in conjunction with Georg Graf's careful outline and study (Graf 1937), while the Muharraq edition of the thirty homilies of St. Gregory Nazianzus may be read alongside the work of Jacques Grand'Henry and collaborators (see, for example, Grand'Henry 1981; Sauget 1983; Tuerlinckx 2001; and the critical editions of some individual homilies from the Arabic collection that have been appearing since 1988 in the Corpus Christianorum, Series Graeca, Corpus Nazianzenum).

3 'Independent reasoning' is probably more accurate than 'ratiocination'—but does not give any sense of the Arabic rhymed title.

4 While I am speaking here of "the manuscript," in fact the Dayr al-Muharraq copy is a pair of volumes, one for each part, bearing the call numbers: Section XI, *kutub lahutiya wa-'aqa'iddiya* 1–2.

5 For purposes of my own study, I have made photocopies of chapters so as, by hand, to add (and occasionally remove) *hamza*, to add (usually) or remove dots so as to distinguish between final *ya'* and *alif maksura*, to add *shadda*, and to punctuate according to the sense of the text rather than according to the printed full stops, which, let it again be said, may reflect markings actually found in the manuscript.

6 Ashraf Najih Ibrahim 'Abd al-Malak is preparing a doctoral dissertation on *al-Hawi* at the Pontifical Urbaniana University in Rome, which hopefully will clarify a number of questions surrounding *al-Hawi* as well as provide us a careful assessment of the published editions.

7 For example, the well-known works of Kamil Salih Nakhlah, Anba Isudhurus, and Iris Habib al-Misri. The introduction also quietly draws on Wadi's important Arabic-language essay on al-Makin 'the elder' (Wadi 1999).

8 In fact, in *Hawi* 1: 280 we find the word *mawdu'*, but this must be corrected to *majmu'* on the basis of both the sense and the self-quotation at page 294.

9 In the background here is the *ummatan wasatan* of Q 2:143. For some understandings of this idea in Islamic tradition, see Griffel 2003.

10 The word *manar* can mean 'lighthouse' or 'minaret.'

14 Egyptian Gnosticism from Its Cradle in the Alexandrian Quarters of the Second Century to Its Jar Tomb in the Upper Egyptian Town of Nag' Hammadi

Hany N. Takla

Introduction

The aim of this study is to try to interpret the fate of Gnosticism in Egypt through a simple investigation of places where texts were found and the historical material available. Our knowledge of the provenance of these texts is not always found in external sources such as historical records or archaeological excavations, but extends to internal textual evidence such as the dialect of the text and indirect evidence found in the literature. In addition, one should keep in mind that not all the Nag' Hammadi texts were Gnostic, but belonged to a Gnostic community, and not all Gnostic texts were found in Nag' Hammadi.

The Original Language of Gnostic Texts

According to James Robinson, the Nag' Hammadi texts, being the largest cache of Gnostic texts found, were translated one by one from Greek into Coptic (Robinson 1990: 2). Many factors justify this view, such as the Alexandrian origin of the texts, Clement's writings against them, and the presence of fragments from the Gospel of Thomas among the papyri fragments of the Middle Egypt Greco-Roman city of Oxyrhynchos. However, Gilles Quispel advanced the premise that the earliest Coptic Gnostic texts to be discovered, Codex Askewianus and Codex Brucianus, were originally written in Sahidic Coptic in Thebes or modern-day Luxor (Quispel 1991: 1148). On the other hand, Bentley Layton in the introduction of his work *The Gnostic Gospels* stresses the point that all Gnostic works discovered were not originally written in Coptic, but Greek (Layton 1987: xxvii).

Ancient Manuscripts and Their Provenance

The list below includes only texts of a Gnostic nature or those that were found in the same corpus as such texts. They are listed in order of discovery.

- *Codex Brucianus*: Papyrus, Sahidic, AD 300–500, discovered in the eighteenth century near Luxor and eventually deposited in the Oxford Bodleian Library in 1769, currently known as OB.Bruce. Ms.96.
- *Codex Askewianus*: Parchment, Sahidic, AD 350–400, discovered in the eighteenth century near Luxor and eventually deposited in the British Library in 1773, currently known as BL.Add.5114.
- *Akhmim Codex*: Papyrus, Sahidic, AD 400–500, discovered in a cemetery in Akhmim and bought by Carl Schmidt for the Berlin Library in 1896, currently known as P.Berol.8502.
- *Oxyrhynchus Papyri*: Papyrus, Greek, third century AD, fragments discovered by B.P. Grenfell and A.S. Hunt and first published in 1897. They are now deposited in three different libraries:
    - P.Oxy.1 in the British Library, London;
    - P.Oxy.654 in the Bodleian Library, Oxford;
    - P.Oxy.655 in Harvard Houghton Library, Cambridge, United States.
- *Nag' Hammadi Papyri*: Payprus, Sahidic, and Lykopolitan, before AD 350, discovered in a cave in 1945 and currently deposited in the Cairo Coptic Museum.
- *Codex Tchacos*: Papyrus, Sahidic, first half of the fourth century AD, discovered circa 1978 about sixty kilometers north of al-Minya in Middle Egypt. Was first kept in Switzerland, but it has been reported that it will be returned to the Coptic Museum after the conservation process is completed and its display to the European public has concluded.

The area of provenance of these codices and fragments begins in the north at the city of Oxyrhynchos and ends in Luxor in the south. With the exception of the Nag' Hammadi codices, the manuscripts are medium to small in size and were most likely to have been discovered in Greco-Roman cemeteries. This meant they were privately owned and did not belong to a large community. The Nag' Hammadi codices were larger in size, however, which suggests that they belonged to a library of an organized community. The dates are only estimates and they span from AD 300 to 500, though that of the community-based collection of Nag' Hammadi seems to be prior to AD 350 according to Layton (Layton 1987: xxvi).

Events Affecting the Birth and Migration of the Gnostic Texts

The beginning and the effective end of Gnosticism in Egypt were significantly affected by a few historical events in Egypt. The following is a brief overview of these events:

1. *The end of the Jewish wars in Alexandria:* In AD 115, a general revolt began among the Jewish communities in various parts of the Middle East as claims by some to be the Messiah circulated. The revolt was very violent on both the Roman and Jewish sides. The eventual outcome in AD 117 was the decimation of the once vibrant and strong Jewish community in Alexandria. This resulted in the emergence of two competing Christian communities that had been hidden behind the strong presence of the larger Jewish community there. One was the Orthodox group that was founded by the preaching of St. Mark, and the other was the eclectic group that is now commonly known as the Gnostics.
2. *Clement of Alexandria versus the Gnostics:* This late second-century Alexandrian philosopher spearheaded the resistance to 'Gnostic' teachings, employing similar philosophical logic to counteract their own. He claimed the title of 'Gnostic' for Christians (Barnard 1991).
3. *The Melitian Schism:* This early schism in the Church of Alexandria began innocently when Melitius, bishop of Lykopolis (Asyut), objected to the terms set by St. Peter I, bishop of Alexandria and martyr, for the readmission of lapsed Christians during the Great Persecution of the early fourth century (Timbie 1991: 1584). Both Peter and Melitius were imprisoned. Peter was imprisoned and exiled twice, ending in his martyrdom, while Melitius was imprisoned once and sent to the mines. This difference in the outcome of their lives made the view of

Peter the orthodox one and Melitius the heretic, as Tim Vivian argued (Vivian 1988: 38).[1] This schism in effect severed Lykopolis from the Orthodox Church in Alexandria. It set Lykopolis up as a rival to Alexandria's ecclesiastical preeminence in Egypt.[2] As a result, it became a haven for every person who had issues with the Church of Alexandria.

4. *Patriarch Dioscorus of Alexandria's anti-heretical crusade, circa* AD *445:* Shortly after St. Dioscorus of Alexandria succeeded St. Cyril of Alexandria, he waged a crusade against the heresies that were allowed to flourish farther away from Alexandria during the time that the Church was involved in defending itself against foreign heresies from Constantinople and elsewhere. He enlisted St. Shenoute the Archimandrite, the Church of Alexandria's de facto ambassador in Upper Egypt, in combating these local heretical groups, as observed in his treatise *Contra Origenistas*, published by Orlandi (Orlandi 1985). The target groups also included Gnostics (Orlandi 2006: 542). According to Stephen Emmel, his influence extended from Hermopolis and Antinoopolis (around al-Minya) in the north to the first Nile Cataract in the south (near Aswan) (Emmel 2004, vol. 1: 12), and so they would have been within his domain.
5. *The demise of the Pachomian federation in the sixth century:* The Byzantine imperial installation of Proterius in place of the exiled Dioscorus as bishop of Alexandria, following the Council of Chalcedon of AD 451, was much resisted by the residents of Alexandria and elsewhere. According to Edward R. Hardy, Proterius's support base outside of Alexandria was ten to twelve bishops and the Pachomian monks of Canopus, the famous monastery near Alexandria (Hardy 1952: 115). This Pachomian monastic support increased due to pressure by the emperor Justinian in the sixth century, which eventually led to the ouster of its federation archimandrite from its headquarters in Pbow (near Nag' Hammadi), Abraham of Farshut (Goehring 2012: 60). Archeological remains of the great basilica of that monastery do not give any clear evidence of the survival of the monastery after the end of the sixth century (Goehring 2012: 62).

The Flight Southward

Now that we have reviewed the manuscript and historical evidence available, we can begin to reconstruct the flight path of the main Gnostic community from Alexandria to Nag' Hammadi as follows:

1. The writings of the community and its early teachers, Valentinus and Basilides, in Alexandria are attested in Greek shortly after the fall of the Jewish community in Alexandria in AD 117.
2. The early third-century philosophical victory of Clement of Alexandria and the conservative nature of the episcopal tenure of Demetrius of Alexandria (AD 189–231) probably hastened their departure from Alexandria.
3. The presence of Greek fragments from the third century in the Greek city of Oxyrhynchos shows that there was a Gnostic presence there at the time, although not for how long. But the limited quantity found does indicate at least that the Greek writings did not last beyond the mid-fourth century, when we have evidence of their translation into Coptic. The history of early Christianity in Egypt does not support an organized campaign against the group until the time of St. Athanasius in the first half of the fourth century.
4. The Coptic Gospel of Judas, discovered along with other Gnostic and non-Gnostic texts in al-Minya, shows that at some time in the early fourth century some individual translations for private individuals were made from a Greek original. The lack of similar dialectal variants in the Nag' Hammadi Codices leads one to believe it was from a Greek original rather than copied from the Coptic ones of that community. The small size of the manuscript is indicative of private ownership. In any case, it does reveal that there was a philosophically-minded, bilingual Copt in that region who read such texts. The lack of existence of another Gospel of Judas in the Nag' Hammadi community may indicate that the community was more conservative-minded than that individual owner and would not accept a work with such a provocative label. Therefore, the al-Minya manuscript represents the first occurrence of a Coptic Gnostic text. Coptic translation was probably a way to mask such texts from the agents of the Alexandrian ecclesiastical authorities, who would obviously be looking for a Greek text, at least at the beginning of the pursuit.
5. Moving southward, we have a clear indication that these texts, probably in Greek, were moved along with what was left of the community to Lykopolis (Asyut). There, they were translated into Coptic. This is clear from the very significant influence of the Lykopolitan Coptic dialect in the Nag' Hammadi texts. One can assume that the

anti-Alexandrian-authority environment of that city, the home of the Melitian Schism, would have provided the necessary haven for translating all the texts into Coptic to shield them from their pursuers and to build a community among the free-thinking residents of the region. Such a peaceful existence would have been possible toward the middle of the fourth century. The large dimensions of the Nag' Hammadi manuscripts indicate that these texts belonged to a significant organized community and not just a random group of individuals.

6. The presence of privately owned copies of Gnostic texts in Akhmim and farther south in Luxor by the middle of the fifth century shows that the influence of the community must have extended somewhat, at least to individuals farther south of their Lykopolitan haven, as observed in the Berlin Akhmim Codex, Codex Brucianus, and Codex Askewianus. However, the private nature of these manuscripts, based on their small sizes, does not indicate the presence of an organized group.
7. The anti-heretical campaign of Patriarch Dioscorus in cooperation with St. Shenoute would definitely have spoiled what would have been a century of peaceful existence for the community in Lykopolis. It is not known how successful the campaign was, considering that the abbot fell ill at least by AD 451, which made him unable to go to Chalcedon at the time. Also, how effective he would have been after his recovery is still a mystery. What can safely be assumed is that sometime after this campaign, the community, with what was left of its members and their texts, moved south and probably west to get away from the hotbed of orthodox zeal of the White Monastery federation of St. Shenoute in the Akhmim–Sohag area. The date of this move could be as early as the second half of the fifth century and as late as the mid-sixth century.[3] What is also known is that, by the time they moved to the new location, the codices were in need of rebinding, as is evidenced by what was found in the cartonnage of the new bindings.
8. The next and final resting place for the community was the area near the modern-day town of Nag' Hammadi, southwest of Akhmim and north of Luxor. They settled in an abandoned Pachomian monastery near its federation headquarters in Faw al-Qibli, to the east. There they rebound their books anew using discarded papyrus fragments and scraps found in the area. If this abandonment of the monastery

was due to the Chalcedonian controversy that arose in the middle of the sixth century at the time of Abraham of Farshut, then a mid- to late sixth-century date would be plausible for their presence there. The early support given to the newly imperially appointed Chalcedonian Proterius by the internationally known Pachomian monastery in Canopus may also have contributed to the abandonment of some of these smaller monasteries at a slightly earlier date. One can be certain of a date after the middle of the fifth century and before the end of the sixth century. In addition, one can be certain of its abandonment by Pachomian monks, Chalcedonian or non-Chalcedonian, before the settlement of this Gnostic community. Among the cartonnage in the codex covers of at least Codex VII of Nag' Hammadi, a fragment was found of a copy of a letter addressed to St. Pachomius (Barns, Browne, and Shelton 1981: 139). It would not have been possible for such a document to be discarded by the Pachomian monks unless they were no longer there.[4]

9. Eventually the community disbanded and the bulk of the library was deposited in a jar near a cliff. The probable reason would be, as Cornelia Römer writes: "The assumption is that these books were once part of a library for which Orthodox Christians were searching and they were therefore hidden from the searchers" (Römer 2009: 627). Also, they could have been kept hidden to preserve what could not be carried away, as happened with the biblical codices of the monastery of Apa Jeremias in Saqqara. Based on the Roman coins found there, Herbert Thompson estimated that they were buried as late as the first quarter of the seventh century (Thompson 1932: x). This would have corresponded to the combined administrative-ecclesiastical rule of Cyrus of Alexandria, who waged a great and indiscriminate persecution of the Copts just prior to the Arab invasion of Egypt. So, based on the type of burial and the political situation in Egypt, the first half of the seventh century would have been the last possible date for the settlement of the Gnostic community last seen in Nag' Hammadi.

Conclusion

Developing a history out of a literary corpus is a difficult task because such literature was designed to be ageless by its writers. A researcher is then left with clues from archaeology, history, paleography, and codicology to uncover its development. In the case of the Gnostics, a community on the run since presumably the third century, the task becomes much harder. From the evidence presented here, one observes an intellectual, eclectic community rising out of the ruins of the Jewish quarter in Alexandria after AD 117, losing the intellectual war in Alexandria by the early third century, and going on the run southward, away from the ecclesiastical authorities in Alexandria. In the process we find it changing the language of its texts to hide them from its pursuers; this language conversion took place in Lykopolis (modern Asyut), as evidenced by the dialect influence of the area. The region's stance against the Alexandria ecclesiastical authority was the attraction to settle there, and eventually the reason to move on as this resistance movement was overcome. Its final resting place was fittingly, as well as ironically, in a ruined Pachomian monastery that became ruined because of its federation alliance with the Alexandrian (Chalcedonian) authority at the time!

Notes

1 It seems that Melitius's first offense was the ordination of bishops in Egypt, contrary to the established tradition that the bishop of Alexandria alone had that authority. The reasons and circumstances are not entirely clear, but the controversy took on a life of its own and plagued the Church of Alexandria for centuries.

2 The First Ecumenical Council of Nicaea in AD 325 put a stamp of approval on the pre-eminence of the Bishop of Alexandria over all of Egypt in response to this schism.

3 When the Gnostic community would have felt the need to move from the friendly confines of Melitian Lykopolis within this time period depends on how strong the Melitian community was at the time. I would argue for a later time rather than earlier unless future archaeological evidence to the contrary is found. In any case, the move to Nag' Hammadi is predicated on the abandonment of the Pachomian monastery there.

4 It should be noted that, based on my arguments above, I would side with those mentioned by Cornelia Römer who dispute the assumption that these books were once owned by Pachomian monks (Römer 2009: 627). The Pachomian monks' ownership was conjectured by such scholars as Elaine Pagels (Pagels 2005: xix).

15 Notes on the Arabic *Life of Ibrahim al-Fani*: A Coptic Saint of the Fourteenth Century

Asuka Tsuji

THE *LIVES* OF COPTIC SAINTS in the later Islamic era fall into the category of sacred biographies that have not attracted much study until recently.[1] This observation does not imply that these *Lives* have little or no historical or literary value. On the contrary, they speak of the struggles and the resilience of the Copts in troubled times, carrying a message that is not lost on us today.[2]

The *Life of Hegumenos Ibrahim al-Fani* is no exception. According to his biography, Ibrahim, or Abra'am, al-Fani was born in Minyat Bani Khasib, modern-day Minya, and died on 9 Hatur AM 1113/AD 1396.[3] He was a disciple of Murqus al-Antuni (d. AD 1386) and a mentor to the eighty-seventh patriarch, Matta'us I (AD 1378–1408). Apart from his *Life,* he is mentioned in the *Majma' al-Qiddisin* (*Mementa Sanctorum*, or 'Commemorations of the Saints') along with St. Murqus al-Antuni and St. Ruways (d. AD 1404), who were his contemporaries, and, in relation to Patriarch Matta'us, in the *History of the Patriarchs*.[4] The only known manuscript of the *Life of Ibrahim al-Fani*, copied in Cairo in 1700, is preserved at the Monastery of St. Antony near the Red Sea.[5] It is a very short hagiography, consisting of only a *Life (Sira)*, with no *Miracles*, in twenty-eight folios.[6] The name of the author is not mentioned.

Ibrahim al-Fani's name appears in a study from the 1980s (Abullif 1998, vol. 1: 19); however, only in 2007 was the *Life* itself mentioned, by Mark N. Swanson. Swanson later discussed its main elements and recognized its importance as a source for understanding the Christian–Muslim relationship of fourteenth-century Egypt (Swanson 2007: 221, 226; Swanson 2010b: 112–13; Swanson 2013a: 226–28). This reading presents the parts of the narrative that have not previously been discussed in order to consider the structure of this *Life* and to inquire into the purpose of its compilation.

Description of the *Life*

Preface

The preface of the *Life* begins by mentioning Ibrahim's death, which is followed by a long lament *(ritha')* over his departure from Fustat (Misr) for his birthplace, Minyat Bani Khasib, where he died. It relates that "we," presumably the author and other followers, begged him not to leave. The author compares his town, the blessed city of Fustat, to a widow and accuses Ibrahim of "abandoning" *(taraka)* the city (*Life*: fols. 3b–6a). Here, he calls on his audience to "let us remember the day Ibrahim left Fustat." These passages relating to the departure of Ibrahim imply that the author was more distressed by Ibrahim's abandonment of Fustat than by his eventual death. This reading suggests that he was a resident of this town and a disciple of Ibrahim.

A panegyric to Murqus al-Antuni, Ibrahim, and their disciples who died as martyrs "in our era" follows the lament (*Life*: fols. 3b–6a).[7] The introduction ends with the author asking Ibrahim for his blessings *(baraka)* and wishing that the story of the saint will be beneficial *(manfa'a)* to those who read or hear his words (*Life*: fols. 6a–9a). It appears that the author sought personal solace in commemorating Ibrahim's life, or perhaps, as a resident of Fustat, he had wished for a relic of Ibrahim to be placed in the town. The phrase "to be beneficial to listeners (readers)" is a topos that is common in prefaces (e.g., Riad 1988: 223–25). As I discuss below, the phrase is, however, suggestive when considering the motive behind the compilation of this *Life* with regard to the social conditions of the Copts.

Ibrahim's Early Life

The account of Ibrahim's life begins with his birth in Minyat Abu Fis (or Fays), which, according to Abu al-Makarim in the *Tarikh al-Kana'is*, is the ancient name for Minyat Bani Khasib (Abu al-Makarim 1984, vol. 2: fol. 78a).[8] His father, for whom he was named, died before his birth, and his mother, Sayyida, raised him. Several episodes from his childhood are recounted, emphasizing Ibrahim's love of study, disregard for earthly pleasure, and yearning for the monastic life from an early age (*Life*: fols. 9b–10a). The *Life* then recounts that one day Ibrahim leaves his home for a monastery in the south without telling his mother, who, believing her beloved son dead, laments. Observing her grief, God sends a Christian man to inform her that Ibrahim is alive and in a monastery. She hastily journeys to the monastery and bids her son farewell at the gate. Her words are so heart-rending, however, that the monks persuade Ibrahim to leave and to remain with his mother until her death (*Life*: fols. 10b–11b).

Ibrahim seems to have returned to the Monastery of Abu Fana after his mother's death.[9] There, he studies books on the saint Abu Fana (Apa Bane, d. ca. AD 385), imitates his life, and copies texts.[10] Here, the story of Abu Fana appears (*Life*: fols. 12a–12b); it is a testament to his veneration in the medieval period.[11] During his time at the monastery, Ibrahim, despite his young age,[12] is ordained as a priest and later as a *hegumenos (qummus)* by a bishop who habitually studied in the monastery's library with him (*Life*: fols. 12a–13a).[13]

The Suffering of Ibrahim

This idyllic period at the monastery is cut short when disaster *(daiqa)* strikes the Christians of Egypt. Unlike most of its monks, Ibrahim refuses to leave the monastery and to go into hiding, a course of action that leads to his arrest and torture by a local official *(mutawalli)*. The author closely narrates the attempts of the authorities to force Ibrahim to abandon his religion. For example, he is tied behind a horse by some soldiers and dragged from village to village. The villagers bribe the official to stop the beatings of Ibrahim, who, rather than complaining, expresses his joy at experiencing the same sufferings as Christ (*Life*: fols. 13b–14a). To paraphrase Swanson, Ibrahim's steadfastness earned him a widespread reputation as a confessor of the faith (Swanson 2013a: 227), with his fame spreading throughout Upper Egypt upon his release and return to the monastery (*Life*: fol. 14a).

Discipleship under Murqus al-Antuni

After cursing an unrepentant deacon, who subsequently dies, Ibrahim experiences much anguish. He leaves the monastery and lives in a cell outside Akhmim. One day, he hears about Murqus al-Antuni and goes to him. Upon meeting Ibrahim, Murqus weeps and admonishes him about the importance of forgiveness. Ibrahim prays for the soul of the dead deacon, and later, upon learning that Murqus has engaged in prayer with the same intention during the same period, Ibrahim leaves Akhmim to live with

Murqus (*Life*: fols. 14a–17a). This episode, which emphasizes mercy, appears in the *Life of Murqus al-Antuni*, where the virtue of mercy is a key theme (e.g., Swanson 2010b: 112).

Following this episode, Ibrahim's time with Murqus at the Monastery of St. Antony, his fight with demons, his naming as Murqus's successor, and his master's eventual death are narrated (*Life*: fols. 17a–22b). Since these stories are essentially in harmony with those of the *Life of Murqus al-Antuni*,[14] it can be assumed that the author had access to the latter text when compiling Ibrahim's biography.

Ibrahim's Sojourn in Fustat

Subsequent to Murqus's death, Ibrahim seems to have traveled to Fustat to meet his brothers and disciples, one of whom is described as Patriarch Matta'us. Here, the narrative changes slightly. Many miracles attributed to Ibrahim are intimately recounted, which conveys the impression that either the author witnessed these events himself or the inhabitants of Cairo and Fustat described them to him (*Life*: fols. 22b–27a).

At this point in the narrative, Ibrahim, with his face shining and with snow-white hair and beard, is pictured as resembling the prophet Aaron. People are struck by his nobleness and humility. This portrayal is followed by various episodes of Ibrahim's time at Fustat: his prophecy of a young man's death, his cautioning a tax collector against cheating, the requests of farmers to bless their crops, his praying for the Nile to rise in the Buheira region of Lower Egypt, and so on. There is even an episode about Ibrahim's prophecy of Cairo's fate, which is an allusion to the Battle of Ankara between the Ottomans and Tamerlane in 1402. This incident strongly suggests that this hagiography was compiled at about that time.

Ibrahim's Death

The *Life* narrates that Ibrahim, realizing that he is near death, expresses a wish to return to his native village, much to the Cairenes' distress. After bidding the people farewell, Ibrahim departs for Minyat Bani Khasib. Upon his arrival, the villagers rejoice, thinking that he has come to sojourn as in the past. However, Ibrahim dies after only a few days. It seems that some of his disciples are at his side. He is buried at the Church of Abu Fis at Minyat Bani Khasib, next to the bishop who ordained him.[15] He is mourned at the Monastery of Shahran by Patriarch Matta'us and at the Monastery of St. Antony (*Life*: fols. 27b–30b).

Authorship

Given the textual evidence, it seems reasonable to assume that the author of the *Life* was a resident of Fustat or Cairo and a disciple of Ibrahim. I cannot determine whether he was a layman or a member of the clergy. The *Life*, probably written at the beginning of the fifteenth century (after 1402), does not show signs of later reworking. The author relied heavily on the *Life of Murqus al-Antuni*, which suggests that this text was in circulation when the *Life of Ibrahim al-Fani* was composed and that Murqus, who died ten years before his disciple, was still held in high esteem in Fustat at that time. As Swanson points out, the author emphasizes the relationship between Murqus and Ibrahim (Swanson 2007: 221; Swanson 2010b: 112). In spite of this observation, I am not certain whether it is accurate to say that Ibrahim was under Murqus's shadow. We learn from the *Life* that he was regarded as possessing unique saintly qualities, so much so as to have merited his own biography and the deep grief of the people of Fustat at his passing.

Purpose of Compilation

The *Life of Ibrahim* sends a clear message to those who read it or who heard it read aloud in church on his memorial day:[16] one should be a good Christian from an early age, honor and cherish one's mother, and follow the lives of the Church fathers and saints, such as Abu Fana, who inspired Ibrahim. Persecutions may occur, but they should be welcomed, for they allow believers to follow in the footsteps of Jesus Christ and his martyrs. However, we must, as Murqus admonished, forgive sinners. God sends holy men, such as Murqus and Ibrahim, to act as intercessors between God and man, and to support the community of believers in perilous times. For this reason, the Coptic communities of Cairo and Fustat are intact and thriving.

The structure of the *Life of Ibrahim* follows a traditional model, and most of its elements are found in other hagiographies. However, some elements, such as the arrest of Ibrahim or the various miracles attributed to him during his stay in Fustat, take the audience to a specific time in history, a period perhaps still fresh in memory. It is widely acknowledged that hagiographies and martyrologies were compiled to meet the religious and social needs of the community they sprang from and thus reflect the concerns of the laity and the clergy of the period (e.g., Heffernan 1988: 18–22; Armanios 2011: 42).[17] It thus appears that the *Life of Ibrahim* served as a witness account of the conditions of the Coptic community in the era in which Ibrahim lived and in which his hagiography was written, the late fourteenth to the early fifteenth centuries. This was a time of persecution and mass conversion for the Christians in Egypt (Little 1976; el-Leithy 2005).[18] During this era, the clergy and the laity demanded the portrayal of a holy man through contemporary and traditional stories.

It is reasonable to affirm, therefore, that this *Life* was written to encourage the Copts in a time of hardship and show the path that good Christians should follow, taking their communal experience and their understanding of it through the *Life* of a saint who was so steadfast in the face of persecution and adversity. In this way, the *Life of Ibrahim* served to strengthen the faith and the resolve of the Christians who were witnessing the diminishing of their community.[19]

Historical Significance of the *Life*

Beyond this inspirational value, the *Life of Ibrahim,* together with those of Murqus al-Antuni, Ruways, and Patriarch Matta'us, offers us a glimpse of the Coptic experiences of the period and the distinct viewpoints of the clergy who sanctioned this *Life*. Moreover, the text attests to the thriving monastic life during this particular era, when the monasteries of St. Antony and Abu Fana, and others, were filled with monks. This vibrant religious life is in stark contrast to the accounts of abandoned monasteries and destitute monks of the late fifteenth and sixteenth centuries (e.g., Gabra 2002: 174). Finally, the *Life* points to an active Coptic community in Cairo, despite the persecutions.

This beautifully executed work indicates the vibrant literary activities of the Coptic Church in the late fourteenth and the early fifteenth centuries. In the former century, the Coptic *Synaxarion*, a collection of brief biographies of saints and martyrs, was completed (Gabra 2008: 245–46). The Coptic community was quite active during this period, despite its persecution, as the production of manuscripts also demonstrates (Youssef 2009a: 108). In some ways, this vigor contradicts the general view that the Church was marginalized during this period (e.g., Little 1976). Had the Church been inactive, such cultural projects would not have been undertaken; thus, even if weakened, the Church still played a vital role in the Coptic community.

In a longer perspective, I suggest that while the eighth century witnessed the 'flowering' of martyrological writing in the Coptic Church (Papaconstantinou 2011: 334), the fourteenth century focused on recording the lives of contemporary holy men, a project that perhaps went hand in hand with the compilation of the *Synaxar*. Each saint's life, his miracles, and his function in the Coptic community varied. As mentioned earlier, it is difficult to tell what the author laments more, Ibrahim's death or his abandonment of Fustat, where his presence was vital to the community.

Whether this *Life* enjoyed popularity or not is hard to determine, as only one known copy of this manuscript survives. However, this evidence could strengthen the argument that this *Life* was compiled to meet a specific requirement of believers at a specific time in history.

Conclusion

Although the power of the patriarch was weak and many Copts were converting to Islam in the fourteenth and fifteenth centuries, the Coptic community, along with its clergy and notables, was still functioning and chose the lives of their holy men as models for all Christians to follow. In terms of the Christian–Muslim relationship, this time is regarded as an era of mass conversion. However, the Coptic Church has survived to the present. I believe that the compilation of saints' *Lives* played a major role in its survival strategy, uniting the people around the faithfulness of holy individuals. Ibrahim's life and biography provides one such story of resilience.

Notes

1 I would like to thank Dr. Gawdat Gabra and Dr. Fawzy Estafanous for giving me the opportunity to present this paper at the symposium and to Fr. Wadi Awad, Dr. Mark N. Swanson, and Dr. Youhanna Nessim Youssef for their encouragement and advice during my work on the *Lives* of Murqus al-Antuni, Ruways, and Ibrahim al-Fani as a part of my dissertation.

2 For an overview of Copto-Arabic hagiographies of holy men, see Graf 1944–53, vol. 2: 474–75; see also the individual entries on each saint for an update by Wadi Abullif (misspelled Abuliff) in the *Enciclopedia dei Santi* (1998) and by Mark N. Swanson in *Christian–Muslim Relations: A Biographical History* (2013a).

3 For the medieval town of Minyat Bani Khasib, see Abu al-Makarim 1984, vol. 2: 78a; al-Maqrizi 2003, vol. 4, pt. 2: 1081.

4 *Kitab al-Ibsalmudiya*: 78; Sawirus Ibn al-Muqaffa' 1970, vol. 3, pt. 2: 137(text), 237 (translation).

5 Dayr Anba Antuni, MS *tarikh* 69 (formerly 75), fols. 3b–31b. Hereafter referred to as *Life*. I am deeply grateful to Dr. Gawdat Gabra for making available a copy of this manuscript.

6 Most Copto-Arabic hagiographies consist of a *Life* and a *Miracle* (e.g., Swanson 2007: 218).

7 While the author of the *Life* clearly admires the martyrs, the author of the *Life of Ruways* has a more ambiguous attitude toward the martyrs of the same era (Swanson 2007: 226–27; Swanson 2010b: 117).

8 For the reading of Fis (as in the text of the *Life*, and not as Qis in the editions of Abu al-Makarim), see Samu'il al-Suriany's note in Abu al-Makarim 1984, vol. 2: fol. 78a.

9 The name of the monastery is only revealed at this point in the narrative. The fifteenth-century historian al-Maqrizi relates that "[the] Monastery of Abu Fana used to house a thousand monks. Now there are only two." Although it is not clear from al-Maqrizi's account at what period the monastery housed so many monks, the passage in the *Life* suggests that this monastery was still prospering in the fourteenth century (al-Maqrizi 2003, vol. 4, pt. 2: 1040).

10 Among the many fourteenth-century saints, Ibrahim is the only one whose studies are mentioned. It is well known that the copying of manuscripts was an important occupation of the monks in the Ottoman period. Here, it is interesting to note that Ibrahim seems to have pursued this occupation (e.g., Armanios 2011: 69; Murre-van den Berg 2006: 17).

11 For the Arabic *Life of Abu Fana*, see Gabra 1990.

12 This reference to his young age is puzzling. In the *History of the Patriarchs,* Ibrahim is reported to have protested against the future Patriarch Matta'us's ordination as a priest, arguing that he was too young (Sawirus Ibn al-Muqaffa' 1979, vol. 3, pt. 2: 137 [text], 236–37 [translation]).

13 I am not certain whether the term *hegumenos* refers to 'the head of the monastery' here. The name of the bishop is not mentioned.

14 The *Life of Murqus al-Antuni* is unpublished. For details about this *Life*, see Swanson 2013a: 203–206. I thank Dr. Gawdat Gabra for providing me with a copy of one of the manuscripts.

15 This church is mentioned by Abu al-Makarim, but not in al-Maqrizi's *Khitat*, which suggests that it was destroyed in the fifteenth century, before al-Maqrizi's time.

16 The preface of the *Life of Barsauma al-'Uryan* calls out to "Christ-loving people, gathered in God's church for the commemoration of our saintly father Barsauma" (Crum 1907a: 143).

17 For Armanios's discussion on the communal ethos depicted in an Ottoman martyrology, see Armanios 2011: 41–47.

18 For a detailed analysis of the conversion process of this period, see el-Leithy 2005.

19 As Armanios notes, this idea of hagiographies used as a tool to strengthen the Christian community has been frequently explored (Armanios 2011: 174 n. 1).

16 Snippets from the Past

Two Ancient Sites in the Asyut Region: Dayr al-Gabrawi and Dayr al-'Izam

Jacques van der Vliet

Asyut/Lykopolis in Late Antiquity

There can be little doubt about the importance of the city of Asyut in the Christian history of Egypt. Even if it is unlikely that Alexander of Lykopolis, the fourth-century author of a witty treatise against the Manichaeans, was really a bishop of that city—as is still occasionally maintained—Melitius, the originator of the Melitian schism, also in the fourth century, certainly was. In the early seventh century, Constantine of Asyut, a contemporary of Patriarch Damian, was one of the prominent bishops of the nascent Severan ('miaphysite') Church, the precursor of the present-day Coptic Orthodox Church. In the period of the persecutions, it was the scene of many martyrdoms, and in the fourth–fifth centuries it was a renowned center of monasticism with which the names of Paul of Tamma and John of Lykopolis remain associated. Still in the early seventh century, John Moschos's *Spiritual Meadow* bears witness to the reputation of its monasteries.

Asyut was a major Christian center, as it still is today, and in late antique and early medieval times its hinterland was covered with monastic settlements and sanctuaries devoted to the cult of the martyrs, many of them centers of pilgrimage. Indeed, historical maps of the region show a remarkable density and concentration of Christian sites, stretching from the region of Abnub on the east bank, via the ancient necropolises of Asyut itself, mainly on the west bank, to the region of Shotb, south of the city (see, for instance, Wipszycka 2009: 142). Yet all these ancient sites left surprisingly few traces in the modern scholarly record. Thus, when one consults the Brussels database of Coptic documentary papyri, the turnout for Asyut is almost nil (see Delattre 2012a, under "Provenance: Assiout"). And even though several of the ancient monasteries around Asyut are honored by an article in *The Coptic Encyclopedia*, they appear to have little to contribute to our knowledge of Coptic Egypt. Hence, while Melitius, Constantine, and John of Lykopolis continue to attract scholarly attention, our picture of the broader Christian landscape of Asyut in premodern times remains hazy and patchy.

The background of this somewhat sad state of affairs is to be sought in the ruthless exploitation of the region by the would-be archaeologists who, in the nineteenth and twentieth centuries, plundered the sites around Asyut, in particular the rich necropolises of the Old and Middle Kingdoms. These dilettanti and treasure hunters were exclusively interested in pharaonic antiquities and hardly ever in more recent material. For the Christian antiquities of the region the loss was disastrous. Architectural remains were destroyed and poorly recorded, if at all. Other evidence, apart from some inscriptions, was sold on the antiquities market to join the mass of objects and documents for which no certain provenance is known and which—as a result—became virtually worthless for historical research.

In the following pages I intend to illustrate these points by briefly evoking the example of two sites that in recent decades have received a certain amount of scholarly interest: Dayr al-Gabrawi (north of Asyut, near Abnub) and Dayr al-ʿIzam (west of Asyut).

Dayr al-Gabrawi: The Martyrium of St. Victor the General?

Dayr al-Gabrawi is famous mostly for its Old Kingdom rock-cut tombs dating from the Sixth Dynasty.[1] These were published in 1902 by Norman de Garis Davies, whose team also copied some of the Coptic inscriptions that are witness to the monastic reuse of the tombs (summarily edited by W.E. Crum in Davies 1902, vol. 2: 45–46). The tombs were republished in more recent years (Kanawati 2005–13), but this new publication is exclusively focused on the Old Kingdom reliefs. In addition to the tombs, there is a Christian village, sometimes called Dayr Abu Buqtur al-Gabrawi, after the patron of its church, St. Victor, a martyr from the era of Diocletian.[2] The present village church appears to be a fairly recent building, but in the immediate neighborhood various remains of a presumably late-antique date have been identified. Among these are a structure described as a Roman basilica and sites locally known as the 'Chapel of Sitt Barbara' and the 'Monastery of Sitt Barbara,' designations that appear to have very little historical foundation.

The various ancient and medieval remains of Dayr al-Gabrawi were the object of a German survey in the early 1980s. This resulted in an inventory of archaeological sites and an archaeological map of sorts (D. Kurth in Kurth and Rößler-Köhler 1987: 186–94, with maps 1 and 3, plans 6–7). Regrettably the architectural remains recorded for Dayr al-Gabrawi gave rise to widely divergent interpretations and—as a result—considerable confusion (see the authoritative discussion in Grossmann 1991b). The site is redeemed by a Latin inscription that—although non-Christian in character—is of great interest for the Christian history of the region. The stone inscription, commonly designated as *CIL* III 22 (= Mommsen 1873: 8, no. 22), has been known since the seventeenth century.[3] According to rumor, the stone was built into the walls of the modern village church as recently as the 1980s, but it has not actually been seen by visitors since the nineteenth century.

The Latin text is dedicatory in nature. It records the construction of the camp *(castra)* of a Roman military division, the First Cohort of the Lusitanians, by the emperors Diocletian and Maximian in AD 288. The establishment of this stronghold was part of the thorough military reorganization of the empire under Diocletian, which for Egypt resulted among other things in the withdrawal of the southern, Nubian frontier to Philae and the building of a chain of fortifications along the Nile (van Berchem 1952: 59–71). The ruins of a so-called 'basilica' on the northeast of the modern village of Dayr al-Gabrawi are most likely remains of this Roman camp (Grossmann 1991b: 171–73; Coquin, Martin, and Grossmann 1991b: 811–12).

The official inscription of the year 288 combined with the plausible archaeological identification of Roman military architecture on site allows a series of important historical inferences (for which, see primarily Horn 1988: xi–xix; Horn 1992: 128–37). A somewhat later Roman source, the *Notitia Dignitatum*, from the end of the fourth century, situates the camp of the First Cohort of the Lusitanians, mentioned in the Latin inscription, near a place called Theraco, a name that is traditionally emended to Hieracon on the authority of another Roman source, the *Antonine Itinerary*.[4] The *Itinerary*, which dates from the time of Diocletian itself, situates the settlement of Hieracon on the east bank of the Nile, south of Antinoopolis, actually at the approximate location of Dayr al-Gabrawi (cf. Bell 1942: 144; Timm 1984–92, vol. 4: 1950–51).

In the medieval hagiographical literature about the military martyr St. Victor, the son of Romanus ('Victor the General'), a *kastron* (fortified settlement) of Hierakion, south of Antinoopolis, is mentioned as the place of his martyrdom and death, most notably in the account of his martyrdom that survives in Sahidic Coptic (Budge 1914: 28; Elanskaya 1969: 47–48). In Jürgen Horn's view, the hagiographic tradition concerning St. Victor can be traced back to the late fourth century, even if the Sahidic version of the martyrdom, which mentions Hierakion, is definitely of a much later date (see Horn 1988: lxxi–lxxiii). In any case, a presumably Sahidic martyrdom of St. Victor circulated already in seventh- and eighth-century Thebes (Crum 1921: no. 281), and his cult is attested for the city of Asyut itself in the sixth century (Papaconstantinou 2001: 63, citing a document that mentions a chapel of the saint), which presupposes the local existence of a martyrology.

Therefore, in spite of the late date of the manuscripts, which are from the tenth century, it seems probable that the *kastron* of Hierakion in the Sahidic martyrdom of Victor preserves the memory of the military camp near Hieracon, likewise situated south of Antinoopolis, which was home to the First Cohort of the Lusitanians at the time of Diocletian.[5] The implication is clear: Dayr al-Gabrawi, where the Lusitanians were stationed, may have been the very place where the military saint Victor suffered his martyrdom. The location of Victor's martyrdom and subsequent cult at Dayr al-Gabrawi would seem to be corroborated by the traditional dedication of the local church to the same St. Victor as well as by other hagiographical traditions. Thus, the medieval literature on St. Claudius of Antioch, whose cult was centered in the Asyut region, locates a sanctuary of St. Victor on the east bank, south of Antinoopolis and north of Asyut, precisely where Dayr al-Gabrawi is situated (Papaconstantinou 2001: 66). The wealth of its church attracted the three robbers in the well-known story, told in a homily attributed to Constantine of Asyut, which relates a predatory foray ending with the arrest and conversion of the thieves by St. Claudius himself (Godron 1970: 640–54; see the reconstruction of their itinerary in Drescher 1942: 77 n. 2, and 85).

Supposing that the various assumptions and identifications proposed above prove to be correct, Dayr al-Gabrawi *might* have housed a major sanctuary of a famous martyr from the great persecutions, Victor the son of Romanus, and the site *might* offer an interesting example of the Christian reuse of Roman military architecture. Regrettably, however, too little archaeological work has been done on the various sites of Dayr al-Gabrawi to be firmly positive on any of these points. Tracing the whereabouts of the Latin inscription of emperors Diocletian and Maximian may be a good starting point for any further research.

Dayr al-'Izam: The Hermitage of John of Lykopolis?

Dayr al-'Izam, or 'the Monastery of the Bones,' is situated in the western necropolis of Asyut.[6] The city's extensive cemeteries are famous as the provenance of many of the Middle Kingdom sarcophagi that bear versions of the so-called Coffin Texts, an important collection of Egyptian funerary rituals. The link with these ancient texts sparked a recent revival of interest in the necropolis as a whole. A German project, directed by Jochem Kahl, not only conducts excavations on site, but also intends to document its history up to modern times (see in particular Kahl 2007a and Kahl 2013). The project also pays due attention to the period of its Christian reuse, and we may hope to be better informed in the near future than we are now.

The monastic site of Dayr al-'Izam was excavated, or rather plundered, by two local amateur diggers in September 1897. A brief report of their most important finds appeared a few years later (Maspero 1900). A very schematic map (after V. de Bock) was published in 1912 by Somers Clarke in his *Christian Antiquities in the Nile Valley* (Clarke 1912: 179). Later accounts are largely dependent on this scarce information, as the site appears to have suffered destruction later on (Coquin, Martin, and Grossmann 1991a). The finds made in 1897 include the sad remains of a medieval monastic library, comprising twenty-four fragments of parchment and paper codices. These texts are still unpublished, but they were briefly analyzed by W.E. Crum shortly after their discovery (Crum 1902: nos. 8080–8103). The find consists of biblical, apocryphal, homiletic, and liturgical texts, predominantly in Sahidic. In spite of its piteous state, the collection has its importance, in particular since Crum was able to link some of the fragments to manuscripts kept in the French National Library, presumably originating from the White Monastery near Sohag. The future study of medieval Coptic literature would undoubtedly benefit from a full publication of the find.

Another important find is an amphora inscribed with a long text in Sahidic Coptic from the year 1155/56 (Crum 1902: no. 8104, plate I). As the inscription is of considerable historical significance it will be translated in full below, at the end of this chapter. It identifies the place where the jar was buried and inscribed as the 'monastery of Apa John of the Desert,' a name that is also found in some other medieval sources (for which, see Coquin, Martin, and Grossmann 1991a; Timm 1984–92, vol. 2: 830–31).

That this 'monastery of Apa John of the Desert' at Dayr al-'Izam is the same as a 'monastery of Apa John of the rock (or mountain) of Siout (Asyut),' known from earlier sources, is possible, but quite uncertain (see Kahle 1954: 24; Timm 1984–92, vol. 2: 829–33). In any case, the Apa John who gave his name to the monastery may well have been—in the opinion of many scholars—none other than John of Lykopolis, a famous monk from the late fourth century, who indeed must have lived at some distance west of Asyut. Hence, Dayr al-'Izam is generally identified as the historical hermitage of St. John of Lykopolis (for instance, both Doresse 2000: 422 and Grossmann 2002: 208 n. 20 find this a likely assumption).

Although the identification is not supported by contemporaneous, late-antique material from the site of Dayr al-'Izam itself, it served as the basis for an interesting hypothesis, brought forward some twenty years ago by the papyrologist Constantine Zuckerman (1995: 188–94). In his view, Dayr al-'Izam would be the likely provenance of the so-called archive of Apa John, a group of Greek and Coptic papyri from somewhere in Middle Egypt that used to be loosely associated with the Hermopolite nome, as are many other Middle Egyptian papyri. The bilingual 'archive' dates from the late fourth century and consists of letters addressing a monk, Apa John, who apparently was well connected with the higher society of his time and who might very well be the sort of influential person John of Lykopolis was.[7] The papyri had appeared on the antiquities market briefly after the amateur diggings at Dayr al-'Izam in 1897 and were soon dispersed over various, mainly British, collections. According to Zuckerman's reconstruction, the amateur excavators of Dayr al-'Izam would have handed some of their finds over to the Antiquities Service, while keeping the more valuable papyri for themselves to bring them piecemeal on the market.

Zuckerman's hypothesis is very attractive (for a generally positive discussion, see Wipszycka 2009: 83–85). It would at once confirm the connection of John of Lykopolis with Dayr al-'Izam and provide us with the social network of an important holy man from late antiquity, known from various literary sources as a major figure in early Egyptian monasticism. Yet it is also very fragile. The provenance of the dossier of Apa John in Dayr al-'Izam is far from proven and—even if it were—John is and was a very common name. There must have been hundreds of 'Apa Johns' in late antique and early medieval Egypt! Hence, Zuckerman's thesis was accepted by some, but received critically by others, for instance by Malcolm Choat, who announced a comprehensive (re-)edition of the archive (see, preliminarily, Choat 2007, in particular 180–83 for a discussion of Zuckerman's thesis). In my opinion, it can at best be accepted as an attractive working hypothesis that can be falsified, not by reflections of a general nature, but only by a prosopographical analysis of the archive of Apa John. Where does the social network of this Apa John fit in topographically: in the Asyut region, or instead more to the north, in the neighborhood of Hermopolis? Another way by which Zuckerman's thesis could be tested would be fieldwork on the spot. Does the medieval 'monastery of Apa John of the Desert' at Dayr al-'Izam indeed hark back to the fourth century? For the time being, unequivocal evidence to this effect, be it archaeological or papyrological, appears to be lacking.

Conclusions

The monasteries of Asyut tell a sad story of destruction and neglect. Asyut must have been an important Christian center in late antiquity, as it is today, but hardly anything survives that can be used to document its history in this period. The connections that have been postulated between Dayr al-Gabrawi and St. Victor the General, and between Dayr al-'Izam and St. John of Lykopolis, and which I have briefly discussed here, rest on slender evidence and the arguments in favor of them are extremely fragile. Only a combination of further research in the field *and* in museum and library collections may help to reconstruct a world that now seems largely lost.

Appendix: The Jar from Dayr al-'Izam

The Sahidic inscription on the amphora mentioned above is historically interesting on various scores. It shows that in the twelfth century Dayr al-'Izam bore the name of 'monastery of Apa John of the Desert,' but also that it maintained contacts with the region of Akhmim farther south. In addition, the text presents a rather gloomy picture of the circumstances under which not only Fatimid rule but also many medieval monasteries succumbed. Yet it has never—to the best of my knowledge—been translated into English (for a French translation, see Mallon 1914: 2866). The following translation is made after the text printed by Maspero (1900: 117–18), but takes into account the important corrections published by V. Loret (1903: 104). I furthermore collated Maspero's readings with the published photograph (Crum 1902: pl. I), which shows only part of the text, however. Later re-editions (such as Hasitzka 1993: no. 299) lack independent value. Crum (1902: no. 8104) provides a detailed description of the jar.

God have mercy on us, me, Papa Basile, and my brother, the deacon Pakire, the sons of the blessed Papa Joseph, from Talmarage (al-Maragha) in the province of Shmin (Akhmim), who assumed—beyond our worth—that name of 'monk' in this monastery of Apa John of the Desert—may his blessings be with us. Amen.

In the brief and insignificant days that we have consumed, this tiny bit of perfume, which is this myrrh, came in and we stored it for who will come after us. Its amount is nine quarters, of which there are twelve in an *oipe*.

(We did this in the year of) the Era of the Martyrs 872 (AD 1155/56), when there was famine in the land of Egypt, in particular the city of Siout (Asyut), and violence from the part of the authorities in charge and unrest from outside, due to the Arabs and the people who had become infuriated with each other. O Lord, help us!

And we believe in the creed that was established in Nicaea by the 318 bishops, which professes the Father and the Son and the Holy Spirit, one single Godhead—to Him be the glory. Amen.

As an afterword, it may be added that the jar and its contents were found sealed and intact, and that since the days of Basile and Pakire no one had apparently made use of the myrrh.

Notes

1 For the pharaonic antiquities of Dayr al-Gabrawi, see now Moreno García 2012.

2 For the toponym, see Horn 1992: 65, with n. 172. The designation 'Dayr' does not necessarily imply that it was the site of an ancient monastery, as it may refer to any ancient Christian settlement. For general accounts of Christian Dayr al-Gabrawi, see Coquin, Martin, and Grossmann 1991b; Timm 1984–92, vol. 1: 41–44 (under Abnub); vol. 4: 1949–52; Horn 1992: 65–66, 128–37.

3 See Sicard 1982a: 14–15, with the notes by M. Martin, about the place where the stone was located in 1716.

4 Cf. the apparatus of the latest edition of the *Notitia*, Neira Faleiro 2005: 254.

5 Note, however, that the Greco-Latin word *kastron*, 'fortified place,' has a different range of meaning than the Latin *castra*, 'army camp'; see, for discussion, Łajtar 1997: 44–45.

6 For general accounts, see Clarke 1912: 178–79; Coquin, Martin, and Grossmann 1991a; Doresse 2000: 418–23, cf. 571–72; Kahl 2007: 99–102; Kahl 2013: 126–29.

7 See, in addition to Zuckerman 1995, van Minnen 1994: 80–85; Choat and Gardner 2006; Choat 2007; Gonis 2008; Wipszycka 2009: 83–85.

17 Liturgy of the Monastery of al-Muharraq

Youhanna Nessim Youssef

THE MONASTERY OF AL-MUHARRAQ has special peculiarities in its liturgical practice.[1] For example, the term used there for 'hymn' is different from all other manuscripts: *luhunat*, rather than *alhan*. There are even differences in the musical instruments, as the monks of the Monastery of al-Muharraq use, in addition to the traditional *naqus* (or *daff*) and the triangle, another instrument called the cymbal *(sanj)* (Moftah, Robertson, and Roy 1991).

This monastery was the only one to survive throughout the Middle Ages in Upper Egypt. Some of its monks were learned people, such as the monk Iqluda (Claudius), who was the brother of Patriarch Gabriel IV and took part in the consecration of the *myron* in the year AD 1374 (Youssef and Zanetti 2014: 22). This monk ordered the copying of important manuscripts, among them the *Philocalia* (Khalil 1993) and the interpretation of the Apocalypse by Ibn Katib Qaysar (Ms 52 Theology—Monastery of St. Antony, dated AM 1117 (AD 1401); the manuscript was copied in the scriptorium of the Monastery of St. Antony).[2] Another example is the monk Girgis, who was the abbot of the Monastery of al-Muharraq (Anba Gregorius 1968: 194; Dayr al-Muharraq 1990: 119) in the late eighteenth century and copied the critical edition of the four gospels of Ibn al-'Assal,[3] now preserved in the Coptic Museum (62 Biblica).[4] (This means that the readership in the monastery was able to appreciate such an important book.)

There are also some oral traditions that have never been recorded before, and that are unique to this monastery. Among them, we can mention that when the priest blesses the people, he turns to his left (which is the right of the altar); the same can be said for the opening of the curtain of the altar, which is also done from the right.[5]

R.F.G. Viaud studied the procession of the Feast of the Cross and noted several peculiarities, such as a station near the tomb of Musa or Salome (Viaud 1967–68).

In a previous article I highlighted the importance of the doxology of the consecration of the sanctuary of the church of al-Muharraq (Youssef 2009b). In this chapter I will highlight some other texts related to the monastery:

- the *tarh* of the consecration of the church of Qusqam (tune Batos and tune Adam)
- the Arabic *tarh* for the same occasion
- the synaxarion (the Upper Egyptian version commemorating the consecration of the church of Qusqam)
- *psalis*, tune Batos and tune Adam
- commemoration of an abbot of al-Muharraq

The liturgy in this monastery is characterized by four features:

1. A local hagiographical tradition through adding the names of many local saints to the *memento sanctorum*, such as Hermina, Isidore, and Sana.
2. The presence of the Holy Family in the place. This is represented by the cult of 6 Hatur, where there is a special rite unique to the monastery, the Feast of the Entry of the Holy Family into Egypt, and special stations in the rite of Palm Sunday. The consecration of the Church of the Virgin Mary on 6 Hatur has a special rite in the Ethiopian Church. For this feast, the *Anaphora* of the Lord is used (Daoud 1959: 98). This liturgy is used only three times a year. The two other occasions are 26 Ba'una, the consecration of the Church of the Virgin in Philippe, and 16 Misra, the ascension of her body. The service on 8 Ba'una marks the consecration of the Church of Mahama—a Lower Egyptian counterpart to the feast of 6 Hatur in Middle Egypt.
3. The rite for the Nile. This rite is performed on the Feast of the Cross, 17 Tut, when the priest offers incense at the highest point reached by the flood.
4. Survival of the Greek language. The region of Asyut in general and the Monastery of al-Muharraq in particular preserved the Greek

language for a long time. The manuscripts of the Basilian anaphora in Greek came from the Asyut region, from places such as Abnub and Asyut itself (Budde 2004: 85–88). There is also an ode of Kiyahk (Youssef 2013), and another hymn for the eve of the Nativity, in which there are stanzas in both Greek and Sahidic; it begins with "Your Star Appeared" (Youssef 2012). This hymn is attested in Manuscript 106, "Liturgy." This manuscript contains the narration of the rite of the consecration of the *myron* that took place under the patriarchate of Gabriel IV, who was, before his ordination, a monk from the Monastery of al-Muharraq. His brother was also a monk from the same monastery (see above) (Youssef and Zanetti 2014).

Hymn for the Eve of the Nativity

It is important to mention that the hymn, "Your Star Appeared," suits the context of Nativity Eve, rather than the consecration of the *myron*. Matthew chapter 2—the visit of the Magi to Christ—is read at the Feast of the Nativity in the Coptic Church and this hymn is the last to be sung during communion on the Eve of the Nativity, as preparation for the congregation for the advent of Christ, as if the Magi were advancing toward Bethlehem. The ideas treated in this hymn resemble those of the Nativity hymn composed by Romanos Melodos (Youssef 1998–99).

O.H.E. Burmester was the first to attract the attention of the scholarly world to the importance of this manuscript in his pioneering study on the *Turuhat* (Burmester 1938: especially 175). We will study Manuscript 323 Lit. Coptic Museum (fol. 161), which contains the commemoration of 6 Hatur and the Arabic *tarh*.[6]

Ms 323 Lit. (Simaika and 'Abd al-Masih 1939: 84, no. 171). Consecration of the Church, 6 Hatur: Coptic Text

ⲤⲞⲨ `ⲘⲠⲒⲀⲂⲞⲦ ⲀⲐⲰⲢ ⲞⲨⲀⲄⲒⲀⲤⲘⲞⲤ `ⲚϮⲈⲔⲔⲖⲎⲤⲒⲀ ⲔⲞⲌⲔⲀⲘ ⲎⲬ
ⲂⲀⲦⲞⲤ

ⲀⲖⲎⲐⲰⲤ ⲀⲒϮ ⲘⲠⲀⲞⲨⲰϢ ⲈⲒ ⲈⲢⲈⲦⲒⲚ ⲘⲠⲞⲨⲢⲞ ⲆⲀⲨⲒⲆ ⲈⲐⲂⲈ ⲠⲦⲀⲒⲞ
ⲘⲠⲀⲒⲘⲀ ⲈⲐ̅ ⲚⲦⲈ ϮⲐⲈⲞⲦⲞⲔⲞⲤ ⲘⲀⲢⲒⲀ

ϨⲒⲚⲀ ⲚⲦⲈϤⲦⲀⲘⲞⲚ ⲈⲠⲰⲞⲨ `ⲘⲠⲦⲀⲒⲞ `ⲘⲠⲀⲒⲚⲒϢϮ `ⲚⲦⲞⲠⲞⲤ ⲈⲦⲀ ⲪϮ
ⲚⲀϢⲰⲠⲒ `ⲚϦⲎⲦϤ ⲚⲈⲘ ⲦⲈϤⲘⲀⲨ `ⲘⲠⲀⲢⲐⲈⲚⲞⲤ

ⲠⲈϪⲈ ⲆⲀⲨⲒⲆ ⲠⲒ ⲈⲢⲞⲮⲀⲖⲦⲎⲤ ϪⲈ ϨⲰⲤ ϨⲀⲚϢⲞⲨⲘⲈⲚⲢⲒⲦⲞⲨ ⲚⲈ
ⲚⲈⲔⲘⲀⲚϢⲰⲠⲒ ⲠϬ̅Ⲥ̅ ⲪϮ ⲚⲦⲈ ⲚⲒϪⲞⲘ ⲠⲈⲚⲚⲞⲨϮ

ⲘⲀⲢⲈⲚⲰϢⲀⲒ ⲚⲀⲚ ⲚⲈⲘ ⲚⲀ ⲚⲒⲪⲎⲞⲨⲒ ϦⲈⲚ ⲪⲀⲒ ⲈϨⲞⲞⲨ[7] ⲈⲐⲞⲨⲀⲂ ⲞⲨⲞϨ
ⲚⲦⲈⲚⲈⲢⲮⲀⲖⲒⲚ ⲚⲈⲘ ⲠⲬⲰⲢⲞⲤ ⲚⲚⲎⲈⲐⲞⲨⲀⲂ

ⲈⲚⲰϢ ⲈⲂⲞⲖ ⲈⲚϪⲰ ⲘⲘⲞⲤ ϪⲈ ⲐⲀⲒ ⲦⲈ ϮⲠⲨⲖⲎ ⲚⲦⲈ Ⲡ̅Ϭ̅Ⲥ̅ ⲈⲢⲈ ⲚⲒⲐⲘⲎⲒ
ⲚⲀϢⲈ ⲈϦⲞⲨⲚ ̀ⲚϦⲎⲦⲤ ⲐⲀⲒ ⲦⲈ ϮⲠⲨⲖⲎ ⲚⲦⲈ ⲦⲪⲈ

ⲐⲀⲒ ⲦⲈ ϮⲈⲔⲔⲖⲎⲤⲒⲀ ⲚⲦⲀⲪⲘⲎⲒ ⲚⲦⲈ ⲚⲒⲀⲄⲄⲈⲖⲞⲤ ⲞⲨⲞϨ ⲠⲬ̅Ⲥ̅
ⲬⲒⲢⲞⲆⲞⲚⲒⲚ ⲚⲀⲤ ϦⲈⲚ ⲦⲈϤϪⲒϪ ̀ⲘⲪⲎⲈⲦϬⲞⲤⲒ

ⲈϪⲈⲚ ⲪⲢⲀⲚ ⲚϮⲐⲈⲞⲦⲞⲔⲞⲤ ⲘⲀⲢⲒⲀ ϮⲠⲀⲢⲐⲈⲚⲞⲤ ϮϢⲈⲖⲈⲦ
ⲚⲔⲀⲐⲀⲢⲞⲤ ⲠϢⲞⲨϢⲞⲨ ̀ⲚⲚⲒⲠⲀⲢⲐⲈⲚⲞⲤ ⲦⲎⲢⲞⲨ

ⲐⲀⲒ ⲦⲈ ⲈⲦⲀϤϢⲰⲠⲒ ⲈⲐⲂⲎⲦⲤ ⲮⲰϮ ⲚⲀⲆⲀⲘ ⲠⲈⲚⲒⲰⲦ ⲈⲂⲞⲖϦⲈⲚ
ϮⲠⲀⲢⲀⲂⲀⲤⲒⲤ ⲈⲦⲀϤⲈⲢⲦⲞⲖⲘⲀⲚ ⲈⲢⲞⲤ

ⲤⲈⲘⲠϢⲀ ⲚⲀⲚ ϦⲀ ⲚⲒⲖⲀⲞⲤ ⲚⲒϢⲎⲢⲒ Ⲛ̀ⲞⲢⲐⲞⲆⲞⲜⲞⲤ ⲈⲚϪⲰ ⲘⲘⲞⲤ ⲚⲈⲘ
ⲆⲀⲨⲒⲆ ⲠⲞⲨⲢⲞ ⲠⲒϨⲨⲘⲚⲞⲦⲞⲤ

ϪⲈ ⲀⲤⲞϨⲒ ⲈⲢⲀⲦⲤ ⲚϪⲈ ϮⲞⲨⲢⲰ ⲤⲀⲞⲨⲒⲚⲀⲘ ⲘⲘⲞⲔ ⲠⲞⲨⲢⲞ ϦⲈⲚ
ⲞⲨϬⲒϨⲰⲂⲤ ⲚⲒⲈⲂ ⲚⲚⲞⲨⲂ ⲈⲤⲤⲈⲖⲤⲰⲖ ϦⲈⲚ ⲞⲨⲐⲞ ⲚⲢⲎϮ

ⲦⲰⲂϨ ⲘⲠ̅Ϭ̅Ⲥ̅ ⲈϨⲢⲎⲒ

ⲚⲐⲞϤ ⲞⲚ ⲀⲆⲀⲘ

ⲀϤϪⲒ ̀ⲘⲠⲈⲚϬ̅Ⲥ̅[8] Ⲓ̅Ⲏ̅Ⲥ̅ ⲈⲠⲦⲰⲞⲨ ̀ⲚⲔⲞⲤⲔⲀⲘ ⲚⲈⲘ ⲦⲈϤⲘⲀⲨ ⲘⲀⲢⲒⲀ ⲚⲈⲘ
ⲚⲈϤⲘⲀⲐⲎⲦⲎⲤ

ⲚⲈⲘ ⲚⲒⲀⲄⲄⲈⲖⲞⲤ Ⲉ̅Ⲑ̅ ⲚⲈⲘ ⲚⲒⲬⲈⲢⲞⲨⲂⲒⲘ ⲚⲈⲘ ⲚⲒⲤⲈⲢⲀⲪⲘ ⲚⲈⲘ
ⲚⲒⲀⲠⲞⲤⲦⲞⲖⲞⲤ

ⲚⲈⲘ ⲚⲒⲠⲀⲦⲢⲒⲀⲢⲬⲎⲤ ⲚⲈⲘ ⲚⲒⲠⲢⲞⲪⲎⲦⲎⲤ ⲚⲈⲘ ⲚⲒϪⲞⲘ ̀ⲚⲦⲈ ⲦⲪⲈ
ⲤⲈⲚⲀⲐⲰⲞⲨϮ ϨⲀⲢⲞϤ

ⲞⲨⲞϨ ⲀϤⲈⲢϨⲎⲦⲤ ⲚϪⲈ Ⲓ̅Ⲏ̅Ⲥ̅ ⲠⲈⲚϬ̅Ⲥ̅ ϦⲈⲚ ⲞⲨⲬⲒⲢⲞⲆⲞⲚⲒⲚ ⲘⲠⲒⲈⲢⲪⲈⲒ
ⲈⲐⲞⲨⲀⲂ

ⲞⲨⲞϨ ⲀⲨ̀ⲒⲚⲒ ϨⲀⲢⲞϤ ̀ⲚⲞⲨⲦⲢⲀⲠⲈⲌⲀ ⲚⲈⲘ ⲞⲨⲀⲪⲞⲦ ⲚⲈⲘ ⲚⲒⲤⲔⲈⲨⲞⲤ
ⲚⲦⲈ ⲠⲒⲘⲀⲚⲈⲢϢⲰⲞⲨϢⲒ

ⲀϤⲦⲰⲚϤ ̀ⲚϪⲈ Ⲡ̅Ϭ̅Ⲥ̅ Ⲓ̅Ⲏ̅Ⲥ̅ ⲀϤⲤⲘⲞⲨ ̀ⲘⲠⲒⲎⲒ ⲞⲨⲞϨ ⲈⲢⲤⲪⲢⲀⲄⲒⲌⲒⲚ
̀ⲘⲘⲞϤ ϦⲈⲚ ⲦⲈϤϪⲒϪ ⲈⲐⲞⲨⲀⲂ

ⲞⲨⲞϨ ⲀϤϤⲀⲒ ̀ⲚⲦⲈϤ ϪⲒϪ ̀ⲚϪⲈ ⲠⲈⲚϬ̅Ⲥ̅ Ⲓ̅Ⲏ̅Ⲥ̅ ⲀϤⲤⲘⲞⲨ ⲈⲢⲞϤ ⲞⲨⲞϨ
ⲀϤϢⲈⲠϨⲘⲞⲦ

ⲈϤⲈⲢⲬⲒⲢⲞⲆⲞⲚⲒⲚ ̀ⲚϮⲈⲔⲔⲖⲎⲤⲒⲀ ⲚⲈⲘ ⲚⲈⲤⲤⲔⲈⲨⲞⲤ ⲦⲎⲢⲞⲨ ⲚⲈⲘ
ⲚⲒⲘⲀⲚⲈⲢϢⲰⲞⲨϢⲒ

ⲈⲦⲀⲤϪⲰⲔ ⲈⲂⲞⲖ ⲘⲠϢⲈⲘϢⲒ[9] ⲠⲈϪⲀϤ ̀ⲘⲠⲈⲚϬ̅Ⲥ̅[10] ⲰⲞⲨⲚⲒⲀⲦⲞⲨ
ⲚⲚⲎⲈⲦⲀⲨⲒ ⲈⲠⲀⲒⲦⲞⲠⲞⲤ ⲈⲐⲞⲨⲀⲂ

ⲞⲨⲞϨ ⲚⲎⲈⲦⲀⲨϬⲒⲂϮ[11] ⲚϨⲖⲒ ⲠⲀⲒⲦⲞⲠⲞⲤ ⲈⲨⲈϢⲰⲠⲒ ⲈⲨⲤⲰⲚϨ ϦⲈⲚ
ⲠⲤⲀϪⲒ ̀ⲚⲦⲈ ⲪϮ

Consecration of the Church, 6 Hatur: English Translation[12] (italics indicate Greek loan words in the Coptic text)

The sixth day of Hatur, the consecration of the church of Qusqam, tune Batos.

Truly I advance to *ask* the king David about the honor of this holy place of the *God-Bearer* Mary, *in order to* inform us about the glory and the honor of this great place where God dwelt with His mother the *Virgin*.

David the *psalmist* said: "How amiable are your dwellings, O Lord of hosts our God."[13]

Let us rejoice with the heavenly beings on that holy day, and let us *praise* with the *choirs* of saints,

Proclaiming and saying: "This is the *gate* of the Lord into which the righteous shall enter."[14] This is the *gate* of heaven.

This is the *true church* of the *angels* and *Christ consecrating* it with His sublime hand,

after the name of the *God-Bearer* Mary *the Virgin*, the *pure* bride, the pride of all the *virgins*.

Through her is the salvation of our father Adam from the *transgression* which he *dared* (to do).

It is worthy for us, *people*, the sons of the *Orthodox*, to praise with David the king, the *praiser*:

"The queen stood at Your right, O King, in clothing wrought with gold (and) adorned in variegated manner"[15]

Pray to the Lord for...

And also the Adam tune:

Our Lord Jesus came to the mount of Qusqam with His mother Mary and his *disciples*

And the holy *angels* and the *Cherubim* and the *Seraphim* and the *Apostles*

And the *patriarchs* and the *prophets* and the might of heaven were assembled to Him

And our Lord Jesus started the *consecration* of the holy sanctuary,

Jesus, our Lord, started with the *consecration* of the holy sanctuary.

And they brought to Him a *table,* a chalice, and the *instruments* of the altar.

Lord Jesus rose and blessed the house and *signed* it with His holy hand.

And our Lord Jesus lifted His hand and blessed it and gave thanks.

He *consecrated* the *church* and its all *instruments* and the altars.

When the service was finished, Our Lord said: "Blessed are those who come to this holy *place.*

And whoever will change anything in this *place* will be bound by the word of God."

Arabic *tarh*

When our Lord Jesus Christ was born from the pure Mary, in Bethlehem, Magi came to Jerusalem when the star appeared to them. When Herod was informed and wished to kill Him, thinking that He was a worldly king, Herod searched for the Child to kill Him. An angel of the Lord appeared to Joseph, ordering him to take the Child and His mother and to go to Egypt. Joseph did according to what had been ordered by the angel of the Lord and took the Child and His mother and came to Egypt and from there to Qusqam. They dwelt in it till the death of Herod, and the angel of the Lord ordered Joseph to return back with the Child and His mother to Jerusalem. When the Lord accomplished His economy on the earth and was baptized, chose His disciples, did miracles, was crucified, and was buried and rose from the dead and ascended to Heaven, He sent His Holy Spirit upon His pure disciples on Pentecost. He sent them to preach His glorious name in the whole world and made the nations return to the knowledge of the truth. Afterwards, our Savior assembled with His pure mother and His disciples in this pure mount and consecrated the house wherein He dwelt with His pure mother Mary on that holy day which is the sixth of Hatur. Let us rejoice, be happy and glad, O all faithful, for this is the day of the Lord, and let us say with the psalmist David: "This is the gate of the Lord wherein the righteous shall enter." Truly, my fathers, this holy house is like Jerusalem. This is the house of the Lord wherein He dwelt in this expatriation. This is the harbor to those who will take refuge in it. We, the poor sinners, we beseech the merciful Lord, through the intercession of His pure mother, Mary, to have mercy upon us and forgive us our sins and to order our lives to what pleases His goodness till our last breath.

Commentary

It is important to highlight the terms of consecration: while the title bears ⲁⲅⲓⲁⲥⲙⲟⲥ (consecration), in the rest of both texts we have ⲭⲓⲣⲟⲇⲟⲛⲓⲛ (ordination). The first term is used in other texts such as in the Sahidic *Antiphonarion* (Cramer and Krause 2008), or the Bohairic text of the consecration of the sanctuary of Benjamin (Coquin 1975b: 72, ll. 12, 26; 112, l. 7; 114, l. 7; 164, ll. 19–20; 168, ll. 4, 16; 170, ll. 1, 12; 172, l. 27; 174, l. 1; 176, l. 6). This means that the author of this text wrote at a time when Coptic was not used as an everyday language.

While the *psali* Batos stresses Biblical allusions, especially the psalms, the *psali* Adam highlights the liturgical aspect, showing not only the consecration of the church but also consecration of all the liturgical instruments of the altar. The text clearly expresses the prayers of thanksgiving and the sign of the cross. The same wording also occurs in the *Synaxarion*.

The *Synaxarion*

Text (Forget 1963: 92)

> On that day also the Lord Christ assembled with His disciples in the mount of Qusqam *and consecrated the sanctuary and the church with His pure hands. He signed the Church and the altar in the name of the Virgin Mary, His mother, and by the hand of the angels Michael and Gabriel. Our good Saviour consecrated the vessel of water* according to what was testified by father Theophilus, the patriarch, and the father Cyril. And this place will not perish till the end of ages according to the promise of our Lord Jesus Christ. May the intercession of all be with us! Amen.

Commentary

The Basset edition omits the italicized text (Basset 1907: 255 [179]). It seems that the consecration with water was a practice of Upper Egypt (cf. Coquin 1993b: especially 50 n. 61). The text refers to the patriarchs Theophilus and Cyril.

While the short text of the *Synaxarion* contains several details about the source of this text, Theophilus and Cyril, and a local practice about the consecration of the church, the *psali*s do not give any extra information regarding the consecration of the sanctuary, and even the name of Qusqam is not mentioned.

The *Psali*

Text

Here in full is the text of the *psali*, both the Batos and the Adam sections (Filotheus al-Maqari 1913: 125–35).

ⲁⲩⲥⲁϫⲓ ̀ⲛϩⲁⲛⲧⲁⲓⲟ ⲉⲑⲃⲏϯ ⲱ ϯⲃⲁⲕⲓ ̀ⲛⲧⲉ ⲫϯ ⲱ ϯϣⲉⲗⲉⲧ ̀ⲛⲕⲁⲑⲁⲣⲟⲥ ⲙⲁⲣⲓⲁ ϯⲑⲉⲟⲧⲟⲕⲟⲥ	They spoke of you, O city of God, O *pure* bride, Mary the *God-bearer*
ⲃⲁⲑⲙⲟⲥ ⲛⲓⲃⲉⲛ ̀ⲛⲧⲉ ⲡⲱⲟⲩ ⲁⲩⲥⲁϫⲓ ⲧⲏⲣⲟⲩ ⲉⲡⲁⲥⲁⲓⲉ ̀ⲛϯⲟⲩⲣⲱ ⲧϣⲉⲣⲓ ̀ⲛⲛⲓⲟⲩⲣⲱⲟⲩ ⲙⲁⲣⲓⲁ ϯⲑⲉⲟⲧⲟⲕⲟⲥ	All *degrees* of glory spoke about the beauty of the queen, the daughter of the kings, Mary the *God-bearer*
ⲅⲉ ⲅⲁⲣ ⲁϥϫⲟⲥ ̀ⲛϫⲉ ⲡⲟⲩⲣⲟ ϫⲉ ⲥⲁⲟⲩⲓⲛⲁⲙ ̀ⲙⲙⲟⲕ ⲡⲟⲩⲣⲟ ⲁⲥⲟϩⲓ ⲉⲣⲁⲧⲥ ̀ⲛϫⲉ ϯⲟⲩⲣⲱ ⲙⲁⲣⲓⲁ ϯⲑⲉⲟⲧⲟⲕⲟⲥ	*For* the king said: The queen sat on the right (hand) of the king, Mary the *God-bearer*
ⲇⲁⲩⲓⲇ ⲅⲁⲣ ⲡⲓⲟⲩⲣⲟ ̀ⲙⲙⲏⲓ ϫⲉ ϥⲟⲩⲁⲃ ̀ⲛϫⲉ ⲡⲉⲕⲉⲣⲫⲉⲓ ⲟⲩⲟϩ ̀ϥⲟⲓ ⲛϣⲫⲏⲣⲓ ϧⲉⲛ ⲟⲩⲙⲉⲑⲙⲏⲓ ⲉⲧⲉ ⲙⲁⲣⲓⲁ ϯⲑⲉⲟⲧⲟⲕⲟⲥ	For David the true king (said): Holy is your sanctuary and truly marvelous, Mary the *God-bearer*
ⲉⲑⲃⲉ ϫⲉ ⲡⲭ̅ⲥ̅ ⲡⲉⲛⲛⲟⲩϯ ⲁϥϭⲓⲥⲁⲣⲝ ⲉⲃⲟⲗⲛϧⲏϯ ⲱ ϯⲥⲕⲩⲛⲏ ̀ⲙⲙⲁϩ ⲃ̅ϯ ⲙⲁⲣⲓⲁ ϯⲑⲉⲟⲧⲟⲕⲟⲥ	For Christ our God was incarnated from you, O second *tabernacle*, Mary the *God-bearer*
ⲍⲱⲟⲛ ⲛⲓⲃⲉⲛ ̀ⲛⲛⲓⲁⲅⲅⲉⲗⲟⲥ ⲁⲩⲓ ⲉϧⲣⲏⲓ ⲉⲟⲩⲱϣⲧ ⲙⲙⲟⲥ ⲉⲧⲉ ϯⲥⲉⲙⲛⲉ ̀ⲙⲡⲁⲣⲑⲉⲛⲟⲥ ⲙⲁⲣⲓⲁ ϯⲑⲉⲟⲧⲟⲕⲟⲥ	All *living-beings* of *angels* came down to worship her who is the undefiled *Virgin*, Mary the *God-bearer*
ⲏⲡⲡⲉ ⲫϯ ⲡⲓⲛⲁⲏⲧ ⲁϥⲣⲉⲕ ⲧⲫⲉ ⲁϥⲓ ⲉⲡⲉⲥⲏⲧ ⲁϥϭⲓⲥⲁⲣⲝ ϧⲉⲛ ϯϣⲉⲗⲉⲧ ⲙⲁⲣⲓⲁ ϯⲑⲉⲟⲧⲟⲕⲟⲥ	Behold, God the Merciful bent heaven and came down. He was *incarnated* from the bride, Mary the *God-bearer*
ⲑⲁⲓ ⲧⲉ ⲓ̅ⲗ̅ⲏ̅ⲙ̅ ⲛⲧⲉ ⲧⲫⲉ ⲧⲡⲟⲗⲓⲥ ̀ⲙⲡⲉⲛⲛⲟⲩϯ ⲧⲉ ϫⲉ ̀ⲛⲑⲟ ϯⲙⲁϩ ⲃ̅ϯ ̀ⲙⲫⲉ ⲱ ⲙⲁⲣⲓⲁ ϯⲑⲉⲟⲧⲟⲕⲟⲥ	This is the heavenly Jerusalem, the city of our God, for she is the second heaven, O Mary the *God-bearer*
ⲓ̅ⲏ̅ⲥ̅ ⲡⲭ̅ⲥ̅ ⲡϣⲏⲣⲓ ̀ⲙⲫϯ ⲉⲧⲟⲓ ̀ⲛϩⲩⲥⲟⲥ ⲛⲉⲙ ⲫϯ ⲁϥϭⲓⲥⲁⲣⲝ ⲉⲃⲟⲗⲛϧⲏϯ ⲱ ⲙⲁⲣⲓⲁ ϯⲑⲉⲟⲧⲟⲕⲟⲥ	Jesus *Christ* the Son of God, being *equal* to God, was *incarnated* from you, O Mary the *God-bearer*
ⲕⲁⲗⲱⲥ ⲉⲑⲃⲏⲧⲥ ⲉⲁⲩⲕⲱⲣϥ ̀ⲙⲫⲙⲟⲩ ⲕⲁⲗⲱⲥ ⲥⲉⲙⲡϣⲁ ̀ⲛϩⲁⲛⲥⲙⲟⲩ ̀ⲛϫⲉ ϯⲡⲁⲣⲑⲉⲛⲟⲥ ̀ⲛⲁⲑⲙⲟⲩ ⲙⲁⲣⲓⲁ ϯⲑⲉⲟⲧⲟⲕⲟⲥ	*Well*, for her sake, death was *well* destroyed, the immortal *Virgin* is worthy of praises, Mary the *God-bearer*
ⲗⲁⲥ ⲛⲓⲃⲉⲛ ⲥⲉⲥⲙⲟⲩ ⲉⲣⲟⲥ ⲗⲁⲥ ⲛⲓⲃⲉⲛ ⲥⲉϯⲱⲟⲩ ⲛⲁⲥ ⲗⲁⲥ ⲛⲓⲃⲉⲛ ⲥⲉϩⲱⲥ ⲉⲣⲟⲥ ⲙⲁⲣⲓⲁ ϯⲑⲉⲟⲧⲟⲕⲟⲥ	All tongues praise her, all tongues glorify her, all tongues sing of her, Mary the *God-bearer*

ⲘⲀⲢⲒⲀ ⲦϢⲈⲢⲒ ̀ⲚⲒⲰⲀⲔⲒⲘ ⲘⲀⲢⲒⲀ ⲦϢⲈⲢⲒ ̀ⲚⲚⲒⲠⲢⲞⲪⲎⲦⲎⲤ ⲘⲀⲢⲒⲀ ⲦϢⲈⲢⲒ ̀ⲚⲚⲒⲠⲀⲦⲢⲒⲀⲢⲬⲎⲤ ⲘⲀⲢⲒⲀ ϯⲐⲈⲞⲦⲞⲔⲞⲤ	Mary the daughter of Joachim, Mary the daughter of the *prophets,* Mary the daughter of the *Patriarchs,* Mary the *God-bearer*
̀ⲚⲐⲞ ⲠⲈ ⲠϢⲞⲨϢⲞⲨ ̀ⲚⲚⲒⲢⲰⲘⲒ ̀ⲚⲐⲞ ⲠⲈ ⲐⲚⲞⲘϯ ̀ⲚⲚⲒϨⲒⲞⲘⲒ ⲦⲈⲚϯⲰⲞⲨ ⲚⲈ ϢⲀ ϯⲤⲨⲚⲦⲈⲖⲒⲀ Ⲱ ⲘⲀⲢⲒⲀ ϯⲐⲈⲞⲦⲞⲔⲞⲤ	You are the pride of men, you are the consolation of women, we glorify you till the end, Mary the *God-bearer*
ⲜⲈⲢⲒⲦⲞⲚ ⲚⲬⲈ[16] ⲠⲈⲦⲞⲨⲂⲞ ϤⲤⲀⲠϢⲰⲒ ⲄⲀⲢ ϦⲈⲚ ⲞⲨⲦⲀⲒⲞ ⲘⲀϯϨⲞ ⲈⲬⲰⲚ ϦⲈⲚ ⲞⲨⲠⲀⲢⲢⲎⲤⲒⲀ Ⲱ ⲘⲀⲢⲒⲀ ϯⲐⲈⲞⲦⲞⲔⲞⲤ	*For* your purity is *especially* (ⲈⲜⲀⲒⲢⲈⲦⲰⲤ) elevated in glory; beseech on our behalf *openly*, Mary the *God-bearer*
ⲞⲨⲀⲒ ⲈⲂⲞⲖϦⲈⲚ ϯⲦⲢⲒⲀⲤ ⲈⲦⲈ ⲠⲈⲚⲟ̅ⲥ̅ ⲒⲎⲤ̅ ⲠⲬⲤ̅ ⲀϤϬⲒⲤⲀⲢⲜ ϦⲈⲚ ϯⲠⲀⲢⲐⲈⲚⲞⲤ ⲘⲀⲢⲒⲀ ϯⲐⲈⲞⲦⲞⲔⲞⲤ	One of the Trinity is our Lord Jesus *Christ,* who was *incarnated* from the *Virgin* Mary the *God-bearer*
ⲠⲰⲚϦ ̀ⲚⲚⲒⲬⲢⲎⲤⲦⲒⲀⲚⲞⲤ ⲠϢⲞⲨϢⲞⲨ ̀ⲚⲚⲒⲠⲀⲢⲐⲈⲚⲞⲤ ⲠⲒⲚⲞⲨⲂ ⲈⲦⲤⲰⲦⲠ ̀ⲚⲔⲀⲐⲀⲢⲞⲤ ⲘⲀⲢⲒⲀ ϯⲐⲈⲞⲦⲞⲔⲞⲤ	Life of *Christians*, pride of *virgins*, the *pure* gold, Mary the *God-bearer*
ⲢⲰⲘⲒ ⲚⲒⲂⲈⲚ ⲤⲈⲤⲘⲞⲨ ⲈⲢⲞⲤ ⲚⲒⲀⲄⲄⲈⲖⲞⲤ ⲤⲈϯⲰⲞⲨ ⲚⲀⲤ ϯⲖⲨⲬⲚⲒⲀ ̀ⲚⲔⲀⲐⲀⲢⲞⲤ ⲘⲀⲢⲒⲀ ϯⲐⲈⲞⲦⲞⲔⲞⲤ	All men praise her, the *angels* glorify her, the *pure lampstand*, Mary the *God-bearer*
ⲤⲘⲞⲨ ⲈⲦⲈⲔⲔⲖⲎⲢⲞⲚⲞⲘⲒⲀ ⲘⲞⲒ ⲚⲰⲞⲨ ̀ⲚⲞⲨⲔⲀϯ ϨⲒⲦⲈⲚ ⲚⲒϯϨⲞ ⲚⲈⲘ ⲚⲒⲠⲢⲈⲤⲂⲒⲀ ⲘⲀⲢⲒⲀ ϯⲐⲈⲞⲦⲞⲔⲞⲤ	Bless Your *inheritance*, give them understanding, through the prayers and intercessions of Mary the *God-bearer*
ⲦⲈⲚϯϨⲞ ⲈⲢⲞⲔ Ⲡⲟ̅ⲥ̅ ⲠⲈⲚⲚⲞⲨϯ ⲘⲞⲒ ⲚⲀⲚ ̀ⲚⲞⲨⲞⲨϪⲀⲒ ⲚⲈⲘ ⲞⲨⲤⲰϯ ϨⲒⲦⲈⲚ ⲚⲒϯϨⲞ Ⲛ̀ϯⲘⲀⲤⲚⲞⲨϯ ⲘⲀⲢⲒⲀ ϯⲐⲈⲞⲦⲞⲔⲞⲤ	We beseech You, Lord our God, grant us salvation and deliverance through the beseeching of the Mother of God, Mary the *God-bearer*
ⲨⲠⲠⲈ ⲄⲀⲢ Ⲡⲟ̅ⲥ̅ ⲠⲞⲨⲢⲞ ⲞⲨⲞϨ Ⲫϯ ̀ⲚⲚⲒⲞⲨⲢⲰⲞⲨ ⲀϤϬⲒⲤⲀⲢⲜ ϦⲈⲚ ϯⲞⲨⲢⲰ ⲘⲀⲢⲒⲀ ϯⲐⲈⲞⲦⲞⲔⲞⲤ	Behold, *for* the Lord, the King and God of kings, was *incarnated* from the queen, Mary the *God-bearer*
Ⲫϯ ⲄⲀⲢ ̀ⲚⲦⲈ ⲚⲒⲚⲞⲨϯ ⲞⲨⲞϨ Ⲡⲟ̅ⲥ̅ ⲚⲦⲈ ⲚⲒⲟ̅ⲥ̅ ⲀϤϬⲒⲤⲀⲢⲜ ⲈⲂⲞⲖ̀ⲚϦⲎϯ ⲘⲀⲢⲒⲀ ϯⲐⲈⲞⲦⲞⲔⲞⲤ	For the God of gods and Lord of lords was incarnate from you, Mary the *God-bearer*
ⲬⲰ ⲚⲀⲚ Ⲡⲟ̅ⲥ̅ ⲚⲚⲈⲚⲀⲚⲞⲘⲒⲀ ⲘⲞⲒ ⲚⲀⲚ ⲚⲞⲨⲤⲰⲦⲎⲢⲒⲀ ϨⲒⲦⲈⲚ ⲚⲒϯϨⲞ ⲚⲈⲘ ⲚⲒⲠⲢⲈⲤⲂⲒⲀ ⲘⲀⲢⲒⲀ ϯⲐⲈⲞⲦⲞⲔⲞⲤ	Forgive us, O Lord, our *transgressions,* grant us salvation through the beseeching and the *intercessions* (of) Mary the *God-bearer*
ⲮⲰϯ ⲄⲀⲢ ⲚⲞⲨⲞⲚ ⲚⲒⲂⲈⲚ ⲞⲨⲞϨ ⲠⲰⲚϦ ⲚⲢⲰⲘⲒ ⲚⲒⲂⲈⲚ ϢⲰⲠⲒ ⲚⲈⲘⲀⲚ ⲚⲤⲎⲞⲨ ⲚⲒⲂⲈⲚ ⲘⲀⲢⲒⲀ ϯⲐⲈⲞⲦⲞⲔⲞⲤ	*For* the salvation of everyone and the life of everyone, be with us forever, Mary the *God-bearer*
ⲰⲚⲦⲞⲤ ⲄⲀⲢ ϦⲈⲚ ⲞⲨⲘⲈⲐⲘⲎⲒ ϯⲂⲰ ⲚⲀⲖⲞⲖⲒ ⲚⲦⲈⲀⲪⲘⲎⲒ ⲐⲘⲀⲨ ⲘⲪϯ ϦⲈⲚ ⲞⲨⲘⲈⲐⲘⲎⲒ Ⲱ ⲘⲀⲢⲒⲀ ϯⲐⲈⲞⲦⲞⲔⲞⲤ	*For also*, truly, the true vine (is) the mother of God truly, Mary the *God-bearer*

Commentary

This *psali* is anonymous. I did not find any link to the monastery of Qusqam (al-Muharraq); moreover, the compiler used ready-made text from previous liturgical texts:

Psali	*Theotokia* of Sunday
ⲀⲨⲤⲀϪⲒ `ⲚϨⲀⲚⲦⲀⲒⲞ ⲈⲐⲂⲎϮ Ⲱ ϮⲂⲀⲔⲒ ⲚⲦⲈ ⲪϮ Ⲱ ϮϢⲈⲖⲈⲦ ⲚⲔⲀⲐⲀⲢⲞⲤ ⲘⲀⲢⲒⲀ ϮⲐⲈⲞⲦⲞⲔⲞⲤ	ϪⲈ ⲀⲨⲤⲀϪϮ ⲈⲐⲂⲎϮ `ⲚϨⲀⲚϨⲂⲎⲞⲨⲒ ⲈⲨⲦⲀⲒⲎⲞⲨⲦ ϮⲂⲀⲔⲒ Ⲉ̅Ⲑ̅Ⲩ̅ `ⲚⲦⲈ ⲠⲒⲚⲒϢϮ `ⲚⲞⲨⲢⲞ
They spoke of you, O city of God, O *pure* bride, Mary the *God-bearer*	They spoke of you with great honor, O holy city of the great King

Psali	*Psali* of Sunday for the Virgin
ⲐⲀⲒ ⲦⲈ Ⲓ̅Ⲗ̅Ⲏ̅Ⲙ̅ ⲚⲦⲈ ⲦⲪⲈ ⲦⲠⲞⲖⲒⲤ ⲘⲠⲈⲚⲚⲞⲨϮ ⲦⲈ ϪⲈ ⲚⲐⲞ ϮⲘⲀϨ Ⲃ̅Ϯ `ⲘⲪⲈ Ⲱ ⲘⲀⲢⲒⲀ ϮⲐⲈⲞⲦⲞⲔⲞⲤ	ⲐⲀⲒ ⲦⲈ Ⲓ̅Ⲗ̅Ⲏ̅Ⲙ̅ ⲦⲠⲞⲖⲒⲤ ⲘⲠⲈⲚⲚⲞⲨϮ ⲦⲈ ϪⲈ ⲠϨⲀⲢⲘⲀ ⲚⲚⲒⲬⲈⲢⲞⲨⲂⲒⲘ ⲈⲦⲞⲒ ⲚⲞⲨⲐⲞ ⲚⲢⲎϮ
This is the heavenly Jerusalem, the city of our God, for she is the second heaven, O Mary the *God-bearer*	This is Jerusalem, the city of our God, the chariot of the cherubim (having) all things

The *psali* of Sunday for the Virgin is attributed to John, bishop of Asyut, Manfalut, and Abu Tig in the fifteenth century (Youssef 2003; Youssef 2008), which means that this *psali* was written after that date. The biblical text:

ⲄⲈ ⲄⲀⲢ ⲀϤϪⲞⲤ ⲚϪⲈ ⲠⲞⲨⲢⲞ ϪⲈ ⲤⲀⲞⲨⲒⲚⲀⲘ ⲘⲘⲞⲔ ⲠⲞⲨⲢⲞ ⲀⲤⲞϨⲒ ⲈⲢⲀⲦⲤ ⲚϪⲈ ϮⲞⲨⲢⲰ ⲘⲀⲢⲒⲀ ϮⲐⲈⲞⲦⲞⲔⲞⲤ	ⲀⲤⲞϨⲒ ⲈⲢⲀⲦⲤ ⲚϪⲈ ϮⲞⲨⲢⲰ ⲤⲀⲞⲨⲒⲚⲀⲘ ⲘⲘⲞⲔ ⲘⲠⲞⲨⲢⲞ
ⲆⲀⲨⲒⲆ ⲄⲀⲢ ⲠⲒⲞⲨⲢⲞ ⲘⲘⲎⲒ ϪⲈ ϤⲞⲨⲀⲂ ⲚϪⲈ ⲠⲈⲔⲈⲢⲪⲈⲒ ⲞⲨⲞϨ ϤⲞⲒ ⲚϢⲪⲎⲢⲒ ϦⲈⲚ ⲞⲨⲘⲈⲐⲘⲎⲒ ⲈⲦⲈ ⲘⲀⲢⲒⲀ ϮⲐⲈⲞⲦⲞⲔⲞⲤ	
For the king said: The queen sat on the right (hand) of the King, Mary the *God-bearer*	Ps. The queen stood at Your right
For David the true king (said): Holy is your sanctuary and truly marvelous, Mary the *God-bearer*	
ⲤⲘⲞⲨ ⲈⲦⲈⲔⲔⲖⲎⲢⲞⲚⲞⲘⲒⲀ ⲘⲞⲒ ⲚⲰⲞⲨ ⲚⲞⲨⲔⲀϮ ϨⲒⲦⲈⲚ ⲚⲒϮϨⲞ ⲚⲈⲘ ⲚⲒⲠⲢⲈⲤⲂⲒⲀ ⲘⲀⲢⲒⲀ ϮⲐⲈⲞⲦⲞⲔⲞⲤ	Bless Your inheritance, give them understanding, through the prayers and the intercessions of Mary the God-bearer

Grammatical inaccuracy:

ⲜⲈⲢⲒⲦⲞⲚ ⲚϪⲈ[17] ⲠⲈⲦⲞⲨⲂⲞ ϤⲤⲀⲠϢⲰⲒ ⲄⲀⲢ ϦⲈⲚ ⲞⲨⲦⲀⲒⲞ ⲘⲀϮϨⲞ ⲈϪⲰⲚ ϦⲈⲚ ⲞⲨⲠⲀⲢⲢⲎⲤⲒⲀ Ⲱ ⲘⲀⲢⲒⲀ ϮⲐⲈⲞⲦⲞⲔⲞⲤ	*For* your purity is *especially* (ⲈⲜⲀⲒⲢⲈⲦⲰⲤ) elevated in glory; beseech on our behalf *openly,* Mary the *God-bearer*

The Adam section provides no better information:

ⲀⲘⲰⲒⲚⲒ ⲘⲀⲢⲈⲚϨⲰⲤ `ⲚⲦⲈⲚϪⲰ `ⲘⲘⲞⲤ ⲈⲂⲞⲖϨⲒⲦⲈⲚ ⲘⲀⲢⲒⲀ ϮⲐⲈⲞⲦⲞⲔⲞⲤ	Come, let us praise, saying through Mary the *God-bearer*
ⲂⲞⲎⲐⲒⲀ ⲚⲒⲂⲈⲚ ⲀⲨϢⲰⲠⲒ `ⲚⲚⲒⲠⲒⲤⲦⲞⲤ ⲈⲂⲞⲖϨⲒⲦⲈⲚ ⲘⲀⲢⲒⲀ ϮⲐⲈⲞⲦⲞⲔⲞⲤ	*For* all *help* takes place through Mary the *God-bearer*
ⲄⲈ ⲄⲀⲢ ⲀϤϢⲰⲠⲒ ⲚⲀⲚ `ⲚⲞⲨⲤⲰϮ ⲀⲖⲎⲐⲰⲤ ⲈⲂⲞⲖϨⲒⲦⲈⲚ ⲘⲀⲢⲒⲀ ϮⲐⲈⲞⲦⲞⲔⲞⲤ	*For truly* every salvation came to us through Mary the *God-bearer*
ⲆⲈⲤⲠⲞⲦⲀ ⲠⲈⲚⲚⲞⲨϮ ⲀϤⲚⲞϨⲈⲘ `ⲘⲠⲈϤⲖⲀⲞⲤ ⲈⲂⲞⲖϨⲒⲦⲈⲚ ⲘⲀⲢⲒⲀ ϮⲐⲈⲞⲦⲞⲔⲞⲤ	*Lord* our God, save His *people* through Mary the *God-bearer*
ⲈⲨⲈⲈⲢϢⲀⲒ `ⲘⲪⲞⲞⲨ `ⲚϪⲈ ⲚⲒⲠⲒⲤⲦⲞⲤ ⲈⲂⲞⲖϨⲒⲦⲈⲚ ⲘⲀⲢⲒⲀ ϮⲐⲈⲞⲦⲞⲔⲞⲤ	The *faithful* rejoice today through Mary the *God-bearer*
ⲌⲰⲎ ⲚⲈ ⲘⲀⲆⲀⲘ ⲀⲨϨⲰⲖ ⲈⲠⲒⲠⲀⲢⲀⲆⲒⲤⲞⲤ ⲈⲂⲞⲖϨⲒⲦⲈⲚ ⲘⲀⲢⲒⲀ ϮⲐⲈⲞⲦⲞⲔⲞⲤ	Eve and Adam went (back) to *paradise* through Mary the *God-bearer*
ⲎⲠⲠⲈ ⲈⲘⲘⲀⲚⲞⲨⲎⲖ ⲀϤⲈⲢⲤⲰⲘⲀⲦⲒⲔⲞⲤ ⲈⲂⲞⲖϨⲒⲦⲈⲚ ⲘⲀⲢⲒⲀ ϮⲐⲈⲞⲦⲞⲔⲞⲤ	Behold, Emmanuel became *flesh* through Mary the *God-bearer*
ⲐⲞⲨⲒⲚⲀⲘ ⲠϬ̅Ⲥ̅ ⲀⲤ`ⲒⲢⲒ ⲚⲞⲨϪⲞⲘ ⲈⲂⲞⲖϨⲒⲦⲈⲚ ⲘⲀⲢⲒⲀ ϮⲐⲈⲞⲦⲞⲔⲞⲤ	The right (hand) of the Lord did power through Mary the *God-bearer*
Ⲓ̅Ⲏ̅Ⲥ̅ ⲀϤⲞⲨⲰⲚϨ ⲈⲂⲞⲖ `ⲚϨⲢⲎⲒ ϦⲈⲚ ⲠⲒⲔⲞⲤⲘⲞⲤ ⲈⲂⲞⲖϨⲒⲦⲈⲚ ⲘⲀⲢⲒⲀ ϮⲐⲈⲞⲦⲞⲔⲞⲤ	Jesus appeared in the *world* through Mary the *God-bearer*
ⲔⲀⲦⲀ ⲞⲒⲔⲞⲚⲞⲘⲒⲀ ⲀϤⲈⲢⲤⲰⲘⲀⲦⲒⲔⲞⲤ ⲈⲂⲞⲖϨⲒⲦⲈⲚ ⲘⲀⲢⲒⲀ ϮⲐⲈⲞⲦⲞⲔⲞⲤ	He became *flesh according to the dispensation* through Mary the *God-bearer*
ⲖⲀⲞⲤ ⲚⲒⲂⲈⲚ ⲈⲨⲘⲈⲨⲒ ⲈⲪⲢⲀⲚ `ⲘⲠⲬ̅Ⲥ̅ ⲈⲂⲞⲖϨⲒⲦⲈⲚ ⲘⲀⲢⲒⲀ ϮⲐⲈⲞⲦⲞⲔⲞⲤ	All the *nations* remember the name of *Christ* through Mary the *God-bearer*
ⲘⲀⲢⲈ ⲪⲢⲀϢⲒ ϢⲰⲠⲒ `ⲚⲚⲒⲞⲢⲐⲞⲆⲞⲜⲞⲤ ⲈⲂⲞⲖϨⲒⲦⲈⲚ ⲘⲀⲢⲒⲀ ϮⲐⲈⲞⲦⲞⲔⲞⲤ	Let joy be to the *Orthodox* through Mary the *God-bearer*
ⲚⲒⲢⲰⲘⲒ ⲈⲨⲈⲢϢⲪⲎⲢⲒ ⲚⲈⲘ ⲚⲒⲀⲄⲄⲈⲖⲞⲤ ⲈⲂⲞⲖϨⲒⲦⲈⲚ ⲘⲀⲢⲒⲀ ϮⲐⲈⲞⲦⲞⲔⲞⲤ	Men and *angels* wonder through Mary the *God-bearer*
ⲜⲘⲀⲢⲰⲞⲨⲦ ⲠϬ̅Ⲥ̅ ⲀⲔ`Ⲓ ⲈⲠⲒⲔⲞⲤⲘⲞⲤ ⲈⲂⲞⲖϨⲒⲦⲈⲚ ⲘⲀⲢⲒⲀ ϮⲐⲈⲞⲦⲞⲔⲞⲤ	Blessed are you, Lord; you came to the *world* through Mary the *God-bearer*
ⲞⲨⲚⲒϢϮ ⲠⲈⲠⲦⲀⲒⲞ ⲈⲦⲀⲚⲈⲢⲘⲠϢⲀ `ⲘⲘⲞⲤ[18] ⲈⲂⲞⲖϨⲒⲦⲈⲚ ⲘⲀⲢⲒⲀ ϮⲐⲈⲞⲦⲞⲔⲞⲤ	Great is the honor that we became worthy through Mary the *God-bearer*

ΠΙϨΙΗΒ `ΜΜΗΙ ⲀϤⲤⲰϮ `ΜΠΕϤⲖⲀⲞⲤ ⲈⲂⲞⲖϨⲒⲦⲈⲚ ⲘⲀⲢⲒⲀ ϮⲐⲈⲞⲦⲞⲔⲞⲤ	The true lamb saved His *people* through Mary the *God-bearer*
ⲢⲀϢⲒ ⲞⲨⲞϨ ⲐⲈⲖⲎⲖ Ⲱ ⲚⲒⲞⲢⲐⲞⲆⲞⲜⲞⲤ ⲈⲂⲞⲖϨⲒⲦⲈⲚ ⲘⲀⲢⲒⲀ ϮⲐⲈⲞⲦⲞⲔⲞⲤ	Rejoice and be happy, O *Orthodox*, through Mary the *God-bearer*
ⲤⲈϪⲒⲘⲒ `ⲚⲞⲨⲚⲀⲒ `ⲚⲚⲒⲬⲢⲒⲤⲦⲒⲀⲚⲞⲤ ⲈⲂⲞⲖϨⲒⲦⲈⲚ ⲘⲀⲢⲒⲀ ϮⲐⲈⲞⲦⲞⲔⲞⲤ	*Christians* find mercy through Mary the *God-bearer*
ⲦⲈⲚⲈⲢⲠⲈⲘⲠϢⲀ `ⲚⲚⲀϨϮ ⲈⲫⲢⲀⲚ `ⲘⲠⲬ̅Ⲥ̅ ⲈⲂⲞⲖϨⲒⲦⲈⲚ ⲘⲀⲢⲒⲀ ϮⲐⲈⲞⲦⲞⲔⲞⲤ	We became worthy to believe in the name of *Christ* through Mary the *God-bearer*
ⲨⲠⲠⲈ ⲀϤⲤⲰϮ `ⲘⲘⲞⲚ `ⲚϪⲈ ⲠⲒⲆⲎⲘⲒⲞⲨⲢⲄⲞⲤ ⲈⲂⲞⲖϨⲒⲦⲈⲚ ⲘⲀⲢⲒⲀ ϮⲐⲈⲞⲦⲞⲔⲞⲤ	Behold, the *Creator* saved us through Mary the *God-bearer*
ⲪⲎⲈⲦⲀϤⲐⲀⲘⲒⲞⲚ ⲀϤⲈⲢⲤⲰⲘⲀⲦⲒⲔⲞⲤ ⲈⲂⲞⲖϨⲒⲦⲈⲚ ⲘⲀⲢⲒⲀ ϮⲐⲈⲞⲦⲞⲔⲞⲤ	He who created us became *flesh* through Mary the *God-bearer*
ⲬⲖⲞⲘ `ⲚⲚⲀⲚⲒⲪⲎⲞⲨⲒ ⲚⲈⲘ ⲚⲒⲘⲀⲢⲦⲨⲢⲞⲤ ⲈⲂⲞⲖϨⲒⲦⲈⲚ ⲘⲀⲢⲒⲀ ϮⲐⲈⲞⲦⲞⲔⲞⲤ	Crown of the heavenly and the *martyrs* through Mary the *God-bearer*
ⲮⲞⲖⲤⲈⲖ ⲚⲚⲈⲚϨⲎⲦ ⲪⲢⲀϢⲒ ⲚⲚⲒⲖⲀⲞⲤ ⲈⲂⲞⲖϨⲒⲦⲈⲚ ⲘⲀⲢⲒⲀ ϮⲐⲈⲞⲦⲞⲔⲞⲤ	Consolation of our hearts and joy of the *people* through Mary the *God-bearer*
ⲰⲞⲨ ⲚⲈ Ⲱ ⲐⲎⲈⲦⲈⲚϨⲞⲦ ⲞⲨⲞϨ ⲈⲦⲤⲘⲀⲢⲰⲞⲨⲦ ⲘⲀϮϨⲞ ⲘⲠϬ̅Ⲥ̅ ⲈϪⲰⲚ ⲚⲦⲈϤⲈⲢⲂⲞⲎⲐⲒⲚ ⲈⲢⲞⲚ	Blessed are you, O entrusted and blessed; beseech the Lord for us in order that He *help* us

The *psalis* for the consecration of the sanctuary of Qusqam are of a late date, as is apparent from:

1. the use of other liturgical texts
2. no allusion to the vision of Theophilus or any patristic text
3. no geographical data (compared with the *psali* of the entry of Jesus to Egypt)
4. the many grammatical inaccuracies

There is a *Psali* Batos for the Feast of the Arrival of the Lord into Egypt, where we read:

ⲨⲆⲈⲞⲚ ϦⲈⲚ ⲞⲨⲈⲢⲞⲨⲰⲦ ⲀⲨⲘⲞϢⲒ ϢⲀ ⲠⲦⲰⲞⲨ ⲔⲞⲤⲔⲀⲘ ⲚϦⲎⲦϤ ⲚϨⲀⲚⲀⲂⲞⲦ ⲀϤⲤⲘⲞⲨ ⲈⲢⲞϤ ϦⲈⲚ ⲦⲈϤⲞⲨⲒⲚⲀⲘ	And also with joy, they walked to the mountain of Qusqam, they stayed for many months, He blessed it with His right hand

However, the mention of Qusqam is absent from the *Antiphonarion* of Upper Egypt (Cramer and Krause 2008: 319).

Commemoration of an Abbot of al-Muharraq

Text

I have identified so far three manuscripts from the monastery of al-Muharraq that are kept in the Bibliothèque Nationale de France: Paris Arabe 4779, 4780, and Paris Copte 123. I have already published the doxology for 6 Hatur contained in Paris Copte 123 (Youssef 2009b). The manuscript Paris Arabe 4779 (Troupeau 1974: 30) (fol. 75v–77r), which was copied in the Monastery of al-Muharraq by the monk Yuhanna al-Atlimidi during the reign of Abbot Bulus al-Dalagawi (later commemorated as a saint), contains a commemoration for 28 Baba. This biography differs from what is reported by Anba Gregorius:

> On this day also reposed our virtuous father Hegumen 'Abd al-Malak. This father was from the city of Asyut and when he was aged fifteen years old in the house of his father, his soul renounced all the delights of this perishable world and he aspired to the monastic life. So he abandoned the world and took refuge in God and became a monk* in the monastery known as al-Muharraq . . . This father was interested in building the monastery and restoring the manuscripts by his own hands as he was a scribe. In the beginning of his abbotship he built a beautiful church in the monastery named after the great saint George and he accomplished it perfectly. (Anba Gregorius 1968: 335–36; here and below, the asterisks mark the end of a page in the manuscript)

Commentary

It is amazing that Gabriel IV, the first patriarch consecrated from the monastery of al-Muharraq, who reposed on 3 Bashans, is not mentioned in this *Synaxarion* (i.e., Paris Arabe 4779) (Khater and Burmester 1970: fol. 239r, 136 (text), 234 (translation)).

Two abbots bore the name of 'Abd al-Malak; one was from Asyut (AD 1772–1808) and the other one from Hur (AD 1838–66) (Anba Gregorius 1968: 193–98; Dayr al-Muharraq 1990: 109–14). Our text was copied during the abbotship of the successor to the latter. The text uses a far past tense, hence the former is being spoken of.

> On this day the Savior assembled with this disciple in Qusqam and performed the first liturgy according to what was witnessed by Saint Theophilus and Saint Cyril. It was a great day with the assembly of our Lord* with his mother and his disciples, and he consecrated this

place with his sublime hand, to whom is the glory forever and may his mercy endure for eternity. Amen. (6 Hatur, fol. 84v–85r)

The Sahidic version of the *Synaxarion* according to the manuscript Paris Arabe 4869 commemorates on 20 Kiyahk the martyrdom of Elias, bishop of al-Muharraq during the time of Arianus. His body was hidden until the time of our father Constantine bishop of Asyut, so his body was translated to Asyut, and when Qusiya (al-Muharraq) was rebuilt, the saint appeared to a merchant asking him to return his body to Qusiya. When the merchant arrived in Asyut, he took the body and nobody prevented him, as the saint had promised. According to the *Synaxarion*, his body is kept in the Monastery of al-Muharraq (Forget 1963: 345–47).

This commemoration brings up several points.

1. The chronology. The foundation of the monastery belongs to St. Pachomius or his immediate successors (Meinardus 2002: 156). (This theory is confirmed not only by tradition, but also by the location of the monastery.) It is known that Pachomius came into contact with Christianity in the year AD 312 and he was baptized later, which means after the Great Persecution (Veilleux 1991).
2. In the Pachomian order, we do not find any bishop as an abbot. Pachomius himself refused the priesthood. So, how can the mention of a bishop of al-Muharraq be accurate?[19]
3. The *Life* of Abba Hermina (around the fifth century) (Muyser 1943) narrates that this saint visited the relics of Elias, which were in Qusiya. It is worth mentioning that the commemoration of Abba Hermina is on 2 Kiyahk and the commemoration of Elias is on 20 Kiyahk.
4. Constantine, bishop of Asyut (early seventh century) (Coquin 1981; Garitte 1950), mentions in his second encomium on St. Claudius that thieves went to the sanctuary of Apa Elias in the city of ⲕⲱⲥ. However, given the context of this text, this city should be identified as Qusiya (Godron 1970: 644 [222]–645 [223]).
5. The *History*[20] *of the Patriarchs* (Atiya, 'Abd al-Masih, and Burmester 1959, vol. 2, pt. 3: 228 (text), 362 (translation)) mentions, in the eleventh century, "In Qusqam [are the relics of] Abu Halis the martyr."[21] It is worth noting that Yuhanna Ibn Said al-Kulzumi, while talking about the Holy Family in Egypt, mentions "Kuskam," and the mountain of "Ishnin" and "al-Muharrakah" (Atiya, 'Abd al-Masih, and Burmester 1959, vol. 2, pt. 3: 361 [translation]).

6. We can see that Elias of Muharraq is not mentioned in either the oral or the written tradition of the monastery, but he is linked mainly to Qusiya; the amalgamation of Qusiya and Muharraq led to confusion.
7. The Monastery of al-Muharraq possesses an additional list of saints commemorated in the monastery who are related to other monasteries of the region: Isidorus and Sana (18 Baramhat) (O'Leary 1937: 160, 257), Olympious of Caw (30 Tuba),[22] Macrobius of Dayr al-Ganadla (Coquin 1991a), Dioscorus and Asklepios (Aesculapius) (O'Leary 1937: 124–25; Coquin and Martin 1991e), and Hermina (Coquin, 1991b).

Notes

1 I would to thank all who helped with this chapter, especially Gamal Hermina for the manuscript from the Coptic Museum, and the monks of al-Muharraq Monastery, Fr. Angelos, Fr. Beniamin, Fr. Ammonius, and the other monks.
2 I would like to thank my friend Jacob Askern for this information.
3 For this edition cf. Wadi 2006.
4 Simaika and 'Abd al-Masih 1939: serial number 35; Graf 1939: no. 16.
5 I would like to thank Fr. Beniamin al-Muharraqi, who drew my attention to these traditions.
6 Simaika and 'Abd al-Masih 1939: 84, no. 171; not in Graf.
7 Read ⲡⲁⲓ ⲉϩⲟⲟⲩ.
8 Read ⲛϫⲉ.
9 Read ⲛϫⲉ.
10 Read ⲛϫⲉ.
11 Read ϣⲃⲓϯ.
12 All English translations are by the author.
13 Psalm 84:1.
14 Psalm 118:20.
15 Psalm 45:9.
16 Read ⲡⲉ.
17 Read ⲡⲉ.
18 This is an Arabism, as the word *karama* is feminine in Arabic while in Coptic it is masculine. It is not a misprint, as the second part always ends with -ⲟⲥ to rhyme with ϯⲑⲉⲟⲧⲟⲕⲟⲥ.
19 Only in the early twentieth century did Pope Cyril V ordain some abbots as bishops.
20 For the sources of this part of the history of the patriarchs, cf. den Heijer 1989: 142–43.
21 There are other Eliases, but, according to the context, the one of Qusiya is meant here; cf. Papaconstantinou 2001: 89–91.
22 For the *Synaxarion* of Upper Egypt, see Coquin 1978: 361; Lefort 1950.

18 *L** as a Secret Language: Social Functions of Early Coptic

Ewa D. Zakrzewska

Introduction

The aim of the present chapter is to reconsider the use of Coptic as attested in the texts belonging to the Manichaean community in Kellis (Ismant al-Kharab, Dakhla Oasis). For this particular variety of Coptic, the siglum *L** has been suggested by W.-P. Funk, who thus qualified it as a variety of the so-called Lykopolitan dialect of Coptic, indicated by the siglum *L* (Gardner, Alcock, and Funk 1999: 90–91). As Lykopolis is the Greek name of the city of Asyut, *L** could also be called a variety of Asyutic Coptic (see the section "What Are *L* and *L**?" below for discussion). The texts in which the variety in question is attested are dated to circa AD 355–80 and thus form one of the oldest Coptic text corpora. The majority of these texts have been edited by I. Gardner and his collaborators (Gardner 1996–2007; Gardner, Alcock, and Funk 1999).

The linguistic features of *L** have been described expertly by Funk in Gardner, Alcock, and Funk 1999: 84–95; see also Shisha-Halevy 2002a. The purpose of this chapter is therefore not descriptive, but explanatory: I will put forward a number of hypotheses in order to reconstruct motivations that could have induced the members of the Manichaean community in Kellis to use Coptic for their writings. This was by no means a trivial matter: from the second to the fourth century AD, it was Greek that functioned as the principal literary and administrative language in Egypt. As

R.S. Bagnall (1993: 238) boldly puts it: "There was no way to have an Egyptian sentence recorded except to translate it into Greek." In the third century AD there were some attempts to write Egyptian texts with Greek characters. However, the idiom of these texts, conventionally called Old Coptic, differs considerably from fully developed Coptic as attested from the fourth century onward (Bagnall 2005). The emergence of Coptic, as it seems, was not preceded by recorded historical development.

Writing in Coptic implied, therefore, a conspicuous break with the existing conventions, a fact that calls for explanation. The main purpose of this chapter is to challenge some traditional explanations of this striking innovation and to present alternative ones. Specifically, I will argue that the Manichaean Coptic text corpus from Kellis provides a convincing piece of evidence to corroborate the hypotheses presented in my theoretically oriented articles on the rise of Coptic (Zakrzewska, forthcoming a; forthcoming b).

The structure of this chapter is as follows. In the first section, I present introductory information about the different varieties of Lykopolitan, *L** among others. The next section summarily criticizes some traditional views on the rise of Coptic. This serves as a background for the third section, in which an alternative scenario is presented. The final section contains the summary and conclusions.

What Are *L* and *L**?

L is a so-called siglum, the symbolic indication of a Coptic dialect group called Lykopolitan after the Greek name of Asyut, Lykopolis (see Kasser 1990: 148). In older studies, this dialect group is sometimes indicated by the siglum *A2* (Asyutic), suggested by M. Chaine (1934). In spite of these designations, the geographical connection of Lykopolitan with Asyut is rather weak: the city could have been "the (more or less) northernmost borderline" of the vast area where *L* was in use (Gardner, Alcock, and Funk 1999: 91 n. 132). The southern border could have been the city of Akhmim, hence the alternative qualification of the variety in question as Sub-Akhmimic (see Nagel 1991: 151–54).

It should be stressed that the so-called Lykopolitan is not a single dialect but a set of geographically dispersed, distinct varieties. Every corpus and even single texts that have been qualified as *L* has its own linguistic peculiarities. Most of the differences concern the divergent use of vowels, thus phonetics (or spelling), but there are also some morphological differences

(Nagel 1991: 155–58). All these peculiarities have been meticulously described by scholars such as Chaine (1934), Vergote (1973–83), Nagel (1991), and Funk (1985; 1990), among others.

The main varieties of Lykopolitan are indicated by the siglum *L* with an index, in most cases a digit, but in our case an asterisk:

- *L4*: Manichaean texts found in Medinet Madi
- *L5*: fragments of the Gospel of John and the Acta Pauli from the Bibliotheca Bodmeriana
- *L6*: part of the Nag' Hammadi texts and the Acta Pauli from Heidelberg
- *L**: the particular variety of Lykopolitan attested in the Manichaean texts from Kellis.

According to current views, the texts written in the diverse varieties of *L* originate for the greatest part in the fourth century AD, with a few exceptions dated to the end of the third century and the fifth century respectively (Nagel 1991: 152–53). They are thus among the earliest texts written in Coptic, which makes them an important subject of research not only as regards their content but also their specific idioms. Moreover, it is significant that these early varieties of Coptic seem to disappear in the fifth century. Both the abrupt emergence and the disappearance of these varieties can tell us a lot about the origins and rise of Coptic literacy. It is this process that I am going to illustrate with the material from Kellis.

Challenging Myths about Early Coptic

There are three persistent myths about early Coptic that I would like to question in this chapter:

1. that early Coptic texts would show us how Egyptians of the fourth century spoke;
2. that, due to contacts with Greek during the preceding centuries, Coptic became so heavily 'Hellenized' that one could qualify it as a "bilingual language variety" (Reintges 2001; Reintges 2004a: 36–43; Reintges 2004b);
3. that Coptic would be used by the Egyptian Christians in order to convert simple people who lacked a command of Greek.

The last two statements are obviously mutually contradictory, as already observed in 1993 by R.S. Bagnall, who also points to the "deliberateness" with which Coptic was "invented" (Bagnall 1993: 238, 253). Still, many a study of Coptic is based on the above unquestioningly accepted assumptions, which can be paraphrased as follows: after the establishment of the Ptolemaic dynasty, which imposed Greek as the language of administration and cultural prestige, more and more Egyptians had to become bilingual and the Egyptian language they spoke became more and more influenced by Greek. When the need arose to translate Christian literature into their native tongue, they were thus compelled to use their heavily Hellenized vernacular, Coptic, for this purpose.

In what follows I would like to present an alternative view on early Coptic and to put forward arguments in favor of the view that it should be seen as a deliberately constructed literary idiom, akin to a secret language and intended for in-group use within particular ascetic communities of fourth-century Egypt. Furthermore, I will argue that the linguistic peculiarities of *L** should be looked at and explained in that light.

The starting point for my argumentation is the above observation that the rise of Coptic as an alternative literary language, despite the dominant position of Greek as the language of culture, administration, and, importantly, Christian discourse, involved a dramatic change in the *linguistic behavior* of certain segments of the Egyptian population. As a change of linguistic behavior is basically a social phenomenon (Milroy 1992: 202), the approach adopted here is a sociolinguistic one: the main explanatory principles that I employ refer to *social functions of language use*. My approach is inspired by insights from the following disciplines:

- Social Network Analysis and its sociolinguistic applications, for example, Barabási (2002), Bruggeman (2008), Kadushin (2012), Scott (2013), Ruffini (2008), Schor (2011), Collar (2013), L. Milroy (1987; 2002), J. Milroy (1992), J. and L. Milroy (1985)
- social dialectology and historical sociolinguistics, for example, Britain and Cheshire (2003), Hernández-Campoy and Conde-Silvestre (2012)
- contact linguistics, for example, Muysken (2000; 2007; 2010), Myers-Scotton (2006), Matras (2009), Johanson (2013)
- literacy studies, for example, Gee (1996), Edwards and Sienkewicz (1990), Hornberger (2003), Street (2000), Wagner, Outhwaite, and Beinhoff (2013).

More relevant references are to be found in my articles (Zakrzewska, forthcoming a; forthcoming b), which form the basis of of the next section, below. In this section, theoretical argumentation from these two articles is illustrated with the data from Kellis. In this way I would like to achieve two aims: first, to illustrate my earlier theoretical studies on the rise of Coptic literacy with actual material and, second, to demonstrate that specific features of this material are best explained in the light of those studies, in other words to demonstrate the explanatory value of my argumentation.

An Alternative View on Early Coptic

Does Coptic Represent Spoken Egyptian?

As I argue in Zakrzewska, forthcoming a and forthcoming b, the above question has to be answered in the negative. Although a substantial percentage of the inhabitants of Egypt in the third to fourth centuries AD must have spoken a form of Egyptian, there is no evidence of what this spoken Egyptian could have been like. What can be studied is *literary Coptic* as represented by various scribal traditions. Instead of speculating about the supposedly high degree of bilingualism in late antique Egypt, we should thus better discuss well-attested *biliteracy*, that is "the use of two or more languages in or around writing" (Hornberger 2003: xii; see also Johanson 2013).

From our ethnocentric perspective we often take it for granted that people write down what they otherwise would say. In a milieu of restricted literacy, however, *literacy practices* can have more symbolic than utilitarian function. This phenomenon can be illustrated by the following quotation from B. Street, one of the pioneers of literacy studies: "Literacy was not simply a set of functional skills, but rather it was a set of social practices deeply associated with identity and social position" (Street 2000: 22–23).

Even in modern highly standardized languages, considerable differences exist between spoken and written linguistic varieties. This was even more so in antiquity when access to literacy was limited. Being literate was the exclusive privilege of the upper strata of society, who could afford education and for whom practicing literacy was a question not only of practical needs but also of social and cultural considerations, such as the expression of a certain lifestyle. As early Coptic texts are often texts of the highest status and the highest literary and intellectual quality (for example, translations of Holy Scripture and of theological and philosophical studies, including Manichaean and Gnostic treatises), it can safely be assumed that their writers tried to distance themselves from any vernacular.

Even in the case of letters, the utilitarian function of the text (conveying a message) was considered subordinate to the symbolic one (evoking the shared social and cultural background of the correspondents). This last function was facilitated by the ample use of appropriate formulary expressions that enhanced the symbolic function of texts, as they allowed both the author and the addressee mutual recognition as members of the educated milieu, sharing the intricate conventions of verbal etiquette. A characteristic example of the superiority of the symbolic function of written texts above the utilitarian one are some letters found in Egypt that consist almost entirely of polite formulae (Bagnall and Cribiore 2006: 12–14). The business-like part of the message, as socially less significant, was considered less worthy of being put down and possibly had to be delivered orally by the carrier of the letter. Another example is provided by some letters from Kellis in which formulary sections are in Greek, the language of higher prestige, while the business-like body of the letter is in Coptic (P.Kell. Copt. 22, 24, 35, 43).

This last phenomenon, a situation in which one text contains chunks in two languages, chunks that are larger than one word or phrase, is a conscious communicative strategy called *alternational code mixing* (Muysken 2000: 96–121; Muysken 2007: 321–22, 332–34; see also Johanson 2013: 299–306). The alternating text chunks are not random but are differentiated with respect to their discourse functions, as, in our case, participant-oriented (formulary) versus business-like. This is a nice piece of evidence which points to conscious use of linguistic means by the members of the Manichaean community, well known for their respect for writing and the written word (Gardner, Alcock, and Funk 1999: 77, 163 n. 19).

Were Coptic Writings Used for Converting Egyptians without a Command of Greek?

My answer is again in the negative. In a culture characterized by restricted literacy, as in late antique Egypt (Goody 1968, 11–20; Bagnall 1993: 259–60), conversions, even of individuals, were primarily a social process more likely to be brought about by the influence of social networks (see "Social Networks and Innovative Language Use," below, and Van der Vliet 2013).

As for the use of Coptic, it is remarkable that from the very beginning texts written in this language show a mature literary idiom in which even the most complicated subject matter can be expressed. This functional versatility of Coptic came at a price. Coptic writers had to adopt not only the Greek alphabet but also literary genres, argumentative structures, and rhetorical figures. Moreover, in order to handle new intellectual notions they had to borrow numerous Greek words. Paraphrasing P. Muysken (2000: 275), one could say that they wanted to express in *Egyptian* the *Christian Greek* conceptual universe. For example, in the Kellis letters, 25 percent of the vocabulary is of Greek origin (see "The Use of Greek Loanwords," below). Therefore, early Coptic writings were simply incomprehensible to people without a thorough Hellenistic education. Nevertheless, the fact that literary Coptic was constructed on the basis of native Egyptian morphosyntax enriched with Greek borrowings, and not the other way around, suggests that Egyptian was the first language of the early Coptic writers.

An obvious question presents itself at this moment: who were these writers and for whom were their texts intended?

Social Networks and Innovative Language Use

As argued above, the use of Coptic as a literary language must have been a matter of choice rather than of necessity. It was also a radical change affecting the long-established linguistic behavior of certain groups of literate inhabitants of Egypt. In order to explain this change, I will resort to the applications of Social Network Analysis (SNA) in the field of sociolinguistics. Specifically, I will refer to the groundbreaking research of Lesley Milroy and James Milroy.

Linguistic changes follow scenarios known from other changes in human behavior, scenarios that have been the subject of much research within the framework of SNA. For a linguistic change to take place, at least two crucial initial stages are required: innovation and diffusion. The present considerations are limited to the first of these stages, innovation (for a reconstruction of the following stages, see Zakrzewska forthcoming a). As argued by J. Milroy, linguistic innovators are typically peripheral members of their community who "are often perceived as underconforming to the point of deviance" (Milroy 1992: 184). For potential innovators it is important not to have particularly *strong ties* within one particular community but to have multiple *weak ties* with members of various communities. Thanks to their multiple and rather loose contacts, or ties, with people from many communities, these peripheral members become aware of new ideas and can become inspired by them. Consequently, they can function as "bridges through which information and influence are diffused" (Milroy 1992: 184; see also Bruggeman 2008: 68–77; Kadushin 2012: 31–31, 42–43). In contrast, having strong ties with other members favors norm-enforcing behavior and quite disfavors the bridging function.

Now, let us return to late antique Egypt. The end of the third century and the first half of the fourth saw the rise of diverse ascetic communities: Catholic, Manichaean, Melitian, Gnostic (Emmel 2008; Goehring 2007; Wipszycka 2009; Wipszycka 2013b). It is within these communities that the locus of the sociolinguistic change that led to the rise of Coptic should be situated. As is well known, these pioneers of the monastic movement consciously distanced themselves from their original social milieu and networks in order to create an alternative lifestyle that can only be characterized as innovative in the extreme. Part of this alternative lifestyle, in line with the revolutionary intellectual dynamism of these religious movements, may have been divergent linguistic behavior, in this case the use of Coptic in writing. To put it somewhat sharply: literary Coptic was thus *constructed* not in order to convert Egyptian peasants but to discuss new ideas with like-minded, well-educated 'counter-culturists.' One of these counter-culturist groups was the Manichaeans from Kellis.

How to Express Exclusion or Solidarity?

The life in the Manichaean community in Kellis, reconstructed on the basis of both textual and archaeological sources, has been summarily described by I. Gardner (Gardner 1996–2007, part 1: vi–xvii; part 2: 3–8; Gardner, Alcock, and Funk 1999: 5–58, 72–83). It is important to emphasize the ambivalent social situation of the members of such an 'alternative' community. On the one hand, they had to loosen their social ties with broad layers of the population and even their networks in the Nile Valley: "probably years might pass before a friend or family member in the valley would be able once again to visit the oasis" (Gardner, Alcock, and Funk 1999: 12). On the other hand, they had to forge strong ties with other members of their own community, a fact revealed by the Kellis letters, which "indicate a particularly close-knit set of family groups" resembling "sectarian movements, particularly in their earlier, world-denying stages" (Gardner 1996–2007, part 1: viii; see also Dal Fiore 2007, Bruggeman 2008: 37–61, and Kadushin 2012: 108–34 for communities vis-à-vis social networks in the context of innovative behavior). This interplay of weak versus strong social ties had clear correlates in the linguistic behavior of the members of the Manichaean community in question, at least as far as the use of Coptic in texts is concerned.

First and foremost, these early Coptic texts written with Greek characters and with a considerable quantity of Greek borrowings were inaccessible to both speakers of Egyptian lacking Hellenistic education and to people literate in Greek without a command of Egyptian. Writing in Coptic thus implied the *exclusion* of potential readers who belonged to either of these two groups, probably a greater part of the potential reading public. This can be interpreted as a so-called *negative act of identity*, underlying the construction of secret languages (see Croft 2003: 65–66).

Another important function of a secret language, beside exclusion of outsiders, is to confirm the *shared social identity* of the group members and their mutual solidarity ("positive acts of identity," Croft 2003: 65). In this context it is significant that potential adepts of the new way of writing could not rely on the traditional system of education, limited as it was to teaching Greek literacy. The education in Coptic at this initial stage took place within one's own community, as illustrated by one of the Kellis letters in which a father instructs his son to do writing exercises every day in order to be able to copy books eventually (P.Kell. Copt. 19, 13–19). Another example is a syllabary with specifically the 'new' (non-Greek) characters of the Coptic alphabet (P. Kell. Copt. 10).

In this way, one acquired linguistic norms that were accepted in this particular community and not outside it. At least two conspicuous linguistic properties of early Coptic, also observable in the Kellis texts, are generally acknowledged as facilitating the expression of the shared social identity: the cultivation of particular spelling conventions and the use of words borrowed from another, more prestigious language, in our case Greek.

Spelling Conventions

A well-known feature of linguistic behavior in close-knit communities is the cultivation of local standards of pronunciation, since even slight phonetic differences allow one to distinguish the members of the in-group from outsiders. For example, Milroy (1987: 116–38) distinguished six phonetic variants of the vowel */a/* in the speech of the inhabitants of certain close-knit Belfast neighborhoods. Milroy (1992: 98) observes that an occasional use of a more standard variant by one of the informants was "loudly mocked by his companions" and concludes that this extensive variation was maintained due to "community pressures."

This phenomenon seems to be reflected, at least to some extent, in a considerable 'dialectal' variation between the early Coptic text corpora. Recall that the differences pertain first of all to the divergent use of vowels ("What Are *L* and *L**?" above). To what degree this variation reflects the actual speaking habits and to what degree the *local scribal traditions* and spelling conventions is of secondary importance. What counts is the very fact that these particular traditions were cherished within the particular communities. Thanks to such linguistic strategies, as a rule meaningless for outsiders, the members of a given community could give expression to their shared experience and solidarity.

Seen in that light, early Coptic "dialect boundaries" could probably better be considered "social boundaries" or community boundaries (Myers-Scotton 2006: 31). This reconsideration of early Coptic dialects explains two things: first, that letters of the members of the Kellis community, written in several regions of Upper Egypt, are linguistically so conspicuously uniform among themselves (Gardner, Alcock, and Funk 1999: 84) and, secondly, that the Kellis texts are at the same time significantly different from texts written in other varieties of so-called Lykopolitan (see "What Are *L* and *L**?" above). These other texts originate, according to my line of reasoning, from different communities, which could also be geographically dispersed. The lack of geographical contingency renders traditional dialectological explanations inadequate.

In contrast, according to social network theory, geographical considerations are of less importance than social and relational ones (Bruggeman 2008: 23).

The Use of Greek Loanwords

Another well-known feature that points to the 'constructed' character of early Coptic is the ample but arbitrary use of Greek lexical borrowings. Much research on language contact has conclusively demonstrated that the 'gap theory,' according to which the function of borrowed words is to fill lexical 'gaps' in the recipient language, is only one part of the story. At least equally important is the symbolic function of borrowings to *express one's social identity* (Muysken 2000: 69; see also Myers-Scotton 2006: 143, 167–69; Matras 2009: 149–53). An interesting property of a 'constructed' code, as opposed to one which arises as a result of 'organic' or spontaneous borrowing over an extended period of time, is different restrictions on lexical borrowings (Muysken 2007: 316–20). In the case of historical borrowing, the use of certain well-established loanwords becomes obligatory, especially as regards the so-called cultural vocabulary, lexical items that designate concepts valid in a specific cultural environment (such as the loanwords in English 'altar,' 'chapel,' 'Mass,' which are all of Latin origin and belong to the semantic domain of Christian worship). In contrast, a 'constructed' code typically displays various lexical idiosyncrasies: stylistic variation or words of native stock where one expects borrowed ones.

The arbitrary character of Greek lexical borrowing in Coptic was already signaled by Steindorff (1950: 201–202) and Kasser (1991: 217–18). As regards the Coptic texts from Kellis, the majority of Greek loanwords are indeed cultural vocabulary items, but some stylistic variation in their use can nevertheless be noticed; for example, the Greek legal term *katēgorein,* 'to accuse,' is used interchangeably with its Coptic equivalent *smme* (Demaria 2005: 111–13). The arbitrary character of Greek borrowings in these texts can be illustrated by the use of two words: *sah,* 'teacher,' versus *kathēkoumenos,* 'catechumen.' Both these words are technical terms that designate a particular position in the hierarchical structure of Manichaean social organization and thus belong to the cultural vocabulary. The term *sah* is used to designate 'the Teacher,' a dignitary holding one of the highest offices in the transnational Manichaean hierarchy and operating outside the Kellis community (Gardner, Alcock, and Funk 1999: 75–76). This dignitary is nevertheless referred to by a 'native Egyptian' word. In contrast, fellow villagers of a low status within the Manichaean hierarchy are referred to with the word *kathēkoumenos*, borrowed from Greek. This points to a deliberate construction of certain terminological conventions rather than to organic development.

As for the proportion of words of Greek origin, these form 25 percent of the lexical entries listed in the Indices of the edited documentary Coptic texts from Kellis (Gardner, Alcock, and Funk 1999: 282–315) and 18 percent of the entries of the literary Coptic texts (Gardner 1996–2007, part 1: 145–69; part 2: 139–56). These percentages may seem high in comparison with pre-Coptic Egyptian, but are not especially impressive from a cross-linguistic perspective. Compared with the results of the Leipzig-based Loanword Typology Project (LWT) reported by Tadmor (2009: 56–57), this particular variety of Coptic could qualify as an 'average borrower,' comparable to Dutch (with 19 percent loanwords) rather than a 'high borrower' like English (41 percent). This is clearly at odds with some rather 'impressionistic' assumptions of an exceptionally high degree of Greek lexical influence on Coptic mentioned in the section above. The actual influence, at least as attested in *L**, appears to be limited to cultural vocabulary adopted in a rather arbitrary fashion and in an average quantity. It is thus much less spectacular than what Reintges' dramatic expression "bilingual language variety" might suggest.

As suggested above, the well-established statements about the excessively high proportion of Greek loanwords in Coptic are influenced by comparisons with the earlier stages of Egyptian, which do not show any significant foreign lexical influence. In this respect, writing in Coptic involved, again, a break with old (and by that time obsolete) literary conventions. From a cross-linguistic and cross-cultural perspective, however, it is these conventions of pre-Coptic Egyptian that should be considered exceptional. In other literary traditions, of which Coptic appears to be an instance, a strategy of adopting diverse elements from a prestige language is quite common and, as Johanson concludes, "the codes representing this type do not seem to deserve characteristics such as 'intertwined,' 'mixed' or 'hybrid,' even if they, as English, manifest excessive copying" (Johanson 2013: 323).

*L** as an In-group Variety: More Indications

The Kellis corpus also includes text fragments written in Sahidic. Significantly, these Sahidic texts are not Manichaean, but Catholic (Gardner 1996–2007, part 1: vii; part 2: 5). This indicates once again that the selection of a particular variety of early Coptic was determined by the wish of its users to express a certain *social meaning*, to mark their allegiance to a particular community.

The important role of *expressive function* of early Coptic may explain the disappearance of most Upper Egyptian varieties toward the end of the fourth century when they were superseded by Sahidic. These sociolinguistic processes coincide with the decline of some of the early ascetic communities and the growth, in both size and importance, of others, in particular the Catholic Pachomian ones. As is well known, Sahidic, which became the most important supra-regional variety of Coptic in the centuries that followed, can hardly be pinpointed as a dialect of a specific locality or region in Upper Egypt. It is tempting to hypothesize that the variety of Coptic conventionally called Sahidic was the one that the successful Catholic communities adopted for their purposes and passed on to their followers. Such a hypothetical scenario is entirely consistent with Social Network Analysis, which ascribes successful diffusion of an innovation not to the original nonconformist inventors, but to well-connected and influential *opinion leaders* (Kadushin 2012: 141–46). Without the slightest doubt, Pachomius and his successors can be considered prominent opinion leaders of their times.

Summary and Conclusions

In this chapter I have argued that early Coptic was not simply an Egyptian vernacular but a deliberately constructed alternative literary language and a prestige variety. In order to stress this point, I have consistently referred to the *writers* or *users*, instead of speakers, of Coptic. I have also refrained from sticking anachronistic 'nationalistic' labels on members of supposedly antagonistic ethnic groups (Egyptians versus Greeks) and from simplistic equations between language use and ethnic identity: "Markos speaks Coptic, so Markos is a Copt" (see also Wipszycka 1992 and Fournet 2009: 432–34). Incidentally, I have carefully avoided using the term 'Copts,' anachronistic for the time before the Arab conquest.

The association of Coptic with Christianity is not due to its alleged function of converting 'indigenous' Egyptians, but to its rise and development within early ascetic communities that were the locus of innovative and highly regarded social practices in late antiquity. I have argued that early Coptic was an in-group variety akin to secret languages, which was used as a linguistic correlate of innovative social practices in these communities. Specifically, one of these early communities comprised the writers and readers of the Manichaean texts from Kellis who, by constructing the variety of Coptic conventionally called *L**, creatively used the Egyptian and Greek linguistic resources at their disposal in order to strengthen their social ties and in-group solidarity. Accordingly, I have argued that the traditional dialect boundaries should be reinterpreted as social boundaries, rather than geographical ones.

As regards the role of Greek lexical borrowings, without denying their rather obvious communicative function of filling semantic 'gaps,' I have emphasized their symbolic function of signaling one's social identity. Moreover, I have argued that the use of Greek loanwords in Coptic, besides being less excessive than is sometimes assumed, was more likely an expedient for constructing novel literary conventions than a reflection of actual bilingual speech.

The interpretation offered here has allowed me to explain in a natural and coherent way several apparent oddities that were left unexplained by traditional accounts, for example:

- The linguistic differentiation of the particular corpora and the proliferation of distinct varieties of early Coptic. This can be explained by referring to particular norms maintained and taught within a particular community.

- The geographical dispersion of these varieties, as social networks are based on relations between their members rather than geographical contingency.
- The arbitrary character of lexical borrowings from Greek as characteristic of deliberate borrowing, in contrast to organic or spontaneous borrowing over a prolonged period of time.
- The sudden appearance and disappearance of most Upper Egyptian varieties of Coptic in the fourth century as corresponding to the rise and decline of diverse ascetic communities in that century, as well as the fact that these varieties were eventually ousted by Sahidic, the idiom of the Catholic communities that came to dominate the Christian landscape of Upper Egypt from the fifth century onward.

19 Bawit in the Twenty-first Century: Bibliography 1997–2014

Dominique Bénazeth

Since the rediscovery of the Bawit monastery in 1900, numerous investigations have covered diverse fields of research. Marie-Hélène Rutschowscaya established a bibliography of the main titles, following the chronological order of publication:

Rutschowscaya, M.-H. 1995. "Le monastère de Baouit. Etat des publications." In C. Fluck, L. Langener, S. Richter, S. Schaten, and G. Wurst, eds., *Divitiae Aegypti: Koptologische und verwandte Studien zu Ehren von Martin Krause*, pp. 279–88. Wiesbaden: L. Reichert Verlag.

In the same book, Anne Boud'hors published "Papyrus de Clédat au musée du Louvre" (pp. 29–35).

Both of these scholars were working on the archaeologist Jean Clédat's unpublished archives and on Coptic texts found by him:

Clédat, J. 1999. *Le monastère et la nécropole de Baouit: Notes mises en œuvre et éditées par Dominique Bénazeth et Marie-Hélène Rutschowscaya, avec des contributions de Anne Boud'hors, René-Georges Coquin, Éliane Gaillard*. Cairo: Institut français d'archéologie orientale.

This publication contains the archives of two campaigns (1904 and 1905), followed by chapters "Ostraca" and "Note sur les papyrus," as well as important indexes, prepared by Anne Boud'hors with the help of René-Georges Coquin (these also cover previous archaeological reports from Jean

Clédat, Émile Chassinat, and Charles Palanque, as well as some significant articles, listed on pp. 397–98). This important book has been reviewed twice:

Bingen, J. 2000. *Chronique d'Égypte* 75, no. 149, pp. 201–203.

Clackson, S.J. 2002. *Bulletin of the American Society of Papyrologists* 39, pp. 189–204.

At the turn of the century, research and projects concerning the site were summarized in a communication:

Rutschowscaya, M.-H., and D. Bénazeth. 1998. "Fouilles de Baouit, passé, présent et futur." *Actes du Symposium des fouilles coptes, Le Caire 7–9 novembre 1996*, pp. 89–92, pls. XXIV–XXV. Cairo: Société d'archéologie copte.

New identifications of texts, the discovery of archives, and reopening the excavation have enlarged our knowledge of the monastery, which has been revisited in two general summaries:

Wipszycka, E. 2009. *Moines et communautés monastiques en Égypte, IVe–VIIIe siècles*, pp. 143–50. Warsaw: Warsaw University.

Bénazeth, D. Forthcoming. "Bawit." In C. Finney and C. Noll, eds., *Encyclopedia of Early Christian Art and Archaeology*. Grand Rapids, MI: Wm. B. Eerdmans Publishing Co.

A large range of specific studies has added considerably to the bibliography. The present list takes into account articles from 1997 to 2014, and also makes mention of forthcoming publications. It is organized into nine classifications, presented in chronological order: texts; artifacts in museums; topography; twentieth-century excavations; twenty-first-century excavations; monuments; sculpture; painting; objects. When a book or article deals with other subjects, only the pages mentioning Bawit are given.

Texts

Life of Apollo and Phib

Vivian, T. 1999. "Monks, Middle Egypt, and Metanoia: The Life of Phib by Papohe the Steward (Translation and Introduction)." *Journal of Early Christian Studies* 7, no. 4, pp. 547–71.

Wadi, A. 2007. "Vita dei santi Apollo e Phib (Abīb)." *Studia Orientalia Christiana Collectanea* 40, pp. 237–91. Turnhout: Brepols.

Pirone, B. 2008. "Vite dei santi Apollo e Phib (Abīb)." *Studia Orientalia Christiana Collectanea* 41, pp. 139–76. Turnhout: Brepols.

Vanthighem, N. 2010. "La vie arabe d'Apollô et Phib." In *Édition, traduction et études de textes hagiographiques arabes traduits du copte*. Master's thesis, Université libre de Bruxelles.

Studies

Clackson, S.J. 1999. "Something Fishy in CPR XX." *Archiv für Papyrusforschung und verwandte Gebiete* 45, no. 1, pp. 94–95.

Clackson, S.J. 2000. *Coptic and Greek Texts Relating to the Hermopolite Monastery of Apa Apollo*. Oxford: Griffith Institute.

Gonis, N. 2000. "Two Fiscal Registers from Early Islamic Egypt (*P. Vatic. Aphrod.* 13, *SB* XX 14701)." *Journal of Juristic Papyrology* 30 (1. *P. Vatic. Aphrod.* 13), pp. 21–25.

Gonis, N. 2000. "Two Poll-tax Receipts from Early Islamic Egypt." *Zeitschrift für Papyrologie und Epigraphik* 131, p. 154, no. 1.

Clackson, S.J. 2001. "Reconstructing the Archives of the Monastery of Apollo at Bawit." In I. Andorlini, G. Bastianini, M. Manfredi, and G. Menci, eds., *Atti del XXII Congresso Internazionale di Papirologia (Firenze 23–29 agosto 1998)*, 1, pp. 219–36, pls. VI–VIII. Florence: Istituto Papirologico G. Vitelli.

Hasitzka, M. 2001. "Brief des Klostervorstehers Theodoros die Aparchè-Sammlung Betreffend." *Journal of Juristic Papyrology* 31, pp. 55–58.

Horak, U. 2001. "Credo mit magischen Zeichnungen." *Analecta papyrologica* 13, pp. 55–61.

Pintaudi, R. 2001. "Filatterio su carta araba orientale: Il simbolo Niceno-Costantinopolitano (*PL* III/960)." *Analecta Papyrologica* 13, pp. 47–53.

Wipszycka, E. 2001. "Le fonctionnement interne des monastères et des laures en Égypte du point de vue économique: A propos d'une publication récente de textes coptes de Bawit." *Journal of Juristic Papyrology* 31, pp. 169–86.

Clackson, S.J. 2002. "Fish and Chits: The *Synodontis schall*." *Zeitschrift für ägyptische Sprache und Altertumskunde* 129, pp. 6–11.

Worp, K.A. 2002. "The Date of O. Crum VC 111 and O. Bawit 56–58 & 62." *Zeitschrift für Papyrologie und Epigraphik* 138, pp. 121–22.

Clackson, S.J. 2003. "Nouvelles recherches sur les papyrus de Baouit." In Chr. Cannuyer, ed., *Études coptes VIII: Dixième journée d'études, Lille 14–16 juin 2001*, pp. 77–84. Lille and Paris: Association francophone de coptologie.

Krause, M. 2003. "Zu den nach Apollo benannten Klöstern in Ägypten." In W. Beltz, U. Pietruschka, and J. Tubach, eds., *Sprache und Geist. Peter*

Nagel zum 65. Geburtstag, pp. 149–66. Halle (Saale): Martin-Luther-Universität Halle-Wittenberg.

Boud'hors, A. 2004. *Ostraca grecs et coptes des fouilles de Jean Maspero à Baouit. O. BawitIFAO 1–67 et O. Nancy*. Cairo: Institut français d'archéologie orientale.

Clackson, S.J. 2004. "Museum Archaeology and Coptic Papyrology: The Bawit Papyri." In M. Immerzeel and J. van der Vliet, eds., *Coptic Studies on the Threshold of a New Millenium*, 1, pp. 477–90. Louvain, Paris, and Dudley, MA: Peeters.

Clackson, S.J. 2004. "Papyrology and the Utilization of Coptic Sources." In P.M. Sijpesteijn and L. Sundelin, eds., *Papyrology and the History of Early Islamic Egypt*, pp. 21–44. Leiden and Boston: Brill.

Delattre, A. 2004. "Un contrat de prêt copte du monastère de Baouît." *Chronique d'Égypte* 79, no. 157–58, pp. 385–89.

Delattre, A. 2004. "P.Yale Copt. 29: Une nouvelle attestation du village de Titkooh (Korr. Tyche 519)." *Tyche* 19, p. 260.

Delattre, A. 2005. "La formule épistolaire copte 'C'est votre serviteur qui ose écrire à son seigneur.'" *Archiv für Papyrusforschung und verwandte Gebiete* 51, no. 1, pp. 105–11.

Delattre, A. 2005. "Une liste de propriétés foncières du monastère d'apa Apollô de Baouît." *Zeitschrift für Papyrologie und Epigraphik* 151, pp. 163–65.

Delattre, A. 2005. "Recherches sur le monastère d'apa Apollô (Baouit): L'organisation du monastère aux VIIe et VIIIe siècles." In X. Luffin and S. Vanséveren, eds., *Orientalia d'hier et d'aujourd'hui, Lettres Orientales* 8, pp. 3–8. Louvain: Peeters.

Wipszycka, E. 2005. "Le nombre des moines dans les communautés monastiques d'Egypte." *Journal of Juristic Papyrology* 35, pp. 274, 301–303.

Boud'hors, A. 2006. "Book Review of M.R. Hasitzka, '*Koptisches Sammelbuch* II, Vienne 2004.'" *Orientalia*, Nova Series vol. 75, no. 1, pp. 134–36.

[Muhs, B.P., K.A. Worp, and] J. van der Vliet. 2006. "Ostraca and Mummy Labels in Los Angeles." *Bulletin of the American Society of Papyrologists* 43, pp. 51–58.

Calament, Fl. 2007. "Des murs et des poteries qui parlent." *Le monde de la Bible* 177, pp. 38–41.

Clackson, S.J. 2007. "Archimandrites and *andrismos*: A Preliminary Survey of Taxation at Bawit." In B. Palme, ed., *Akten des 23. Internationalen Papyrologenkongresses (Wien 22.–28. Juli 2001)*, pp. 103–107. Vienna: Verlag der Österreichischen Akademie der Wissenschaften.

Delattre, A. 2007. "La collection papyrologique copte des Musées Royaux d'art et d'histoire de Bruxelles." In N. Bosson and A. Boud'hors, eds., *Actes du huitième congrès international d'études coptes (Paris 2004)*, 1, pp. 79–84. Paris and Louvain: Peeters.

Delattre, A. 2007. "Une lettre copte du monastère de Baouît: Réédition de *P.Mich.Copt.* 14." *Bulletin of the American Society of Papyrologists* 44, pp. 87–95.

Delattre, A. 2007. *Papyrus coptes et grecs du monastère d'apa Apollô de Baouît conservés aux Musées royaux d'Art et d'Histoire de Bruxelles*. Académie royale de Belgique, Mémoire de la Classe des Lettres, 3e série, tome 43, no. 2045. Brussels: Académie royale de Belgique.

Delattre, A. 2007. "La réutilisation des protocoles aux époques byzantine et arabe." In J. Frösen, T. Purola, and E. Salmenkivi, eds., *Proceedings of the 24th International Congress of Papyrology, Helsinki, 1–7 August, 2004*, 1, pp. 219–20 (Annexe: La réutilisation des protocoles au sein du monastère de Baouît). Helsinki: Societas Scientiarum Fennica.

Van Neer, W., W. Wouters, M.-H. Rutschowscaya, A. Delattre, D. Dixneuf, K. Desender, and J. Poblome. 2007. "Salted Fish Products from the Coptic Monastery at Bawit, Egypt: Evidence from the Bones and Texts." In H. Hüster Plogmann, ed., *The Role of Fish in Ancient Times: Proceedings of the 13th Meeting of the ICAZ Fish Remains Working Group on October 4th–9th, Basel/August 2005*, pp. 147–59. Rahden/Westf: Verlag Marie Leidorf.

Calament, Fl. 2008. "Nouvelles inscriptions à Baouît (campagnes de 2003 et 2004)." In A. Boud'hors and C. Louis, eds., *Études coptes X: Douzième journée d'études (Lyon, 19–21 mai 2005)*, pp. 23–38. Paris: De Boccard.

Clackson, S.J. 2008. *It Is Our Father Who Writes: Orders from the Monastery of Apollo at Bawit*. Cincinnati, OH: American Society of Papyrologists.

Delattre, A. 2008. "Ordres de paiement bilingues du monastère de Baouît." *Chronique d'Égypte* 83, no. 165–66, pp. 385–92.

Delattre, A. 2008. "Remarques sur quelques inscriptions du monastère de Baouît." *Bulletin de l'Institut français d'archéologie orientale* 108, pp. 69–81.

Delattre, A. 2008. "La vie quotidienne dans les monastères égyptiens." In H. Froschauer and C.E. Römer, eds., *Spätantike Bibliotheken: Leben und Lesen in den frühen Klöstern Ägyptens*, pp. 55–58, cat. 44 [*Alltag in den frühen Klöstern Ägyptens*, pp. 67–70]. Vienna: Phoibos Verlag.

Saeed Abd Elhameed Ahmed, S. 2008. *A Group of Unpublished Coptic Ostraca in the Cairo Museum*, 1. Cairo: al-Zaim li-l-Khadamat al-Maktabiya.

Youssef, Y.N. 2008. "Book Review: A. Delattre, *Papyrus coptes et grecs* (2007)." *Bulletin de la Société d'archéologie copte* 47, pp. 161–63.

Boud'hors, A., J. Clackson, C. Louis, and P. Sijpesteijn, eds. 2009. *Monastic Estates in Late Antique and Early Islamic Egypt: Ostraca, Papyri, and Essays in Memory of Sarah Clackson*. Cincinnati, OH: American Society of Papyrologists.

Boud'hors, A., and S. Clackson. 2009. "O. Clackson 1–17. Ostraca de Baouît conservés à l'Institut d'égyptologie d'Heidelberg." In Boud'hors, Clackson, Louis, and Sijpesteijn 2009, pp. 1–22.

Delattre, A., and N. Gonis. 2009. "P. Clackson 36–43. Le dossier des reçus de taxe grecs du monastère d'Apa Apollo à Baouit." In Boud'hors, Clackson, Louis, and Sijpesteijn 2009, pp. 61–71.

Fournet, J.-L. 2009. "Conversion religieuse dans un graffito de Baouit? Révision de *SB* III 6042." In Boud'hors, Clackson, Louis, and Sijpesteijn 2009, pp. 141–47.

Krause, M. 2009. "Die koptischen Kaufurkunden von Klosterzellen des Apollo-Klosters von Bawit aus abbasidischer Zeit." In Boud'hors, Clackson, Louis, and Sijpesteijn 2009, pp. 159–69.

Richter, T.S. 2009. "The Cultivation of Monastic Estates in Late Antique and Early Islamic Egypt: Some Evidence from Coptic Land Leases and Related Documents." In Boud'hors, Clackson, Louis, and Sijpesteijn 2009, pp. 205–15.

Sijpesteijn, P.M., and S.J. Clackson with N. Gonis. 2009. "Appendix: P. Clackson 45–46: A Mid-eighth-century Trilingual Tax Demand Related to the Monastery of Apa Apollo at Bawīt." In Boud'hors, Clackson, Louis, and Sijpesteijn 2009, pp. 102–21.

Torallas Tovar, S. 2009. "P. Clackson 47: A Fragment of a Coptic Document from the Monastery of Apa Apollo." In Boud'hors, Clackson, Louis, and Sijpesteijn 2009, pp. 122–23.

Torallas Tovar, S., and K.A. Worp. 2009. "P. Clackson 48–50: Three Greek Montserrat Texts Related to the Monastery of Apa Apollo." In Boud'hors, Clackson, Louis, and Sijpesteijn 2009, pp. 124–28.

Benaissa, A. 2010. "A Usurious Monk from the Apa Apollo Monastery at Bawit." *Chronique d'Égypte* 85, no. 169–70, pp. 374–31.

Delattre, A. 2010. "L'administration de Baouît au VIIIe siècle. À propos des documents peneiôt petshai." *Chronique d'Égypte* 85, no. 169–70, pp. 391–95.

Delattre, A. 2010. "Une curieuse table d'ombres au monastère de Baouît." *Le Muséon* 123, no. 3–4, pp. 273–86.

Delattre, A. 2010. "Des linteaux et des noms: Une enquête prosopographique à Baouît." In A. Boud'hors and C. Louis, eds., *Études coptes XI: Treizième journée d'études (Marseille 7–9 juin 2007)*, pp. 25–30. Paris: De Boccard.

Delattre, A. 2010. "P.Heid. inv. K. 98: Une nouvelle lettre de Baouît?" *Bulletin of the American Society of Papyrologists* 47, pp. 236–37.

Bucking, S.C. 2011. *Practice Makes Perfect: P. Cotsen–Princeton 1 and the Training of Scribes in Byzantine Egypt*. Los Angeles: Cotsen Occasional Press.

Calament, Fl. 2011. "Book Review: Boud'hors, A., J. Clackson, C. Louis, and P. Sijpesteijn (2009)." *Journal of Coptic Studies* 13, pp. 220–25.

Hasitzka, M.R.M., ed. 2011. *Koptische dokumentarische und literarische Texte: First International Summer School in Coptic Papyrology 2006 in der Papyrussammlung der Österreichischen Nationalbibliothek*, pp. 6–12, 66. Berlin and New York: W. de Gruyter.

Albarrán Martínez, M.-J. 2012. "A New Coptic Text from Bawit: P. Palau Rib. Inv. 352." In P. Schubert, ed., *Actes du 26e Congrès international de papyrologie (Genève, 16–21 août 2010)*, pp. 7–10. Geneva: Droz.

Delattre, A. 2012. "Book Review: Bucking (2011)." *Chronique d'Égypte* 87, no. 174, pp. 393–94.

Delattre, A. 2012. "Deux ordres du supérieur du monastère de Baouît P.Duk. Inv. 259 et 1053." *Bulletin of the American Society of Papyrologists* 49, pp. 167–74.

Delattre, A. 2012. "Trois papyrus du monastère de Baouît." *Bulletin de l'Institut français d'archéologie orientale* 112, pp. 101–10.

Fournet, J.-L. 2012. "La 'dipintologie' grecque: Une nouvelle discipline auxiliaire de la papyrologie?" In P. Schubert, ed., *Actes du 26e Congrès international de papyrologie (Genève, 16–21 août 2010)*, p. 249–58. Geneva: Droz.

Blumell, L.H. 2013. "Two Coptic Ostraca in the Brigham Young University Collection." *Chronique d'Égypte* 88, no. 175, pp. 182–83, 186–87, fig. 2.

Delattre, A. 2013. "Nouveaux papyrus du monastère de Baouît." In A. Boud'hors and C. Louis, eds., *Études coptes XII, Quatorzième journée d'études (Rome, 11–13 juin 2009)*, pp. 61–73. Paris: De Boccard.

Vicens, X.M. 2013. "Un papyrus de Baouît conservé à l'Archive et Bibliothèque Épiscopale de Vic." *Zeitschrift für Papyrologie und Epigraphik* 185, pp. 232–34.

Clarkson, S.J., and A. Delattre. 2014. *Papyrus grecs et coptes de Baouît conservés au musée du Louvre*. Bibliothèque d'études coptes 22. Cairo: IFAO.

Delattre, A. 2014. "Le monastère de Baouit et l'administration arabe." In A.T. Schubert and P.M. Sijpesteijn, eds., *Documents and the History of the Early Islamic World*, pp. 43–49. Leiden and Boston: Brill.

Calament, Fl. Forthcoming. "L'apport des nouvelles découvertes épigraphiques de Baouît (2006–2012)." In A. Camplani and P. Buzi, eds., *Acts of the Tenth International Congress of Coptic Studies (Rome 2012)*. Louvain-la-Neuve: Peeters.

Calament, Fl. Forthcoming. "Un 'Père du *topos*' à Baouît: L'apa Danièl." In A. Boud'hors and C. Louis, eds., *Études coptes XIII, Quinzième journée d'études (Louvain-la-Neuve, Université catholique, 12–14 mai 2011).* Cahiers de la Bibliothèque copte 20. Paris: De Boccard.

Calament, Fl., and H. Rochard. Forthcoming. "Les peintres à l'œuvre à Baouît: témoins iconographiques et épigraphiques." In *Mélanges dédiés à Catherine Jolivet-Lévy.* Travaux et mélanges du centre d'Histoire et Civilisation de Byzance. Paris: Collège de France.

Delattre, A. Forthcoming. "Le monastère de Baouit et l'administration arabe." In P.M. Sijpesteijn, ed., *Proceedings of the Third International Society for Arabic Papyrology Conference (Alexandria, 2006).* Leiden: Brill.

Delattre, A. Forthcoming. "Remarques sur la taxation au monastère de Baouît au début de l'époque arabe." In A. Kaplony and C. Römer, eds., *Proceedings of the Fourth International Society for Arabic Papyrology Conference, Vienna, 2009.* Leiden: Brill.

Delattre, A. Forthcoming. "La traduction des institutions administratives dans les monastères égyptiens (VIIe–VIIIe siècles)." In *Interpretatio: Traduire l'altérité culturelle dans les civilisations de l'Antiquité.* Strasbourg.

Legendre, M. Forthcoming. "Arabic Sources and Coptic Monasteries: An Impossible Dialogue? The Case of Bawit after the Islamic Conquest" and "New Developments for the Study of Bawit after the Islamic Conquest." In A. Kaplony and C. Römer, eds., *Proceedings of the Fourth International Society for Arabic Papyrology Conference, Vienna, 2009.* Leiden: Brill.

Schenke, G. Forthcoming. "Micro- and Macro-Management: Responsibilities of the Head of the Monastery of Apa Apollo at Bawit." In A. Camplani and P. Buzi, eds., *Acts of the Tenth International Congress of Coptic Studies (Rome 2012).* Louvain-la-Neuve: Peeters.

Schenke, G. Forthcoming. "Monastic Control over Agriculture and Farming: New Evidence from the Egyptian Monastery of Apa Apollo at Bawit." In A. Delattre, M. Legendre, and P.M. Sijpesteijn, eds., *Authority and Control in the Countryside: Late Antiquity and Early Islam, Continuity and Change in the Mediterranean, 6th–10th Century.* Greenwich: Darwin Press.

Artifacts in Museums

Bénazeth, D. 1997. "Un monastère dispersé: Les antiquités de Baouit conservées dans les musées d'Égypte." *Bulletin de l'Institut français d'archéologie orientale* 97, pp. 43–66.

Giroire, C., D. Ibled, and B. Lafay. 1997. "Une église égyptienne ressuscitée au musée du Louvre." *Revue du Louvre. La revue des musées de France* 5/6, pp. 95–102.

Rutschowscaya, M.-H. 1998. *Le Christ et l'abbé Ména*. Paris: Réunion des musées nationaux.

Guillain, A. 1999. *Inventaire de la collection égyptienne du musée d'Auch*, pp. 106–19. Montpellier: Université Paul Valéry Montpellier III.

Exhibition catalog 2000. *L'art copte en Égypte: 2000 ans de christianisme*, pp. 108–11, 113, 116–17, 148, 150. Paris: Institut du monde arabe/Gallimard.

Bénazeth, D. 2002. *Baouit: Une église copte au Louvre*. Paris: Réunion des musées nationaux.

Auth, S.H. 2005. "Brother George the Scribe: An Early Christian Panel Painting from Egypt in Context." *Eastern Christian Art* 2, pp. 19–36.

Daoud, G. 2005. "Les monastères coptes en Egypte [al-Adura al-Qibtiya fi Misr]." *Bulletin de la Société d'archéologie copte* 44, pp. 133–44, pls. XX, XXI.

Saeed Abd Elhameed Ahmed, S. 2008. See the section "Texts," above, for the Coptic ostraca in the Egyptian museum; some of them could be from Bawit.

Exhibition catalog 2009. *Une autre Égypte: Collections coptes du musée du Louvre* (Musée de Tessé, au Mans; Musée de Millau et des Grands Causses; Musée du pays de Sarrebourg), pp. 152–59, 164–69. Paris: Somogy.

Exhibition catalog 2009. *Un monastère égyptien: L'héritage de Jean Clédat*. Périgueux: Musée d'art et d'archéologie du Périgord. CD-ROM.

Rutschowscaya, M.-H. 2009. "Baouit." In *Objets d'Égypte: Des rives du Nil aux bords de la Seine*, pp. 51–65. Paris: Musée du Louvre/Le Passage.

Exhibition catalog. 2010. *Coptic Art Revealed*. Ph. Whitfield, N. Tomoun, and S. Marei, eds., pp. 37–39, 110–13, 124–25, 128–35. Cairo: Supreme Council of Antiquities.

Bénazeth, D. 2011. "Etude du matériel provenant de l'église nord du monastère de Baouit: Identification, raccords, analyses, restauration." In M.C. Guillard-Le Bourdellès, ed., *La recherche au musée du Louvre 2010*, p. 36. Paris and Milan: Musée du Louvre/Officina Libraria.

Exhibition catalog 2011. *Un altre Egipte: Colleccions coptes del Museu del Louvre* (Catalan) and *Otro Egipto: Colecciones coptas del Museo del Louvre* (Spanish and French), pp. 154–81, 184–87. Barcelona: Obra Social, Fundació "la Caixa."

Delattre, A. 2012. See the section "Texts," above, for the papyri in the Coptic Museum, Cairo.

Exhibition catalog 2012. *Byzantium and Islam: Age of Transition. 7th–9th Century*. H.C. Evans and B. Ratliff, eds., pp. 81–82, 83–86, 195–96. New York: The Metropolitan Museum of Art.

Bénazeth, D. 2013. "Le bassin fatimide du Musée Copte, inv. 5919, et sa surprenante provenance de Baouit." In A. Boud'hors and C. Louis, eds., *Études coptes XII, Quatorzième journée d'études (Rome 11–13 juin 2009)*, pp. 151–68. Paris: De Boccard.

Bénazeth, D. 2013. "Le cavalier qui avait traversé la mer: Note sur une sculpture de Baouit au musée copte du Caire et au musée du Louvre." In Y.N. Youssef and S. Moawad, eds., *From Old Cairo to the New World: Coptic Studies Presented to Gawdat Gabra on the Occasion of his Sixty-fifth Birthday*, pp. 15–28. Louvain, Paris, and Walpole, MA: Peeters.

Topography

Herbich, T., and D. Bénazeth. 2008. "Le *kôm* de Baouît: Étapes d'une cartographie." *Bulletin de l'Institut français d'archéologie orientale* 108, pp. 165–204.

Marchand, S., Gr. Marouard, M. Mossakowska-Gaubert, Fl. Calament, and C. Meurice. Forthcoming. "Survey du monastère d'*apa* Apollô de Baouît: Données archéologiques et analyses préliminaires de la céramique et du verre des ermitages de la montagne." In V. Ghica and Gr. Marouard, eds., *Ermitages d'Égypte au premier millénaire*. Cairo: Institut français d'archéologie orientale.

Twentieth-century Excavations

Rassart-Debergh, M. 2000. "Notes sur les églises de Baouît: Une relecture du dossier de Clédat." In A. Boud'hors, ed., *Études coptes VI: Huitième journée d'études (Colmar 29–31 mai 1997)*, pp. 69–94. Paris and Louvain: Peeters.

Gabra, G. 2002. *Coptic Monasteries: Egypt's Monastic Art and Architecture*, pp. 116–19, pl. 12, 1–5. Cairo: The American University in Cairo Press.

Wipszycka, E. 2002. "L'ascétisme féminin dans l'Egypte de l'antiquité tardive: *Topoi* littéraires et formes d'ascèse." In *Le rôle et le statut de la femme en Égypte hellénistique, romaine et byzantine: Actes du colloque international, Bruxelles–Leuven 27–29 novembre 1997*, pp. 369–72. Paris and Louvain: Peeters.

Gabra, G. 2004. "'New' Discoveries of Coptic Monuments: Problems of Their Preservation and Publication." In M. Immerzeel and J. van der Vliet, eds., *Coptic Studies on the Threshold of a New Millenium*, 2, pp. 1069, 1070. Louvain, Paris, and Dudley, MA: Peeters.

Bénazeth, D. 2005. "Calques de Baouit archivés à l'IFAO." *Bulletin de l'Institut français d'archéologie orientale* 105, pp. 1–11.

Gaillard, É. 2008. "Jean Clédat et la photographie." In A. Boud'hors and C. Louis, eds., *Études coptes X: Douzième journée d'études (Lyon, 19–21 mai 2005)*, pp. 51–61. Paris: De Boccard.

Meurice, C. 2008. "Baouît: Notes sur l'élaboration des publications de l'IFAO (1902–1916)." In A. Boud'hors and C. Louis, eds., *Études coptes X: Douzième journée d'études (Lyon, 19–21 mai 2005)*, pp. 77–87. Paris: De Boccard.

Torp, H. 2008. "The *Laura* of Apa Apollo at Bawit: Considerations on the Founder's Monastic Ideals and the South Church." *Arte medievale*, new series 5, no. 2, pp. 9–46.

Meurice, C. 2011. "La parenthèse égyptienne de Charles Palanque (1865–1909)." *Bulletin de la Société Archéologique, Historique, Littéraire et Scientifique du Gers* 399, pp. 69–71.

Rochard, H. Forthcoming. "Les fouilles de Jean Maspero à Baouit: Relecture de la documentation ancienne." In N. Bosson and A. Boud'hors, eds., *Études coptes XIV: Actes de la Seizième journée d'études (Genève 2013)*. Paris: De Boccard.

Chassinat, E. Forthcoming. *Fouilles à Baouît*. Vol. 2. Edited by Dominique Bénazeth and Cédric Meurice. Cairo: IFAO.

Twenty-first-century Excavations (Louvre–Institut français d'archéologie orientale du Caire)

Bénazeth, D. 2002–2008. "Travaux de l'Institut français d'archéologie orientale," ed. B. Mathieu, L. Pantalacci, and S. Denoix. *Bulletin de l'Institut français d'archéologie orientale*. Cairo: IFAO.

Bénazeth, D. 2004–2008. "Fouilles et travaux en Égypte et au Soudan," ed. N. Grimal, E. Adly, and A. Arnaudies. *Orientalia* 73–77.

Bénazeth, D. 2004. "Recherches archéologiques à Baouit: Un nouveau départ." *Bulletin de la Société d'archéologie copte* 43, pp. 9–24, pls. I–II (the plates are reversed).

Bénazeth, D., and M.-H. Rutschowscaya. 2005. "Neue Grabungen im Kloster von Bawit (2003–2004)." *Kemet* 14, no. 1, pp. 56–59, pl. p. 99.

Boutros, R., and M.-H. Rutschowscaya with contributions from S. Marchand and M. Mossakowska. 2005. "Sondages dans le monastère de Baouit—2003." *Bulletin de l'Institut français d'archéologie orientale* 105, pp. 13–34.

Rutschowscaya, M.-H. 2005. "Fouilles du monastère copte de Baouit

(Moyenne Égypte): Musée du Louvre–Institut français d'archéologie orientale du Caire: Saisons 2002–2003." *La Revue des musées de France. Revue du Louvre* 2, pp. 27–30.

Bovot, J.-L. 2007. "Archéologie d'un couvent égyptien." *Le monde de la Bible* 177, pp. 43–45.

Laurant, S. 2007. "Une journée à Baouit avec les archéologues du Louvre" and "Entretien avec Dominique Bénazeth." *Le monde de la Bible* 177, pp. 15–21.

Rutschowscaya, M.-H. 2007. "Reprise des fouilles françaises à Baouit Louvre/IFAO 2002–2003." In N. Bosson and A. Boud'hors, eds., *Actes du Huitième congrès international d'études coptes (Paris, 28 juin–3 juillet 2004)*, 1, pp. 311–22. Louvain, Paris, and Dudley, MA: Peeters.

Van Neer, W., W. Wouters, M.-H. Rutschowscaya, A. Delattre, D. Dixneuf, K. Desender, and J. Poblome. 2007. See "Studies," above, p. 203.

Bénazeth, D. 2008. "Baouit, le monastère retrouvé." *Grande Galerie: Le Journal du Louvre* 4, pp. 84–89.

Bénazeth, D. 2008. "L'église sud de Baouit retrouvée." *Bulletin de la Société d'archéologie copte* 47, pp. 9–23, pls. 1–4.

Bénazeth, D. 2008. "Nouvelle campagne de fouille à Baouit (2004)." In A. Boud'hors and C. Louis, eds., *Études coptes X: Douzième journée d'études (Lyon, 19–21 mai 2005)*, pp. 11–22. Paris: De Boccard.

Hadji-Minaglou, G. 2008–10. "Travaux de l'Institut français d'archéologie orientale," ed. L. Pantalacci, S. Denoix, and B. Midant-Reynes. *Bulletin de l'Institut français d'archéologie orientale.* Cairo: IFAO.

Bénazeth, D. 2010. "Nouvelles campagnes de fouilles à Baouit (2005, 2006)." In A. Boud'hors and C. Louis, eds., *Études coptes XI: Treizième journée d'études (Marseille 7–9 juin 2007)*, pp. 17–24, pl. 1. Paris: De Boccard.

Del Francia Barocas, L. 2010. "Ricerche archeologiche e restauri recenti nell'Egitto copto." In Fr. Raffaele, M. Nuzzolo, and I. Incordino, eds., *Recent Dicoveries and Latest Researches in Egyptology: Proceedings of the First Neapolitan Congress of Egyptology, Naples, June 18–20 2008*, pp. 41–42, figs. 4, 5:3. Wiesbaden: Harrassowitz.

Hadji-Minaglou, G. 2011. "Baouît." In B. Midant-Reynes and S. Denoix, eds., *Rapport d'activité 2010–2011*, pp. 54–55. Cairo: Institut français d'archéologie orientale.

Hadji-Minaglou, G., Fl. Calament, and C. Meurice. 2011. "Fouilles de Baouit, Égypte (saison 2010)." In M.C. Guillard-Le Bourdellès, ed., *La recherche au musée du Louvre 2010*, pp. 118–20. Paris and Milan: Musée du Louvre/Officina Libraria.

Hadji-Minaglou, G. 2012. "Baouît." In B. Midant-Reynes and S. Denoix, eds., *Rapport d'activité 2011–2012*, pp. 132–37. Cairo: Institut français d'archéologie orientale.

Hadji-Minaglou, G. 2013. "Baouît." In *Rapport d'activité 2012–2013*, pp. 201–208. Cairo: IFAO.

Calament, F., and G. Hadji-Minaglou. 2014. "Les fouilles de Baouit (Moyenne-Egypte)." In *La recherche au musée du Louvre 2012*, ed. M.C. Guillard-Le Bourdellès, pp. 178–79. Paris and Milan: Musée du Louvre, Officina Libraria.

Hadji-Minaglou, G. Forthcoming. "Découvertes récentes à Baouît." In A. Camplani and P. Buzi, eds., *Acts of the Tenth International Congress of Coptic Studies (Rome 2012)*. Louvain-la-Neuve: Peeters.

Hadji-Minaglou, G. Forthcoming. "L'église principale de Baouît: Etat des lieux à l'issue de la campagne de fouilles 2013." In N. Bosson and A. Boud'hors, eds., *Études coptes XIV: Actes de la Seizième journée d'études (Genève 2013)*. Paris: De Boccard.

Institut français d'archéologie orientale. http://www.ifao.egnet.net/archeologie/baouit/

Monuments

Bénazeth, D. 2002. See "Artifacts in Museums," above, for the South church in the Louvre.

Grossmann, P. 2002. *Christliche Architektur in Ägypten, Handbuch der Orientalistik*, 62. Leiden, Boston, and Cologne: Brill.

Bénazeth, D., and M. Gourdon. 2007–. "L'église sud de Baouit en 3D." http://musee.louvre.fr/expo-imaginaire/baouit/fr/index.html

Boutros N., T. Sehad, and O. Bouet. 2008. "Expériences pédagogiques: Communication hypermédia de reconstructions archéologiques hypothétiques." In R. Vergnieux and C. Delevoie, eds., *Actes du colloque Virtual Retrospect 2007 (Pessac (France), 14–15–16 novembre 2007)*, pp. 137–39. Bordeaux: Ausonius.

Bovot J.-L., and A. Del. 2008. "La modélisation de l'église copte de Baouit (Égypte): L'exemple d'une démarche commune entre archéologues et architectes." In R. Vergnieux and C. Delevoie, eds., *Actes du colloque Virtual Retrospect 2007 (Pessac (France), 14–15–16 novembre 2007)*, pp. 167–77. Bordeaux: Ausonius.

Bénazeth, D. 2012. "L'église de l'archange Michel du monastère copte de Baouit." In M.C. Guillard-Le Bourdellès, ed., *La recherche au musée du Louvre 2011*, pp. 90–91. Paris and Milan: Musée du Louvre/Officina Libraria.

Bénazeth, D. 2013. "L'église de l'archange Michel à Baouit." In C. Askeland, A. Boud'hors, A. Delattre, and G. Schenke, eds., "Selected Papers from the ICCoptS 9 (Cairo 2008)." *Journal of Coptic Studies* 15, pp. 3–20. Louvain: Peeters.

Bénazeth, D., O. Bouet, J.-L. Bovot, Fl. Calament, R. Cortopassi, A. Del, A. Delattre, M. Dupéron, Chr. Guilbaud, St. Lazare, Chr. Lyon-Caen, T. Magnaudet, S. Marchand, C. Meurice, M. Mossakowska-Gaubert, A. Nageh, A. Savy, W. Van Neer, and N. Vanthieghem. Forthcoming. *L'église de l'archange Michel dans le monastère copte de Baouit*. Cairo: Institut français d'archéologie orientale.

Sculpture

Bénazeth, D. 2000. "Les sculptures de Baouit réemployées au XIXe siècle." In A. Boud'hors, ed., *Études coptes VI: Huitième journée d'études (Colmar 29–31 mai 1997)*, pp. 50–67. Paris, Louvain: Peeters.

Enss, E. 2005. *Holzschnitzereien der spätantiken bis frühislamischen Zeit aus Ägypten: Funktion und Dekor.* Wiesbaden: L. Reichert Verlag.

Bénazeth, D. 2013. See "Artifacts in Museums," above, for the sculptured niche from the North church.

Rutschowscaya, M.-H. 2013. "Gabriel et Michel, les deux archanges à Baouit." In A. Boud'hors and C. Louis, eds., *Études coptes XII: Quatorzième journée d'études (Rome 11–13 juin 2009)*, pp. 215–21, pl. 4–6. Paris: De Boccard.

Meurice, C. Forthcoming. "La sculpture copte: Découvertes récentes à Baouit." In A. Camplani and P. Buzi, eds., *Acts of the Tenth International Congress of Coptic Studies (Rome 2012)*. Louvain-la-Neuve: Peeters.

Painting

Iacobini, A. 2000. *Visioni dipinte: Immagini della complazione negli affreschi di Bawit*. Rome: Viella.

Kakovkine, A. 2000. "A Group of 6th–9th Century Murals in the Chapels of Baouit." *Coptica Hermitagiana*, pp. 69–92. (In Russian; English summary, pp. 104–105.)

Coupry, Cl. 2003. "Peintures coptes sur bois: Analyse de pigments." In Chr. Cannuyer, ed., *Études coptes VIII: Dixième journée d'études, Lille 14–16 juin 2001*, pp. 99–106. Lille and Paris: Association francophone de coptologie.

Zibawi, M. 2003. *Images de l'Egypte chrétienne: Iconologie copte*, pp. 72–84, fig. 128. Paris: Picard.

Auth, S.H. 2005. See "Artifacts in Museums," above, for the painted wood in Newark.

van Loon, G.J.M. 2005. "A Note to the Provenance of the Panel of 'Brother George the Scribe.'" *Eastern Christian Art* 2, pp. 37–38.

van Loon, G.J.M. 2006. "The Virgin Mary and the Midwife Salomé: The So-called Nativity Scene in Chapel LI in the Monastery of Apa Apollo in Bawit." In *Eastern Christian Art* 3, pp. 81–103.

Bolman, E. 2007. "Depicting the Kingdom of Heaven: Paintings and Monastic Practice in Early Byzantine Egypt." In R.S. Bagnall, ed., *Egypt in the Byzantine World 300–700*, pp. 418–27. Cambridge: Cambridge University Press.

Rutschowscaya, M.-H. 2007. "Visages de l'art copte." *Le monde de la Bible* 177, pp. 46–50.

Rutschowscaya, M.-H. 2010. "Ce que racontent les murs d'un ermitage copte . . . ." In Fr. Briquel Chatonnet and M. Debié, eds., *Sur les pas des Araméens chrétiens*, pp. 311–23, figs. 1–16. Paris: Geuthner.

Rutschowscaya, M.-H. 2010. "Nouvelles peintures découvertes dans le monastère de Baouit." In A. Boud'hors and C. Louis, eds., *Études coptes XI: Treizième journée d'études (Marseille 7–9 juin 2007)*, pp. 45–51, pls. 2–3, 4A. Paris: De Boccard.

van Loon, G.J.M. 2011. "Priest and Father, Prophet and Martyr: Zacharias, Parent of Saint John the Baptist." In M. Eaton-Krauss, C. Fluck, and G.J.M. van Loon, eds., *Egypt 1350 BC–AD 1800: Art Historical and Archaeological Studies for Gawdat Gabra*, pp. 94–96. Wiesbaden: Reichert Verlag.

Thomas, Th.K. 2012. "Mimetic Devotion and Dress in Some Monastic Portraits from the Monastery of Apa Apollo at Bawit." *Coptica* 11, pp. 15–57.

Calament, F., and H. Rochard. Forthcoming. See "Texts" and "Studies," above.

Objects

Bénazeth, D. 2005. "Trouvaille de vitrages dans le monastère copte de Baouit (7e–10e siècle)." In exhibition catalog *De transparentes spéculations: Vitres de l'Antiquité et du Haut Moyen Âge (Occident–Orient). Id'Antique*, 4, pp. 127–30. Bavay: Musée/site archéologique de Bavay. See also in the same volume: D. Foy, pp. 113, 115, 116, 132, and M.-D. Nenna, pp. 120, 126.

Cortopassi, R. 2006. "Monastère de Baouit: Premiers textiles." *Archaeological Textiles Newsletter* 43, pp. 12–17, figs. 8–12.

Marchand S., and D. Dixneuf, with contributions from M.-H. Rutschowscaya. 2007. "Amphores et conteneurs égyptiens et importés du VIIe siècle apr. J.-C: Sondages récents de Baouît (2003–2004)." In S. Marchand and A. Marangou, eds., *Amphores d'Égypte de la Basse Epoque à l'époque arabe*, 1, pp. 309–43. Cairo: Institut français d'archéologie orientale.

Cortopassi, R. 2008. "Datation au 14C de neuf toiles brochées du Louvre." *Archaeological Textiles Newsletter* 47, pp. 3–6.

Dixneuf, D. 2008. "Un lot d'amphores de la première moitié du VIIe siècle à Baouit (Moyenne Égypte): Campagne 2004—'Sondage 3.'" In A. Boud'hors and C. Louis, eds., *Études coptes X: Douzième journée d'études (Lyon, 19–21mai 2005)*, pp. 39–49. Paris: De Boccard.

Lyon-Caen, Chr. 2008. "Bouchons d'amphore et bouchons de jarre du site de Baouit: Problématique et premier récolement." In A. Boud'hors and C. Louis, eds., *Études coptes X: Douzième journée d'études (Lyon, 19–21 mai 2005)*, pp. 63–75. Paris: De Boccard.

Romanus, K., W. Van Neer, E. Marinova, K. Verbeke, A. Luypaerts, S. Accardo, I. Hermans, P. Jacobs, D. De Vos, and M. Waelkens. 2008. "Brassicaceae Seed Oil Identified as Illuminant in Nilotic Shells from a First Millenium AD Coptic Church in Bawit, Egypt." *Analytical and Bioanalytical Chemistry* 390, pp. 783–93.

Lyon-Caen, Chr. 2010. "Les lampes du monastère de Baouit." In A. Boud'hors and C. Louis, eds., *Études coptes XI: Treizième journée d'études (Marseille 7–9 juin 2007)*, pp. 31–44. Paris: De Boccard.

Dixneuf, D. 2011. *Amphores égyptiennes: Production, typologie, contenu et diffusion (IIIe siècle avant J.-C.–IXe siècle après J.-C.)*, pp. 236–38. Alexandrie: Centre d'études alexandrines.

Południkiewicz, A., and A. Konstantinidou. 2012. "Bawit—Church 'D.' IFAO—Louvre." *Bulletin de liaison de la céramique égyptienne* 23, pp. 91–99.

Bouet, O. Forthcoming. "La chaire de Baouit: Hypothèses de restitutions à partir de modèles numériques." In A. Camplani and P. Buzi, eds., *Acts of the Tenth International Congress of Coptic Studies (Rome 2012)*. Louvain-la-Neuve: Peeters.

20 Children's Burials from Antinoopolis: Discoveries from Recent Excavations

Cäcilia Fluck

Introduction

Exploration of Antinoopolis—the well-known city founded by the Roman emperor Hadrian around AD 130 to honor his beloved Antinous after his legendary death in the Nile—began in the late nineteenth century.[1] In January 1896, Carl Schmidt (1868–1938), a German scholar, undertook a first small excavation in the northern cemetery (Fluck 2000: 175–76). In the same year, the French scholar Albert Gayet (1856–1916) started a large mission at this site. Continuously between 1896 and 1911, excavation took place in the entire ancient town (Calament 2005: 110–50).

From 1913 to 1914 the Egypt Exploration Fund under the leadership of John de Monins Johnson (1882–1956) excavated the rubbish heaps along the ancient city wall in the southwestern and eastern section of the town. The findings are spread over various collections in Britain, the majority now in the British Museum (Andorlini 1998; Pritchard 2013; O'Connell 2014).

Since winter 1935/1936 the site has been under Italian auspices under the direction of the Istituto G. Vitelli in Florence and the University of Rome. After a long interruption due to the vicissitudes and the aftermath of the Second World War, excavations were re-established in 1965 (Pensabene 1993: 273–88; Manfredi 1998; Donadoni, Spallanzani Zimmermann, and Bongrani Fanfoni 1974). Since 2000, an international team of specialists under the leadership of Rosario Pintaudi has been exploring the entire ancient town, including, for instance, areas in the northern necropolis that had never been touched by previous excavations (Pintaudi 2008).[2]

In particular, the cemeteries of Antinoopolis that were discovered during the various campaigns are considered an inexhaustible source for artifacts and objects of daily use—especially textiles in which the bodies were dressed and wrapped. The variety and quantity is enormous, ranging from little fragments and simple shrouds to almost complete garments and furnishing textiles. These textiles were often beautifully and richly decorated. The findings are distributed in museums and collections, particularly in France and some other European countries (Calament 1989; Rassart-Debergh 1997: 53–56; Calament 2005: 438–48; Linz and Coudert 2013: 493). A recent exhibition "Antinoé, à la vie, à la mode: Visions d'élégance dans les solitudes" in the Musée de Tissus in Lyons (from 1 October 2013 to 28 February 2014) gave a lively impression about fashion and style in ancient Antinoopolis. Burials and textiles from Antinoopolis in the collection of the museum were shown and published in a splendid catalog by Maximilien Durand and Florence Calament, which includes a comprehensive bibliography that reflects the research on textiles from Antinoopolis from the late ninteenth century till today (Cat. Lyon 2013).

Children's Burials from the 'Peristyle Complex'

This chapter is part of a study carried out in the context of "DressID: Clothing and Identities: New Perspectives on Textiles in the Roman Empire," a project funded by the cultural program of the European Commission that ran between 2007 and 2012. It focuses on textiles from four children's burials that Rosario Pintaudi and his team excavated in a 'peristyle' complex at the eastern edge of the northern cemetery at Antinoopolis in 2007.[3]

This complex most probably served as a meeting place for descendants to commemorate the dead before parts of it were converted into living quarters (Grossmann 2008: 42–44). Many coins and papyri were found in this area that date from the third to the seventh centuries AD—a period to which the majority of the textile finds belong (Pintaudi 2008: 12).

During the campaigns in January, February, and October 2007, some corpses and lots of single pieces of textile were found there.[4] Most of the corpses were not in their graves any more but dispersed in the dump. We do not know when this happened exactly. It might be that the area was plundered at some unknown date. But it cannot be excluded either that the inhabitants of the dwellings, which were installed in the colonnade when the cemetery was not in use any more, destroyed the place, or even that Gayet's staff used it as a deposit for all the material not meant for export to Europe (Pintaudi 2008: 11–12; Grossmann 2008; Fluck 2013: 89–91).

Nevertheless, a few graves remained still untouched. Some were found in situ under the pavement of the peristyle court (Pintaudi 2008: 14); others were in the eastern boundary wall.[5]

Newborn Buried with His Mother (Kind 1)

One of these intact graves was that of a mother buried together with her newborn. It was discovered in January 2007 in the center of the court.[6] Both corpses were wrapped in shrouds and fixed by bands arranged in the form of a lozenge pattern. This wrapping was typical for burials not only in Antinoopolis, but all over Egypt in the late antique and early Christian periods.

Due to the decomposition of the skeleton of the baby, it was not possible to determine its sex. It was dressed in four tiny garments worn one upon the other and a shawl that was put around its neck (Fluck 2010: 182–84, figs. 3–7).

All the garments were made of linen basic weaves. Their measurements vary between 38 and 43 centimeters in length and 32 to 42 centimeters in width, including the sleeves.

1. A simple, undecorated tunic (Kind 1: T_2009.03) fitted out with a hood and sewn together from six pieces of a discarded linen fabric; plain weave with self bands; height 38 cm, width 35 cm, length of sleeves 14 cm, height of hood 17 cm, width of hood 26 cm, length of neck slit 16 cm.
2. A hooded tunic (Kind 1: T_2009.02) made of seven pieces from two different linen fabrics; both are in plain weave with self bands; height 41 cm, width 32 cm, length of sleeves 13.5 cm (left) and 18 cm (right), height of hood 18 cm, width of hood 25 cm, length of neck slit 17 cm; sections at armpits are left open. Only the hood is decorated, with four little tassels of black and red wool at the top.
3. A little dress with flared sides (Kind 1: Kleid_2009.01, fig. 20.1), a type of garment that was inspired by Persian or Syrian fashion. It is made out of eight pieces of a linen fabric; plain weave; height 40.5 cm, width 42 cm, length of sleeves 15.5 cm, length of neck slit (back) 19.5 cm. The front and back parts—both including the upper parts

Fig. 20.1. Dress with flared sides (Kind 1: Kleid_2009.01). © Harald Froschauer.

of the sleeves—are cut to shape separately, and then sewn together on the shoulders. The lower parts of the sleeves were joined to the upper parts. They taper toward the ends. Two gores on each side were added to the lower part of the dress to give it its flared shape. The neck opening is cut out in a semicircle and ends in a slit on the left shoulder. A cord of red and white wool served to fasten the slit. The neck opening and the lower ends of the sleeves are decorated with a band of little squares, embroidered in green wool. The back of the dress is left undecorated, and the middle of the front is emphasized by a cross within a corona hanging down from a chain. The decoration, made of green and yellow wool, is unusual in that it is embroidered.[7]

4. A hooded sleeveless tunic (Kind 1: T_2009.01) served as an outer garment. The body and hood are made of two different linen fabrics; both in plain weave with self bands; height 43 cm, width 36 cm, height of hood 20 cm, width of hood 28 cm, length of neck slit 19 cm. The tunic is decorated with tiny *clavi* consisting of a brown stripe between red lines running down toward the lower end. Going out from the neck slit, on the front and the back sides, there are five vertical lines of twined additional weft threads: two long lines of red

and white wool run parallel to the inner side of the *clavi* and three short lines of red wool lie between them. The hood is embellished with red circles, each filled with a cross, in tapestry technique; its front edge is trimmed with a red braid and fringes are on the top.

5. A simple scarf (Kind 1: Schal_2009.01), found wrapped around the neck, completed the baby's equipment. It was cut out from a linen fabric, most probably from the same cloth used for the tunic T_2009.03; plain weave with self bands; length 75 cm (weft direction), width 11.5–12 cm.

Textile Equipment of a Little Boy's Burial (Kind 2)

Fifteen textiles from a boy's burial are preserved.[8] His corpse was found in the peristyle court on the same level as the newborn with its mother. The boy was dressed in three tunics (fig. 20.2) and his head was covered with fragments of different cloths. He was laid on two wooden beams before being wrapped in several layers of sheets, which were fixed on top by bands arranged in a lozenge pattern as usual.

The tunics, all made of linen, were worn one upon the other. Two are almost completely preserved. From one tunic one half of the front is missing. Their length varies between 45 and 50 cm, the largest neck slit is 23 cm long, and the sleeves measure between 12.5 and 17 cm. They could fit a child of an age of approximately one year.

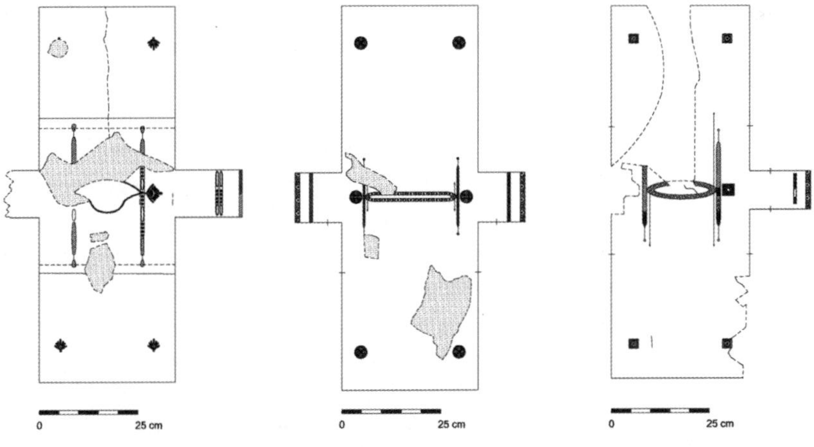

Fig. 20.2. The three tunics of 'Kind 2.' © Andreas Wietheger and Cäcilia Fluck, after drawings by Harald Froschauer.

1. Innermost, a cross-shaped linen tunic woven in one piece (Kind 2: T_2009.02, fig. 20.2, middle); plain weave; height 47 cm, width 35 cm, length of sleeves 12.5 cm, neck opening 23 cm; sections at armpits are left open. Roundels decorate the shoulders and the edges of the tunic's lower part, and *clavi* run down from the shoulders and end in ovals. They are done in tapestry technique and show white or yellowish circles on a red ground. From the decorative stripes that were woven into the sleeves, only remnants of red wool and traces of a tapestry in bright-colored linen are preserved. The trimmings at the end of the sleeves and around the neck opening are made using tablet weaving with a lozenge pattern in red wool and undyed linen.
2. The middle tunic (Kind 2:T_2009.03, fig. 20.2, right) is of the same type, but with a horizontal tuck in the middle; plain weave; height 50 cm, width 37.5 cm, length of sleeves 17.5 cm, neck opening 21 cm. The neck opening and the lower end of the sleeve are again trimmed with a small braid in very fine tablet weaving, but now the geometric pattern is carried out in blue wool and undyed linen. At the right shoulder can still be seen remnants of a small ribbon that served to fasten a neck slit, which is typical for children's tunics. The tunic is decorated with tiny *clavi* that consist of a row of alternating red, yellow, and green heart-shaped leaves that run into a *sigillum* in the form of a leaf. Blossoms in red, yellow, and green decorate the little tunic on both shoulders and at the lower edges. A small band on the sleeve consists of a row of red rods and green leaves. *Clavi*, blossoms, and the sleeve band are done in tapestry and inserted into the basic weave of the tunic.
3. The upper tunic (Kind 2: T_2009.01, fig. 20.2, left)—again of the woven-to-shape type—is badly damaged. The front, larger parts of the back and one sleeve are well preserved; plain weave; height 45 cm, width 34.5 cm, length of sleeves 14.5 cm, neck opening 18 cm. The *clavi* and the squares on one shoulder and at the lower edges are done in tapestry. They contain circles, dots, and little squares in green and yellow wool or undyed linen. The stripes on the sleeves show a band of red and green rods. The trimmings at the neck opening and the end of the sleeves are again in tablet weaving, corresponding to the above-mentioned style (Kind 2:T_2009.02).

The corpse of the little boy was wrapped in seven linen sheets, five of a coarse quality and two of a finer quality. One of them belongs to a special type of shroud with a striking brocaded red cross on one or two of the edges that was frequently found in this part of the cemetery (Kind 2: Tuch_2009.02). The other sheets lack any colored decoration. Only five have fringes (Kind 2: Tuch_2009.02, Tuch_2009.03a–b, Tuch_2009.04a–o, Tuch_2009.06a–b, Tuch_2009.07a–b), three of them are fitted out with self bands—stripes of similar colors created by at least two weft threads in the same shed (Kind 2: Tuch_2009.04a–b, Tuch_2009.06a–b, Tuch_2009.07a–b), and another is structured by a thick weft yarn that was inserted at regular intervals, creating a wavy selvedge (Kind 2: Tuch_03a–b). Remnants of the trimming and fixing band at the neck of tunic T_2009.01 were found on Tuch_2009.07a–b, so it must have been the undermost shroud. Tuch_2009.04a–o was the uppermost because it shows traces of the diamond-shaped lacing.

Fragments of the strings were used to fix the sheets around the corpse (Kind 2: Ba_2009.01a–b, Ba_2009.02, Ba_2009.03). A little bundle of strong linen threads (Knäuel_2009.01) bringing to mind tied-up oracular requests on papyri repeatedly found in the northern part of this cemetery (Cat. Florence 1998: 100–101, no. 86), and rags that were used as filling material, among them a checkered linen weave in blue and bleached linen with a slightly shimmering surface in a fine quality (Kind 2: UF_2009.01), also belonged to this burial.

The Burial of a Naked Boy (Kind 3)

Another corpse found below the floor of the peristyle court belongs to a boy who was buried on a wooden panel that imitates the outline of the body. His equipment was much poorer than those of the two other children.[9] It consists only of several layers of cloth that were wrapped around his naked body. Two of them belong to the type of fringed shroud with one or two of the edges decorated by a red cross in brocading (Kind 3: Tuch_2009.01 (fig. 20.3) and Tuch_2009.03). Two were made out of coarse linen yarns and have long fringes (Kind 3: Tuch_2009.02 and Tuch_2009.04), while the uppermost sheet is made out of a woolen fabric in a striking peach color that is slightly napped on both sides.[10] Traces of the original lacing and also remnants of the woolen strings can still be clearly seen on the surface. Some torn rags of different sizes, together with a piece of a linen hairnet in sprang technique with remnants of a decoration in red wool (Kind 3: Haarnetz_2009.01), were used as filling material.

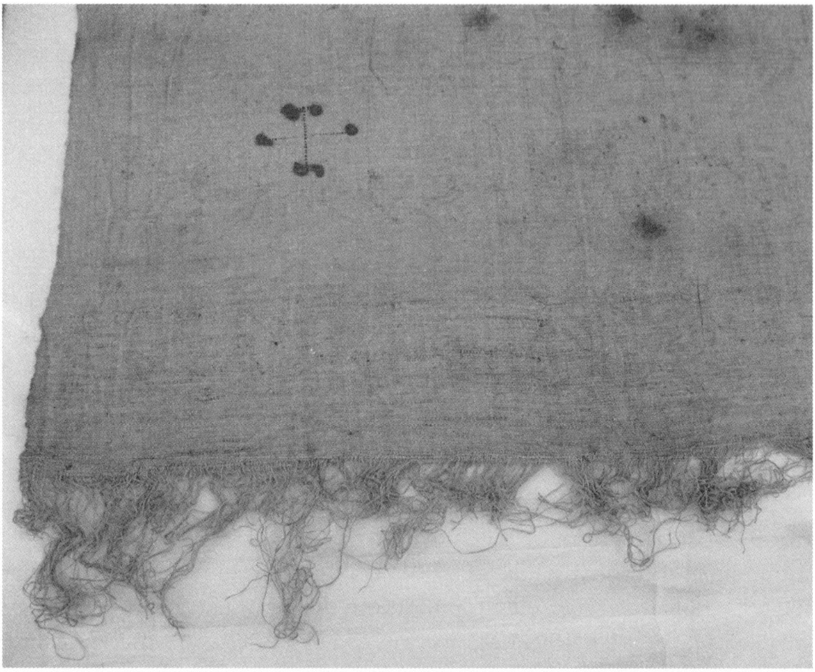

Fig. 20.3. Shroud with cross motif. © Harald Froschauer.

Dispersed Items of Children's Clothing

Two infant tunics

Among the dispersed finds in the peristyle complex in October 2007 were the remnants of the corpse of a baby dressed in two linen tunics.[11] The arms of the child were not put into the sleeves but through the open edges at the armpit.

1. The tunic next to the body (T_2010_04) is of the cross-shaped type, woven in one piece. It is completely preserved; plain weave with self bands in regular intervals; height 34 cm, width 32 cm, length of sleeves 12 cm; neck opening 15 cm (measured from the back); sections at armpits are left open. The neck opening is semicircular; a band to close the opening is attached on the left part of the rear edging. A vertical red woolen stripe of triple weft threads on both sides marks the transition from the front and back part of the tunic to the sleeves. The decoration, done in tapestry, consists of tiny *clavi* showing bright circles on a red ground; the *sigilla* at the

end are of leaf shape. The same pattern occurs in the stripes on the sleeves. Little roundels of a diameter of only 2 cm are inserted at the shoulders and symmetrically in the lower edges of the tunic. Each contains a little rosette in a circle and is framed by the so-called 'running wave' motif.

2. The upper tunic (T_2010.03, fig. 20.4) is of the same type, again completely preserved and fitted out with a semicircular neck opening. It is torn at the left shoulder and vertically on the rear; plain weave with self bands; height 35 cm, width 31 cm, sleeves 11 and 12 cm, neck opening 12.5 cm (measured from the back); sections at armpits are left open. The transition between front and back and sleeves is marked by twined linen weft threads. Two red woolen weft threads are inserted on the right shoulder. The tunic is decorated with simple triple stripes made of blue wool in plain weave that run down from the shoulders to the tunic's lower edge. A fastening band for the neck opening, partly torn off now, was stitched to the left shoulder. A comparable piece was found by Albert Gayet (Coudert, Cortopassi, and Médard 2013: 271, no. 93).

Fig. 20.4. Child's tunic with blue stripes. © Harald Froschauer.

A girl's veil

A small veil with a wreath on top (Schleier_2009.01, fig. 20.5) is to date unique among the finds from the peristyle complex (Fluck 2010: 184–85, fig. 8; Fluck and Froschauer 2011: 63, figs. 10–11); height 20.5 cm, width 32 cm; length of wreath 17 cm, diameter of wreath 1.5 cm; plain weave. The veil is made of a rectangular piece of a fine linen fabric. A selvedge at the bottom marks its lower end. The original width of the piece cannot be determined. The weave at the upper end of the veil is gathered and rolled to form a wreath. The latter is fixed by linen and wool yarns in three colors (undyed linen and apricot and turquoise wool) alternating regularly at intervals of about 1 cm. The wreath is fixed to the veil by a few threads of linen yarn in simple stitches.

Given the dimensions of the piece, it seems that the veil is almost completely preserved. Only a few centimeters are missing from the sides and from the wreath. Most probably the veil once belonged to a little girl. Similar veils but in larger dimensions, or mantles and hairnets combined with wreaths, were uncovered in Antinoopolis in connection with female burials (Fluck and Froschauer 2011: 63 with further references).

Fig. 20.5. A girl's veil. © Harald Froschauer.

A child's hood

Another piece of headgear, a little hood (Kapuze_2010.01, fig. 20.6), belongs to the isolated finds from the peristyle complex (Fluck and Froschauer 2011: 60, fig. 6). It consists of a rectangular piece of cloth trimmed with a rolled hem all around, originally folded along the vertical axis, sewn together at the upper edge and then pleated into a triangular form; plain weave with self bands in the upper part; height 28 cm, width 39 cm (unfolded); the upper edges are destroyed. The top and the sides are decorated with carefully constructed braids of plaited linen and wool threads (undyed linen, wool in red and green colors). One of the wool threads is cut off to create small fringes. The lateral braids end 4 cm above the lower edge, where remnants of the sewing thread are visible.

Hooded tunics seem to be restricted to children's graves. They were found not only in Antinoopolis, but at other sites as well. In this context it is worth mentioning that some church fathers, such as Evagrius, Palladius, Sozomenus, and others, describe the hood as a typical element of children's clothing that influenced the monk's habit. The *koukoullion*—the monk's cowl—was regarded as a symbol of the innocence of childhood (Giorda 2011: 183–84).

Fig. 20.6. A child's hood. © Harald Froschauer.

Conclusion

The textiles from children's burials that were discovered in the peristyle complex are of a solid but not outstanding quality, like some of the children's garments with elaborate decoration that go back to Albert Gayet's excavations between 1896 and 1911 (for example, Calament 2005: 26, fig. 26a; Cat. Lyon 2013: 194–97, nos. 59 and 62; Linz and Coudert 2013: 222–29, nos. 58–61; Coudert, Cortopassi, and Médard 2013: 267–68, nos. 88–89, and 272–73, no. 96).

As usual, children's garments imitate those of the adults, but on a miniature scale, with the exception of hooded tunics, which are a special item of children's apparel. All of the tunics presented in this study are made out of linen; most of them are woven to shape and—like their 'adult' models—decorated with symmetrical tapestry work. However, some undergarments are made of several pieces cut out from torn-off fabric and sewn together in a tunic shape. All garments, including headgear, analyzed so far are fabricated very accurately and with care for tiny details. They resemble some pieces found during Gayet's excavations (Coudert, Cortopassi, and Médard 2013: 271, nos. 93–94, and 275, nos. 100–101), and later, during the 1930s campaigns of the Italian Mission in the northern necropolis in the vicinity of the peristyle complex (Cat. Florence 1998: 230, nos. 315–16).

Three of the children were dressed in at least two tunics and then wrapped in shrouds; only one boy was found naked. Some of the shrouds show red crosses on one or two edges. Such shrouds were found frequently in this part of the cemetery, and not only in connection with children's burials. They attest the Christian belief of the deceased.

In none of the children's graves were toys or other attributes found. Only a small bundle of linen threads could have been used as a sort of amulet. Judging from the medium quality of the textiles, the reduced decoration, and the fact that some garments were made of reused fabrics, it seems that the children belonged to middle-class families. The fact that the corpses of the deceased children were treated the same way as that of adults—dressed in their clothing and wrapped up carefully—reflects a respected status afforded to children in Antinoopolis in late antiquity.

Notes

1 Sporadically, European travelers have visited the site since the sixteenth century (Calament 2005: 82–93). Some monuments and an excellent topographical map were published in the *Description de l'Égypte*, a monumental œuvre of eleven

volumes that resulted from the Napoleonic expedition to Egypt in the years 1798–1801 (*Description* 1822, vol. 4: pl. 53–58).

2 See also Antinoupolis Foundation, http://www.antinoupolis.org/.

3 I am deeply grateful to the field director, Rosario Pintaudi, for admitting me to his excavation team and for his permission to publish the findings related to children's burials here. Many thanks are owed to Harald Froschauer for providing me with drawings and images for this chapter.

4 The textile finds from the burials and the debris were put into storage in the house of the Italian Mission. Recording started in the winter campaign 2008; conservation of the first pieces began in the autumn season 2007. It has been carried out by Mohammed Saleh Ahmed and Nasr Ahmed Mohammed from the National Museum of Egyptian Civilization and Somaya Abdelkhalek from the Museum of Islamic Art, both institutions in Cairo.

5 For the finding circumstances, see Pintaudi 2008: 11–14, pls. XIV–XVII, figs. 74–94, and pls. XXIV–XXV, figs. 134–44; Minutoli 2008: 61–62.

6 Found 10 October 2007, northern necropolis, Kom Est, quadrant E1, level I.

7 A fourth-century child's garment with an embroidered cross motif was found in Kellis (personal communication from Rosanne Livingstone, March 2013). For a brief description of this find, see Livingstone, Chandler, and Martin 2008: 36.

8 Found 3 February 2007, northern necropolis, Kom Est, quadrant D1, level I; unwrapped 4 February 2007.

9 Found 1 January 2007, northern necropolis, Kom Est, quadrant D1/A4, level I.

10 Comparable to the treatment of the fabrics used for the famous Persian riding coats and gaiters found by Albert Gayet and Carl Schmidt: see Cat. Florence 1998: 193, no. 233 (= Louvre inv. E29410); Fluck 2004: 142 and 144; Linscheid 2004: 154; Mälck 2004: 166–68, 170; Cat. Lyon 2013: 62–64, no. 4; 90–93, no. 18; 98–103, no. 20; 120–30, nos. 29, 30; 136–43, nos. 34–35; 164–67, no. 46; 176–78, no. 51; 184–85, no. 54; 190–93, no. 58; 198–204, nos. 63–64; 218–19, no. 72; 308–309, no. 123; 320–23, no. 132; 392–95, no. 157. For the peach color, compare other fragments from Antinoopolis in Cat.Lyon 2013: 160–61, no. 43, and 292–93, no. 111.

11 Found 10 October 2007, northern necropolis, Kom Est, quadrant E1, level I.

21 Recent Excavations at Bawit

Gisèle Hadji-Minaglou

The remains of the Bawit monastery, founded by Apa Apollo, are located near Dashlout, about twenty-five kilometers south of Hermopolis (today Ashmunayn).[1] The *kom* covers an area of forty hectares. Apa Apollo's monastery was one of the most important monasteries of Middle Egypt and the site of Bawit has indubitably yielded the richest papyrological and epigraphical documentation in the region.[2]

The Monastery of Bawit has been identified with that of Apa Apollo by both Walter Crum and Jean Clédat (Clédat 1902: 525–31). According to chapter 8 of the *Historia Monachorum in Aegypto*, Apollo founded his monastery around 386–88.[3] Although tradition has placed the foundation of Apa Apollo's monastery at the end of the fourth century, no archaeological evidence has come to light to confirm this dating. The oldest remains discovered on the site so far go back to the end of the sixth century, while the written documentation and the majority of monuments show that the monastery reached its peak during the seventh and eighth centuries. Furthermore, inscriptions attest to the existence of the monastery until the tenth century (Bénazeth 2008: 406; Calament, in press), and according to the surface pottery, the site was deserted toward the end of the eleventh century or the beginning of the twelfth century.[4] At that time the monastery was no longer in operation and there was a cemetery in the eastern part of the site.[5]

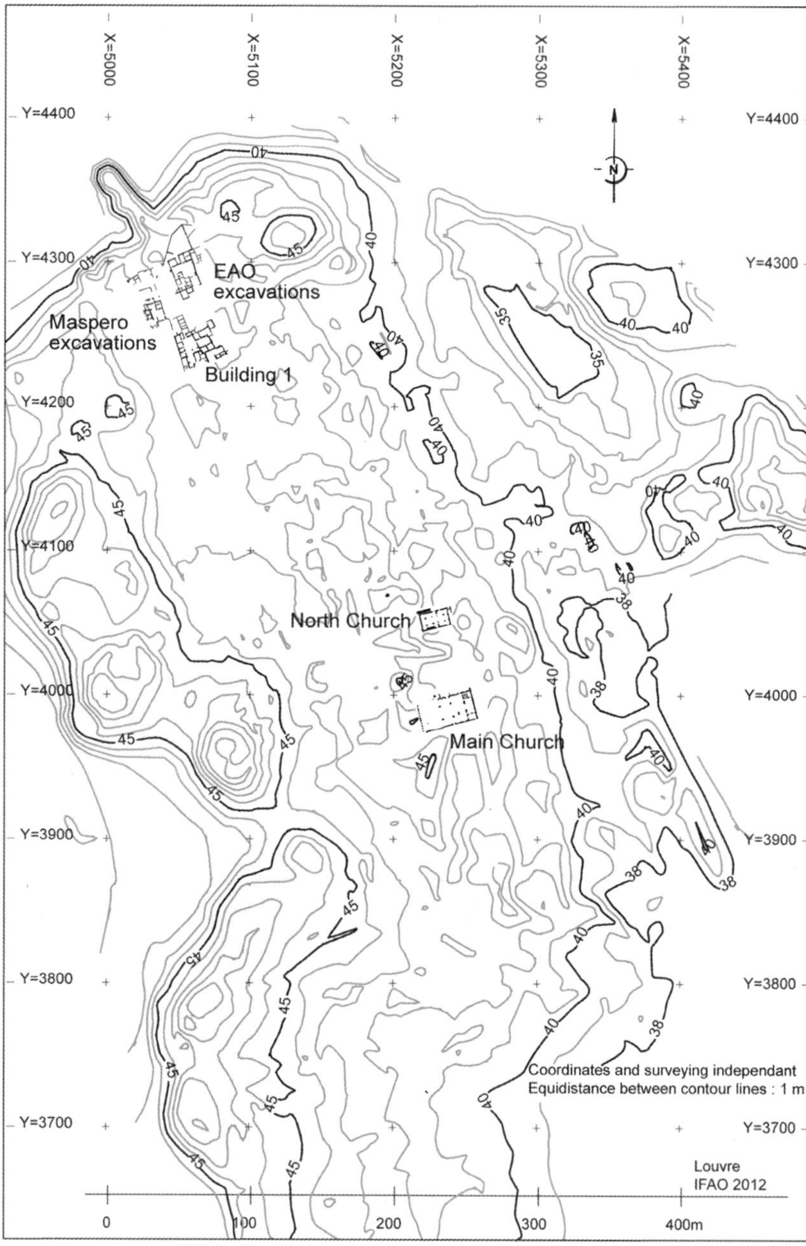

Fig. 21.1. Topographical map of Kom Bawit. © Louvre Museum/IFAO.

The Former Excavations

Jean Clédat was the first scholar to visit Bawit. Resident at the French Institute of Oriental Archaeology (Institut français d'archéologie orientale [IFAO]), he was then working at the nearby necropolis of Meir, about fifteen kilometers south of Bawit. After a survey of the site at the beginning of 1901, assisted by Émile Chassinat and Charles Palanque,[6] he started an official dig for the IFAO at the end of the same year. He worked at Bawit until 1905 and unearthed many constructions, most of them scattered in the northern half of the *kom*. Among Clédat's discoveries are the two churches known as "Église nord" (North Church) and "Église sud" (South Church), both located in the central area of the site.[7]

After an interruption of seven years, in 1913 the excavations started again under the supervision of Jean Maspero, then an IFAO resident (Maspero 1931–43). After Maspero's death, in 1915, the site was abandoned to its fate and was gradually covered over by the wind-blown sand. The discoveries of both Clédat and Maspero have been located again thanks to the magnetic survey of the site carried out by Tomasz Herbich in 2004–2007.[8] Except for limited excavations by the Egyptian Antiquities Organization in 1976 and 1984–85,[9] the *kom* was deserted until 2002, when the joint mission of the IFAO and the Louvre Museum undertook new field research at Bawit.

The Sectors of the Current Excavations (fig. 21.1)[10]

Since work resumed, the dig has taken place in two sectors: in the northern and the central parts of the *kom*. At the northern sector a dwelling quarter has been discovered, and in the central part the North Church has been unearthed again.[11] South of it, a new church, without any doubt the main church of the monastery, was discovered and has been in the process of being excavated since 2008.

The Dwellings of the Northern Area

In 2003–2004, three trenches were dug in the northern part, near the buildings discovered by Jean Maspero and by the Egyptian Antiquities Organization (Boutros and Rutschowscaya 2005). One of the trenches, sondage 3, has been widened and has revealed dwellings of which only one, Building 1, has been unearthed.

Building 1 (fig. 21.2) belongs to a large block, the extent of which is unknown. Dated to the first half of the seventh century, Building 1 consists of several rooms surrounding a courtyard. On the western side of the

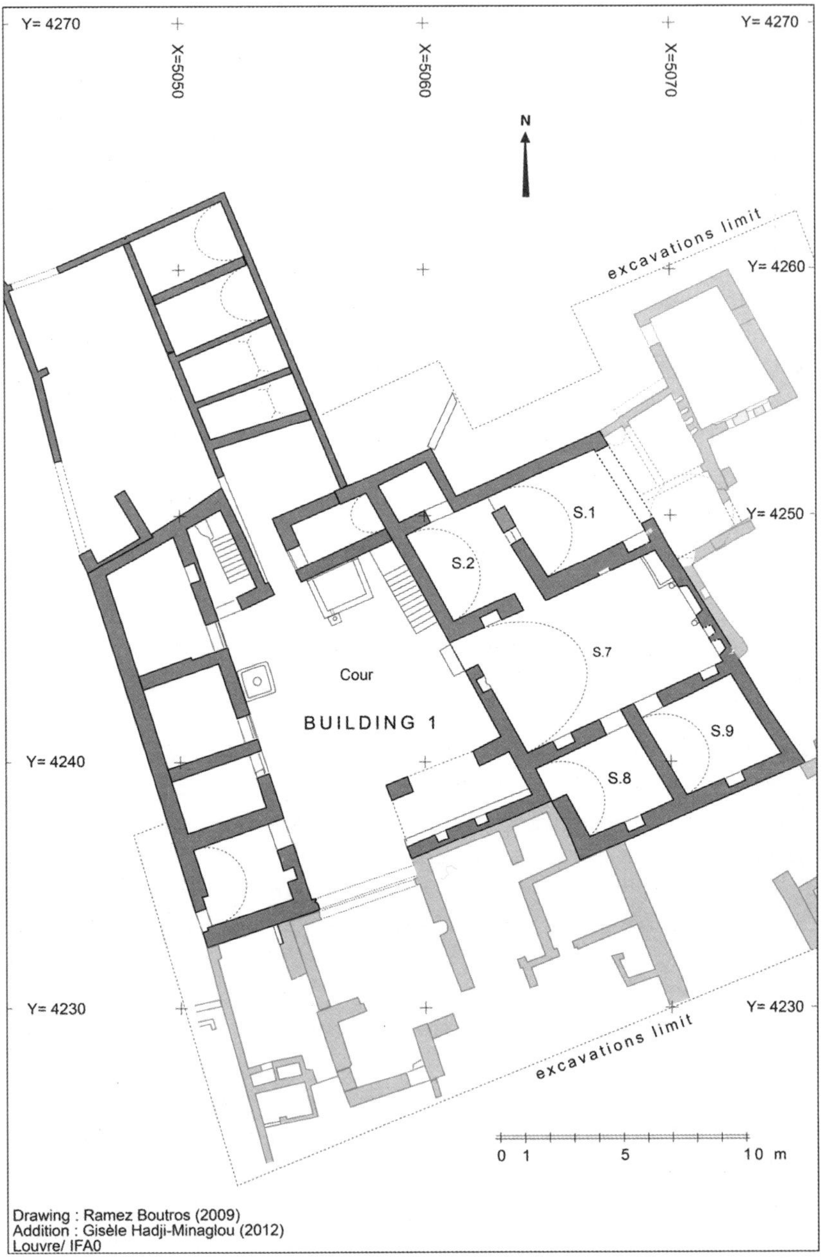

Fig. 21.2. Plan of Building 1. © Louvre Museum/IFAO, R. Boutros, and G. Hadji-Minaglou.

courtyard are four rooms that do not communicate with each other: the entrance to Building 1 is on the southernmost side of these four rooms. On the northern side of the courtyard, two rooms stand on either side of a corridor leading to a kitchen and storerooms. The courtyard was delimited to the south by a wall that separated Building 1 from its neighbor. This wall has been destroyed and we do not know if there was any communicating door there. On the eastern side of the courtyard is a complex of five vaulted rooms. This complex is composed of a large (9 x 5.35 m) rectangular central room (S.7) from which one has access to the four other rooms, almost square in plan. These rooms are symmetrically set, two by two, to the north (S.1 and S.2) and the south (S.8 and S.9) of the largest room.

The walls and the vault of room S.7 were decorated with paintings. A large part of the vault collapsed after the building was abandoned, pulling down the west wall toward the interior of the room. The paintings preserved on the vault were cleared from 2005 to 2007 (Rutschowscaya 2010a),[12] and the west wall, almost completely destroyed, was cleared in 2012 (fig. 21.3). It was decorated with three niches: one in the middle and two smaller ones on the south side of the wall. The central niche was once flanked by two columns, of which only the stone bases are now preserved. In this niche was originally painted the image of Christ in majesty,

Fig. 21.3. Bawit, Building 1, the eastern wall of S.7, seen from the west. © Louvre Museum/IFAO, M. Perraud.

surrounded by seraphs and the four evangelists. In the next niche was represented a saint of whom only the lower part of the body can be seen. On the north side of the wall, north of the central niche, were represented the Magi. The central niche was flanked by two wooden sculptures that were originally embedded in the wall. These elements were found in the rubble. One of them, which was on the south side, represents the Archangel Michael and the other, which was on the north, represents the Archangel Gabriel.[13] They were both sculpted from one single piece of wood, cut lengthwise. A certain Victor, either sculptor or painter, has affixed his name on one side of the piece that represents Gabriel.

The Main Church (figs. 21.4 and 21.5)

When Clédat excavated the South Church, he also uncovered, to the south of it, a part of a room that he named with the letter D (Chassinat 1911: pl. VII). This room, in fact, is the naos of a large basilica, which appears to be, without any doubt, the main church of the monastery.

The basilica has three aisles. The walls are made of kilned bricks, with an external facing of limestone blocks. The limestone blocks have been left bare, while the internal brick facing was plastered with a lime rendering and a whitewash that has disappeared almost everywhere. Traces of color and inscriptions can be seen where the whitewash has been preserved. The many fragments of coating found in the sand covering the ruins show that the interior of the whole building was decorated with paintings. From the sand have also been collected carved elements of architecture, broken into pieces: epistyles, friezes, capitals, and jambs. These fragments, together with the large pick marks in the walls, are to a large extent the result of the work of the *sebakhin*. The *sebakh* consisted of decomposed mud brick, a material rich in nitrates, which provided an excellent agricultural fertilizer. In the late nineteenth and early twentieth centuries, farmers were allowed to collect this material from ancient mounds and, as elsewhere in Egypt, they were very active at Bawit (Palanque 1906: 1–14, pl. II). Nevertheless, some limestone blocks and shafts of column, also thrown into the sand, have obviously been cut up to be used in the lime kiln that was lying on the surface of the *kom*, some meters south of the church (Hadji-Minaglou 2012: 133, fig. 84).

The excavation of the basilica began in 2008 and now progresses from east to west. At the present time, the sanctuary and a large part of the naos have been uncovered.[14] As a whole, the width of the building is 21.2 meters on the eastern side and 20.7 meters on the west. The length is 39.6 meters.

Fig. 21.4. Bawit, the main church, seen from the northeast. © Louvre Museum/ IFAO, G. Poncet.

The naos is divided into three aisles and the sanctuary into three sections with the bema in the middle. The narthex, if there is one, has not yet been uncovered. The plan, as it appears today, is the result of many alterations.

The sanctuary covers a surface area of 21.2 by 7.15 meters. The external facing of the eastern wall of the sanctuary is flat. There, nothing shows the position of the bema, while the position of each lateral chamber was marked by a shallow quadrangular niche. The northern niche is clearly delimited by the limestone blocks of the masonry, and the position of the southern niche has been determined thanks to the remains of its wooden base. In the central part of the bema, the bases of two small columns indicate the position of the altar. Behind these bases, two jambs, 4.9 meters apart, are built in the eastern wall and delimit a square niche that takes the place of the apse. The jambs might have supported arches, which were also leaning on the west wall of the bema. Another rectangular and smaller niche is situated in the southeast corner of the room. This was originally flanked by two small columns. There is no symmetrical niche in the northeast corner of the room, but instead, a door leading to the north lateral chamber. In the western wall of the bema are three openings leading to the nave: the northern and the southern ones were closed by wooden doors, while the middle opening was closed with a wooden chancel of which only the base has been found, completely rotten and pulverized. The pavement of the bema is made of limestone slabs with some elements of white marble. It is divided into two areas different in width, the eastern part raised about twenty-five centimeters above the western one. Originally, the pavement of the bema was all at one level and the heightening of the eastern part is the result of repair work. At the emplacement of the altar, the two preserved bases have been included in the new pavement and, underneath, the imprint of the slabs of the previous pavement can be seen. The western part of the pavement has also been repaired, the central slabs having been replaced with fragments of stones and bricks installed without care.

The south lateral chamber has not undergone any major transformation: apparently, the level of the floor, simply made of clay with a lime covering, is the original one. To the north of the bema is an area divided into two parts almost equal in surface. In the northern part is a chamber, paved with kilned bricks, while in the southern part is a staircase. The stairs lead to the gallery, if there was one, which would have extended over the northern aisle, or to the roof. Usually this staircase is located in the western part of the church, and the fact that it is in the east and in the sanctuary makes it particularly notable. In three other basilicas located in Middle Egypt, the staircase is also established in the eastern part of the building. In the church of the south cemetery of Antinoopolis, the stairs are at the north extremity of the sanctuary and start in the nave. At the southeast church of Dayr al-Bala'iza, the staircase is situated north of the northern lateral chamber, from where it has its access. At the White Monastery in Sohag, the stairs are established north of the triconch and have two entries, one from the sanctuary and one from the nave (Grossmann 2002: figs. 55, 148, and 150).

The naos is divided into three aisles. The nave is 9.5 meters wide and the side aisles are each 4.75 meters in width. The east-to-west interaxial distance between two columns is 4.1 meters. The monolithic columns and their bases stood on pedestals of kilned bricks. Not all of the columns are preserved and only four pairs have been exactly located. The position of the pair closest to the sanctuary is known thanks to the trace of its pedestal under the stone pavement. The next pair, which is located five meters from the western wall of the sanctuary, is the best preserved: the pedestal and the stone base of both columns are visible and half of the broken southern column is still standing. The third pair has been incorporated into L-shaped pillars. The pedestal and base of the southern column of the fourth pair

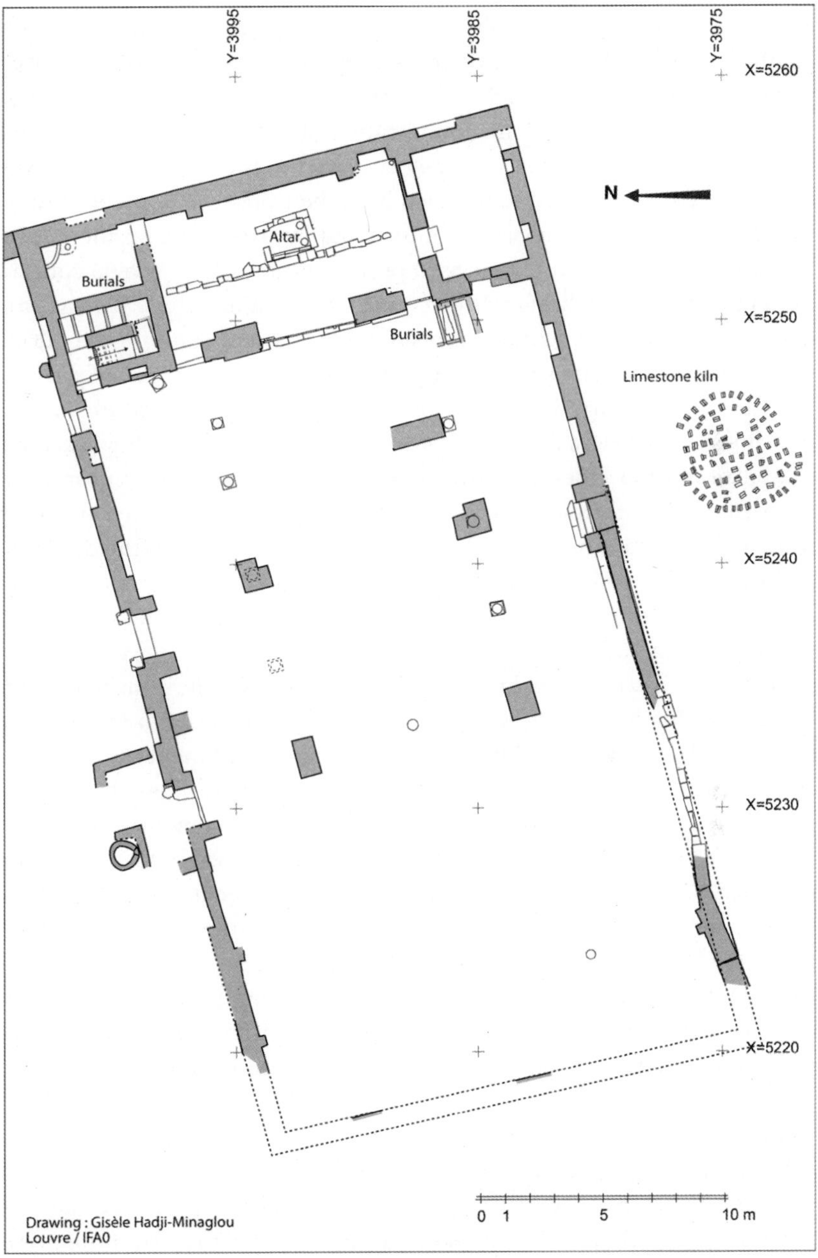

Fig. 21.5. Bawit, plan of the main church. © Louvre Museum/IFAO, G. Hadji-Minaglou.

are still in position, while only the trace of the pedestal of the northern column is visible. A fifth pair of columns may have been incorporated in two rectangular pillars, which have not yet been completely uncovered. The L-shaped pillars have no foundation and rest directly on the pavement of the naos. The naos had three entrances to the north aisle and one to the south. The northwest entrance is the best preserved. It was flanked by two engaged columns on the outside and by two pillars on the inside. The south entrance was once closed off by a wall made of several courses of kilned bricks alternating with a course of reused limestone blocks. The same type of implementation has been used for the masonry of the pillars of the nave. The blocking up of the south door and the masonry of the pillars are contemporary with the reconstruction of part of the south wall of the church. The original wall had probably fallen after an earthquake. Like the pillar and the blocked door masonry, the wall was built with reused material. Most of the blocks have been placed on their edge and many have painted inscriptions on them. One of these inscriptions bears the date 625 and five others the date 632. All these inscriptions are contemporary and commemorate the same event. They allow us to date the rebuilding of the wall to the beginning of the seventh century.

The naos has had two successive floors. The first one is made of clay, covered with a lime wash, lying on a layer of clean sand. On the surface, parallel and perpendicular lines imitating a regular pavement of rectangular slabs have been imprinted by means of a stretched rope. The second floor, which covers the first one, is a pavement of rectangular limestone slabs placed upon clean sand. Two stelae have been reused in the pavement. One had been placed in the nave, in front of the bema: it concerns Apa Daniel, archimandrite of the monastery at the beginning of the eighth century. The other one is a funerary stela situated in front of the south door. Dated to the beginning of the ninth century, it bears the epitaph of a certain Hor and his wife. These two inscriptions do not help us to determine the date of the abandonment of the church; nevertheless, they do give us a *terminus post quem*.[15]

The Burials (fig. 21.5)

A trench made in the southern aisle of the naos, in front of the sanctuary, on a spot where both the stone pavement and the clay floor have disappeared, has revealed the presence of burials underneath the church. One grave has been emptied of the sand covering the corpse. After the photographic record had been made, the corpse was left in its original position and reburied. The grave is dug into the rock and is delimited by thin walls of mud bricks. It was sealed with a pavement of mud bricks lying on the sand that filled the hole and then covered with smoothed clay. The deceased was buried in a west–east orientation, the face looking toward the east. He is still wrapped in a shroud, and a coin, by now eroded, was placed upon his heart. Five other graves have been found under the staircase. They are of the same type as the one discovered in the southern aisle. They were also sealed with a covering of mud bricks. These graves have not been excavated because of the lack of space. The graves show that the church was probably built over a cemetery. In the staircase, the layers excavated over the burials and under the pavement of the church have yielded some coins dating to the end of the sixth century[16] and pottery dating to the end of the sixth century or the beginning of the seventh century. These help us to date the construction of the basilica to the very end of the sixth century or the beginning of the seventh century.

Conclusion

A very small percentage of the *kom* of Bawit has been excavated. The most ancient remains, the South Church and the main basilica, go back to the beginning of the seventh century. The seventh century in its entirety is represented by the constructions in the northern area. In the main basilica we have traces of rebuilding and refurbishment until the beginning of the ninth century, the most important phase having taken place soon after the construction of the building. The North Church was built at the end of the seventh century or the beginning of the eighth century. The seventh and eighth centuries have also yielded a large majority of the written documentation. What can be said about the vestiges of the ninth, tenth, and eleventh centuries that the pottery survey leads us to expect? And what can be said about the late fourth-century remains that tradition invites us to find? The answers to these questions are what we hope to discover in the future.

Notes

1 The results of the Bawit excavations presented here are those achieved at the end of the 2012 season. A French version is in press: Hadji-Minaglou, in press a. The results of the 2013 season will be presented in Hadji-Minaglou, in press b. I am grateful to Vivienne G. Callender who has kindly revised my English.

2 The reference papyrological bibliography is given in Wipszycka 2009: 86–87.

3 For the Greek text, see Festugière 1961: 46–71; for the French translation, see Festugière 1964: 46–63, especially 48, l. 36: commentaire. An English translation is available in Russell 1981: 70–79.

4 The results of this survey are not yet published. For the moment, the results of the survey in the hermitages situated over the cliff, at the west of the *kom*, are presented in Marchand et al., forthcoming.

5 A burial has been discovered over the main church (Bénazeth 2007: 282), and, in the same area, the disrupted surface layers contained human remains such as bones and clothes.

6 Émile Chassinat was then director and Charles Palanque resident at the IFAO.

7 The 1901 and 1902 seasons are published in Clédat 1904–1906; the 1903 to 1905 seasons are partly presented in Clédat 1916 and Clédat 1999.

8 The located buildings appear in dark blue in the topographical map of the site, published in Bénazeth and Herbich 2008.

9 The results of these excavations have not been published. Nevertheless, a general publication including the discoveries made at Bawit has been announced: Abdal-Tawab and Grossmann, forthcoming.

10 The topographical map of figure 21.1 has been drawn up by students of the École Supérieure des Géomètres Topographes du Mans: J. Boerez and S. Griffet (2003), and T. Touzé and J. Sarret (2006 and 2007). I have simplified the map and completed it with the vestiges brought to light since 2008. The remains excavated by the Egyptian Antiquities Organization in 1976 and 1984 have also been added. I thank Peter Grossmann for the plan he has kindly given me.

11 The North Church was excavated by Émile Chassinat and Charles Palanque in 1902 and remained unpublished. In 2003–2005, it was cleared again by Dominique Bénazeth and Jean-Luc Bovot. The manuscript of the publication presenting the works is near completion: Bénazeth, forthcoming. At the moment, one can find a brief description of the building in Pantalacci 2005: 441, and a plan in Lyon-Caen 2010: 33, fig. 2.

12 Only the lower part of the vault is preserved and a large part of the paintings has fallen into the rubble, with the rest of the vault. The fragments of painting have been collected and the reconstitution of the scenes is still in progress.

13 The two pieces are now exhibited in the Coptic Museum in Cairo, where they are registered under numbers 12816 and 12821: see Rutschowscaya 2010b and Rutschowscaya 2013.

14 The results obtained from 2008 to 2010 are presented in Hadji-Minaglou 2008, Hadji-Minaglou 2009, and Hadji-Minaglou 2010. No excavations took place in 2011. The report concerning the 2012 season is in Hadji-Minaglou 2012.

15 The inscriptions on the south wall and the stelae reused in the pavement are being studied by Florence Calament: see Calament, in press.

16 I wish to thank Professor Olivier Picard for his details about the dating of the coins found in the main basilica.

22 Funerary Aspects in the Paintings from the Apollo Monastery at Bawit

Karel Innemée

Introduction

Much has been written about the monastic settlement of Bawit and it seems a daring task to try and add something substantially new to this. First of all we have limited access to the material on which we can base our conclusions. Only a small part of the total area occupied by the monastic settlement was investigated, and if one makes a rough estimate it may not be more than about 5 percent (Torp 1957: 513). The excavations by Clédat, Chassinat, Palanque, and Maspero in the beginning of the twentieth century were carried out according to the standards of those days and the material published by the excavators is fragmentary and leaves us with many questions. Even the valuable addition to the publication of Clédat by Dominique Bénazeth and Marie-Hélène Rutschowscaya (Bénazeth and Rutschowscaya 1999) is not sufficient to answer all these questions.

One of the basic questions concerns the function of the buildings that have been called *chapelles* by Jean Clédat and *salles* by Gaston Maspero. In this chapter I will try to shed light on this function on the basis of the iconography of the mural paintings that have been found here. When Clédat excavated the site of Bawit he mistakenly supposed he was dealing with a monastic cemetery and, as a result, named the non-ecclesiastical buildings that he found *chapelles*. When Maspero continued the work from 1913, he corrected this after discovering that no tomb was to be found under any of the buildings and, more appropriately, interpreted them as the living quarters of the monks of the settlement, giving them the name of *salles* in his publication (Maspero 1932–43, vol. 5). The names by which the buildings were indicated was changed, but this does not imply that all questions surrounding their functions have been solved. In his lemma on the architecture of Bawit in *The Coptic Encyclopedia*, H.-G. Severin remarks:

> Of building operations in the area of the *kom* of Bawit, at least in the fifth and sixth centuries, we know nothing for certain (extent, architectural form, and function), and therefore, for the time being, should rule out neither any future confirmation of the conventional interpretations nor the possibility of perhaps surprising new insights (such as the possibility that the first building phase was a cemetery). (Severin 1991: 366)

There are reasons to believe that at least a number of the buildings were not just cells, but had other functions. As in the monastery of Apa Jeremias in Saqqara, many cells were equipped with an oriented niche containing painted decoration that resembled the paintings in apses. Some of these rooms have an elongated shape, with a width that is a multiple of its depth. This is the case in, for instance, *salles* 5 and 6 (Maspero 1932–43: pl. I). In other cases, rooms are more or less square or rectangular, but for none of them does a liturgical function seem likely. The presence of an apse-like niche, however, suggests that they were used for devotional purposes, in the case of the elongated rooms allowing the monks to stand next to each other in a row, facing the apse/niche.

According to the *Historia Monachorum in Aegypto*, the monks would celebrate the liturgy daily, apparently in one of the churches (Rufinus, *Historia Monachorum* 7: 13,4; Schulz-Flügel 1990: 302). That could mean that the *chapelles* or *salles* were mainly used as *oratoria* for the prayers of the hours and other prayers. This is not a new conclusion, but the next question would be what the painted decoration in these rooms can tell us about their use and function. The decoration in the eastern niches, as mentioned, has in most cases a clear reference to apse decoration and as such raises no specific questions, but a number of recurring subjects on the walls of these rooms, such as hunting scenes, are more difficult to explain in the context of *oratoria* for groups or individual monks.

In 1957, Hjalmar Torp published an article in *Byzantion* that apparently and unfortunately has remained unnoticed by many. It is rarely mentioned in publications concerning the use and function of the architecture of Bawit, but it could give us a clue nevertheless concerning additional aspects of the rooms in Bawit and their decoration. Torp draws a parallel between the construction of monastic dwellings such as the ones in Bawit and the architecture of late antique and early Christian tombs. Of the approximately seventy buildings unearthed in Bawit, more than forty have barrel vaults, mostly in combination with remains or evidence for the existence of an upper floor. These upper floors were not supported by the barrel vault, but by wooden beams, a construction highly unusual in house architecture, but all the more usual in tombs, such as those in the cemetery of Tuna al-Gebel, fifteen kilometers north of Bawit (Torp 1957: 526–29). Torp's explanation for the resemblance between tombs and monastic buildings is that the latter consisted of an upper story that functioned as the living quarters for the monks, while the vaulted ground floor rooms were intended as funerary chapels for burial and commemoration rites (Torp 1957: 530–38). In this conclusion, Torp returns partially to the interpretation of Clédat, who also attributed a funerary function to the *chapelles*. This remarkable conclusion raises at least two questions. The first one is whether the painted decoration of these rooms can support Torp's view. A second question is why so many funerary chapels are present within the compound of a monastery. Would a church not be sufficient for such funerary rituals? In order to go deeper into this matter we will have to take a closer look at a number of iconographical themes that recur in the decoration of these presumed funerary chapels. Although certain themes are unique, others can be found in a number of varieties. If Torp is right, these paintings should have a link with funerary iconography.

Hunting Scenes

A small group of mural paintings that seems difficult to explain in a Christian monastic context depicts hunting scenes. One example can be found in *chapelle* XVIII, where we see representations of two childlike hunters, dressed in short tunics and trousers, and a gazelle in octagonal frames that are part of a geometrical pattern (Clédat 1916: pls. LXIV, LXV) (fig. 22.1). In *chapelle* XII, a hunter with bow and arrow is depicted as he shoots an arrow through the head of a lion (Clédat 1904–1906: pl. XXXVII). The most elaborate, though only partly preserved, hunting scene known so far is

Fig. 22.1. Bawit, watercolor after a detail from *chapelle* XVIII: a boy hunting a gazelle (Clédat 1904–1906).

Fig. 22.2. A boy hunting a boar, detail from a tomb in Silistra (Bulgaria) (Dorigo 1971).

in *chapelle* XXXVII, where a group of hunters (four are visible) are involved in a hunt for deer. Their dress also consists of short tunics and trousers. We know examples of hunting scenes from various contexts in late Roman art, such as floor mosaics, but from 220–30 onward they also occur in considerable numbers in so-called hunting sarcophagi (Koch and Sichtermann 1982: 92–97; Andreae 1980). They represent the hunt of various kinds of game, such as deer and wild boar in, for instance, a sarcophagus from Arles[1] or of lions as depicted in a sarcophagus from Spoleto.[2] Hunting scenes must have occurred frequently, not only as reliefs on sarcophagi, but also in the painted decoration of Roman tombs, though fewer of these tomb paintings have survived. A provincial example of such a hunting scene was found in a tomb in Pantikapaion (nowadays Kerch, Ukraine) (Rostovtzeff 1919: pl. LXXIX). A good parallel for the hunting boys from *chapelle* XVIII is a painting from a Roman tomb in Silistra (modern Bulgaria), where a small boy, also painted in an octagonal frame, hunts a wild boar (Dorigo 1971: fig. 184) (fig. 22.2).

The *Imago Clipeata*

In a number of rooms in Bawit, we encounter representations of busts in a round frame *(clipeus)* supported by winged figures, in this Christian context to be identified as angels. In *chapelle* XVIII, for instance, over the niche in the eastern wall, two angels lift a *clipeus* that most probably contained a bust of Christ (Clédat 1916: pl. LIX). In 1976, a painting of a bust of Christ in a *clipeus*, lifted by two angels, was excavated in Bawit by the Egyptian Antiquities Organization and moved to the Coptic Museum (Gabra 2006: fig. 56) (fig. 22.3). Not only Christ, but also saints have been represented in a similar

Fig. 22.3. Bust of Christ in a clipeus, supported by angels, from Bawit, now in the Coptic Museum, Cairo (Gabra 2006).

Fig. 22.4. Roman sarcophagus, third quarter of the third century, with an *imago clipeata* of the deceased, now in the Pushkin Museum, Moscow (http://ancientrome.ru/art/artworken/img.htm?id=3757).

way. In *chapelle* XXXII, for instance, John the Baptist and Zachariah have been painted in this way in niches on the northern and eastern walls (Clédat 1904–1906: pl.VIII). The origin of this *imago clipeata* lies in the Roman iconography of the apotheosis, a theme often occurring in a funerary context, in which the portrait of a deceased is supported by *genii* or *erotes*. As such it occurs frequently on marble sarcophagi[3] (Koch and Sichtermann 1982: 238–41) (fig. 22.4), and also in mural paintings, such as, for instance, in the tomb of Aelia Arisuth in Gargaresh (Libya) (Dorigo 1971: fig. 165).

Men in the Fiery Furnace

A third theme that can be found frequently in both a monastic and a funerary context is that of the three Hebrews in the fiery furnace, the biblical story taken from Daniel 3. In Bawit it was represented ín *salle* 30 (Maspero 1932–43: pl. XLV), but reference to the story can also be found in the form of graffiti, such as the ones in *chapelle* XIX, on the western wall, where two graffiti just give the names of the three Hebrews (Clédat 1916: 112). In the monastery of Apa Jeremias in Saqqara, the subject was painted in chapel F (Quibell 1908: pl. LVII). The painting that was found in Wadi Sarga by R. Campbell Thompson in 1913/14 and that shows the scene of the Three Hebrews may have been made for a monastic dwelling as well.[4] In early Christian Roman art the same theme occurs frequently in a funerary context, specifically in catacomb paintings and sarcophagi reliefs.[5] The theme can be found not only in the Mediterranean area, but also in the necropolis of al-Bagawat (mausoleum of the Exodus) (Cipriano 2008: 145–46). Its popularity as a funerary theme can be explained by the fact that the Three Hebrews are mentioned in the *Commendatio animae*, the prayer for the salvation of the soul of the deceased that was in use from the third century on. Here, the deliverance of the soul is compared to a number of biblical stories in which faith or the mercy of God save the just in danger (Brown Tkacz 1991: 488).

Not only do we have iconographical parallels for the theme in funerary contexts, there is also an apothegm that refers to the Three Hebrews and compares the cell of the monks directly to the furnace:

> An elder said: "A monk's cell is the furnace of Babylon, in which the three children found the Son of God, and the pillar of cloud, from which God spoke with Moses." (*Apophthegmata Patrum*, Anonymous series, Wortley 2013: 147 [N.206/7.46])

From this short aphorism, we learn that the cell is considered the place where the monk communicates with God and, implicitly, a place of salvation.

Decorative Patterns; Floral and Animal Decoration

Apart from iconic and narrative themes, we find a number of elements in the geometrical, floral, and animal decoration of rooms in Bawit that have clear correspondences with paintings from late Roman tombs. The painting of the hunting boy from *chapelle* XVIII (Clédat 1916: pls. LXIV, LXV) shows a geometrical framework that consists of octagons and cross shapes, filled in with a meander pattern. This pattern may have been used in several situations, ranging from floor mosaics to ceiling decoration in private houses, but two close parallels happen to be from Roman tombs, one in a third- or fourth-century tomb in Abila (Jordan) (Ling 1991: fig. 208), the other one in cubiculum N in the catacomb of the Via Latina (Ferrua 1960: pl. CXI; Ferrua 1991: fig. 124).

There are more elements in the decorative painting from Bawit for which parallels can be found in a funerary context. The grapevines that come out of a jar on the south wall in *chapelle* XIX (Clédat 1916: pls. LXXXII, LXXXIII) could of course be interpreted as purely decorative, but in late Roman funerary art they are used frequently, in both non-Christian and Christian symbolism, to refer to the cult of Dionysos-Bacchus or the blood of Christ, respectively (Thomas 1990: col. 494–95). The same can be said of the peacocks, painted flanking a cross on the west wall of the same room (Clédat 1904–1906: pl. XXIX) (fig. 22.5), a motif that occurs frequently in tomb decoration, in the Mediterranean area and also in Egypt, as a symbol of eternal life and a reference to Paradise (Kramer 1990: col. 409–11) (fig. 22.6).[6]

Fig. 22.5. Bawit, two peacocks flanking a cross, western wall of *chapelle* XIX (Clédat 1904–1906).

Fig. 22.6. Theodosia between Saints Colluthos and Maria, watercolor after the painting in her tomb in Antinoë (Zibawi 2003).

Other animals that occur in paintings in Bawit are gazelles and birds of prey (eagles). In *chapelle* XXVII, for instance, we find an eagle with triple *bulla* around the neck (Clédat 1904–1906: pl. XCIII). Gazelles are found in a number of paintings, especially in *chapelle* XVII where they accompany standing figures of monks and the personification of Ekklesia.

A close parallel for representations of these animals in the context of a tomb chamber is the recently discovered tomb with chapel near Dayr Anba Shenoute near Sohag. In the underground vault, the decoration consists of crosses flanked by gazelles and eagle-like birds, framed by decorative borders with meander patterns (Bolman, Davis, and Pyke 2010). Not only the shape of the architecture, but also the decoration, shows that the rooms in Bawit have in many cases a close similarity to tombs.

The Monk's Dwelling as a Tomb

On balance, after analyzing the iconography of a number of paintings from rooms in Bawit, we can come to the conclusion that there are close parallels to themes that occur frequently in late Roman funerary art, ranging from reliefs on sarcophagi to paintings in Christian catacombs. Elisabetta Lucchesi-Palli, after analyzing the iconography of the hunting scenes and decorative and floral patterns in Bawit, came to the conclusion that the painters who decorated these rooms must have had an elaborate knowledge of Roman paintings and mosaics, especially from the Syro-Palestine region (Lucchesi-Palli 1988 and 1990). If we go one step further in our analysis we can say that they were also well informed about funerary iconography. None of the themes discussed above have a purely funerary character—hunting scenes, grapevines, and peacocks occur in house decoration as well—but it is their occurrence in combination with each other that reinforces the similarity with tomb decoration. Hjalmar Torp came to the conclusion that the construction of these rooms, in their architectural resemblance to tombs, was to be explained by their function as commemorative chapels. This aspect may certainly not have been absent, but primarily these so-called chapels bear a resemblance to tombs, and this cannot be a coincidence. From a number of texts, especially the *Apophthegmata Patrum,* we know that the monk considered his cell a tomb, either in a metaphorical sense or literally. From countless cases in Egypt we know that rock-cut tombs were transformed into cells or small monasteries (the west banks of Thebes and Aswan are just two examples) or that monastic settlements were built on necropolises, as in the case of Apa Jeremias's monastery near Saqqara. On one hand, this had the practical advantage of having ready-to-use accommodation or building material to be reused at hand, while on the other, there was the ideological reason of seeking confrontation with the pagan spirits as part of a life of *askesis.*[7] But even more important was the ideal of the monk becoming 'dead to the world,' reaching a state of *apatheia* in which the monk would be indifferent to scorn or praise, as Macarius advised a young brother in one of the apothegms (Macarius 23, Ward 1975: 132). We find the same advice in different wordings, such as in an apothegm of Moses:

> A brother questioned Abba Moses saying, "I see something in front of me and I am not able to grasp it." The old man said to him, "If you do not become dead like those who are in the tomb, you are not able to grasp it." (Moses 11, Ward 1975: 140–41)

As a consequence, the tomb is considered a place of salvation of the soul:

> A brother said to Abba Poemen, "What should I do?" The old man said to him, "When Abraham entered the promised land he bought a sepulcher for himself and by means of this tomb he inherited the land." The brother said to him, "What is the tomb?" The old man said, "The place of tears and compunction." (Poemen 50, Ward 1975: 173)

The cell as a tomb can be seen as a metaphor, but in some cases we can see how certain monks took it literally. In one of the anonymous apothegms a Father from Sinai goes to Egypt with his pupil and comes to the town of Kuno. In the morning, they see the people of the town go to the cemetery to lament their dead till the third hour. The Father then proposes that his pupil erect tombs for the two of them after coming back to their cells to lament their own souls (Anonymous series, N. 592, 1, Wortley 2013: 401).

The Aspect of the Oratorium

The themes depicted on the walls of the rooms in Bawit strongly suggest a metaphorical character as a tomb for the monk(s) living on the upper floor of the same building. But, on the other hand, there is the aspect of a prayer room, as we have seen, clearly indicated by the presence of the miniature apses in the eastern walls. Judging from the number of these rooms in the complex, it seems unlikely that they were used for funerary ritual only, as Torp suggested, but rather for the daily liturgy of the hours. In that case, the monks would be standing next to each other in lines, facing east. In a number of rooms there are rows of persons depicted on the western wall, as is the case of, for instance, *chapelles* XVII, XVIII, XXVI, and XXVIII (Clédat 1904–1906: 79, 92–94, 133, 157–58). These persons can be saints, but often we find representations of monks and saints standing side by side. Some of these monks are standing with their hands raised, in a gesture of prayer, as in *chapelle* XXVI (Clédat 1904–1906: pl. LXXXVII). We do not know whether these monks were portrayed during their lifetime, but it is perhaps more likely that what we have here are commemorative representations, again comparable to funerary paintings such as the painting of Theodosia from Antinoë, standing with raised arms between Saints Colluthos and Maria (fig. 22.6). We find similar representations in Roman catacombs, where families are reunited after death by their representations in the tomb.[8] In several rooms, names of monks and saints have been added on the western (and other) walls, apparently in addition to the paintings. Thus the representations of the monks and saints on the western walls of the *oratoria* and the names added later may have been intended as their literal *re-presentations*, images that substitute the real presence of persons, joining the living monks in their daily prayers.[9] In this way, the living monks would be reunited with their spiritual ancestors in their praise of God. A parallel for such an iconographical composition outside of Bawit can be found in the church of the Holy Virgin in Dayr al-Suryan. On two half-columns in the *khurus*, facing east, are the representations of two monks. One painting cannot be identified with certainty, but may represent St. Macarius, while the other one, standing again in a gesture of prayer, is identified as St. Apollo of Bawit (Innemée, Van Rompay, and Sobczynski 1999: 175–76; Innemée and Van Rompay 2002: 248, fig. 5). It seems they were intended as representatives or personifications of Egyptian monasticism, literally and metaphorically backing the monks standing in the *khurus* during prayers and liturgies.

Conclusions

The last word about the function of the rooms called *chapelles* by Clédat has not been said, and it will take more fieldwork to come to well-founded conclusions. Hjalmar Torp seems right when he draws a parallel with tomb architecture, but his supposition that the ground-floor rooms were only commemorative chapels seems less convincing. On the basis of the material available so far, we can say that these rooms most probably were the place for daily prayers and, in addition to this, had clear references to funerary architecture and its iconography. This fits the ideal of the monk to be 'dead to the world' and the metaphor of the cell as a tomb. The cell of the monk, and especially its prayer room, has a number of connotations, but generally it is considered the place where the monk finds salvation.

Living monks and their deceased predecessors were reunited here in praise of God. The 'absent' monks (deceased, or alive but physically not present) were represented by their image or a graffitto of their name on the wall. The cell combines the aspects of living quarters with those of a tomb and/or funerary chapel. The monk thus lives and prays in a cell that is at the same time a tomb, reminding him of the fact that he is dead to the world. The funerary character of the decoration underlines the view that the monk is dead to the world and illustrates his communion with his deceased 'spiritual ancestors.'

The so-called *chapelles* in Bawit were parts of the living quarters of the monks and were used for devotional purposes, most likely the liturgy of the hours and possibly also commemorative gatherings, and in their decoration they refer to church interiors (apse decoration, narrative cycles) as well as to tombs.

The funerary themes depicted show the painters' familiarity with late Roman traditions and iconography, a phenomenon that is also apparent in the church decoration of the Red and White Monasteries near Sohag.

Notes

1 The sarcophagus is now in the Musée de l'Arles et de la Provence antiques. For a photograph, see: http://upload.wikimedia.org/wikipedia/commons/4/4e/Arles_sarcophagus_hunting_scene.jpg.

2 The sarcophagus is in the Piazza del Duomo: Database of Ancient Art, http://ancientrome.ru/art/artworken/img.htm?id=4414.

3 A fine example is a third-century sarcophagus in the Pushkin Museum, Moscow: Database of Ancient Art, http://ancientrome.ru/art/artworken/img.htm?id=3757

4 The painting is no longer in context, but was brought to the British Museum: British Museum, http://www.britishmuseum.org/research/research_projects/all_current_projects/wadi_sarga.aspx.

5 Of the many examples we can mention: Catacomb of Priscilla, Capella Graeca (Crippa and Zibawi 1998: fig. 73); Catacomb of Priscilla (Crippa and Zibawi 1998: fig. 90); Catacomb of the Via Latina (Ferrua 1991: fig. 144); sarcophagus of Marcia Romana Celsa, Arles (Crippa and Zibawi 1998: fig. 122).

6 A good example of a pair of peacocks, this time flanking a bowl of fruit, can be found in cubiculum E of the catacomb at the Via Latina (Ferrua 1991: fig. 77). From

Egypt, the best-known example is the painting from the tomb of Theodosia in Antinoë, where the deceased is represented between two saints, with two peacocks in the pendentives over the painting (Zibawi 2003: fig. 9).

7 As in the case of Macarius, who spent the night in a pagan temple and used mummies as pillows, provoking a spiritual fight with evil spirits (Macarius 13, Ward 1975: 130).

8 An example is the so-called cubiculum of the Five Saints in the San Callisto catacomb, where five members of a family are represented with raised arms, in a gesture of prayer (Crippa and Zibawi 1998: pl. 9).

9 The veneration of funerary portraits and of icons of saints are closely related in late antiquity. On this topic, see Belting 1994: 78–98.

23 The Cave of John of Lykopolis

Jochem Kahl

Gebel Asyut al-Gharbi

Gebel Asyut al-Gharbi, a limestone mountain located to the west of Asyut at the edge of the Libyan Desert, provides much information on ancient Asyut (Kahl 2007a: 59–106). The mountain rises to a height of up to two hundred meters above sea level. During the pharaonic period, Gebel Asyut al-Gharbi served as a necropolis for the inhabitants of Asyut, high officials among them, as well as for sacred animals. In addition to this, several areas of the mountain were exploited as a quarry. In the Christian era, Christian anchorites used the numerous tombs as cells or dwellings (Kahl 2007a: 71–72) (fig. 23.1). The walls of the tombs, decorated with ancient Egyptian pictures and hieroglyphs, were either merely covered with a rough mud plaster by the anchorites, or whitewashed and decorated with inscriptions and paintings. Monasteries were also erected on Gebel Asyut al-Gharbi, with Dayr al-Meitin and Dayr al-'Izam being especially noteworthy examples, both of which were abandoned during the fifteenth century AD at the latest. Today, most of the Christian wall decorations have perished. The destruction took place especially during the nineteenth and twentieth centuries, when substantial losses occurred.

Thanks to research carried out by geologists Klemm and Klemm (Kahl 2007a: 59–61; Klemm and Klemm 2008: 112–15), it is possible to divide the mountain into eleven geological steps, which also correspond to eleven

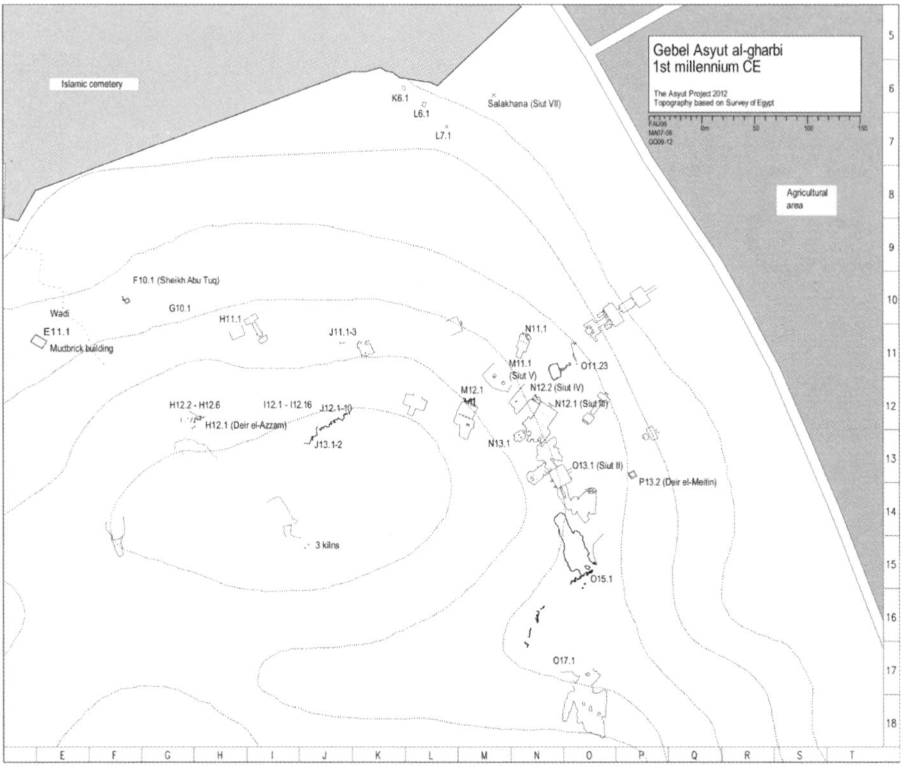

Fig 23.1. Gebel Asyut al-Gharbi in the first millennium AD. © Cornelia Goerlich, The Asyut Project.

steps of pharaonic tomb architecture. At steps 6 and 7, later also at step 2, rock tombs for the nomarchs of the First Intermediate Period and of the Middle Kingdom (approximately 2160 to 1900 BC) were driven horizontally into the mountain. With their monumental size, these tombs surpass the dimensions of coeval sepulchral structures intended for non-royal persons. The inner hall of Tomb III from the First Intermediate Period covers six hundred square meters (Kahl 2007a: 74–77); Tomb II from the early Middle Kingdom features an inner hall with a height of over twelve meters (Kahl 2007a: 85–86). Some of the proprietors of the tombs were posthumously venerated as saints (Kahl 2012), for example Djefai-Hapi I (the owner of Tomb I), Iti-ibi (the owner of Tomb III), and Khety II or Khety I (the owners of Tomb IV and Tomb V, respectively). Besides these large tombs, more than a thousand smaller burial sites were hewn into Gebel Asyut al-Gharbi, giving it the appearance of a honeycomb.

John of Lykopolis

John of Lykopolis (310/320–394/395), seer and prophet, lived as an ascetic and recluse in a cave in the western mountain of Asyut (Greek: Lykopolis). Many people consulted him. Even Emperor Theodosius trusted in John to foretell his future (Schaff and Wace 1995: 226).

Several sources written in Greek, Latin, and Coptic provide information regarding John's life and works. He was born in Asyut to Christian parents. According to the *Historia Lausiaca,* he learned the trade of carpenter while his brother became a dyer. After the death of his parents, John went into the Scetis Desert (the Wadi al-Natrun) and became a monk. He was educated in different monasteries between the ages of twenty-five and thirty, studying with Apa Isidor and Apa Poemen. John's name became famous in distant monasteries because of his firm fasting and praying. Then the angel of the Lord appeared to him and instructed him to return to his hometown and teach the way of righteousness there. John consequently returned to Asyut, where he lived in a hermitage situated in the western mountain on the desert escarpment in accordance with the principles of early monasticism (*Historia Monachorum in Aegypto* I, 6; Kahl 2007a: 138–39).

The Cave of John of Lykopolis

According to *Historia Lausiaca* XXXV, John made himself three cells on the actual summit and then went in and immured himself. The building had no door. Accordingly, John did not leave his hermitage for forty (*Historia Monachorum in Aegypto* I, 4) or forty-eight (*Historia Lausiaca* XXXV) years. Disciples gave him food and drink through a window (*Historia Lausiaca* XXXV). As John ate nothing apart from fruit, the ascetic life wore out his body so that his beard no longer grew on his face at the age of ninety years (*Historia Monachorum in Aegypto* I, 17). Through the window, John communicated with the world outside, receiving visitors on Saturdays and Sundays. The visitors had to be male; John refused to receive women. A small church (Devos 1969b: 194) and a shelter (*Historia Monachorum in Aegypto* I, 16; Russell 1981: 54) in the vicinity of John's cell were at the disposal of the visitors (Kahl 2007a: 139).

Nevertheless, the exact location of John's hermitage is still disputed. Dayr al-'Izam, situated on top of the mountain plateau, has been proposed

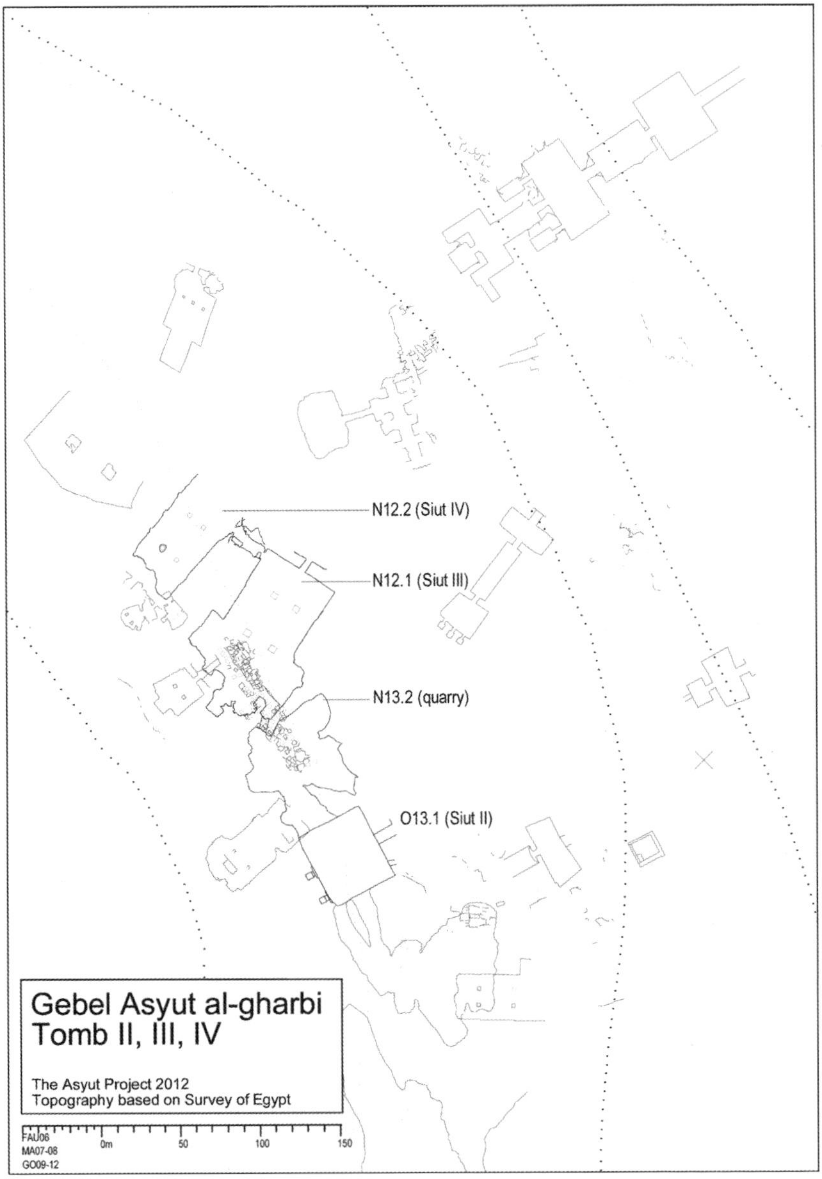

Fig. 23.2. The hermitage of St. John of Lykopolis (Asyut, Tomb II, III, IV). © Cornelia Goerlich, The Asyut Project.

by several authors (Coquin and Martin 1991c; Zuckerman 1995), but the tripartite complex of Tomb II (and later quarry N13.2)/Tomb III/Tomb IV (N13.2/N12.1/N12.2) with its late antique corridors connecting the individual tombs should be considered as well (fig. 23.2).

A jar found at Dayr al-'Izam bears a Coptic inscription dated 1156 and naming the site "Apa John of the Desert" (Crum 1902: 33–34, pl. 1; *JdE* 3145; CG 8104). Therefore, Dayr al-'Izam is often referred to as the hermitage of St. John of Lykopolis (cf. Coquin and Martin 1991c; Grossmann 2002: 208). However, it remains unclear where the three rooms that served John for the rest of his life were located.

The fact that the earliest findings of pottery in Dayr al-'Izam can be dated no further back than the fifth to seventh century AD, according to the 2009 survey (Eichner and Beckh 2010: 207), as well as the fact that a building with three rooms, which could have served as John's hermitage, cannot be detected either today or in the excavation report from 1900 (Maspero 1900), are arguments against the assumption that Dayr al-'Izam is the site of the hermitage of St. John of Lykopolis.

The situation is different as far as the nomarch tombs of the First Intermediate Period and the Middle Kingdom are concerned: a perusal of the sources that provide us with an idea of the architecture of the hermitage show a number of congruities with Tombs II, III, and IV (fig. 23.3). An approximately two-meter-high passageway (fig. 23.4) connects Tombs IV and III, and makes it possible for a man to traverse it effortlessly in an upright position. The connection between Tombs IV and III, which dates from Christian times, is complemented with a connection between Tomb III and N13.2. The latter designates a quarry that came into operation during or after the New Kingdom and that stretches north from the inner hall of Tomb II. This quarry reached to the rear wall of Tomb III, where a passageway to Tomb II was constructed in the southwest corner (fig. 23.2). This connection of three rooms is consistent with the description in the *Historia Lausiaca*. According to *Historia Lausiaca* XXXV, John inhabited a hermitage with three rooms on the outskirts of Asyut. One chamber was for his bodily needs, another was where he worked and ate, and the third was where he prayed.

A window situated in the wall of St. John's hermitage served as a connection to the outside world, according to the *Historia Monachorum* (I, 5; I, 15). Even though the fronts of Tombs II, III, and IV were completely destroyed by mining activities in the nineteenth century (Kahl 2013: 84–85), the

Fig. 23.3. Asyut, Tombs III, IV, and V in 2007. © Frith Barthel, The Asyut Project.

Fig. 23.4. Asyut, Tomb IV: passageway connecting Tomb IV and Tomb III, 2007. © Manja Maschke, The Asyut Project.

Fig. 23.5. Asyut, Tomb III (left) and Tomb IV (right) in 1799 (Description de l'Égypte 1822, vol. 4: pls. 48.10, 48.4).

architectural drawings of the 1799 French Expedition (fig. 23.5) show that the front of Tomb III featured two window-like openings in addition to the entrance (*Description de l'Égypte* 1822, vol. 4: pl. 48.10), which cannot be part of the original design from the pharaonic period. It seems likely that these openings are identical with the window mentioned in the *Historia Monachorum*.

Remains of a ceiling painting are extant in the entrance area of the inner hall of Tomb IV (fig. 23.6). The remains show a bust portrait of a male figure contained in a medallion. In the man's left hand, the depiction of the upper part of a book survives; above his left shoulder, the letters Iota and Omega can still be discerned. These are the initial letters of the name Ιωάννης (Eichner and Beckh 2010: 210). The northwest pillar of Tomb IV is the only one that remains today. Its shape and the typical Coptic chisel

Fig. 23.6. Asyut, Tomb IV, inner hall, ceiling painting, after restoration in 2012. © Fritz Barthel, The Asyut Project.

traces indicate a remodeling that took place in Christian times, apparently in order to utilize the inner hall of Tomb IV as a sacred space (El-Khadragy 2006: 89–90). The assumption that a saint named John was venerated in this tomb in the Christian period suggests itself—in all likelihood, the saint in question was St. John of Lykopolis.

These observations support a thesis I put forth as early as 2007, according to which Tombs II, III, and IV constituted the hermitage of St. John of Lykopolis (Kahl 2007a: 139; Kahl 2007b).

Tombs III and IV have fulfilled multiple purposes over time. During the First Intermediate Period, they initially served as tombs for the nomarchs and their relatives; they subsequently became the location for the ritual veneration of the deceased nomarchs during the Twelfth Dynasty (Rzeuska 2012: 209–10). During the Amarna Period, Tomb IV was ultimately used as a quarry (Kahl 2007a: 61–62). In Tomb III, on the other hand, pottery and *ushabtis* from the New Kingdom period were recovered, which makes it likely that the tomb was used for secondary burials at this point. During the Third Intermediate Period and/or Late Period, secondary burials certainly took place in Tomb III. This is clearly evidenced by findings from Shaft 4, which was rediscovered by the Asyut Project after going unnoticed since premodern times (Kahl, El-Khadragy, and Verhoeven 2006: 243). Only some twenty- to forty-centimeter-deep recesses hewn into the rock floor suggest further burials in pre-Christian times. Findings of late Roman, Byzantine, Coptic, and Mamluk pottery attest to the vivid Christian and post-Christian history of the tomb. To give an example, the floor of the tombs was surfaced with a layer of bones and bandages 50 to 100 centimeters thick in post-Christian times. The required building materials probably originated from the nearby Tomb of the Dogs (cf. for Tomb V, Kahl and Malur 2011: 182).

The treatment of Tombs III and IV by the archaeologists of the early twentieth century constitutes an obstacle to the interpretation of their history of usage. The Italian archaeologist Ernesto Schiaparelli and his assistant Virginio Rosa, as well as the British archaeologist David George Hogarth and the French archaeologists Émile Chassinat and Charles Palanque, all used Tombs III and IV as the base of operations for their excavations on Gebel Asyut al-Gharbi (Kahl 2007a: 30–33; cf. the picture in D'Amicone 2009: 40–41). They ate and slept in the tombs and stored their findings there. Accordingly, the cleaning of Shaft 1 in Tomb III revealed numerous 'leftovers' from the Italian and French archaeologists: not only cigarette boxes, wine labels, papers, and newspaper clippings, but also, for example, 1,200 fragments of *ushabti*s that surely did not originate from Tomb III. As a consequence of its use as a base camp, it has to be expected that findings from different tombs on Gebel Asyut al-Gharbi were brought there before a decision was made whether the artifacts were to be sent to Europe or to the Egyptian Museum in Cairo, or whether they were simply to be left in the tomb, like the *ushabti* fragments.

Although we may justifiably assume that some of the findings from Tomb III do in fact stem from this burial site, a great many other findings certainly cannot be associated with this tomb originally. Unfortunately, it is frequently impossible to ascertain which scenario is the case. This also holds true for the post-Christian findings that are my main concern here. It is not possible to determine with certainty in every individual case that they originally derive from Tomb III.

The interpretation of Tombs II, III, and IV as the hermitage of St. John of Lykopolis is at the very least not called into question by the existence of findings from the fourth century AD (pottery, oil lamps, wooden figurine), even if all due caution is applied to the question of their original context of usage. In Tomb III, during the first millennium AD, the main activity of occupation started in the fourth century and lasted through the whole period, but it looks as if the greatest intensity of occupation took place between the fifth and the seventh century (that is, after St. John's death).

As a consequence of the identification of Tombs II, III, and IV as the hermitage of St. John, a cross-cultural continuity in relation to the veneration of saints becomes evident: as already mentioned, the owners of Tombs III and IV (or possibly of the neighboring Tomb V), Iti-ibi and Khety, were venerated as saints in the second millennium BC. Their tomb inscriptions formed part of the cultural memory of ancient Egypt as late as the second century AD, as findings of papyri in Tebtynis in the Fayoum attest (Osing 1998; Kahl 1999; Kahl 2012). The tombs with their function as memorial sites for ancient Egyptian saints also served as memorial sites for a Christian saint, and the fact that Dayr al-Meitin was constructed in close vicinity to Tombs II, III, and IV in the fifth century AD, that is, immediately after the death of St. John, is unlikely to be a coincidence.

24 Al-Shaykh Sa'id Revisited: A Reassessment of the Spatial Layout of a Monastic Community

Gertrud J.M. van Loon

AL-SHAYKH SA'ID (Middle Egypt) covers the southern part of the archaeological concession area of the Dayr al-Barsha Project (Research Group Egyptology, KU Leuven),[1] directed by Harco Willems.[2] The site is named after the nearby tomb of a local saint. An ensemble of Old Kingdom tombs (end of Fifth Dynasty–beginning of Sixth Dynasty) was cut into the steep western cliff face of an outcrop between two wadis, Wadi Jamus to the north and Wadi Zabayda to the south (figs. 24.1–3). Monumental tombs line the principal ridge, with a lower and a higher level of smaller tombs and shafts. Steep paths connect the long narrow terraces. A lower range of jagged cliffs and rifts separates the tomb complex from the floodplain.

Fig. 24.1. View of the range of Old Kingdom tombs. © G.J.M. van Loon 2013.

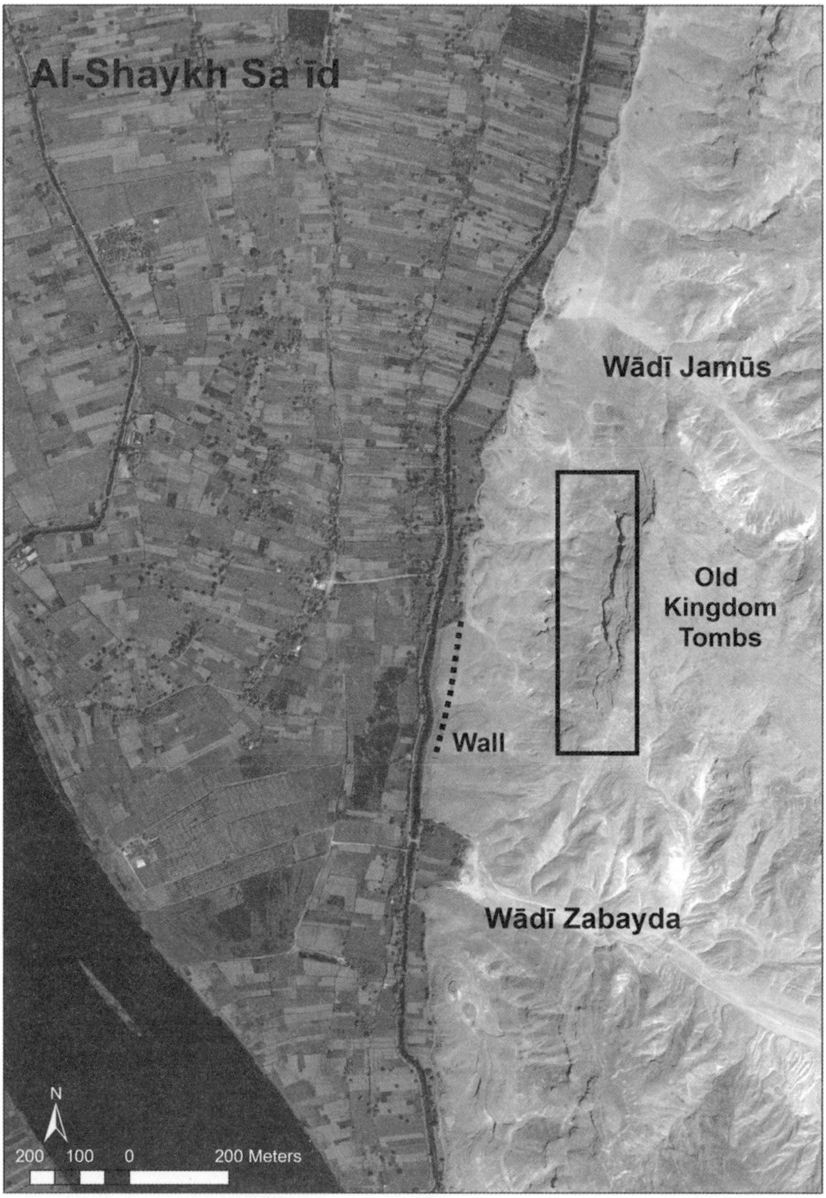

Fig. 24.2. Map of al-Shaykh Sa'id.

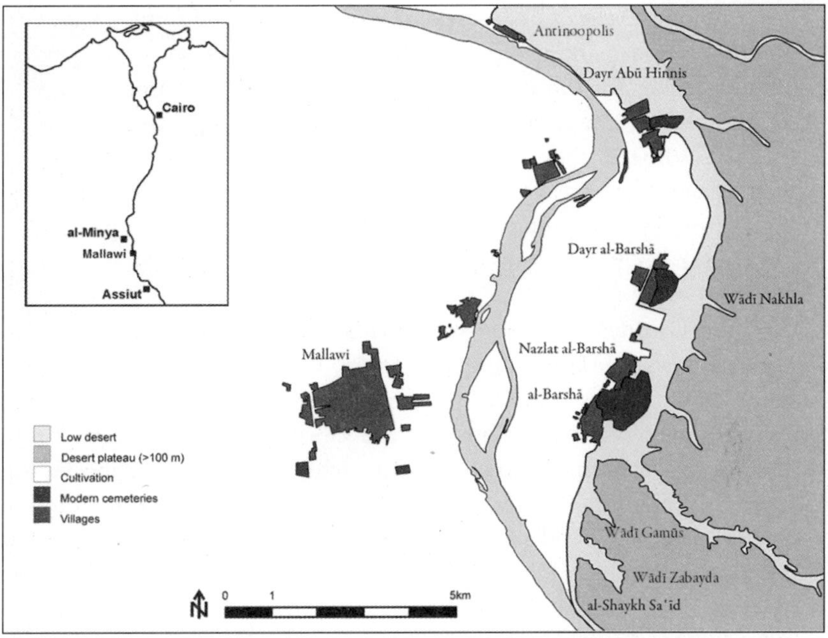

Fig. 24.3. Map of the greater Dayr al-Barsha region. Courtesy Chr. Peeters, Dayr al-Barsha Project.

At the end of the nineteenth century, Norman de Garis Davies studied and documented the tombs (Davies 1901). They have received little attention since,[3] but the Supreme Council of Antiquities restored the most important tombs in 2002–2003. Davies was one of the few late nineteenth-century Egyptologists who also documented Christian remains. A number of tombs show traces of reuse as habitation, and, on the terraces in front, wall remains testify to the construction of walled courtyards and additional buildings. Tomb 25, the tomb of Werirni,[4] was remodeled as a church. Inscriptions found in some of the tombs confirm that a monastic community once inhabited the site (Davies 1901; Timm 1984–92, vol. 5: 2327; Jones 1991: 141–42; van Loon 2010; van Loon and Delattre 2014, with an appendix on the inscriptions by A. Delattre).

Only a handful of early travelers and scholars seem to have visited the tombs. The British diplomat and antiquarian William Richard Hamilton stopped at the site in the winter of 1801–1802. On the tomb of Werirni, he wrote:

> On the inner walls of one of the catacombs we found some curious sculptures and paintings. It had long served as a Greek or Coptic church, either for the inhabitants of the town, or for some devout hermits who in the early ages of Christianity may have dwelt in these caverns. Whoever they were, they have given vent to their religious fury against the idols of Paganism, by mutilating all the prominent figures and by concealing the paintings under a thick coat of plaister. (Hamilton 1809: 275–76)[5]

Sir John Gardner Wilkinson visited al-Shaykh Sa'id in 1824–25. In his famous guidebook, *Modern Egypt and Thebes,* he describes pharaonic reliefs in some of the tombs and adds, "Before several of the grottoes are crude brick walls, built when inhabited by the Christians, who converted one of them into a church, cutting a circular niche into the rock opposite the entrance" (Wilkinson 1843, vol. 2: 70). The Coptic inscription in Tomb 6, a series of names of monks that he copied in his notebook, was not added (Oxford, New Bodleian Library, Ms. Wilkinson dep. C 5 fol. 4, unpublished;[6] see Davies 1901: 35; edited by Delattre in van Loon and Delattre 2014).

The French Egyptologist and artist Nestor l'Hôte was in al-Shaykh Sa'id in 1838. He was the first to call this settlement "Deyr-abou-fâm" (l'Hôte 1840: 51; see Davies 1901: 10; Coquin and Martin 1991f; Timm 1984–92, vol. 2: 572; al-Suriany 1990: 115; Jones 1991: 141). His unpublished notebook contains a sketch of the niche in the "Tombeau dont les premiers chrétiens ont fait une église," which he dated to the third–fourth century (Paris, BnF, NAF 20396: 273 verso).[7]

When exactly these tombs were reused by monks is not known. So far, no historical documentation of a monastic settlement at al-Shaykh Sa'id has been found. Dates of habitation vary. Petrie dated fragments of glass and ceramics found near Tombs 61–62 to the fourth century (Davies 1901: 4). Jones dated ceramics to the period of the fifth to the eighth centuries (1991: 143). The themes of the paintings in the church have been known since the fourth to fifth centuries, but cannot be narrowed down to a more specific period of time (Van Loon 2010: 171–75). One of the texts in Tomb 39 contains a fragmentary date, pointing to the twelfth century (Davies 1901: 36; Delattre in van Loon and Delattre 2014).

One remarkable feature of this site is the remains of a large wall at the foot of the hills, to the southwest of the group of tombs. On satellite imagery, a stretch of about 270 meters of this mud-brick wall running parallel to the

Fig. 24.4. The wall at the foot of the tomb complex, al-Shaykh Sa'id. © G.J.M. van Loon 2013.

Nile can still be traced in the desert environment. To the north, it disappears below cultivation. Part of it is still standing (approximatey 6.50 m long, 1.6 m thick, and 3.50–4 m high; figs. 24.2 and 24.4).[8] This enigmatic wall had already intrigued Hamilton (1809: 275), Edmé François Jomard, who wrote about it in the *Description de l'Egypte* (1822, vol. 4: ch. 16, "Description de l'Heptanomide," 322–24), and Wilkinson (1843, vol. 2: 70; Oxford, New Bodleian Library, Ms. Wilkinson dep. C 5 fol. 4, unpublished). Ideas about the age and function of this once huge wall differ, but one of the theories is that it might have been part of a monastic valley settlement that was related to the community living in the tombs (Kemp 2005: 37–38, 54).

In all probability, the monks who settled in the tombs of al-Shaykh Sa'id adhered to a semi-anchoritic lifestyle. They had chosen to live on their own or share a dwelling with a disciple. The community would meet once a week for mass and a communal meal. To supply their everyday needs, there might have been other services such as a bakery or kitchens (Wipszycka 2009: 288–90). The degree of organization in such a group varied. The physical surroundings of their chosen location, pre-existing spaces such as tombs or, in other places, quarries or natural caves, partly dictated building activities and subsequently the size of the community and how the monks organized their lives. The interior could, within boundaries, be adapted to their wishes and, if space were available, additional rooms or buildings could be constructed or a courtyard could be fenced off with a wall (van Loon and Delattre 2014; van Loon and De Laet, 2014).

This chapter explores the way monks adapted the tombs of al-Shaykh Sa'id to a monastic community as well as the role of the wall in front of the cliffs. Was it part of the layout of the settlement or did it serve another purpose?

Living at al-Shaykh Sa'id

In order to be able to analyze the settlement pattern, a distribution map was constructed, showing the exact location of the tombs and the road system. For each tomb, markers of habitation (building activities [interior or exterior], decoration, and inscriptions) were noted. Using this sort of map, the diffusion of reused tombs and spaces that had a specific function began to emerge. Paths were revealed to point to particular areas, showing the internal structure of the settlement as well as links to the outside world.

The area was mapped using very high spatial resolution satellite imagery (Quickbird-2) combined with the maps Davies published in 1901 (pls. I–II). Remote sensing implies a spatial context of the features analyzed; a basic map can be created that serves as a starting point for field survey. A field survey (carried out in 2012–13) included taking GPS readings of the entrances of the tombs (using a Trimble® GeoExplorer® 2005 GeoXT™ handheld GPS) and documenting characteristics related to their reuse. Paths were examined and their context recorded.

The features of each tomb were set out in Microsoft Excel and, in conjunction with the GPS readings, imported into the ESRI/ArcGIS® module ArcMap. If GPS readings for tombs were absent (mainly because of the falling away of the satellite signal caused by the steep rock faces), points were digitized in ArcGIS on the basis of photographic documentation and a comparison with Davies' maps. Data analysis was performed using selection queries as implemented in the ArcGIS software.

Three general objective characteristics, 'building activities,' 'decoration,' and 'inscriptions,' were chosen as markers for habitation. These are all features that can be observed, as none of the tombs or the spaces in front of the tombs were excavated. Evidence for 'building activities' includes, for example, stone or mud-brick walls, windows, doorways, floors, cupboards, benches, and niches. 'Decoration' applies to painting and sculpture.

'Inscriptions' merely indicates the presence or absence of inscriptions and graffiti, not language or content.

In total, Davies numbered 102 tombs, located on the main ridge and on terraces above and below this, plus a few tombs scattered in between these levels. Some of these tombs are currently inaccessible. Examples are Tomb 18, located high up in a virtually perpendicular cliff face, or Tombs 94–102, which have now almost completely filled up with sand and debris. Moreover, Davies counted, indiscriminately, monumental tombs, small tombs, low tombs of approximately 1 cubic meter, with or without a shaft, mere niches, and 'pit-tombs,' single square shallow shafts with a low vault in one of its sides. It is clear that the latter three types were not suitable to habitation, although the low tombs could be incorporated in a complex, for example, as storerooms. All tombs were mapped and subsequently those tombs qualifying as a dwelling place were filtered out. Of the 102 tombs counted by Davies, only twenty-five were large and high enough for this purpose. Further analysis was performed on the latter group.[9]

A glance at the distribution map (fig. 24.5) makes it clear that the best possible use was made of the existing situation. The main ridge of the natural outcrop houses monumental tombs, which were remodeled. Dividing walls between small tombs could be dismantled in order to create an acceptable space, as in Tombs 70–71, in which a doorway was cut and windows, seats, and steps were carved (Davies 1901: 8–9). Another way to connect tombs was to build a communal courtyard, as in front of Tombs 61 and 62 (61 is low and very small). Davies states that the floor of the courtyard was plastered and contained two receptacles, sunk in the floor (Davies 1901: 4 and 8, pl. XVII ["Tombs arranged as a dwelling"]; van Loon 2010: 163).

The mud-brick or stone structures in front of the tombs show that full use was made of the space on the terraces. These terraces are currently very narrow and often steep, but building remains (for example, near Tombs 37 and 39) indicate that originally these ridges must have been wider in some spots. A relatively wide and flat area in front of Tombs 24–28, where Davies excavated a small building in front of the church (Davies 1901: 4, pl. XVII ["Brick house outside tomb of Urarna"]; Jones 1991: 141–42, pl. XII-1), and extending to the southwest near Tombs 29–30, shows a concentration of mud-brick remains. These constructions were built of bricks of various sizes laid in different bonds. Further analysis of the bricks and the scatter of pottery sherds among the wall remains (planned for the mission of 2014) will give more insight into the date and function of these buildings.

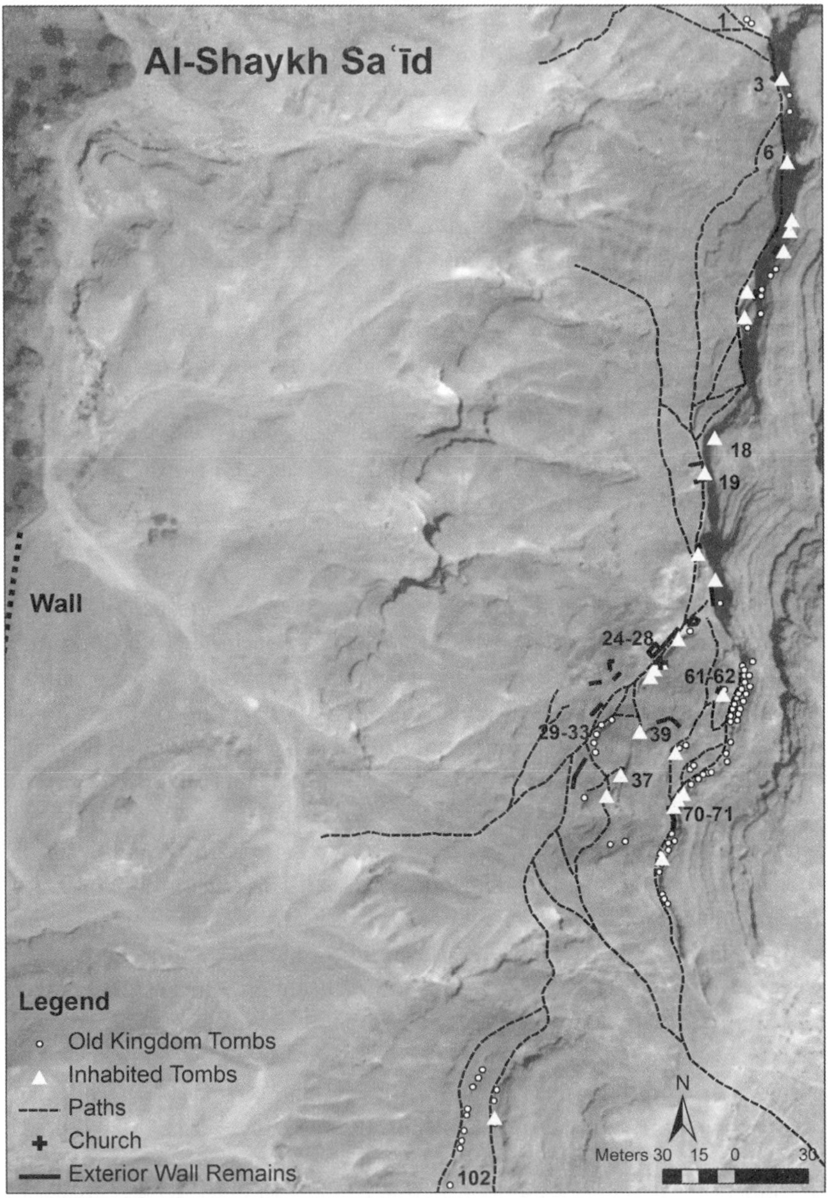

Fig. 24.5. The settlement pattern at al-Shaykh Sa'id.

However, it is clear that this pottery belongs roughly to either the Late Roman or the Byzantine period.

Only Tomb 25, the tomb of Werirni, in which a church was installed, could be assigned a special function. The original intermediate wall dividing the present chamber into two was removed. A large niche was cut in the southeast wall, flanked by pilasters with sculpted capitals. The conch is painted with a winged creature and is rimmed with a white decorative border on a dark background. To the right of the niche, fragments of a military saint (St. Phoibammon/Abu Fam?) can be distinguished, and on the southwest wall are the fragments of a unicorn, an ankh cross, and a species of deer (Davies 1901: 16–17, pl.VII, XIII–B, XIV; van Loon 2010: 164–75). The layout and decoration of the eastern part of the church featuring such a spacious absidal niche fits into a series of churches installed in tombs and quarries in this region. Similar niches can be found in Amarna (Tomb of Panehsy; Davies 1905: 9, 11–13; Pyke 2008), Dayr al-Dik (Quarry 13; Martin 1971: 27–33; van Loon 2008: 182–90) and Speos Artemidos (Martin 1971: 62; van Loon, in press).

The most elaborate interior can be found in Tomb 39. It seems highly likely that this tomb was never finished or decorated. It contains a large number of wall niches (four large ones hold beds), which were painted with geometrical designs in red, black, and yellow (fig. 24.6; Davies 1901: 36, pl. XXXIII; van Loon 2010: 163–64). Apart from the church and this tomb, decoration is sparse. Pilasters flank a small niche in Tomb 37 and Davies noted a painted decorative pattern in Tomb 18 (Davies 1901: 31). The entrance to Tomb 30, which is low and shows no further adaptation, is flanked by engraved crosses (Davies 1901: 7). Only Tombs 6, 19, 25, and 39 preserve inscriptions, mainly monks' names and a dated dedication in Tomb 39 (twelfth century; Davies 1901: 16–17, 29, 35–36, pl. XIV–B/D; see van Loon 2010: 176; Delattre, in Van Loon, in press a).

The infrastructure of paths in the tomb complex is the result of frequent use following a least-cost trajectory (fig. 24.5). None of the paths show built, paved, or cut sections. Consequently, they are almost impossible to date. The north and south paths leading from the valley, which ascend to the main ridge, were most probably the old principal entrance routes. Likewise, the paths connecting the terraces must have already existed during the time this area was used as a cemetery. Avoiding the sharp elevations and deep rifts, there are some walking paths leading up directly from the floodplain to the main ridge, ending in front of Tombs 1–3 and Tombs

Fig. 24.6. Al-Shaykh Sa'id, Tomb 39, view to the southwest, with three niches holding beds. © G.J.M. van Loon 2008.

24–33. It is hard to say to which period the latter paths date. Although they are steeper than the northern and southern routes, they do lead directly to the monumental tombs and they might have been in use since the Old Kingdom. These connections are all located between the floodplain and tomb complex and within the complex itself, with one exception: from the main and upper ridge a path runs in a southeasterly direction and ends in the Wadi Zabayda. This wadi runs southeastward for about 5.5 kilometers and ends among the North Tombs of Amarna, the site of a contemporaneous Christian settlement, inhabited from about the fourth to the ninth century (Jones 1991; Kemp 2005).

At al-Shaykh Sa'id, a small compact monastic settlement was developed. Tomb 25 was probably chosen as a church because it is located in the center of the site with easy access on all sides, including the area occupied by mud-brick structures that extends to the southwest near Tombs 29–33. So far it has been impossible to identify workshops or rooms set aside for specific use. Barry Kemp (2005: 37) has estimated that this group of dwellings could have housed approximately thirty monks at any one time, and that is, in my opinion, a reasonable estimate. His theory of a group of hermitages dependent on a mother community in the plain, of which the wall fragment formed a part, will be examined below.

The Wall (figs. 24.2 and 24.4)

In the *Description de l'Égypte* Edmé François Jomard, an engineer and cartographer in Napoleon's retinue of scholars who explored Egypt in 1798, noted:

> Au-dessous de ce point, il y a encore d'autres carrières qui annoncent que les Égyptiens ont faits des grands travaux dans la montagne. Un long mur égyptien, en briques d'une grande épaisseur, qu'on trouve près du Nil, et tracé parallèlement au fleuve, confirme cette idée. Les briques sont énormes, et les habitans disent que c'est l'ouvrage de la plus haute antiquité. Je crois très probable, quoique la géographie n'en fasse point mention, qu'il a existé une position ancienne dans cet endroit; il est possible que le Nil, en abandonnant Meylâouy, et se portant à l'est, ait détruit les vestiges de cette ancienne ville. (*Description de l'Égypte* 1822, vol. 4: vol. 4: 323–24)

In the adjoining map of the region a "mur de briques" is indicated. Around 1800, the Nile flowed much closer to the hills than it does nowadays (Jacotin 1876: feuille 13; cf. Kemp 2005: fig. 1.17).

Hamilton describes the construction of the wall. He writes that on this spot

> are the vestiges of an antient [sic] Egyptian town, marked out by its wall of bricks baked in the sun, and the catacombs in the cliff. This wall is in some parts entire; but, unlike most other Egyptian walls, the bricks never present outwards their long sides; and over each layer of bricks placed edgeways on their narrow sides, are placed two layers of the same sized bricks on the flat sides. (Hamilton 1809: 275)

Both men thought this remnant was once part of a town wall and that the town itself, located to the west of the wall, had disappeared, swallowed up by the meandering of the Nile.

In his journal of 1824–25, Wilkinson notes "a long cr.[ude] br.[ick] wall, inclosing perhaps the burying ground, for below the T[om]^{bs} in the rock are these of cr. br. for poorer people."[10] However, in his later *Handbook for Travellers* he has this to say about this wall: "At Isbáyda [= Zabayda, the name of the southern wadi] there is another portion of the Gisr el Agoós" (Wilkinson 1843: 70–71). Norman de Garis Davies records that the wall, which could be followed for about 275 meters, had served as a defense against the Bedouins. He adds: "Such walls are found elsewhere in similar situations to the north and south . . . , and bear the name *Gisr el Agûz*, 'Dike of the Old Man,' perhaps because the Arabs see how ill-fitted they are to serve as dams. The size of the bricks (10¼ x 3 x 5 inches (Mr. J. Newberry))[11] may give the clue to the age of the construction" (Davies 1901: 5). Note that he translates *el Agûz* as 'old man,' instead of the more usual 'old woman.'

The Old Lady's Dike or Old Lady's Wall figures in an old and popular tale about the mythical queen Daluka, who reigned in Egypt after Pharaoh and his army drowned in the Red Sea while pursuing Moses and his people. According to tradition, she surrounded Egypt with a wall, either to protect the country or to protect her son.[12] Isolated (strong) wall remains parallel to the Nile, which had no obvious context, were often identified with Queen Daluka's wall, even though there is no evidence at all that such a wall ever existed (Sijpesteijn 2011 discusses the Arabic narrative tradition but the story has older origins: H. Willems, personal communication).

As set out above, Kemp proposes that the remains were the outer perimeter wall of a monastic complex whose buildings were destroyed by the meandering of the Nile. This 'parent community' would have had satellite hermitages in the converted tombs in the cliffs. He writes that the building method "is not inconsistent with the Late Roman period" (Kemp 2005: 37–38, 54).

Research by the KU Leuven team confirms that the masonry of the wall fragment at al-Shaykh Sa'id contains Late Roman ceramics (Willems et al. 2009: 293). The Late Roman date is consistent with the archaeobotanic analysis of one of its mud bricks (Marinova et al. 2011). In 2007, the team surveyed the area to the west of the wall, which covers about 800–950 meters to the current river bank, but no building remains were found in this area.

To sum up, the wall, which once ran along in front of the cliff of al-Shaykh Sa'id, parallel to the Nile, can be dated to the Late Roman period (c. third–sixth century). The trace is still about 275 meters long, but its original length is not known. To the west there are no building remains, and to the east the nearest constructions (mud-brick in front of the tombs) are located around 240 meters from the wall trace, with some steep low cliffs and a plain strip of desert in between.

As a consequence, Jomard and Hamilton's idea of an ancient city wall, whether pharaonic or from later times, can be abandoned. Wilkinson's hypothesis of a wall enclosing a cemetery is doubtful. The only mud-brick constructions are those at the foot of the rock-cut Tombs 25–33. Although these structures require further research, they seem to be of a much later date. A continuous wall as a defensive structure (Davies) was almost certainly never a reality. Finally, Kemp's theory, a wall surrounding a monastery, comes up against a similar problem to that of the lost-city theory of Jomard and Hamilton: no building remains to the west of the wall have ever been found.

The idea of a wall delimiting the area belonging to the monastic settlement in the cliffs springs to mind. For example, Dayr al-Bala'iza (near Asyut, abandoned in the ninth century), where a church was installed in a quarry and a large monastic complex with several churches built on the steep ascending hill, did have a surrounding wall (Grossmann 1993). However, in contrast to al-Shaykh Sa'id, Dayr al-Bala'iza was a sizable cenobitic community in which a wall to separate monastic life from worldly affairs was a necessity. Furthermore, physically, the latter wall, like the other known contemporary monastic boundary walls, was a much more modest structure than the wall at al-Shaykh Sa'id (Grossmann 1993: 173–74; Grossmann 2002: 307–309). Defensive walls in (semi-)anachoritic communities are known to have been developed from approximately the ninth century. They were never built around a complete settlement, but around a nucleus containing the most important buildings (Grossmann 2002: 309–13). Moreover, such a large and massive wall as in al-Shaykh Sa'id has not been encountered in monastic architecture so far (P. Grossmann, personal communication).

A parent community in the floodplain with a satellite settlement in the cliffs has long been proposed for monastic habitation patterns on the east bank in Middle Egypt (Martin 1971; Kemp 2005: 54–55, although Kemp recognizes the risk of oversimplification). In my opinion, every site needs to be assessed individually. For example, recent research on the monastic hill settlement and the village of Dayr Abu Hinnis, about 8.5 kilometers north of al-Shaykh Sa'id, has led to new insights into the habitation pattern (van Loon and De Laet, 2014). Al-Shaykh Sa'id, with its own church, most probably functioned as an autonomous community. Situated not far from the river, it had ties with the outside world in the near vicinity in order to obtain necessary provisions as well as for trade, and contact with neighboring communities, as the southeastern path in the direction of Amarna suggests. So far, no indication of a corresponding valley settlement has been found.

Therefore, for the time being, the function of the large wall in the floodplain has to remain a mystery. Sadly, it will probably have to remain an unsolved mystery. The wall traces are in imminent danger of destruction. In the hope of attracting tourists to Amarna, the Ministry of Tourism has decided to build a new road suitable for buses along the east bank. For various reasons, the trajectory does not follow the existing dirt road, but cuts through the strip of desert at the foot of the cliffs. At al-Shaykh Sa'id, it will run directly along the wall. In April 2013, the new road had already reached Wadi Jamus, the wadi to the north of the Old Kingdom rock tombs, thereby destroying a First Intermediate Period cemetery that had not yet been investigated. Owners of the land adjacent to the new road had building plans. The road and other developments will probably have reached an advanced state by now, thereby forever shattering the peace and quiet that once attracted the desert fathers.[13]

Notes

1 The current research is part of the author's EU-funded Marie Curie Fellowship at KU Leuven, "A View from Heaven: Exploring the Potential of Remote Sensing Techniques to Study Spatial Patterns of Monastic Habitation on the East Bank of the Nile in Middle Egypt" (FP7-MC-IEF 254243), and is being carried out within the framework of the Dayr al-Barsha Project (Research Group Egyptology, KU Leuven), which is funded by research grants from FWO Vlaanderen and the Bijzonder Onderzoeksfonds of KU Leuven (http://www.dayralbarsha.com).

2 The concession also includes Dayr al-Barsha and Dayr Abu Hinnis, which are together called the "Greater Dayr al-Barsha Region."

3 Most of the ground plans of the tombs have been copied from plans made on site by John Newberry in 1892 (Davies 1901: preface, xi–xii). For the history of research before 1900, see Davies 1901: 10 (correction: Lepsius, *Denkmäler* 2, 120–23).

4 Numbering of the tombs according to Davies. Modern orthography prefers Werirni to Urarna or Ouramou as found in older literature.

5 For this reference, I thank Christoph Peeters, Dayr al-Barsha Project.

6 I would like to thank Colin Harris (Modern Papers & John Johnson Reading Room) for his friendly welcome and help.

7 For this reference, I thank Marleen De Meyer, Dayr al-Barsha Project.

8 Measurements taken in 2008. At that time, it had deteriorated only slightly since Davies measured it (Davies 1901: 5).

9 Between Tombs 6 and 7, a tomb was used as a quarry. Davies indicated this place as "ruined tombs," but did not number the spot (Davies 1901: pl. I). The space has not preserved any traces of reuse for habitation and is not included in the analysis. Tombs 94–102 are not included either as they are now almost completely hidden by sand and debris. Davies (1901: 9) says that 94 and 101 were small chambers, 95–99 were very small and rough, and 100 and 102 were not cleared at that time.

10 Oxford, New Bodleian Library, Ms. Wilkinson dep. C 5 fol. 4 (unpublished).
11 The brick size corresponds to the measurements given by Kemp 2005: 37.
12 In some versions of this story, Queen Cleopatra was the builder of the wall (Sijpesteijn 2011: 90, 99).
13 Special thanks go to Rosemary Robson-McKillop for correcting my English.

25 Toward the Documentation of the Monastery of the Holy Virgin at al-Muharraq, Asyut

Howard Middleton-Jones

The site of Dayr al-Muharraq is located at the foot of the mountains of Qusqam (Coptic Syowt and present day al-Qusiya), GPS location Latitude 27.38491 Longitude 30.77989. Nothing is known for certain about the date of the foundation of this monastery (Coquin and Martin 1991d: 841). According to tradition, found in a sermon attributed to Pope Theophilus of Alexandria, the Holy Family stayed at this site for a period of six months, and Jesus returned here after the resurrection to consecrate the altar mentioned in Isaiah 19:19.

The site encompasses a number of unique and important architectural elements, including a marbled-top stone altar, and a unique collection of beautifully illustrated icons. It is therefore vital that these important examples of art and architecture, representing the Coptic tradition, be collated and recorded for the heritage of the Coptic culture. In addition, by standardizing the documentation record, a similar system may be employed at many other early Christian sites in Egypt toward a universal catalog, which in turn may be maintained and referenced for the legacy of the Coptic people.

Method of Documentation

In January 2011, a short while after the tragic church bombing in Alexandria and only a week prior to the Egyptian revolution, an important presentation was given at the Patriarchate in Cairo (Middleton-Jones 2011). Its premise was to offer a system of documentation whereby a national 'register' could be developed for the churches and monasteries of Egypt. The register would maintain the full records of all associated architectural elements, artwork, and important archaeological finds. Unfortunately, due to the political upheaval and unrest since 2011, energies have been concentrated on other more important matters, and thus the formulation of such a register was never further discussed or implemented. The development of such a register would provide the foundations and impetus for the cultural growth of the Coptic heritage, while simultaneously promoting public awareness of these important early Christian sites and monuments.

By developing and maintaining such records, especially those of a photographic nature, the register documentation would provide an important tool in aiding the conservators toward a correct and individual approach to the conservation of each site. A register would also be beneficial in maintaining an archaeological record, especially in connection to any 'at risk' sites, thus providing vital documentation toward future management programs, including applications for conservation funding. This register would differ slightly from that of the Coptic Monasteries Multi-Media Database (Middleton-Jones 2010) in that the documentation would be more of an 'in-house' record that would be individually suited for each unique Coptic site and recorded on site.

Dayr al-Muharraq Documentation

Throughout the monastery there are many diverse and important examples of unique Coptic art and architectural elements; thus it is vital to develop a standardized system whereby these elements and objects may be recorded for posterity. Much work has already been carried out by Fr. Athanasios al-Muharraqi and the brothers at the monastery, especially in the recording of the history of the site and the cataloging of the beautiful icons (Dayr al-Muharraq 2012). The incorporation of such a register, utilizing a standard recording technique (Middleton-Jones 1997) for this and other sites, would provide an important documentation package for the continued preservation of the monastery. In addition, with the increasing use of the many available photographic packages incorporating digital enhanced software, high-resolution images of objects may be reproduced. The resulting images would be of great advantage especially in deciphering inscriptions and analyzing artwork. The high-resolution process would offer clarity toward recognizing the origins of texts and illustrations alike, a technique that would prove invaluable in studying icon images. A similar photographic survey was utilized at the site of the church remains at Qubbat al-Hawa, Aswan (Middleton-Jones and Dekker 2010) (fig. 25.1). The important apse and wall illustrations along with the associated inscriptions are rapidly eroding at this site, and without any recording or documentation the site may be lost forever. While using this technique of high-resolution image photography, a new discovery of a hitherto unknown wall illustration was revealed, that of a painting of an outline of a priest (fig. 25.2). This proved to be an effective demonstration of what may be discovered during a survey and the post-editing of high-resolution site images.

In order to carry out such a photographic recording program, the minimum equipment required would be a standard SLR (single lens reflex) camera such as a Canon 550D, a sturdy tripod, and post-editing software such as Photoshop (minimum CS5). The actual photographing of any object or site in general should be carried out with the 'RAW' option available with the camera, and it may be also advantageous to combine the RAW with the JPEG (.jpg) setting. Utilizing this combination would make it easier when selecting the images on the computer prior to post-editing. This is due to the fact that RAW files only show up as a file, not as an image, while JPEG images show the actual image. This

Fig. 25.1. Qubbat al-Hawa corridor wall illustration of individual priests, showing erosion and damage. Photograph by Howard Middleton-Jones.

Fig. 25.2. New discovery of illustration of a priest on a cornerstone, Qubbat al-Hawa. Photograph by Howard Middleton-Jones.

Fig. 25.3. Dayr al-Muharraq, icon showing two monastery abbots: Father Hegomen 'Abd al-Malak al-Asyuti (AD 1771–1802), right, and Father Hegomen Girgis al-Dwairi (AD 1808–13). Photograph by Fr. Maximos al-Muharraqi.

Fig. 25.4. Dayr al-Muharraq, icon of Queen St. Mary the Virgin. Photograph by Fr. Maximos al-Muharraqi.

way the viewer is able to quickly select the required image by opening the adjacent corresponding RAW file in the post-editing suite.

The advantage of shooting in RAW is that the intention of the process is to capture as closely as possible the characteristics of the image or scene. Because RAW file images contain unprocessed qualities they are much larger files than normal JPEG files. Often RAW files are 28–30 megabytes

Fig. 25.5. Close-up of a section of fig. 25.4 showing enhanced detail. Photograph by Fr. Maximos al-Muharraqi.

in size compared to the smaller 3–5 megabyte JPEG files. Therefore, a reasonably sized memory card must be used in the camera, such as a 16 gigabyte card, to hold the larger files. Thus, selecting the RAW files and opening in Photoshop, for example, and ultimately converting to .jpg will offer a detailed image with greater clarity, providing more options for future publications and use in advanced digital programs.

Fig. 25.6. Dayr al-Muharraq, marble icon of St. Mark the Apostle dated to the nineteenth century, by either Nicola Tawdary or Demitry Gurges, both of Jerusalem. Photograph by Fr. Maximos al-Muharraqi.

Utilizing the above method would be extremely advantageous when documenting icon images, for example, where the high-resolution images may be edited and enhanced to allow detailed study. This would be especially true when looking for faded inscriptions, or even where the artist or writer has overlaid a second text.

Method of Recording and Documentation

Prior to any recording or documentation, a 'standard' recording document, or 'caption' or 'style' sheet, should be developed (Middleton-Jones 2010). Utilizing such a template would ensure the uniformity of documentation for a diverse array of objects and sites, but also allow the option of customization to each individual unique site. An example of a blank 'caption sheet' and a completed one are provided below.

Caption Sheet

Inventory number (a reference unique to that site or object)
Date recorded (the date when the object was documented or photographed)
Category (architectural element/painting/icon/carving/textile)
Material (stone/wood/textile)
Period (date of manufacture or origin)
Measurements (in centimeters and millimeters)
State of preservation (complete/fragment/condition)
Location of object (current location of object)
Description (free textual description, history and original location when found, and description of individuals in the scene)
Artist or author (if known)
Images (photographs/drawings of object)
Bibliography (references)
Archaeological records (past or current excavations)
Restoration (description of any past or current conservation work)
Comments (additional information that may be of interest relating to the object)
Keywords (separated by commas, such as artist, icon, image, stone, sculpture, wood, period, etc.—any information that would assist in retrieving the documentation if maintained in electronic form)
Documenter signature (name of person who recorded the information)

Example of Completed Caption Sheet

Inventory number: MUR/005
Date recorded: 25 November 2013
Category: icon painting
Material: wood
Period: 19th century
Measurements: 98.5 cm x 77 cm
State of preservation: complete, in good condition

Location of object: Church of the Holy Virgin, mounted on the southern wall of the first section
Description: icon of Queen St. Mary the Virgin
Artist or author: Anastasy al-Romy
Images: al-Muharraq image library
Bibliography: Dayr al-Muharraq. 2012. *The Monastery of the Holy Virgin, al-Muharraq*. Asyut: Dayr al-Muharraq.
Archaeological records: N/A
Restoration: none recorded
Comments: The publication Dayr al-Muharraq 2012, produced by the brothers especially for the sixth International Symposium of Christianity and Monasticism at the Monastery of al-Muharraq, contains information on this and other icons in addition to other important architectural elements of the monastery.
Keywords: icon, painting, wood, Virgin, Mary, Church, southern, wall, Anastasy, al-Romy, Asyut, Jesus, al-Muharraq
Documenter signature: xxxxxxxxxx

Comments

As can be observed with the above example of completed documentation, it is important to enter the maximum amount of data possible, especially when formatting the information for wall illustrations and icons. Including such information would prove highly advantageous for any restoration program by providing the restorer with the necessary detailed information on the artwork to be restored. In this way, the optimum planning and method of restoration can be carried out with the minimum of alteration or damage to the original artwork.

An additional advantage of this type of standardized recording is that related objects, not only from the same site, but also from other sites, may be discovered by cross-matching keywords and descriptions. This in turn may assist in completing a jigsaw or mosaic of the overall and larger picture of the Coptic past.

Conclusion

The Coptic Church was and is the backbone of Christianity in Egypt, a central hub from which the growth of not only the spiritual, but also the cultural, Coptic identity permeates throughout Egypt and beyond. It is vital that the cultural heritage of the Coptic period be maintained and enhanced by documenting these unique and important artifacts belonging to the early Christian sites. This would not only maintain the communal and religious identification of the Coptic people, but enhance general awareness in the public domain of this unique heritage.

There are also many advantages in documenting records on a more local level, such as assisting in the daily administration of a site, maintaining a 'watching brief' (care and upkeep of the buildings and associated architectural elements), reporting any site erosion or damage, and recording visitor numbers to the site. More importantly, by maintaining a record, site security may be improved, so that the future of the site can be protected by implementing methods to safeguard it, especially in the more isolated locations.

This type of documentary record, in conjunction with a site register, would provide the resources and information for a cultural heritage program in education, conservation, and preservation. Ultimately, a correctly maintained record would be of the utmost importance for any future management plan of the site, and would assist applications for funding and aid for the many unique, but often overlooked, early Christian sites.

Acknowledgments

I would like to thank Fr. Athanasios al-Muharraqi and his brothers at the monastery of al-Muharraq for kindly providing and allowing the use of the icon images presented in this chapter.

26 The Monastery of the Holy Virgin Mary at al-Muharraq, Mount Qusqam: Reflections of Its Monks Today

Fr. Philoxenos al-Muharraqi and
a group of the monastery's monks

Introduction

The value of ancient monuments, sometimes, is not in the material they are made of, but rather in their living heritage and ancestral spirit.[1] How much more it is if these were blessed by the Lord himself, such as the deserted house in which He dwelled as a child and which later became the ancient church of Our Lady in the monastery today. The site gained worldwide fame, for generations, as a place of pilgrimage. Whenever an opportunity arose, there were renovations or a new expansion of the buildings in order to accommodate pilgrims and others who frequented the monastery.

Hence, today, there are no surviving remains of the ancient walls and buildings, except for those in the 'archaeological area' (fig. 26.1) and a remaining portion of the walls on the southern and eastern sides dating back to the nineteenth century.

Before giving a detailed description of the archaeological area in the monastery, it should be noted that in the first quarter of the twentieth century an engineering committee of archaeologists was formed to study the monastery. The committee delegated Dr. Ugo Monneret de Villard to prepare a comprehensive survey of the churches and buildings of the monastery.

Subsequently, he meticulously and skillfully completed the task of preparing architectural drawings with detailed cross-sections of vertical elevations, side views, and horizontal plans of the area (Dayr al-Muharraq 2012: 14, 24, 28–30; Monneret de Villard 1928). The book was published in Milan in 1928.

Description of the Ancient Monuments of the Monastery

The Holy Virgin Mary Ancient Church

This church is the oldest one in the monastery and is unique in its simple structure. It cannot be categorized under the common architectural styles found in any Coptic church. It is built out of sun-dried bricks with asymmetrical walls. There are no ornamental ancient Coptic patterns, engravings, dappling, variegations, or drawings on its walls.

It is known that ancient architecture, especially that of Coptic churches, has its own unique architectural features that can identify the time of construction by a building's style and interior division. Yet the simple structure of this church—unlike ancient churches in general—makes it difficult to draw any conclusions.

The simplicity and lack of unique features are a testimony to its antiquity and originality. Despite the repair and renovations performed in the church, it has always been the deliberate practice of the monks living there to keep the simplicity of the style intact. Although they could have built a cathedral

Fig. 26.1. Qusqam, the archaeological area. Photograph by Fr. Maximous al-Muharraqi.

honoring and befitting the status and prestige of the place, which the Holy Family blessed during their visit and stay, they chose not to. Despite the customary practice in some Coptic church building of adding more lavish architecture and art as a part of the renovation work, this was not the case with this ancient church throughout the various repairs and renovations up to the nineteenth century. The only exceptions were the construction of two rooms, one on each side of the sanctuary, at an unknown time period prior to the erection of three domes on top of the church in the sixteenth century. It has become a deep-rooted feeling in the hearts and minds of the monastery's fathers not to change the church. This can be attributed to a divine order that the church must be as it has always been, a witness through generations to the meekness of the only-begotten Son who took upon himself the form of a servant, and was made in the likeness of men to save his people.[2]

The following is a detailed description of the church.

The sanctuary

The eastern apse in a Coptic church is referred to as the bosom of God the Father, as it symbolizes God's longing for His Church, which is waiting for His Second Coming. It is a curved semicircular area in the eastern wall of the sanctuary. Two other rooms were built on either side of the sanctuary. They are also of simpler architecture, matching that of the ancient structure. The left (northern) room is used as a sacristy, a dressing room for the clergymen, and has no door entry to the nave of the church. The right (southern) room is for the deacons' service, where the Holy Communion set is kept. It is worth mentioning that during the restoration and renovation of the church in the year 2000, it was discovered that the eastern wall is a double wall with enough space in between for one person to stand. This space had an opening to the southern room of the sanctuary. The three sixteenth-century domes are atop the sanctuary and the two rooms.

The altar is the most important part of the sanctuary. It is cubical rather than rectangular. On its surface there is a marble top with a semicircular edge,[3] with an engraved Greek inscription. It reads: "O Lord, give rest to the blessed Colluthos," and is dated 15 Kiyahk AM 463 (11 December AD 746).[4] According to church tradition, four pillars symbolizing the four Evangelists must be erected around the altar. However, due to the narrow space of the sanctuary, only three were erected and fixed to the right and left walls. The fourth pillar was added later, during the 2000 restoration mentioned above.

Entries to the sanctuary are all low-rise, which makes the believer passing through them bow his head in humility and respect for the house of the Lord. According to the Coptic Church tradition, the altar of the Holy Virgin Mary Church is located "in the midst of the land of Egypt." This is understood as a fulfillment of the prophesy of Isaiah, "In that day there shall be an altar to the Lord in the midst of the land of Egypt, and a pillar at the border thereof to the Lord" (Isaiah 19:19).

The nave

Nothing remains of the ancient nave except for the southern wall, extending from the first to the second sections. The other walls—the southern wall of the third section, as well as the western and the northern walls—were all constructed in the nineteenth century. As is customary in Coptic churches, the nave is divided into three main sections. The first section is for the believers, the second for the penitents, and the third for the catechumens or those not yet baptized. Seven domes were also built over the nave, carried by squinches on top of four circular pillars, made of red and black bricks.

The narthex

This is built with two pillars in the middle with a wooden roof. At a later date the church of the Ethiopians was built on top of it. However, in the 1930s this church was removed because it was feared that it might affect the structure of the ancient church. In 2000, the following restoration and renovation work took place:

1. Two additional domes were built on top of the nave, for a total of nine domes. The old layer of gypsum on the walls was replaced with a new one.
2. During the restoration in the southern wall, two doors were found hidden under the old layer of gypsum, so they were reopened (Dayr al-Muharraq 2012: photographs nos. 2 and 3).
3. A door was reopened in the western wall of the external narthex of the church. This door existed in the nineteenth century.

Wood-carved iconostases

The iconostasis, forming a complete visual and physical barrier, is adorned with beautiful icons and carved wooden crosses facing the congregation. It represents an open book written in an easy and simple language, announcing to all generations God's love for humans. There are two iconostases in the church (fig. 26.2):

Fig. 26.2. Qusqam, two iconostases in the ancient Church of the Holy Virgin Mary. Photograph by Fr. Maximous al-Muharraqi.

1. The first iconostasis has a wooden plaque with a Coptic–Arabic phrase inlaid in silver lettering, reading: "Hail to the sanctuary of God, Hail to St. Mary Mother of God." It appears that the arch of this part of the door is made of wood older than the rest of the iconostasis. It has some anonymous carved inscriptions on its back. In the center of the arch is a metal ring to hang the thurible (censer) during the liturgy. Due to the sacredness of the sanctuary, no layman is allowed inside it. Hence, there is a small window on each side of the main door for the congregation to receive Holy Communion. Currently, communion is administered to the congregation in the nave of the church, in front of the main door. In the 1940s, the iconostasis was disassembled because of termite infestation and the damaged sections were removed. This restoration resulted in the reduction of the overall size of the iconostasis.

2. The second iconostasis was removed from the Ethiopian church and is placed adjacent to the first iconostasis. On the arch of its door it similarly has a wooden plaque inlaid with silver lettering, but with different Coptic–Arabic phrases, which date back to the nineteenth century. They read: "Glory to God in the highest, and on earth peace, good will toward

men. Hail to the sanctuary of God the Father. A sanctuary dedicated to the name of Peter and Paul the Apostles."

The church icons

In the Orthodox tradition, the icon is a highly stylized religious painting. The subject and placement of the icons is significant, as an uneducated person could learn the whole Bible just by looking at them. The icons are fixed to the iconostasis in order to attract the soul to long for eternal glory. In 1996, the monastery paid special attention to the preservation and cataloging of these icons, which date back to the eighteenth and nineteenth centuries (Dayr al-Muharraq 2012: 19–22).

Oil lamps and ostrich eggs

The oil lamps are placed in front of icons during the liturgy and lit with pure olive oil. Currently, the only remaining oil lamp in the church is that of the east wall within the sanctuary; it is always lit so that no strange (i.e., outside) fire is used in the church. This is symbolic of what the Lord said to Moses regarding oil lamps being constantly lit (see Exodus 27:20–21). The east lamp also symbolizes the star that appeared to the wise men from the east in the Levant. Ostrich eggs in the church symbolize the divine providence and resurrection of the Lord. They are usually hung in front of the iconostasis.

Two Other Ancient Churches

Historical documents of the monastery mention two other churches, but today they no longer exist.

St. John the Baptist Church

This church was dedicated to the Ethiopian monks. Its date of construction is unknown; the oldest evidence found so far of its existence dates back to the middle of the seventeenth century. The church was in close proximity to the ancient Holy Virgin Church, on its north side. It was demolished in the nineteenth century and replaced by the new narthex and its attached rooms. What remains today are only the stone altar and some icons.

St. Takla-Haymanot Church

Although the iconostasis bears the name of the Apostles Peter and Paul, the name 'St. Takla-Haymanot' was prevalent throughout the church. It was also dedicated to the Ethiopian monks and built on the roof of the ancient church narthex in the nineteenth century. It too was demolished in the 1930s due to the weakness of the ancient church building. The iconostasis of this church was placed inside the ancient church, as mentioned above.

The Ancient Keep

Keeps were built to protect the monks from fierce barbarian raids. One of the oldest and largest known keeps is that of the Monastery of St. Macarius in Wadi al-Natrun (al-Maskin 1984: 394–95; 591–620). The keep, in structure, is a fortified building with one entrance accessed by a wooden drawbridge. The shape of its openings (windows) in cross section is conical, a design that allows the viewer from inside to observe what is outside, while not giving the viewer from outside the same privilege. The keep needed to be designed and well-enough equipped to give the monks maximum protection for as long as a siege would last. It is also arranged to allow the monks to perform their ascetic practices as well as to sustain them physically during their stay.

The essential elements of a keep

The keep contained the following for use during a siege:

1. *A source of drinkable water*: As this keep had no well, there must have been a link between the well of the ancient Church of the Holy Virgin Mary and the lupine basin in a room on the ground floor. Another possibility is that there was an old well to the east of the keep connected to the lupine basin. When water was needed, the basin inlet was opened to let water flow.

2. *Sufficient amounts of food*: Only lupine could be stored during any siege, as all other food would soon rot. This would be sufficient for sustaining the monks regardless of how long the siege lasted.

3. *Cells or living rooms*.

4. *A place for worship*: In this keep there is one chapel, dedicated to the Archangel Michael, that he might intercede on the monks' behalf and protect them from evil.

5. *One or more small burial rooms*: In the event of a monk dying during the siege, he would be buried in a designated area that at al-Muharraq was usually located between the roof of the keep and the ceiling of the chapel.

6. *Emergency caches*: These were constructed in case the attackers succeeded in breaking through to kill the monks. The most important is

situated under the sanctuary. If a breach of the defenses took place during the liturgy, the priest and those who served with him, if possible, would escape there to hastily receive the Holy Communion before it fell into the hands of the attackers.

Key features of the al-Muharraq keep

1. *The dimensions of the keep*
   - Base area: 10.53 m × 10.10 m
   - Upper area: 9.60 m × 8.80 m
   - Height: 16.57 m

2. *The keep chapel*: This is dedicated to the Archangel Michael. It has one altar and its nave is divided into two small sections by two pillars and a wooden partition in between. It seems that the two pillars are probably from ancient times and possibly taken from a nearby pagan temple that existed during the earliest period of Christianity, as evidenced from the broken capital of one of them. Standing at the front of the nave is a wooden lectern from which the 'lectionary book'—the book of ritual readings—is read. It is believed to date as far back as the twelfth century, when the keep was renovated. The door of the church, as well as the other doors, is of the same design as those of the ancient Church of the Holy Virgin Mary. We have had no information to date to confirm whether the keep was ever utilized. Yet it has been renovated and restored at different times: in the twelfth, sixteenth, eighteenth, nineteenth, and twentieth centuries. In 2001 a complete exterior and interior renovation was carried out.

3. *The hemicycle sundial*: This consists of a fixed gnomon in the middle of the diameter of a semicircle, carved on the southern wall of the keep. The time is read from the shadow of the gnomon falling on the time scale.

The Holy Virgin Mary Church, also known as St. George Church

The church was established in the late eighteenth century with meager resources. In 1878 a new church called 'the Holy Virgin Mary' was built over the ruins of this church. It was finished in 1880. The northern altar was named after John the Baptist, the southern one after St. George, and the middle one after the new name of the church, the Holy Virgin Mary. A number of biblical verses are engraved on its iconostasis in a most beautiful Arabic calligraphy, along with other decorative ornamental elements (fig. 26.4).

Fig. 26.3. Qusqam, selected ornamental carvings on the outside walls of the keep. Photographs by Fr. Maximous al-Muharraqi.

Fig. 26.4. Qusqam, marble iconostasis of St. George Church. Photograph by Fr. Maximous al-Muharraqi.

The church icons

a. Icons mounted on the marble iconostasis (Dayr al-Muharraq 2012: 38), in the Byzantine style, painted by two renowned iconographers from Jerusalem in the nineteenth century: Nicola Tawdory of Jerusalem and Demitry Girges of Jerusalem
b. Icons mounted on the walls and Holy Icon (Dayr al-Muharraq 2012: 39, 40), dating back to the nineteenth century.

The nave

The nave is designed following the medieval pattern, in which women had a private place on the second floor over the church's nave. The interior of the church was renovated in 1990. After the renovations, it was consecrated on the commemoration of our Father Hegomen Mikhail al-Buhairy's repose. His relics were moved to a handmade wood-carved reliquary and placed in a magnificent Epitaphios canopy in the nave during a ceremony attended by His Grace Bishop Sawiros, abbot of the monastery, along with thirteen other Coptic bishops on 16 Amshir AM 1707 (23 February 1991).

Fig. 26.5. Anba Abram, bishop of the Fayoum and Giza (left); St. Hegomen Mikhail al-Buhairi al-Muharraqi (right). Photograph by Fr. Maximous al-Muharraqi.

This holy father pursued the monastic life during the tenure of Abbot Fr. Boules al-Delgawy (AD 1866–70), who later became known as Anba Abram, bishop of the Fayoum and Giza, and was renowned for his holiness.[5] St. Mikhail al-Buhairi was also famous for his virtues and his holiness; he reposed on 23 February 1923. The Holy Synod proclaimed him a saint in 1963 along with his spiritual father, Anba Abram (fig. 26.5).

The southeast, outside the nave

The baptistery is located here. Also, underneath, there is a sepulcher for the abbots of the monastery. The last monks to be honored by being buried there were Fr. Benjamin al-Muharraqi and Fr. Aghabius al-Muharraqi, who were martyred at the monastery's main gate on 11 March 1994.

The outside of the church's eastern wall

Here is found a wall painting of two martyrs: St. George on the southern side and St. Mercurius Abu Sayfayn on the northern side.

More Recent and Modern Buildings

The monastery buildings consist of many different architectural styles, depending on the time of their building and the needs they serve. It is worth mentioning that all recent renovations of and restorations to the monastery churches (previously mentioned), as well as all new construction dating from 1977 to the present time, were accomplished under the guidance and blessings of His Grace Bishop Sawiros, bishop and abbot of the monastery.

The New Church of the Holy Virgin Mary (built 1964)

This church has three altars. The middle or main one is dedicated to the Holy Virgin Mary; the southern altar was originally named after St. George and later rededicated to St. Abram, bishop of the Fayoum and Giza; and the northern altar is named after St. Takla-Haymanot the Ethiopian. All the icons in the church were painted by the iconographer Yacoub Fanous.

Abbot's Residence

This is the official place of residence of the abbot. It also functions as a residence for visiting senior dignitaries of the Church, such as patriarchs, bishops, and so on. Its architecture is Italian in style. It was built in 1910, during the tenure of His Grace Bishop Pachomius I, abbot of the monastery from 1896 to 1928.

Educational Ministry

Education in monasteries has great importance for students and scholars as it provides the means to develop their intellect spiritually and scientifically, while also being immersed in the monastic life. The following are institutions of education at the monastery:

The theological seminary

The purpose of this seminary is to prepare qualified clergymen for the Church. The seminary offers a four-year bachelor's degree program in theology.

St. Didymus Institute for Cantors

The purpose of this institute is to train cantors and chanters who perform an essential role in churches. The institute offers a five-year study program to enable students to learn other curricula besides chants, melodies, and rites of the church.

Visitors' and Pilgrims' Buildings

Throughout the year, the monastery celebrates all Coptic Orthodox Church feasts, especially those of the Holy Virgin Mary. Multitudes of visitors and pilgrims attend these occasions in the monastery, to receive blessings and, for some, to baptize their infants. Accordingly, the monastery is equipped with many facilities, such as several guest accommodations and a celebration yard.

Walls and Gates

The monastery walls and gates have the following features (Dayr al-Muharraq 2012: 46, 47):

1. Sun-dried brick walls from the nineteenth century.
2. Stone walls dating back to the first half of the twentieth century, designed by the professional committee that commissioned the survey (as mentioned in the introduction). This portion of the wall is modeled on the walls of Jerusalem and has two gates.
3. A section of red-brick walls with reinforced concrete was built in 1978 to replace the sun-dried brick wall. It has two gates. The main gate was renovated during 2003–2004 to make it architecturally worthy of the monastery's historical status.

A Selection of Antiquities from the Monastery's Collection

Some of the notable antiquities found in the monastery are as follows (fig. 26.6):

1. The holy wooden plate of the Ethiopian church.
2. Wooden, silver-plated Gospel casket decorated with crosses, foliage ornaments, and Arabic and Coptic inscriptions (twelfth/thirteenth century).
3. Decorated silver cover of an oil lamp.
4. Pottery vessel.
5. Granite font.
6. Column capitals, limestone.
7. Wooden lectern (twelfth century).
8. Stone baptistery font.
9. Stone altar of the Ethiopian church.

Fig. 26.6. Qusqam, selected collection of antiquities. Photographs by Fr. Maximous al-Muharraqi.

Conclusion

This chapter presents a brief survey of the architecture and the contents of al-Muharraq monastery, presented as reflections of the monk-fathers of the monastery. It is considered one of the holiest places in Egypt: the site hosted the Holy Family during their flight to Egypt, and Church tradition tells us that its ancient church was dedicated by the Lord and His Apostles. This truly represents an altar in the middle of Egypt, as Isaiah the prophet wrote hundreds of years before the advent of Christ.

Notes

1 This chapter is based on Dayr al-Muharraq 2012, published on the occasion of the convening of the sixth International Symposium of Christianity and Monasticism in Middle Egypt, at the Monastery of al-Muharraq, Egypt.

2 This is based on the Holy Virgin Mary's instruction to Pope Theophilus of Alexandria (twenty-third Pope of Alexandria, AD 385–412), as recorded on page 88 of Manuscript 9/14 in the monastery library.

3 This semicircle of marble is a peculiar shape found in ancient Coptic altars in Egypt. The idea of such a shape comes from an old Coptic motif that first appeared in the Last Supper icons, where the table is semicircular.

4 See "History and Heritage" in Dayr al-Muharraq 2012, and figure 8.6 in this volume.

5 He reposed in 1914.

27 An Overview of Rock-cut Coptic Sites in Asyut

Ashraf Nageh and Mary Kupelian

Introduction

This research is an attempt to provide an overview of some of the most remarkable rock-cut monasteries in Asyut Governorate. The Asyut plateau was a suitable area for monastic settlement as it is bordered on the east and the west with mountains flanking the agricultural land. Only four sites were selected for this study. They are, from north to south: Dayr al-Mu'allaq or Dayr Mar Mina al-Agaybi (literally, the 'Hanging Monastery'), Dayr Durunka, the churches of Dayr Rifa, and Dayr al-Ganadla. Dayr Mar Mina is located on the eastern side of the Nile, while the other three sites, namely Durunka, Rifa, and al-Ganadla, are located on the western side. The caves and rock cuts in these mountains provided hermits and monks with ready-prepared isolated shelters just adequate to their needs.

The objective of this short overview is to shed light on the importance of this type of monastery and church, examples of which are scattered along the Nile Valley in Asyut. They provide important evidence and comprise elements that are of equal significance to other monasteries throughout Egypt.

The ancient Egyptian quarrymen were clever in extracting blocks of stones from different kinds of rocks that were accessible in Egypt. They used the limestone hills deposited from Cairo to Esna along the Nile Valley to obtain limestone blocks for construction and ornamental purposes such

Fig. 27.1. Unquarried pillar to support the rock-cut church in Dayr al-Ganadla. Courtesy of St. Mark Foundation, 2011.

as temples, tombs, sarcophagi, and statues (Harrell and Storemyr 2009: 8). These hills also functioned as sites for rock-cut tombs.

Mostly, the quarrying started in the form of open pits and trenches, and then continued into the mountains to produce caves or large galleries. To support these galleries, rock pillars were left to carry the roofs (fig. 27.1). The quarrying of limestone was achieved by using copper (and later bronze) chisels and picks. These tools did not change from the Dynastic Period until the Late Period. This basic process of softstone (limestone and sandstone) quarrying remained unchanged through the ancient Egyptian and Roman periods, but the picks and chisels were later made of iron. Hammered iron wedges were also used occasionally to split limestone and sandstone (Harrell and Storemyr 2009: 29).

Limestone quarrying was active all along the Nile Valley: eighty-nine ancient quarry sites are known (Harrell 2012: 6). It is worth mentioning that some thirty-six ancient quarry sites are known on the east and west sides of the Asyut area alone. Later on, many of the limestone galleries, especially in Minya and Asyut, were transformed into Coptic Christian hermitages and monasteries, and some of them are still functioning today (Harrell and Storemyr 2009: 29).

Locations of Reference Sites in Asyut

Asyut Governorate is located almost in the middle of Egypt (about 375 kilometers south of Cairo) between the coordinates 27°11′00″N / 31°10′ 00″E and 27.18333°N / 31.16667°E. It stretches for about 120 kilometers from north to south along the Nile River and is bordered on the east by Asyut Eastern Mountain, on the west by Asyut Western Mountain, on the north by Minya Governorate, and on the south by Sohag Governorate. Nowadays it is considered the most important city of Upper Egypt.

On the Eastern Mountain, Dayr Mar Mina is located near al-Ma'abda (27°21′27.49″N / 31° 0′43.08″E). It belongs to the Diocese of Abnub and al-Fath. It is about 35 kilometers northeast of Asyut city and located at an elevation of 170 meters above ground level. It was established in ancient Egyptian quarries, utilizing a big cave in the mountain.

On the Western Mountain, the other three referenced sites are located from north to south: Dayr Durunka, Dayr Rifa, and Dayr al-Ganadla, respectively.

Dayr Durunka belongs to the Diocese of Asyut. It is situated on Durunka Mountain, above the village of Durunka (27°6′44″N / 31°10′ 5″E). It is about eleven kilometers southwest of Asyut and located at an elevation of 100 meters above sea level. It is where the Holy Family visited during their flight into Egypt, according to Coptic tradition.

The churches at Rifa also belong to the Diocese of Asyut and are located about four kilometers south of Dayr Durunka. They are situated on the cliffs of Durunka Mountain. Rifa churches lie at 27° 4′29.16″N / 31°11′5.72″E and at an elevation of 66 meters above sea level. The cliff churches of Dayr Rifa are not regarded as a monastery, but they reuse ancient Egyptian tombs.

Dayr al-Ganadla belongs to the Diocese of Abu Tig. Its coordinates are 26°56′38″ N / 31°17′49″ E. It is located at an elevation of 54 meters above sea level. It was established in ancient Egyptian quarries that lie to the west of the village of al-Ganadla, about 25 kilometers southwest of Asyut and about 30 kilometers south of Durunka.

General Geological Setting

Along the Nile Valley, nearly all the limestone came from Tertiary formations (mainly Eocene). Generally, the ancient quarries located in the hills and cliffs border the Nile Valley between Cairo in the north and Esna in the south (Harrell and Storemyr 2009: 15).

The geological setting of the Asyut area represents a part of the Nile Valley zone of Egypt. The carbonate succession in this area is subdivided mainly into the Minya and Durunka formations (Klitzsch, List, and Pöhlmann 1987) (fig. 27.2).

Dayr Mar Mina is located at Gebel Abu Foda. The rocks of Gebel Abu Foda belong to the Minya formation. This formation was introduced by Said (1961). It also underlies the Salamut formation (Bishay 1961) and overlies the Thebes formation. This formation was thought to be Middle Eocene (Said 1960), but Boukhary and Abdelmalik (1983) put this formation within the late Early Eocene time span. The thickness of the Minya formation ranges from 35 meters to over 80 meters (Issawi, el Hinnawi, and Mazhar 1999). It is formed of hard bedded limestones and ranges in color from white to gray (Klemm and Klemm 2001: 638).

Microscopically, the rocks of the Minya formation are fine- to medium-grained wackestone and packstone to less often grainstone, with mainly echinoids and foraminifera (especially alveolinids and nummulitids) and lesser amounts of other invertebrates and non-skeletal peloids. It is essentially non-silty/sandy, non-clayey, and non-dolomitic, but slightly to moderately siliceous with silt-sized quartz grains (Harrell 2012: 14).

Dayr Durunka, Dayr Rifa, and Dayr al-Ganadla are located in Gebel Durunka, which belongs to the Durunka formation. This formation was first described by El-Naggar (1970). It overlies the Minya formation. The thickness of the Durunka formation ranges from 35.5 meters to over 133 meters. It is composed of Lower Eocene limestone: hard, crystalline, massive to thin laminated limestones (Khalifa et al. 2004: 236). Its color ranges through grayish white, yellowish white, white, and snow-white. Microscopically, it is represented by grained mudstone and grainstone to mainly wackestone and packstone, with primarily foraminifera, echinoids, and non-skeletal peloids, and lesser amounts of other invertebrates, mostly bivalves, gastropods, and calcareous algae. It is essentially non-silty/sandy and non-dolomitic, but occasionally clayey (marly) and slightly to moderately siliceous with few detretal grains (Harrell 2012: 15).

Dedication of the Monasteries

The four sites are dedicated to two of the most popular saints in Egypt. Durunka, Rifa (one church), and al-Ganadla are dedicated to the Virgin Mary and located on the western side of the Nile. The annual festival of the Holy Virgin is celebrated in August (7 to 22 August).

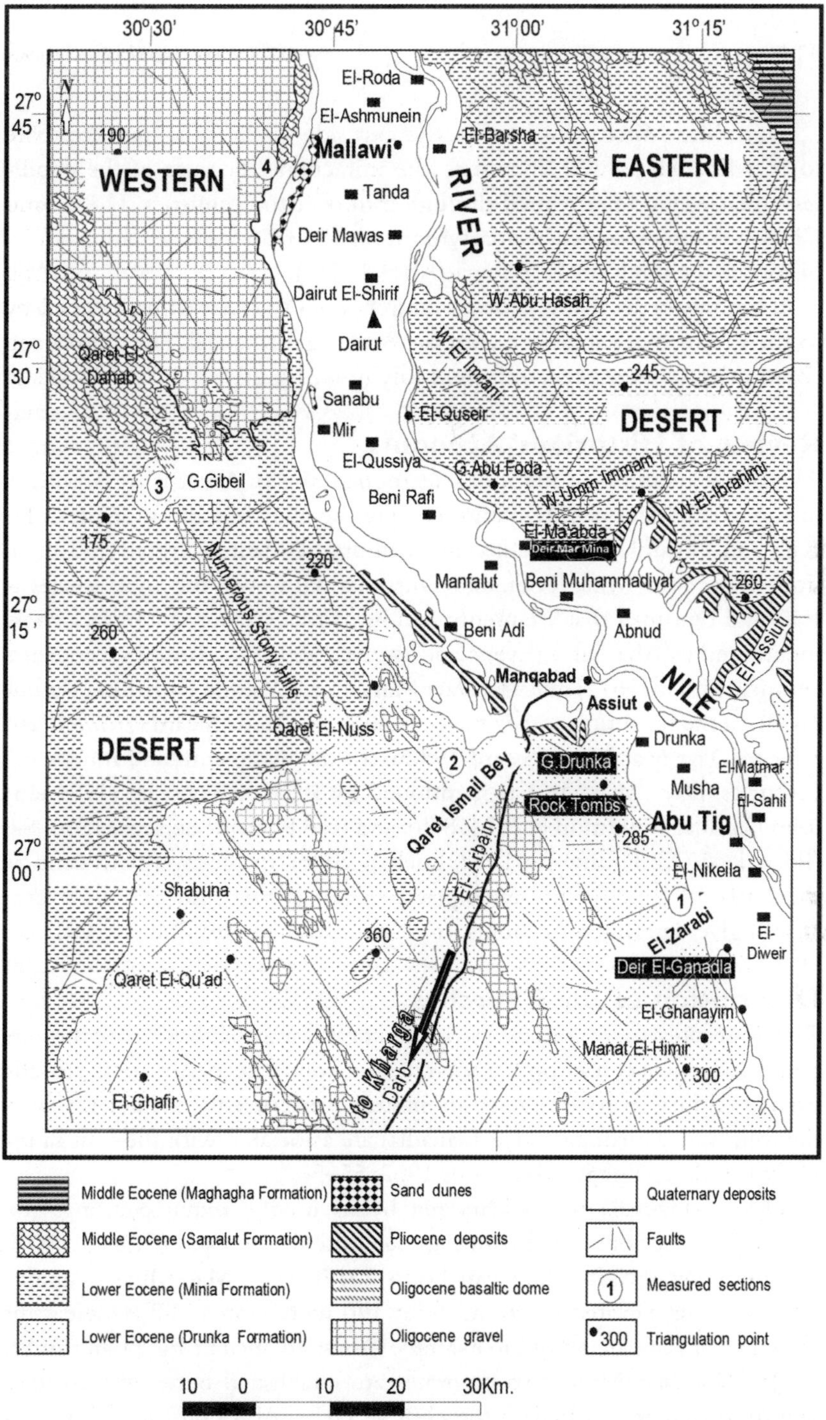

Fig. 27.2. Geological map of the studied monasteries in Asyut (Khalifa et al. 2004).

Dayr Mar Mina is located on the east side of the Nile and dedicated to St. Mina. He is well known as 'the miraculous' because of the countless miracles God performed through him over the centuries. The Coptic Church commemorates his martyrdom on 15 Hatur and the dedication of his original church on 15 Ba'una (Atiya 1991b).

It is noteworthy that one of the churches of Dayr Mar Mina is dedicated to the Virgin Mary together with the Archangel Michael. The annual celebration at the monastery is from 8 July to 8 August.

Review of Historians' Accounts

The oldest mention of the rock-cut monasteries of Asyut is by Abu Salih in the twelfth century. He mentions only the churches and monasteries at Rifa and Durunka. In the fifteenth century, al-Maqrizi visited and mentions Dayr Mar Mina, Rifa, and Durunka. However, the monasteries at Rifa and Durunka that are mentioned by al-Maqrizi are not, in fact, those mentioned by Abu Salih (Evetts and Butler 1969: 214). In the seventeenth century, Vansleb (1672) refers to Dayr Mar Mina, Rifa, and Durunka (Vansleb 1678). In the meantime, other travelers, such as Claude Sicard (1677–1726), refer to Dayr Mar Mina (Sicard 1982b). In the eighteenth and nineteenth centuries, Dayr Mar Mina is mentioned by Richard Pococke (1704–65), John Gardner Wilkinson (1797–1875), and Karl Richard Lepsius (1810–84) (Pococke 1743; Thompson 1992; Loeben 2008). In the twentieth century, the Duke of Saxony, the Jesuit priest Jullien (1901), and Somers Clarke (1930) give descriptive accounts of the four studied sites (Jullien 1901).

Description of the Churches

The four sites each contain two churches. Some of these churches are completely quarry or tomb rock-cut and some are partly rock-cut and partly masonry structures. Each monastery has a specific character. Two of the four sites (Durunka and al-Ganadla) are associated with the visit of the Holy Family to Egypt (Meinardus 1963: 55–56).

Dayr al-Ganadla is characterized by its unique mural paintings (for detailed descriptions of the paintings, see Buschhausen and Khorshid 1998; van Loon 2004; Gabra and van Loon 2012). Dayr Mar Mina is unique because of its elevated location, about 170 meters on a cliff, whereas the churches of Rifa are a unique example of reused ancient Egyptian tombs.

At Dayr Mar Mina, two churches are established between two massive rocks and are located in the cliffs of Gebel Abu Foda, just above the village of al-Ma'abda (Cruz-Uribe 2004). The first church is situated in a big quarry, rock-cut in the mountain. Inside the church there is a carved altar dedicated to Mar Mina. The second church is named after the Virgin Mary and the Archangel Michael. This church is also a rock-cut quarry in the mountain. To the north of the second church there is an ancient keep situated in rocks lower down. This keep is partly built of brick and partly rock-hewn, and is divided into three floors. The first floor is mainly occupied by cells for the monks. The second floor consists of three rooms used as a sacrificial hall in honor of the saint. The third floor leads to the top of the keep, where the two churches of the monastery are located. Also, there are two modern buildings constructed beside the ancient keep.

Dayr Durunka is also called the Monastery of the Virgin. The site was excavated by A. Kamal in 1916 and produced some finds that date back to the ancient Egyptian and the Coptic periods. The monastery consists of two separate rock-cut quarries. The old church is named after the Virgin Mary (fig. 27.3 C). The west end of the church is a rock-cut quarry, while the eastern part is constructed upon an artificial platform.

The second church is dedicated to the Archangel Michael (fig. 27.3 B). The plan of this church is traditional: the western division is for women, then comes the division for men, followed by the *khurus,* and at the end there is the *haykal.* The northern altar is dedicated to Anba Bishoi and the central one to the archangel. The six eastern areas of the church are covered with brick domes. The rest of the church, westward, is roofed with beams on which are laid reeds covered above with flat mud bricks (Clarke 1912: 175). The rock-cut churches are adjacent to modern buildings that were built on the slope of the mountain to serve as accommodation for pilgrims. Although this monastery has no ornamental elements, it is one of the largest and most popular pilgrimage destinations for Christians in Egypt.

Dayr Rifa is a complex of large reused rock-cut ancient Egyptian tombs. This site was excavated by W. Petrie in 1907, when a large number of Coptic, Greek, and Arabic manuscripts were found. The site seems to have been inhabited until the eighth century. Dayr Rifa comprises two churches situated in two ancient tombs. They are separated from each other by approximately one hundred meters. The first church is dedicated to St. Theodore and the second to the Virgin Mary. The Church of St. Theodore was built inside a tomb with two columns at the entrance and has a small mud-brick structure roofed with a little dome. The church has one *haykal* and included a smaller shrine of St. Theodore (Meinardus 2002: 227). This

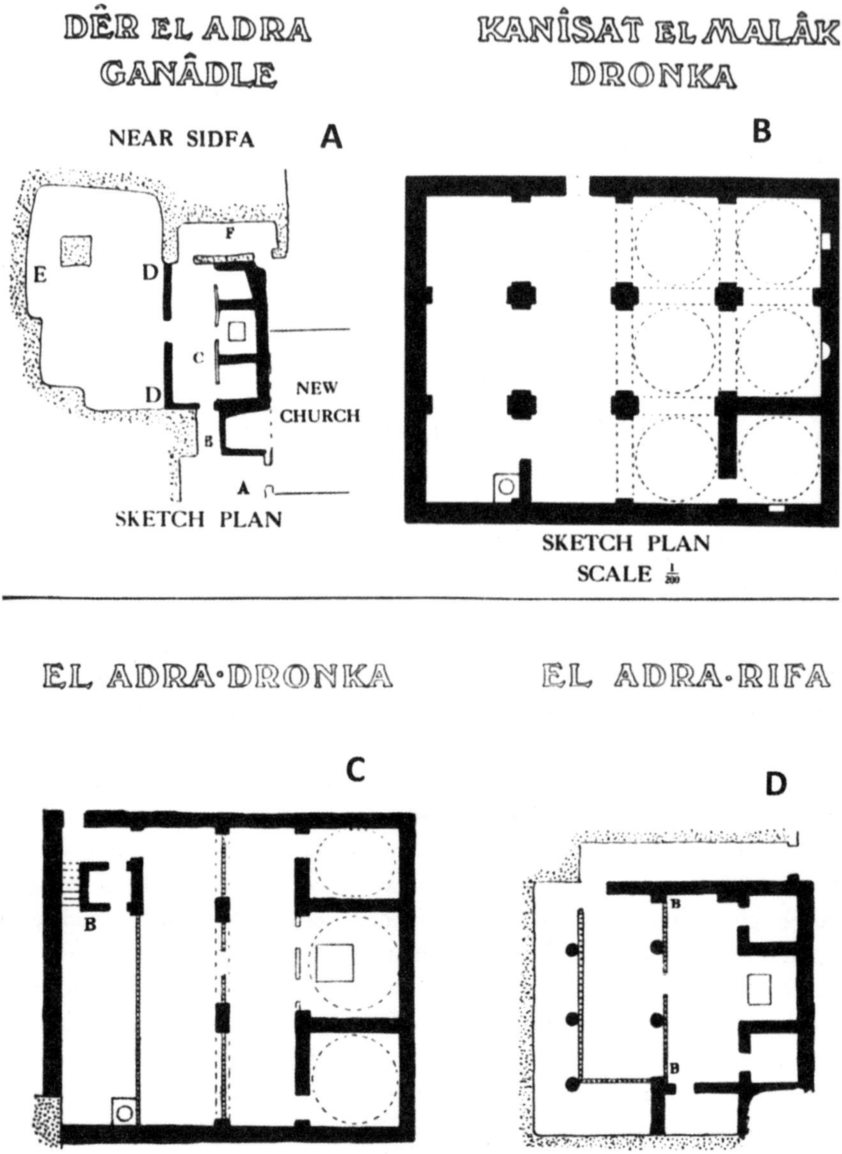

Fig. 27.3. Plans of rock-cut churches in Asyut (Clarke 1912).
A: The rock-cut church of the Virgin Mary in Dayr al-Ganadla.
B: The rock-cut church of the Archangel Michael in Dayr Durunka.
C: The rock-cut church of the Virgin Mary in Dayr Durunka.
D: The rock-cut church of the Virgin Mary in Dayr Rifa.

church is divided into sections: the women's section, the men's section, the *khurus*, and the *haykal*. In addition, there are two chambers sited on the north and the south of the *haykal* (fig. 27.3 D).

The second church, of the Holy Virgin, is sited inside a rock-cut tomb located to the left of the previous one. This church is divided into sections, such as the *khurus*, the men's section, and the women's section, by lattice screens. The church is lit by a hole in the roof just in front of the *haykal*. It includes a wooden inlaid screen before the *haykal*, while inside the *haykal* there is an altar dedicated to the Virgin Mary. The church is decorated with a number of icons.

Dayr al-Ganadla is also called the Monastery of the Virgin. It is composed of two churches built into old quarries. The older one is dedicated to the Virgin Mary and contains an altar dedicated to Abu Maqrufa. The monastery itself is sheltered by walls on three sides, while its western wall is formed by the cliff.

The Church of the Holy Virgin is built in an ancient quarry (fig. 27.3 A). Several wall paintings are found on the walls of the cave. All the architectural elements of the niches, walls, and ceilings in the church were painted, probably in the sixth century. These early murals were plastered over in the eleventh or twelfth century and repainted with a series of saints and angels. Also, on the north wall, part of the scene of the Communion of the Apostles is still preserved.

There are some comparative remarks to be made about the paintings and the architectural elements of this church. First of all, the gable-shaped niches cut into the walls are similar to the niches in the monasteries near Sohag, namely the Red and the White Monasteries. Second, the interiors of the niches are decorated with crosses, inscriptions, and ornamental borders consisting of branches and leaves that are similar to the patterns represented in the chapels at Bawit. Third, the sculpture executed on the northern and eastern walls of the church is similar to the friezes found in the monastery of Apa Jeremias in Saqqara. Fourth, the acanthus leaves and the crosses in this church bear a resemblance to those in Dayr Abu Hinnis in Minya (Gabra, van Loon, and Sonbol 2012). Another interesting point of comparison is the presence of the Armenian salvation sign, which is visible on the wall of this church and also existed in the scene of Christ in Majesty in the White Monastery.

The altar screen is built of masonry and reused pieces of sculpture, decorative borders, and stelae, probably dating from the original church building. The eastern wall with the sanctuary is made of brickwork and probably dates back to the nineteenth century.

The second church, dating back to the 1860s, is dedicated to the Apostles and is located to the east of the old church. It has three domes and three *haykals*, dedicated to St. Macrobius (north), Ss. Peter and Paul (center), and St. George (south) (St. Mark's Foundation 2011).

Dating

The rock-cut monasteries in this study were all ancient Egyptian quarries, but the churches of the Dayr Rifa cliff were ancient Egyptian tombs. The two quarries of Durunka and al-Ganadla were used from the Old Kingdom through to the Late Period, but the quarry site of Dayr Mar Mina is of unknown date (Harrell and Storemyr 2009). The Middle Kingdom tombs of Dayr Rifa are typical of private tombs of that period, which were cut high in the cliff (Dodson 1991: 20). The style of their contents largely belongs to the Twelfth Dynasty and earlier (Petrie 1907).

The dating of the rock-cut monasteries around Asyut can be problematic and may need further research. However, hermits in the Asyut area began to settle in caves and ancient Egyptian rock-cut galleries and tombs around the fourth and fifth centuries, when monks used to live in a variety of places, without any uniform manner of settlement. For example, some solitary monks lived in caves, like St. Yuhanna al-Asyuti, while others lived in monastic communities. All either settled at the edge of the agricultural land or lived deep in the desert. This could be the beginning of monastic communities at that time. Dayr Durunka benefited from its renown as one of the stations that the Holy Family visited during its flight into Egypt. Traditionally, it is said to date from the first century (Coquin and Martin 1991b: 799).

The site of al-Ma'abda village, with Dayr Mar Mina in the cliffs above, was occupied from the Twenty-sixth Dynasty through the seventh century AD. As a result of excavation on the western edge of the town, many houses and a small temple were discovered (Cruz-Uribe 2004: 8).

Dayr al-Ganadla is decorated with two superimposed layers of wall paintings, the older probably dating from the sixth century and the upper layer from the twelfth to thirteenth century. This evidence shows that the monastery was established about the fifth to sixth century and existed during the twelfth to thirteenth centuries.

Conclusions

The monasteries in this study were founded on the basis of there being ready-excavated 'rooms' created by ancient Egyptian quarries in the limestone mountains. The Eastern Mountain of Asyut belongs to the Minya formation and the Western Mountain to the Durunka formation.

The monasteries located on the western side are dedicated to the Virgin Mary. Two of the monasteries studied are associated with the Flight into Egypt. The elevation of Dayr Mar Mina is a remarkable 170 meters in the cliff above ground level. Dayr al-Ganadla is unique with its rare wall paintings that were applied onto the rock-cut surface. Unfortunately, these paintings were unprofessionally restored. The churches of Dayr Rifa are situated in reused ancient Middle Kingdom tombs. Although the dating of the monasteries is problematic, most probably all can be dated to the fifth to sixth century.

Finally, this chapter demonstrates the importance and the need for more sustained archaeological work in these rock-cut churches and monasteries, which are distinguished by their unique architecture. Modern methods of excavation, documentation, conservation, and restoration have been utilized at many Coptic sites, but the only rock-cut church to have benefited from this is Dayr Abu Hinnis. The further application of these methods to these sites will help to protect this important heritage from being lost.

28 Architectural Typology of Historic Coptic Churches from Oxyrhynchos to Dayr al-Ganadla

Sami Sabri Shaker

THE AIM OF THIS STUDY is to correct the common notion that the architectural design of the typical Coptic Orthodox church either has a cruciform plan or is in the form of Noah's Ark, which reflects a lack of awareness and lack of study of the rich and diverse Coptic architectural heritage throughout the ages. It will be concerned primarily with the categorization of the historic churches of Middle Egypt, in the region from Oxyrhynchos to Dayr al-Ganadla. This categorization will be based on the nave's formation and the roofing system, excluding cave and rock-cut churches. Basic architectural elements and one or more distinctive examples of each type will be illustrated.

With respect to the design of the nave and its roofing system, the architectural typology of historic Coptic churches in Middle Egypt can be summed up by seven types, as follows:

1. Churches with domed nave
2. Churches with nave roofed with a combination of domes and vaults
3. Churches with square nave
4. Transverse churches
5. Basilican-plan churches
6. Basilican-plan churches with triconch sanctuary
7. Basilican-plan churches with transepts (cruciform plan)

Churches with Domed Nave

Nave covered with a single dome surrounded by U-shaped flat-roof aisles

1. A single-dome nave surrounded by three aisles. This type could also be described as being made up of two *khuruses* (choirs), a front *khurus* and a back one. Examples include Mar Qulta (St. Colluthos) Church at Rifa (fig. 28.1) and al-Amir Tadros (St. Theodore) Church at Dayr Bisra (fig. 28.2).

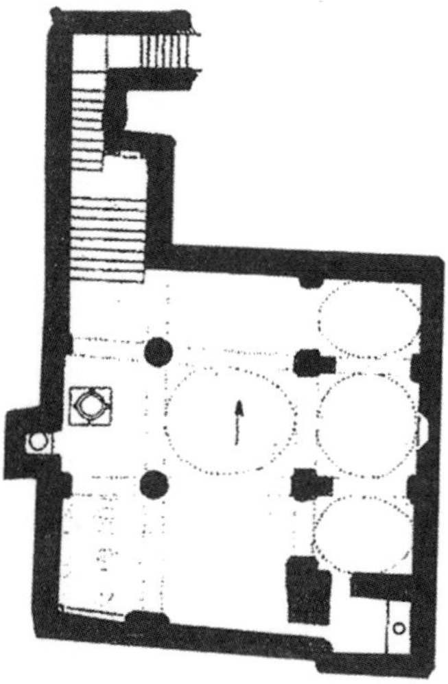

Fig. 28.1. Mar Qulta (St. Colluthos) Church at Rifa (al-Suriany and Habib 2002: 172).

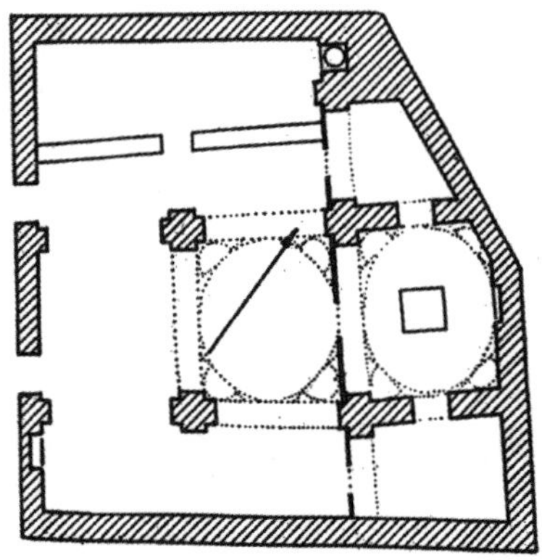

Fig. 28.2. Al-Amir Tadros (St. Theodore) Church at Dayr Bisra (al-Suriany and Habib 1990: 98).

2. Nave consisting of a large central dome on brackets on a square space, bounded by a double-height *khurus* of the same width. The dome and *khurus* are surrounded by three flat-roofed aisles: the northern, the southern, and the western. The latter is also known as the inner narthex or the return aisle. Above the three aisles there is a U-shaped mezzanine floor (gallery) overlooking the nave. Next to the sanctuary there is the cave where the Holy Family stayed during their flight into Egypt. The dark hatched areas on the ground floor plan are rock-cut, while the rest of the walls are composed of masonry constructed during the 1938 renovation. The baptismal font is cut into a southern rock column of the nave (fig. 28.3).

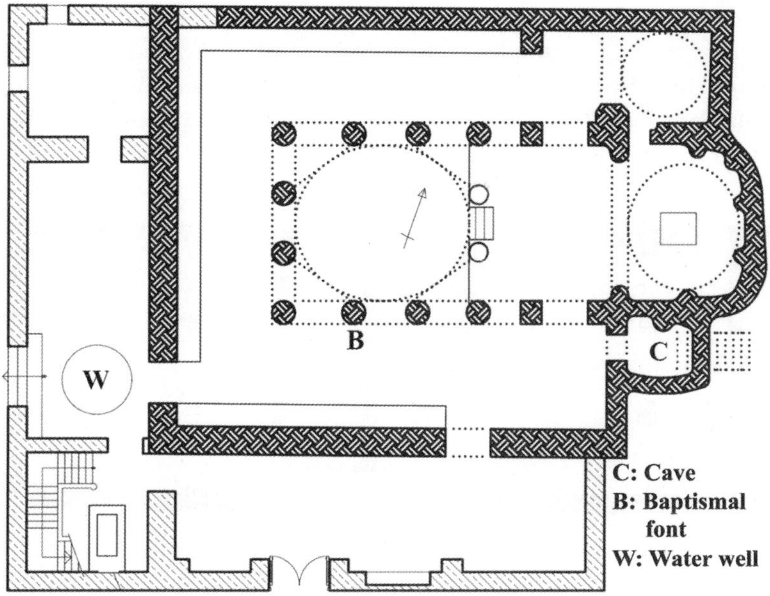

Fig. 28.3. The church of Dayr al-'Adra in Gebel al-Teir, Samalut. Redrawn by the author from Suriani and Habib 1990: 129.

Nave covered with six domes

1. A nave covered with six domes forming two *khurus*es, where the front *khurus* is slightly larger. The sanctuary area is also covered with three domes; this design is known as the 'nine-dome church.' In general, the church's highest dome is the one facing the main sanctuary. The church of Dayr al-Ganadla at Abu Tig is a good example (fig. 28.4).

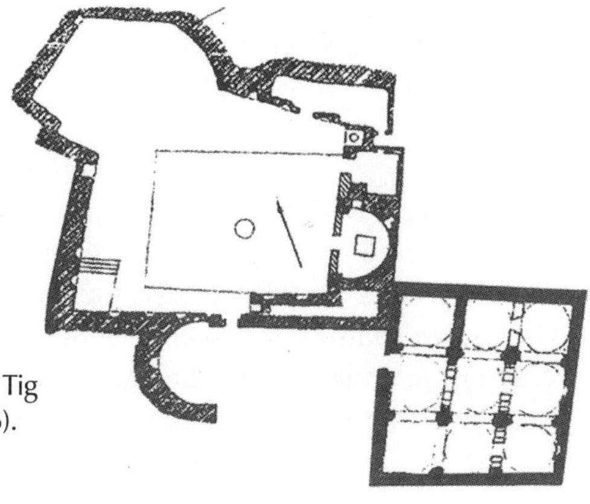

Fig. 28.4. Dayr al-Ganadla, Abu Tig (al-Suriani and Habib 2002: 176).

2. A nave covered with six domes forming two *khuruses*, in addition to an inner narthex. Examples include Dayr al-Meshreki at Ezbet Doss, Dayrut (fig. 28.5); St. Mary Church at Bani Adi, Manfalut (fig. 28.6); al-Malak at Bani Magd, Manfalut (fig. 28.7); and Dayr Mar Mina near Sanabu (fig. 28.8).

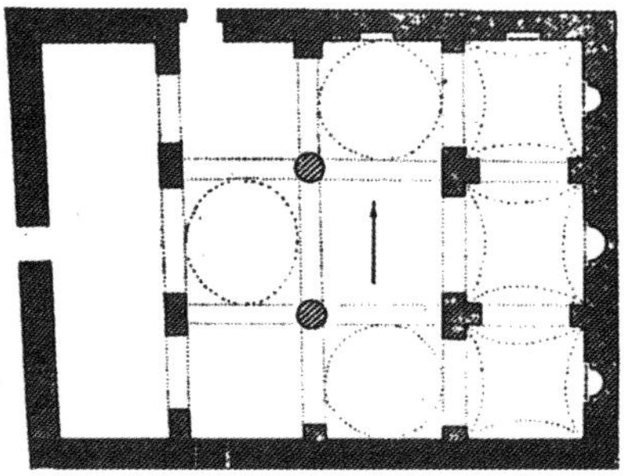

Fig. 28.5. Dayr al-Meshreki at Ezbet Doss, Dayrut. Redrawn by author from al-Suriani and Habib 1990: 110.

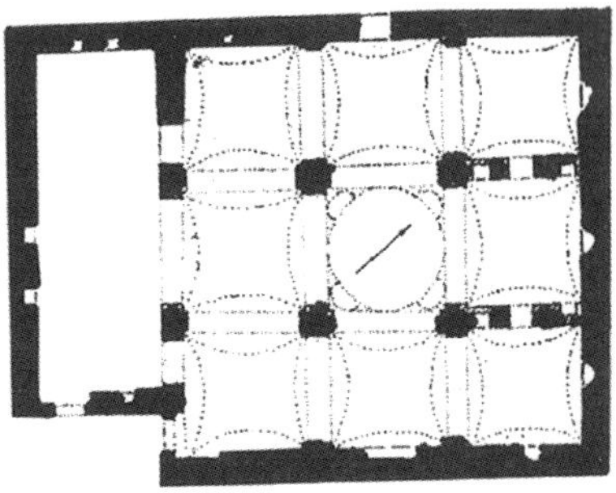

Fig. 28.6. St. Mary Church at Bani Adi, Manfalut (al-Suriani and Habib 2002: 164).

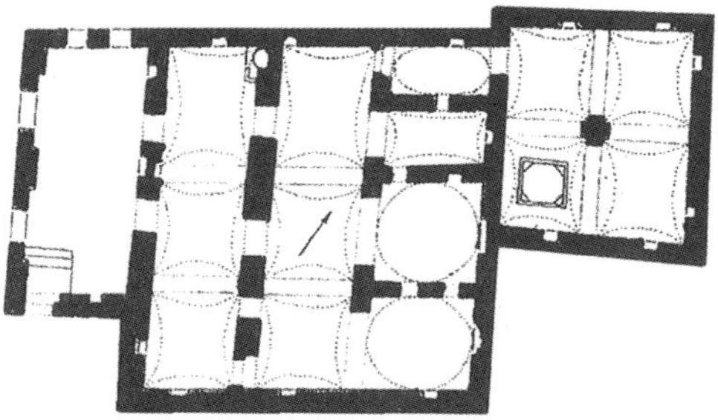

Fig. 28.7. Al-Malak (the Angel) Church, Bani Magd, Manfalut (al-Suriani and Habib 2002: 162).

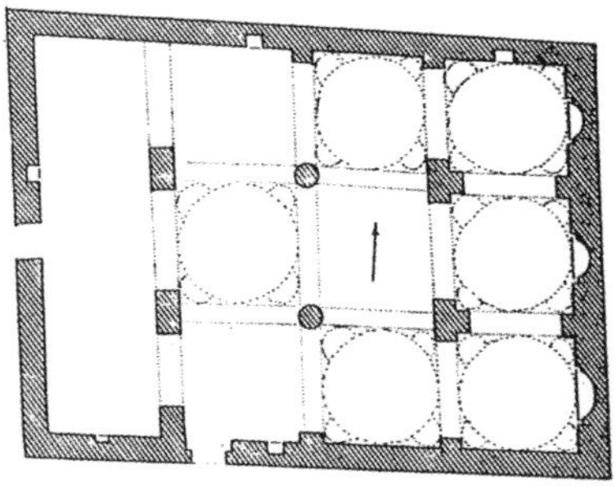

Fig. 28.8. Dayr Mar Mina near Sanabu (al-Suriani and Habib 1990: 109).

Nave covered with nine domes

1. Nave covered with nine domes of equal size. This type is known as the 'twelve-dome church,' because the sanctuary area is covered with three domes, in addition to the nine above the nave, all of which are generally of the same size, height, and structure. Seven churches of this type can be found in the region: the Church of Dayr al-Sanquriya in Bani

Mazar (with two exo-narthices) (fig. 28.9); Anba Athanasius Church in al-Qufur (fig. 28.10); Anba Pigul Church in Tallah (fig. 28.11); al-Malak Church in Buq (fig. 28.12); al-Malak Church at Hur, Mallawi (fig. 28.13); the Church of Dayr al-Malak at al-Rayramun, Mallawi (fig. 28.14); and the Church of Dayr Mar Boctor at Shu, Abnub (fig. 28.15).

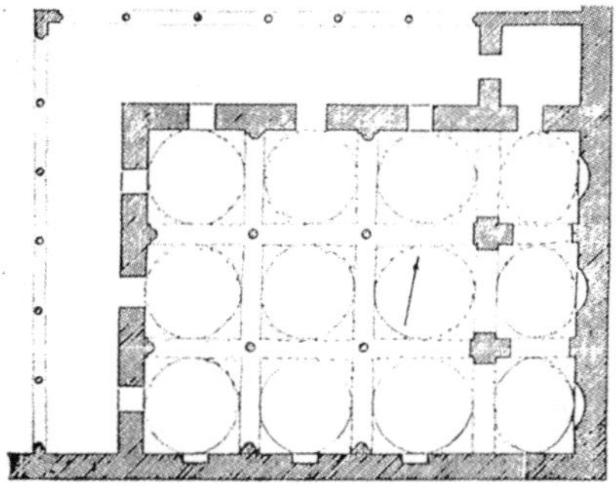

Fig. 28.9. Dayr al-Sanquriya, Bani Mazar (al-Suriani and Habib 1990: 135).

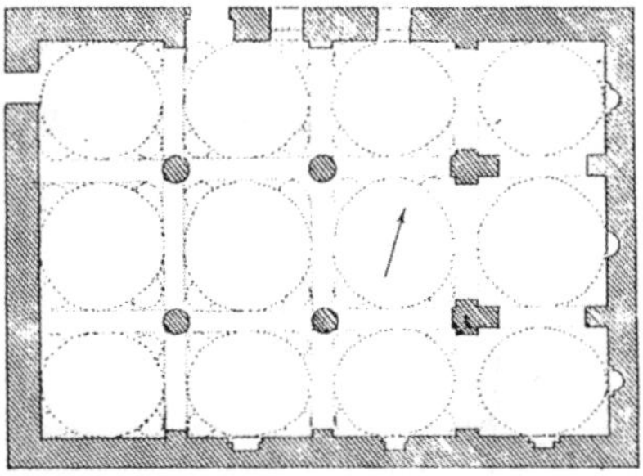

Fig. 28.10. Anba Athanasius Church, al-Qufur, Mataï (al-Suriani and Habib 1990: 133).

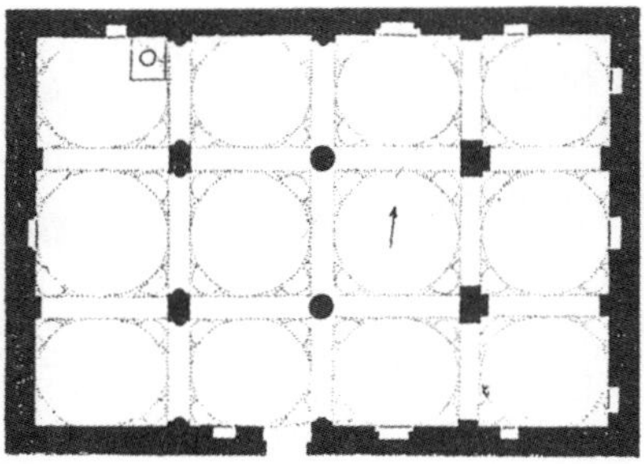

Fig. 28.11. Anba Pigul Church, Tallah (al-Suriani and Habib 1990: 126).

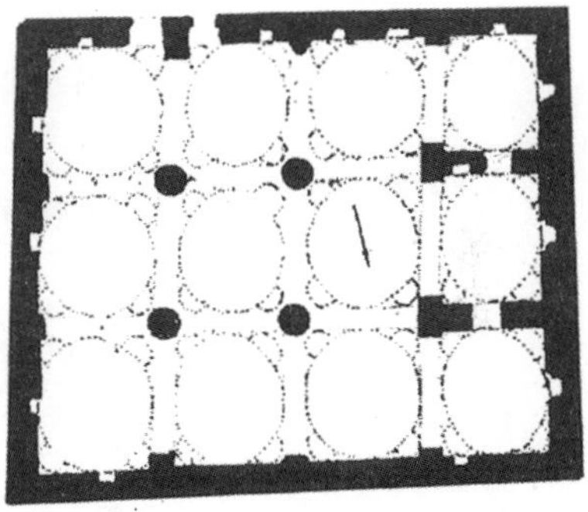

Fig. 28.12. Al-Malak (the Angel) Church at Buq, al-Qusiya (al-Suriani and Habib 2002: 161).

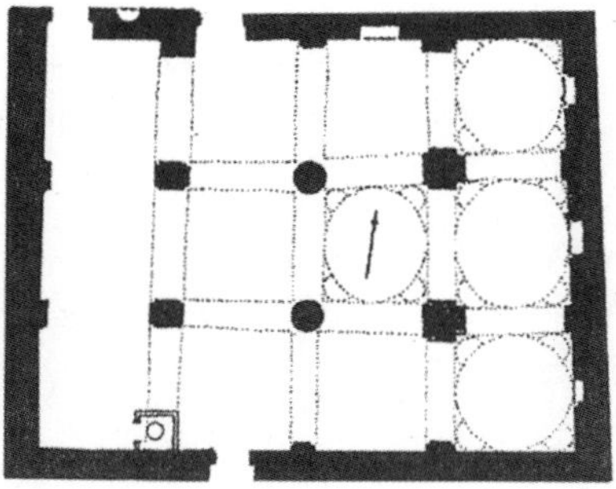

Fig. 28.13. Al-Malak (the Angel) Church at Hur, Mallawi (al-Suriani and Habib 2002: 150).

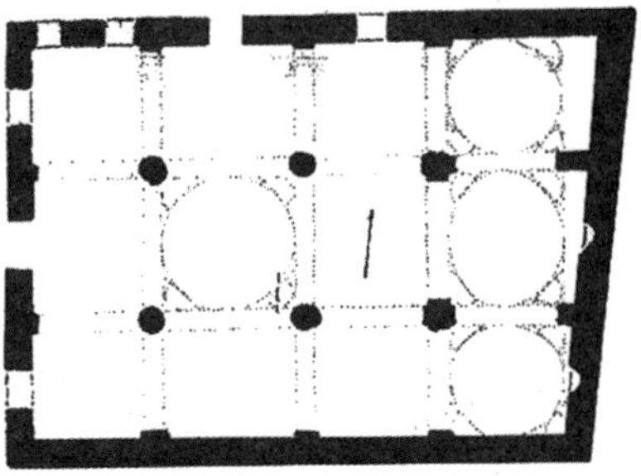

Fig. 28.14. Dayr al-Malak at al-Rayramun, Mallawi (al-Suriani and Habib 2002: 151).

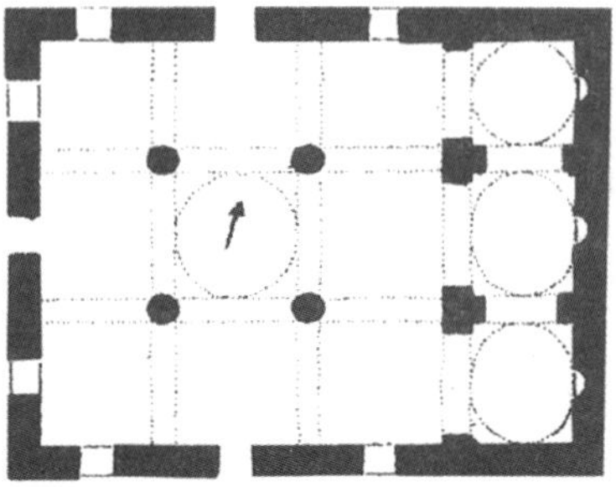

Fig. 28.15. Dayr Mar Boctor at Shu, Abnub (al-Suriani and Habib 2002: 166).

2. Nave covered with nine domes of unequal size
   a. This type is also known as the 'twelve-dome church,' because the sanctuary area is covered with three domes, in addition to the nine above the nave. Nevertheless, here the domes have neither the same height nor the same shape. The Church of Dayr Anba Sarabamun at Dayrut al-Sherif (fig. 28.16) and Abakir and Yuhanna Church at Manhari (fig. 28.17) are examples of this type.

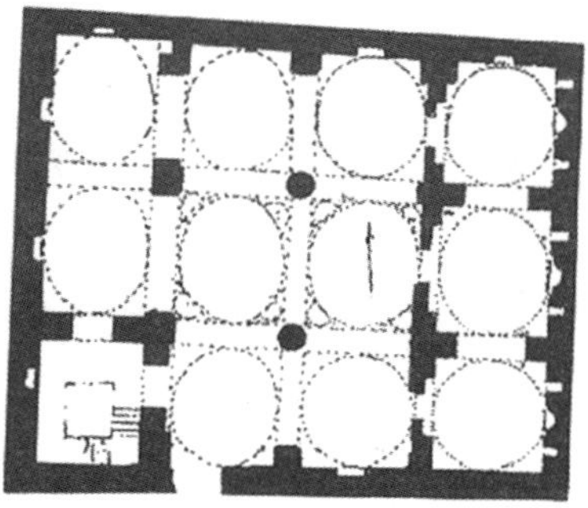

Fig. 28.16. Dayr Anba Sarabamun at Dayrut al-Sherif (al-Suriani and Habib 2002: 158).

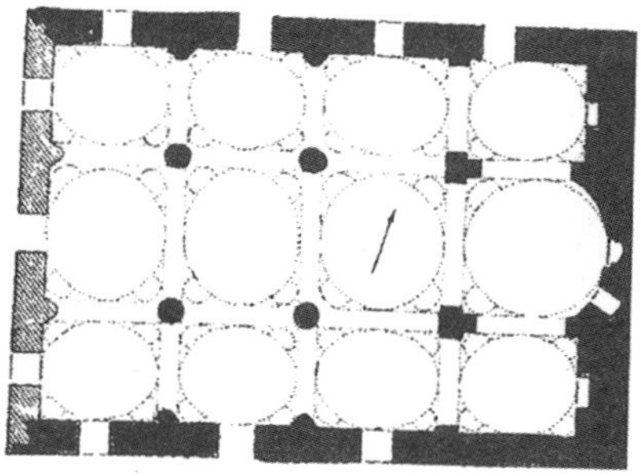

Fig. 28.17. Abakir and Yuhanna Church at Manhari, Abu Qurqas (al-Suriani and Habib 2002: 148).

   b. This type is similar to the previous one, with the addition of an inner narthex. An example is Anba Athanasius church at Dayr al-Zawya (fig. 28.18).

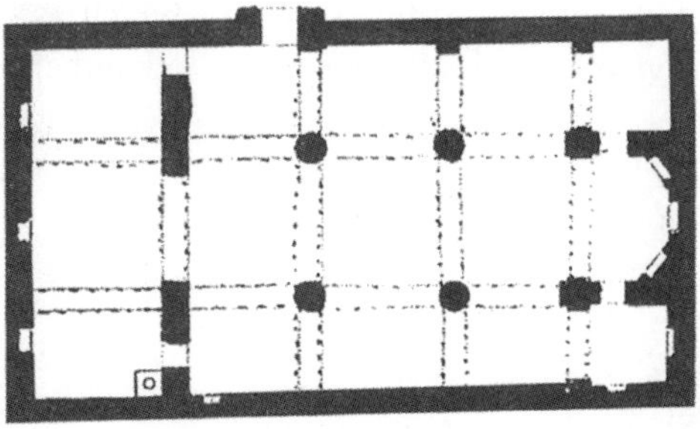

Fig. 28.18. Anba Athanasius Church at Dayr al-Zawya (al-Suriani and Habib 2002: 173).

c. Another variation of the nine-dome nave is characterized by the presence of an exo-narthex, for example, in Dayr al-Muharraq in al-Qusiya (fig. 28.19) and St. Mary Church at Delga, Dayr Muwas (fig. 28.20).

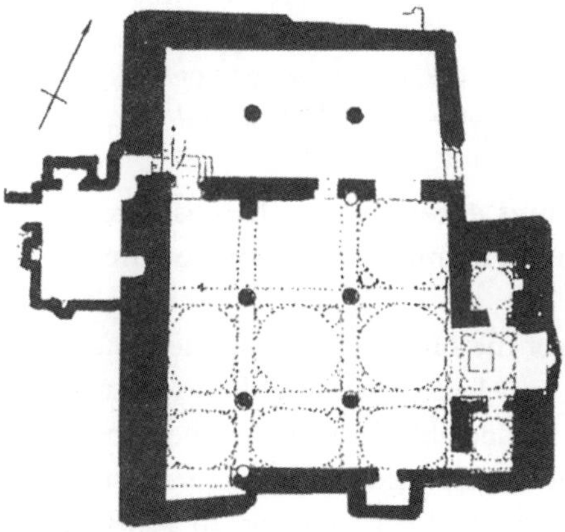

Fig. 28.19. Dayr al-Muharraq, al-Qusiya (al-Suriani and Habib 2002: 160).

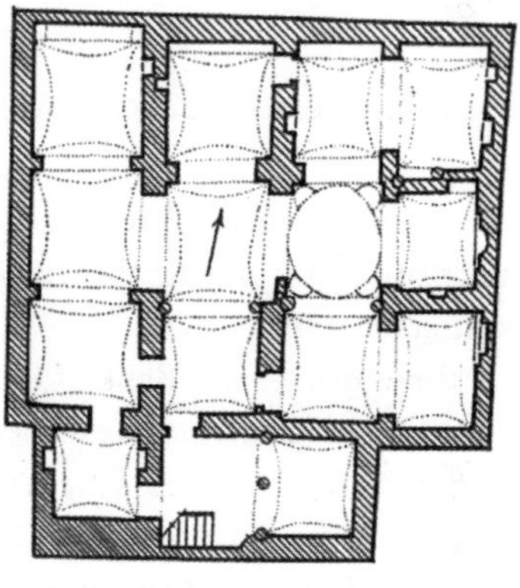

Fig. 28.20. St. Mary Church at Delga, Dayr Muwas (al-Suriani and Habib 1990: 113).

Churches with Nave Roofed with a Combination of Domes and Vaults

Nave consisting of a central dome and four umbrella vaults perpendicular to it, where each of the half domes at the end of the vault is based upon a half-cylindrical apse containing a small niche

This type of church can also be described as a 'tetraconch church,' with a central dome surrounded by four half-umbrella vaults, such as the church of Dayr al-Dik (fig. 28.21). This church is considered a perfect bi-axial design. The church's only altar lies in its northeastern side. In the four corners of the church there are four square chambers, two of which are connected to the sanctuary and serve as sacristies *(diakonia)*; these chambers were probably roofed with domes.

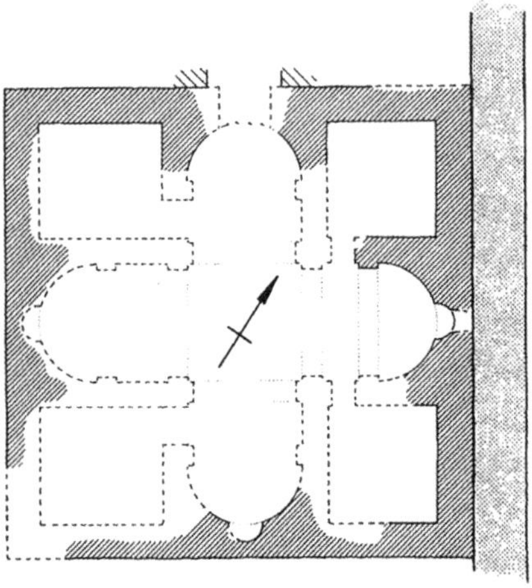

Fig. 28.21. The church of Dayr al-Dik, in Antinoë (east of Mallawi) (Grossmann 2002: pl. 51).

Nave consisting of three central domes extending in the east–west direction, lying along the nave's axis of symmetry, in front of the main sanctuary

The three domes are flanked on each of the northern and southern sides by three umbrella vaults, each ending in a half dome. The dome situated directly in front of the sanctuary is considerably larger than the others. There is a vaulted exo-narthex on the western side of the church, such as at the Church of Dayr Abu Hinnis, south of Antinoë (fig. 28.22). This church originally had one sanctuary, but then the first *khurus* was extended northward, creating an additional sanctuary.

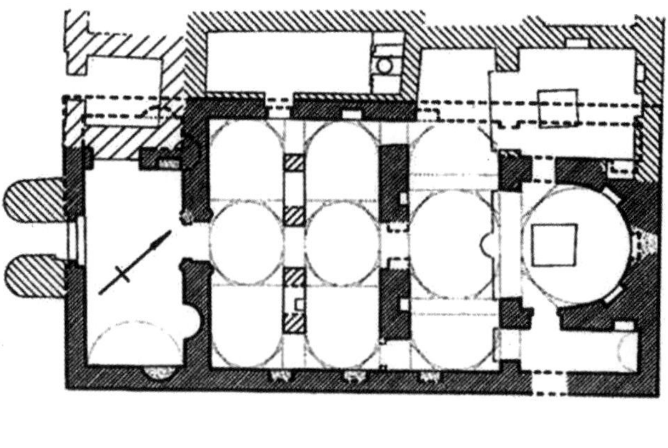

Fig. 28.22. The Church of Dayr Abu Hinnis, south of Antinoë (Grossmann 2002: pl. 141).

Churches with Square Nave

Churches in this style have a large central dome that lies in the middle of the square nave, carried on four columns with a round, square, or cruciform cross section. The central space is surrounded by a U-shaped balcony (on the northern, western, and southern sides). Above the balcony, there are four small equal domes, one in each of the nave's corners. In between these domes, there are four rectangular spaces, each covered with a vault or flat ceiling, resulting in a bi-axial design.

On the ground floor, there is often an exo-narthex enveloping the nave on the outside (on one, two, or three sides) and adding more space to the balcony, in addition to the environmental and aesthetic benefits resulting from it. There is always an inner narthex, in order to straighten the external form of the building. The sanctuary area extends through the whole width of the building, and this type of church usually has three altars. The exterior of the building is a clean-cut rectangle, free of any projections.

This architectural type occurs in the Church of al-Shahid Tawadros (St. Theodore the Martyr) in Abu Qurqas (fig. 28.23), the Church of Anba Qustur in Bardanuha (fig. 28.24), and the Church of Mar Boctor (St. Victor) in Musha (fig. 28.25).

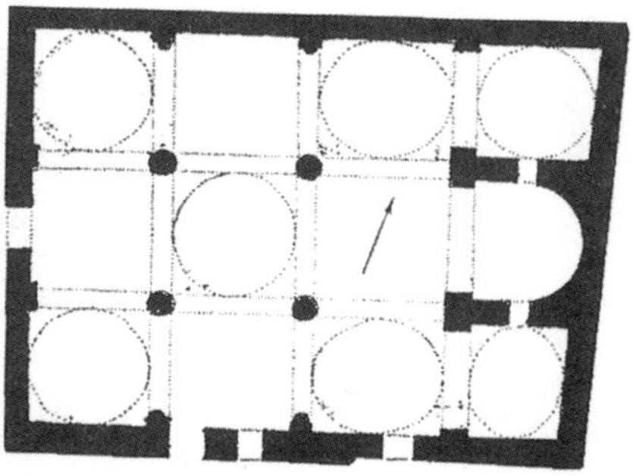

Fig. 28.23. Al-Shahid Tawadros Church, Abu Qurqas (al-Suriani and Habib 2002: 148).

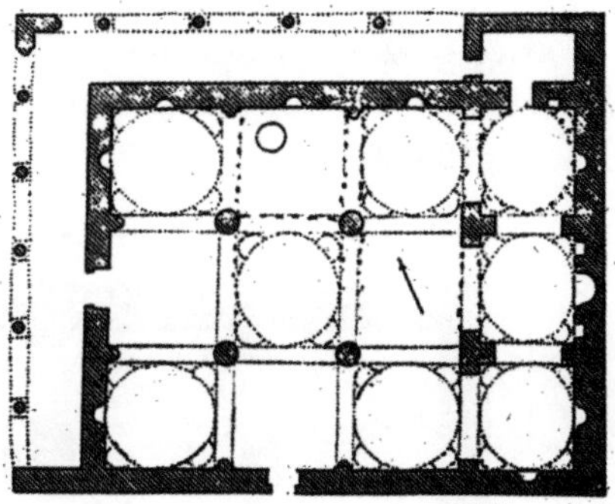

Fig. 28.24. Anba Qustur Church, Bardanuha, Mataï (al-Suriani and Habib 1990: 134).

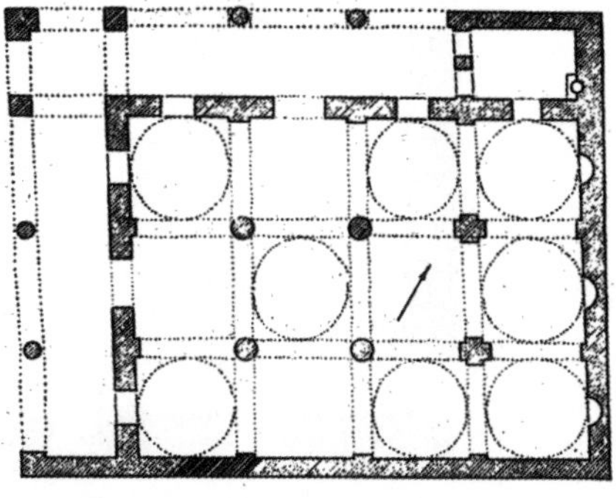

Fig. 28.25. Mar Boctor Church, Musha (al-Suriani and Habib 1990: 91).

Transverse Churches

'Transverse churches' are also known as 'Akhmim churches,' where the width of the church building is larger than its length—that is, the nave's extension in the north–south direction is larger than its east–west extension. For this reason, they are also known as 'short churches.' These churches are divided into two *khuruses*, and usually have multiple parallel/adjacent altars and a nave with multiple domes, the highest of which is the dome opposite the main altar in the central bay.

These churches are often extended northward and southward by adding to each side two bays and a sanctuary, or *diakonia*. The sanctuary area consists generally of three parallel half-cylindrical sanctuaries, roofed with three domes.

In Dayr Anba Hermina at 'Ezbet al-Aqbat, al-Badari, probably built in two or three phases, one can easily identify that the first phase included a semicircular sanctuary, centrally located with respect to the original design (fig. 28.26).

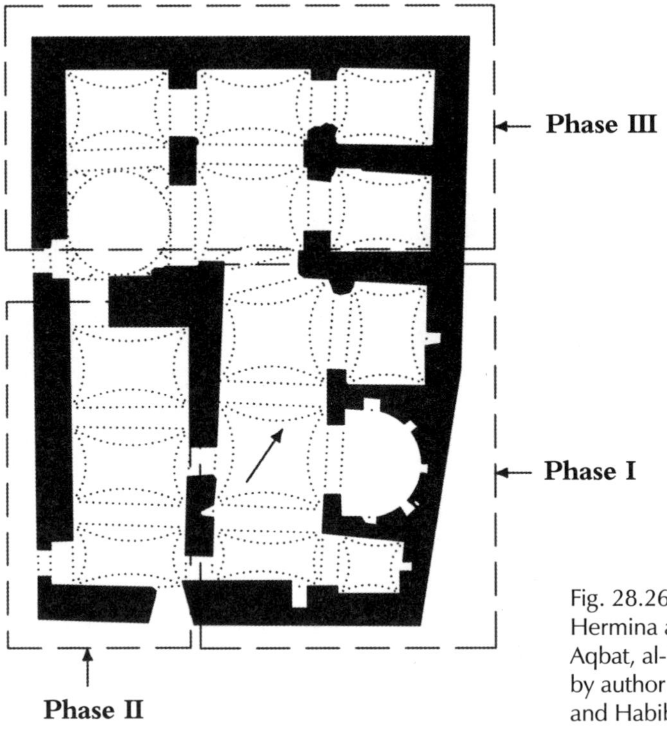

Fig. 28.26. Dayr Anba Hermina at 'Ezbet al-Aqbat, al-Badari. Redrawn by author from al-Suriani and Habib 2002: 169.

Basilican-plan Churches

These churches have a wide middle nave running east to west, are high-roofed with a wooden truss and clerestory windows, and are flanked by three aisles on the northern, western, and southern sides. The sanctuary area is of great depth, and there is usually a wooden dome known as the ciborium (or baldachin) above the altar, carried on four marble columns. The sanctuary area is characterized by the presence of a large synthronon *(thronos).* There is a mezzanine floor (gallery) above the three aisles, overlooking the nave.

1. Typical basilican-plan church, such as the church of Dayr al-Bala'izah, west of Abu Tig (fig. 28.27).

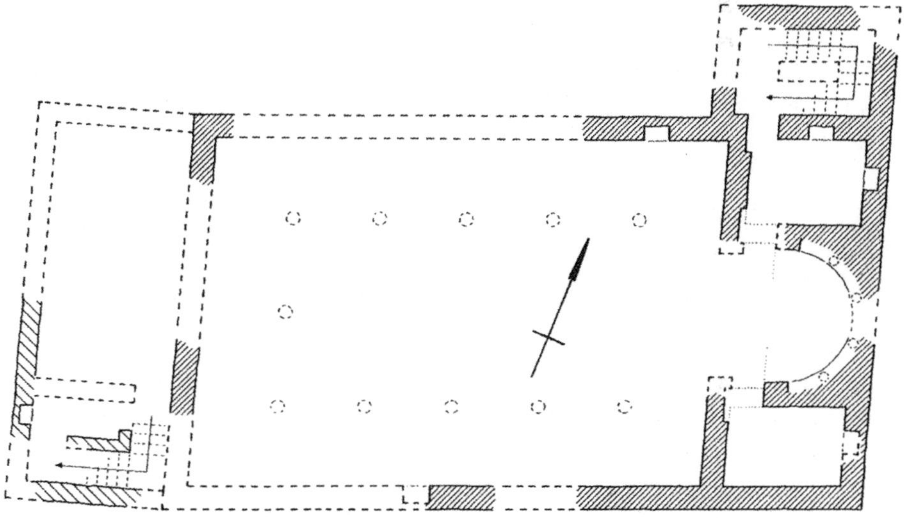

Fig. 28.27. Dayr al-Bala'iza, west of Abu Tig (Grossmann 2002: pl. 148).

2. Basilican-plan church without the return (western) aisle, such as the church of Dayr Anba Apollo at Bawit, Dayrut (fig. 28.28).

   The basilica plan was greatly influenced by the design of the hypostyle hall in ancient Egyptian temples, for example at Karnak temple, with its high and wide central nave, flanked by short and narrow side aisles, in addition to the clerestory windows admitting natural lighting and ventilation for the nave.

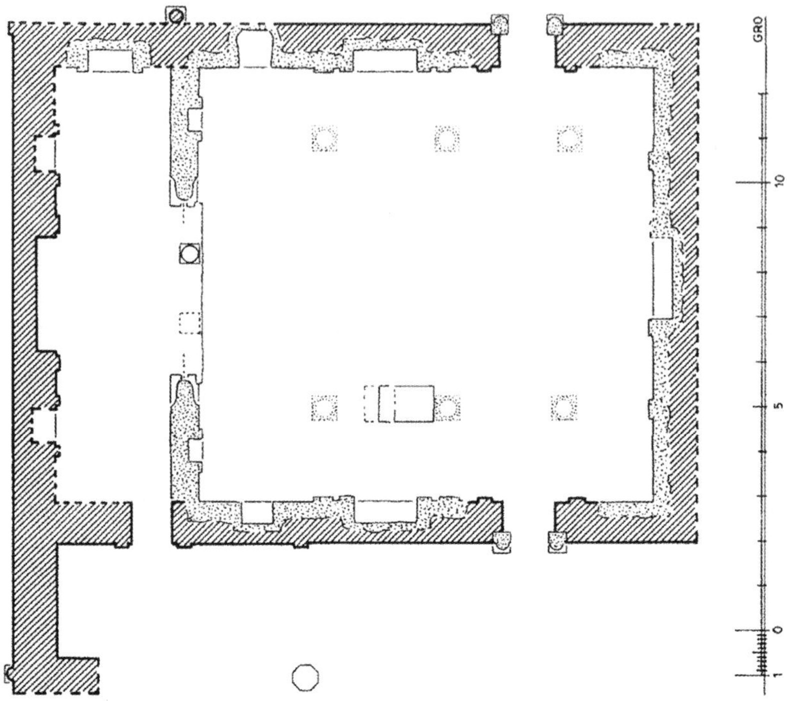

Fig. 28.28. Dayr Anba Apollo at Bawit, Dayrut (Grossmann 2002: pl. 142).

Basilican-plan Churches with Triconch Sanctuary

A wide, high-roofed, short central nave running east to west, with an unequal triconch

The nave was once roofed with a brick vault and is currently roofed with a flat wooden ceiling. There are three aisles around the nave, such as at the church of Dayr Abu Fana in Mallawi (fig. 28.29). There, the current sanctuary lies within a large eastern apse, of nearly the same width as the middle nave, with a fresco depicting the largest Iota cross in all of Egypt. The sanctuary and the *khurus* form together an unequal triconch, because the eastern apse is much larger than the two apses of the *khurus*.

The monastery is also known as the Monastery of the Crosses, due to the fact that, in addition to the large Iota cross, there are other wall paintings depicting different sizes and forms of crosses.

This architectural type also applies to the basilica of Kom Namrud, west of Samalut (fig. 28.30).

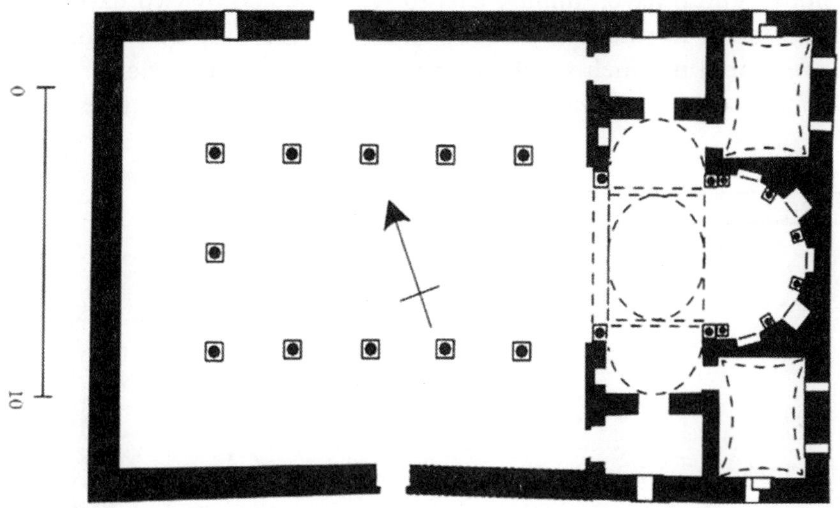

Fig. 28.29. The church of Dayr Abu Fana (St. Epiphanius), Mallawi. Redrawn by author from Grossman 2002: 136.

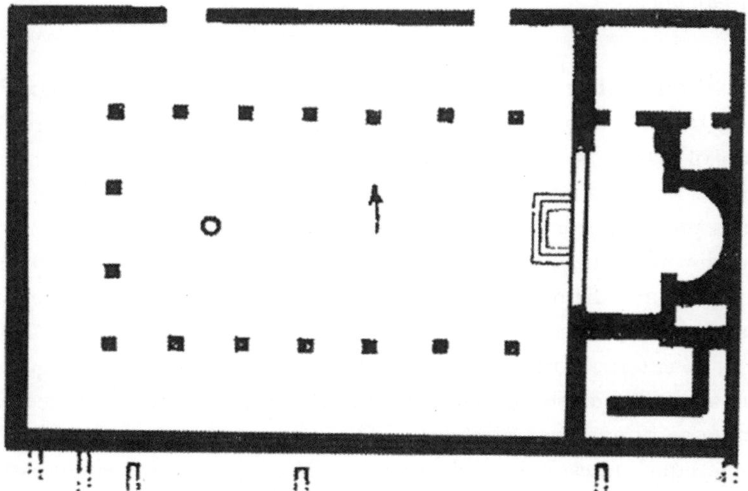

Fig. 28.30. The basilica of Kom Namrud, west of Samalut (al-Suriani and Habib 2002: 142).

A long central nave, running east to west, flanked by two narrow aisles on the northern and southern sides, with a separate defined *khurus* and a triconch sanctuary, but without a return aisle
Dayr al-'Izam, Mount Durunka (fig. 28.31) is an example of this type.

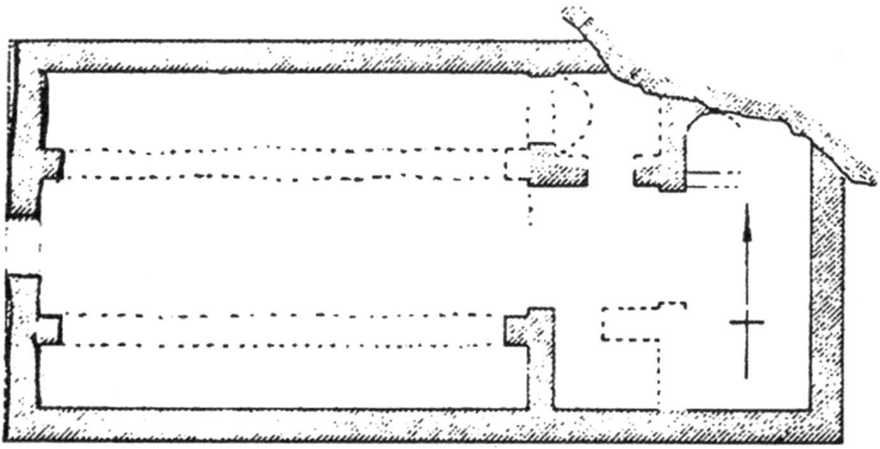

Fig. 28.31. The church of Dayr al-'Izam, Mount Durunka (al-Suriani and Habib 1990: 96).

Basilican-plan Churches with Transepts (Cruciform Plan)

This type of church comprises a large central nave, flanked by three aisles, one of which is the return aisle. The central nave is about forty-three meters long and not more than fifteen meters wide. Two semicircular transepts protrude from the church building, each of which includes a large middle aisle flanked by two narrower ones, and ends in a semicircular apse with an inner diameter of twelve meters, which is equal to the diameter of the eastern apse, such as at the Basilica of al-Ashmunayn (fig. 28.32).

The external form of the Basilica of al-Ashmunayn is rectangular, and the apses cannot be discerned from the outside. It is distinguished by the presence of an inner narthex as well as an exo-narthex, and also by its three equal apses. The total inner length of the central eastern–western nave (excluding the depth of the eastern apse) is nearly equal to the inner distance between the northern and southern walls of the transepts.

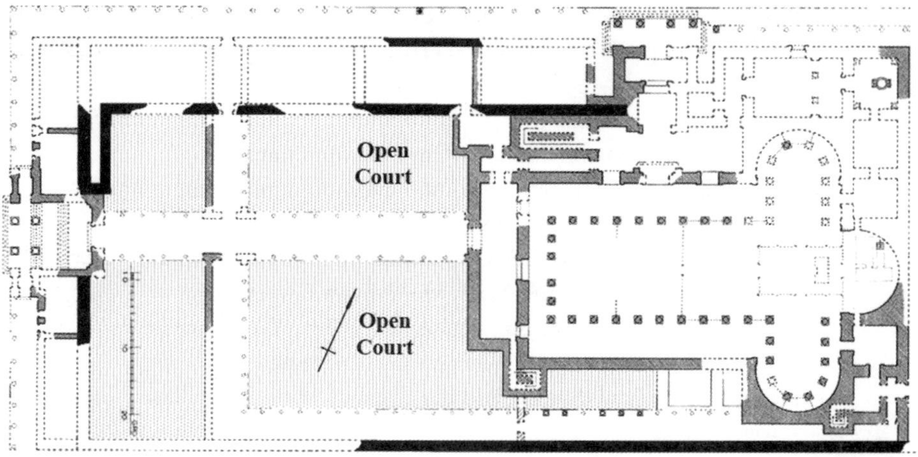

Fig. 28.32. The Great Basilica, Hermopolis Magna (al-Ashmunayn). Redrawn by author from Grossmann 2002: pl. 59.

The Ruined Churches of Manqabad

These two chapels, recently discovered by the Sohag University expedition in the northeast of Asyut, do not fit into any of the previous categories, being unique in their architectural formation (fig. 28.33). Each has a defined *khurus* and an oblong nave with no columns or other form of support. It is difficult to determine the roofing system in their current state; however, the short six-meter span of one church could have had a brick vault running in the east–west direction, and the 7.8-meter span of the other church suggests a wooden truss.

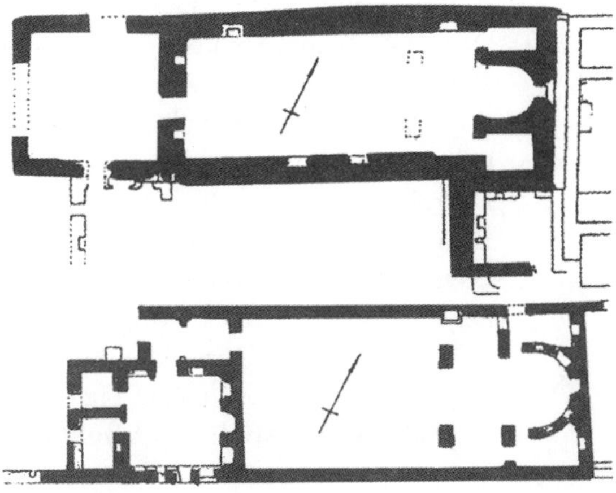

Fig. 28.33. The ruined churches of Manqabad (al-Suriani and Habib 2002: 165).

Appendix: Historic Monasteries and Churches of Middle Egypt from Oxyrhynchos to Dayr al-Ganadla[1]

Historic Monasteries

Dayr al-Sanquriya, Bani Mazar—Minya Governorate
Dayr al-'Adra, Gebel al-Teir, Samalut—Minya Governorate
Dayr Abba Hor at Sawada—Minya Governorate
Dayr al-Agaibi at Manhari, Abu Qurqas—Minya Governorate
Dayr Abu Fana at Qasr Hur, Mallawi—Minya Governorate
Dayr al-Malak at al-Rayramun, Mallawi—Minya Governorate
Dayr al-Dik, east of Mallawi—Minya Governorate
Dayr Sunbat, Dayr al-Nasara, and the ruins of Antinoë, Mallawi—Minya Governorate
Dayr Abu Hinnis, Mallawi—Minya Governorate
Dayr al-Barsha, Mallawi—Minya Governorate
Dayr Abu Fam at the cave tombs of al-Shaykh Sa'id, al-Barsha—Minya Governorate
Dayr Anba Sarabamun at Dayrut al-Sherif—Asyut Governorate
Dayr Anba Apollo at Bawit, Dayrut—Asyut Governorate
Dayr al-Meshreki at Ezbet Doss, Dayrut—Asyut Governorate
Dayr Mar Mina near Sanabu—Asyut Governorate
Dayr al-Quseir, east of al-Qusiya—Asyut Governorate
Dayr al-Muharraq, al-Qusiya—Asyut Governorate
Dayr al-Amir Tadros, Bani Shuqair, Manfalut—Asyut Governorate
Dayr Mar Mina al-Mu'allaq (the Hanging Monastery), east of Manfalut—Asyut Governorate
Dayr al-Gabrawi, Abnub—Asyut Governorate
Dayr Mar Boctor at Shu, Abnub—Asyut Governorate
Dayr Abu Ishaq at Arab al-'Awamir, Abnub—Asyut Governorate
Dayr Tassa—Asyut Governorate
Dayr Anba Hermina at 'Ezbet al-Aqbat, al-Badari—Asyut Governorate
Dayr al-'Izam, Mount Durunka—Asyut Governorate
Dayr al-Mouttin, Mount Durunka—Asyut Governorate
Dayr al-'Adra, Mount Durunka—Asyut Governorate
Dayr Rifa, Mount Durunka—Asyut Governorate
Dayr al-Bala'iza, west of Abu Tig—Asyut Governorate
Dayr al-Ganadla, Abu Tig—Asyut Governorate

Historic Churches

Church of Anba Qustur, Bardanuha, Mataï—Minya Governorate
Church of Anba Athanasius at al-Qufur, Mataï—Minya Governorate
Basilica of Kom Namrud, west of Samalut—Minya Governorate
Church of Abu Sayfayn, al-Tayeba, Samalut—Minya Governorate
Church of Mar Mina, Taha al-A'meda, west of Samalut—Minya Governorate
Church of Abaskhyron al-Kelliny, al-Baihu, south of Samalut—Minya Governorate
Church of Anba Pigol, Tallah—Minya Governorate
Church of Abakir and Youhanna, Manhari, Abu Qurqas—Minya Governorate
Church of al-Shahid Tawadros, Abu Qurqas—Minya Governorate
Church of al-Malak at Hur, Mallawi—Minya Governorate
Basilica of al-Ashmunayn, Mallawi—Minya Governorate
Church of al-'Adra, Mallawi—Minya Governorate
Bishopric of Mallawi church, Minya Governorate
The church at the ruins south of Antinoë—Minya Governorate
Church of al-'Adra at Delga, Dayr Muwas—Minya Governorate
Church of Mar Girgis at Sanabu—Asyut Governorate
Church of al-Malak at Buq, al-Qusiya—Asyut Governorate
Church of al-Shahid Tawadros at al-Temsahiyah, al-Qusiya—Asyut Governorate
Church of al-Shahid Youhanna al-Heraclye at Om al-Qusour, Manfalut—Asyut Governorate
Church of al-Malak, Bani Magd, Manfalut—Asyut Governorate
Bishopric of Manfalut church—Asyut Governorate
Church of al-'Adra at Bani Adi, Manfalut—Asyut Governorate
Church of Abu Seifein at al-Gawli, Manfalut—Asyut Governorate
The Ruined Churches at Manqabad—Asyut Governorate
The old reconstructed churches of Abnub, such as Yuhanna al-Ma'madan (St. John the Baptist) church, al-'Adra church, and Abu Fam church
Church of Mar Girgis, Bani Mur—Asyut Governorate
Church of al-Amir Tadros at Dayr Bisra—Asyut Governorate
Church of al-Amir Tadros at Bawit—Asyut Governorate
Church of al-Malak, Dayr Durunka village—Asyut Governorate
Church of Mar Qulta at Rifa—Asyut Governorate
Church of Mar Boctor, Musha—Asyut Governorate

Church of al-Amir Tadros al-Shatby at Shutb–Asyut Governorate
Church of al-Shahid Philotheos, Muti'a—Asyut Governorate
Church of al-Shahid Claudius of Baqur—Asyut Governorate
Church of Anba Athanasius at Dayr al-Zawya—Asyut Governorate

Notes

1 The churches/monasteries indicated in italics in this appendix are illustrated and included in this chapter. Within each table, the monasteries and churches are listed in geographical sequence from north to south.

Abbreviations

AEH	*African Economic History*
AI	*Annales islamologiques*
ASAE	*Annales du Service des antiquités de l'Egypte*
BASP	*Bulletin of the American Society of Papyrologists*
BIFAO	*Bulletin de l'Institut français d'archéologie orientale*
BSAC	*Bulletin de la Société d'archéologie copte*
BSOAS	*Bulletin of the School of Oriental and African Studies*
CBC	Cahiers de la bibliothèque copte
CIM	Centro Italiano Microfiches
CSCO	Corpus Scriptorum Christianorum Orientalium
IFAO	Institut français d'archéologie orientale
IJMES	*International Journal of Middle East Studies*
JAC	*Jahrbuch für Antike und Christentum*
JARCE	*Journal of the American Research Center in Egypt*
JCS	*Journal of Coptic Studies*
JEA	*Journal of Egyptian Archaeology*
JECS	*Journal of Eastern Christian Studies*

JJP	*Journal of Juristic Papyrology*
JJS	*Journal of Jewish Studies*
JTS	*Journal of Theological Studies*
MES	*Middle Eastern Studies*
MIFAO	Mémoires de l'Institut français d'archéologie orientale du Caire
PL	*Patrologia Latina*
PSI	*Papiri greci e latini*. Pubblicazione della Società Italiana per la ricerca dei papiri greci e latini in Egitto
SAK	*Studien zur Altägyptischen Kultur*
SKCO	Sprachen und Kulturen des Christlichen Orients
SOCC	*Studia Orientalia Christiana Collectanae*
ZÄSA	*Zeitschrift für Ägyptische Sprache und Altertumskunde*
ZPE	*Zeitschrift für Papyrologie und Epigraphik*

Bibliography

Abba Demetrius. 2000. *Rihlat al-'a'ila al-muqadasa fi Malawi*. Malawi: Mutraniya Malawi Printing House.

———. 2007. *Tahqiq al-Bardiya alati hasamat al-fatra alati qadaha al-rab Yasu' fi Misr.* Malawi: Mutraniya Malawi Printing House.

'Abd al-Latif al-Baghdadi. 1910. *Kitab al-ifada wa-l-i'tibar fi-l-umur al-mushahada wa-l-Hawadit al-mu'ayana bi-'ard Misr, Relation de l'Égypte par 'Abd al-Latif al-Baghdadi*, trans. and ed. M. Silvestre de Sacy. Paris: Imprimerie impériale.

'Abd al-Masih, Y., and O.H.E. Burmester, trans. and eds. 1959. *History of the Patriarchs of the Egyptian Church, Known as the History of the Holy Church.* Texts and Documents, vol. 2, part 3. Christodoulus-Michael (AD 1046–1102). Cairo: Société d'archéologie copte.

Abdal-Tawab A.-R., and P. Grossmann. Forthcoming. *Archaeological Researches of the Egyptian Antiquities Organisation in Christian Monuments of Upper and Lower Egypt.*

Abdeltawab, S. 2013. "Karst Limestone Foundation Geotechnical Problems, Detection and Treatment: Case Studies from Egypt and Saudi Arabia." *International Journal of Scientific and Engineering Research* 4, no. 5, pp. 376–88.

Al-Absalmûdiyya al-Sanawiyya al-Muqaddasa. 1992. 9th ed. Cairo: Central Association for the Renewal of Coptic Orthodox Churches of Cairo.

Abu al-Makarim. 1895. *The Churches and Monasteries of Egypt and some Neighbouring Countries,* attributed to Abu Salih the Armenian. T.A. Evetts and A.J. Butler, eds. Oxford: Clarendon Press.

———. 1984. *Tarikh Abu al-Makarim: al-kana'is wa-l-adyura fi al-qarn al-thani 'ashar*, vol. 2, ed. Samu'il al-Suriany. Wadi al-Natrun: Dayr al-Suryan.

Abullif, W. 1998. "Abramo l'Egumeno." In J.N. Cañellas and J. Virgulin, eds., *Enciclopedia dei santi: Le Chiese orientali*, 2 vols., vol. 1, p. 19. Rome: Città Nuova.

Adli, N. 1999. *Hikayat al-hurub (rihlat al-'a'ila al-muqadasa ila Misr)*. Cairo: al-Masriyin Printing House.

Afifi, M. 1999. "The State and the Church in Nineteenth-century Egypt." *Die Welt des Islams*, New Series 39, no. 3, pp. 273–88.

Albarrán Martínez, M.J. 2011. *Ascetismo y monasterios femininos en el Egipto tardoantiguo: Estudio de papiros y ostraca griegos y coptos*. Montserrat: Publicacions de l'Abadia de Montserrat, S.A.

'Ali Mubarak. 1887. *al-Khitat al-tawfiqiqiya al-gadida li-Misr al-Qahira wa muduniha wa biladiha al-qadima wa-l-shahira*, vol. 11, 1st ed. Cairo: al-Matba'a al-Kubra al-Amiriya.

Amélineau, É. 1887. *Étude sur le christianisme en Égypte au septième siècle*. Paris: Ernest Leroux.

———. 1890. *Actes des martyrs de l'église copte*. Paris: Ernest Leroux.

———. 1893. *La géographie de l'Égypte à l'époque copte*. Paris: Imprimerie nationale.

'Anan, M.A. 1999. *Mu'arikhu Misr al-islamiya wa masadir al-tarikh al-misri*. Cairo: al-Hay'a al-Misriya al-'Ama li-l-Kitab.

Anba Abraam. 2004. *Ibarshiyat al-Fayyum bayn al-madi wa al-hader*. Cairo: al-Karma Printing House.

Anba Gregorius. 1968. *al-Dayr al-Muharraq: tarikhahu wa wasfahu wa kul mushtamalatahu*. Cairo: Bishopric of Scientific Research and Coptic Culture.

Andorlini, I. 1998. "Gli scavi di John de Monins Johnson ad Antinoe (1913–1914)." In Cat. Florence, F. Del Francia-Barocas, ed., *Antinoe cent'anni dopo* (Exhibition catalogue Palazzo Medici Riccardi, Florence), pp. 19–22. Florence: Istituto papirologico G. Vitelli.

Andreae, B. 1980. *Die Sarkophage mit Darstellungen aus dem Menschenleben, Zweiter Teil: Die römischen Jagdsarkophage*. Berlin: Gebr. Mann Verlag.

Ansari, H.N. 1984. "The Islamic Militants in Egyptian Politics." *IJMES* 16, no. 1, pp. 123–44.

Armanios, F. 2011. *Coptic Christianity in Ottoman Egypt*. New York: Oxford University Press.

Athanasiyus al-Maqqari. 2007. *Al-Kana'is al-sharqiya wa awtaniha*. Vol. 2. Kanisat Misr, Cairo: Dar Nubar Shubra.

———. 2012. *Fihris kitabat aba' kanisat al-Iskandariya: al-kitabat al-'arabiya*. 2 vols. Cairo: Matabi'ah al-Nubar.

Atiya, A.S., ed. 1991a. *The Coptic Encyclopedia*. New York: Macmillan.

———. 1991b. "Martyrs, Coptic." In A.S. Atiya, ed., *The Coptic Encyclopedia*, vol. 5, pp. 1550b–1557b. New York: Macmillan, http://ccdl.libraries.claremont.edu/cdm/ref/collection/cce/id/1330

Atiya, A.S., Y. 'Abd al-Masih, and O.H.E. Burmester, eds. 1959. *History of the Patriarchs of the Egyptian Church known as the History of the Holy Church*. Vol. 2, part 3. Textes et documents 5. Cairo: Société d'archéologie copte.

Baer, G. 1959. "The Dissolution of the Egyptian Village Community." *Die Welt des Islams*, New Series 6, no. 1/2, pp. 56–70.

———. 1967. "Slavery in Nineteenth-century Egypt." *Journal of African History* 8, no. 3, pp. 417–41.

———. 1969. "The Beginnings of Urbanization." In G. Baer, ed., *Studies in the Social History of Modern Egypt*. Chicago, IL: University of Chicago Press.

Bagnall, R.S. 1993. *Egypt in Late Antiquity*. Princeton, NJ: Princeton University Press.

———. 1995. *Reading Papyri, Writing Ancient History*. New York: Routledge.

———. 2005. "Linguistic Change and Religious Change: Thinking about the Temples of the Fayoum in the Roman Period." In G. Gabra, ed., *Christianity and Monasticism in the Fayoum Oasis: Essays from the 2004 International Symposium of the Saint Mark Foundation and the Saint Shenouda the Archimandrite Coptic Society in Honor of Martin Krause*, pp. 11–19. Cairo: The American University in Cairo Press.

Bagnall, R.S., and R. Cribiore. 2006. *Women's Letters from Ancient Egypt, 300 BC–AD 800*. Ann Arbor, MI: University of Michigan Press.

Bagnall, R.S., and D.W. Rathbone, eds. 2008. *Egypt from Alexander to the Copts: An Archaeological and Historical Guide*. Cairo: American University in Cairo Press.

Bahr, S. 1991. "Coptic Congress of Asyut." In A.S. Atiya, ed., *The Coptic Encyclopedia*, vol. 2, pp. 602–603. New York: Macmillan.

al-Bakri. 1992. *al-Masalik wa-l-mamalik*. Cairo: al-Dar al-Arabiya li-l-Kitab.

Barabási, A.-L. 2002. *Linked: The New Science of Networks*. Cambridge, MA: Perseus.

Barnard, L.W. 1991. "Clement of Alexandria." In A.S. Atiya, ed., *The Coptic Encyclopedia*, vol. 2, pp. 562–63. New York: Macmillan.

Barns, J.W.B., G.M. Browne, and J.C. Shelton. 1981. *Nag Hammadi Codices: Greek and Coptic Papyri from the Cartonnage of the Covers*. Leiden: Brill.

Baron, B. 1994. "Readers and the Women's Press in Egypt." *Poetics Today* 15, no. 2, pp. 217–40.

Basset, R., ed. 1907. *Le synaxaire arabe jacobite (Rédaction Copte)*, vol. 2, *Les mois de hatour et de kiahk*. Patrologia Orientalis 3.3, 13. Paris: Firmin-Didot.

———. 1922. *Le synaxaire arabe jacobite (Rédaction copte)*, vol. 4, *Les mois de barmahat, barmoudah et bachons.* Patrologia Orientalis 16, 2. Paris: Firmin-Didot.

Bastianini, G., and R. Pintaudi, eds. 2008. *Antinoupolis I: Scavi e materiali.* Florence: Istituto papirologico G. Vitelli.

Baumeister, T. 1972. *Martyr Invictus: Der Martyrer als Sinnbild der Erlösung in der Legende und im Kult der frühen koptischen Kirche: Zur Kontinuität des ägyptischen Denkens.* Forschungen zur Volkskunde 46. Münster: Regensberg.

Bausi, A. 2010. "Qʷəsqʷam (Koskam) in Ethiopian Tradition." In S. Uhlig and A. Bausi, eds., *Encyclopaedia Aethiopica*, vol. 4, p. 318. Wiesbaden: Harrassowitz.

Bell, D.N. 1983. *Besa: The Life of Shenoute.* Cistercian Studies 73. Kalamazoo, MI: Cistercian Publications.

Bell, J. 1942. *Egypt in the Classical Geographers.* Survey of Egypt. Cairo: Ministry of Finance.

Belting, H. 1994. *Likeness and Presence: A History of the Image before the Era of Art.* Chicago and London: University of Chicago Press.

Bénazeth, D. 2007. "Baouît." In L. Pantalacci and S. Denoix, "Travaux de l'Institut français d'archéologie orientale en 2006–2007." *BIFAO* 107, pp. 280–84. Cairo: IFAO.

———. 2008. "Baouît." In L. Pantalacci and S. Denoix, "Travaux de l'Institut français d'archéologie orientale en 2007–2008." *BIFAO* 108, pp. 403–407.

Bénazeth, D., O. Bouet, J.-L. Bovot, Fl. Calament, R. Cortopassi, A. Del, A. Delattre, M. Dupéron, Chr. Guilbaud, St. Lazare, Chr. Lyon-Caen, T. Magnaudet, S. Marchand, C. Meurice, M. Mossakowska-Gaubert, A. Nageh, A. Savy, W. Van Neer, and N. Vanthieghem. Forthcoming. *L'église de l'archange Michel dans le monastère copte de Baouit.* Cairo: Institut français d'archéologie orientale.

Bénazeth, D., and T. Herbich. 2008. "Le kôm de Baouît. Étapes d'une cartographie." *BIFAO* 108, pp. 165–204.

Bénazeth, D., and M.-H. Rutschowscaya. 1999. *Le monastère et la nécropole de Baouit.* MIFAO 111. Cairo: IFAO.

Bishay, Y. 1961. *Biostratigraphy Study of Eocene in the Eastern Desert between Samalut and Assiut by Large Foraminifera.* Alexandria: Third Arab Petroleum Congress.

Blanc, C. 1966. *Origène: Commentaire sur saint Jean. Tome 1 (Livres I–V).* Sources Chrétiennes 120. Paris: Les Éditions du Cerf.

Boinet, A. 1899. *Dictionnaire géographique de l'Égypte.* Cairo: Imprimerie nationale.

Boismard, M.-É. 2003a. "Étude sur le papyrus copte de l'évangile de Matthieu provenant de la collection Schøyen." *Revue Biblique* 110, no. 3, pp. 387–98.

———. 2003b. *L'Évangile selon Matthieu d'après le papyrus copte de la collection Schøyen: Analyse littéraire.* Cahiers de la Revue Biblique 55. Paris: Gabalda.

Bolman, E.S., S.J. Davis, and G. Pyke. 2010. "Shenoute and a Recently Discovered Tomb Chapel at the White Monastery." *Journal of Early Christian Studies* 18, no. 3, pp. 453–62.

Booth, M. 2002. "'She Herself Was the Ultimate Rule': Arabic Biographies of Missionary Teachers and Their Pupils." *Islam and Christian–Muslim Relations* 13, no. 4, pp. 427–48.

Bosson, N. 2006. "Le Codex Schøyen (Évangile de Matthieu). Études pour servir à l'identification d'un nouveau dialecte de Moyenne-Égypte." In L. Painchaud and P.-H. Poirier, eds., *Coptica—Gnostica—Manichaica: Mélanges offerts à Wolf-Peter Funk*. BCNH, Section "Études" 7, pp. 19–79. Quebec: Les Presses de l'Université Laval Québec; Louvain and Paris: Editions Peeters.

Boud'hors, A. 2005. "Manuscripts and Literature in Fayoumic Coptic." In G. Gabra, ed., *Christianity and Monasticism in the Fayoum Oasis*, pp. 21–31. Cairo: The American University in Cairo Press.

Boud'hors, A., and R. Boutros. 2000. "La Sainte Famille à Gabal al-Tayr et l'Homélie du Rocher." *Etudes coptes* 7, CBC 12, pp. 59–76. Louvain: Peeters.

———, trans. 2001. *L'homélie sur l'église du Rocher attribuée à Timothée Aelure*. Patrologia Orientalis 49, fascicule 1, no. 217. Rome: Pontifico Istituto Orientale.

Boud'hors, A., and Ch. Heurtel. 2010. *Les ostraca coptes de la TT 29: Autour du moine Frangé*. Brussels: CReA Patrimoine.

Boukhary, M., and W.M. Abdelmalik. 1983. "Revision of the Stratigraphy of the Eocene Deposits of Egypt." *Neues Jahrbuch für Geologie und Paläontologie* 6, pp. 321–37.

Boutros, R., ed. 1999. *Malaf Khass 'an hurub al 'aela al muqadessa ila ard Masr*. Shoubra, Cairo: n.p.

Boutros, R., and M.-H. Rutschowscaya. 2005. "Sondages dans le monastère de Baouît—2003," with contributions by S. Marchand and M. Mossakowska. *BIFAO* 105, pp. 12–34.

Bovon, F., and P. Geoltrain, eds. 1997. *Ecrits apocryphes chrétiens*, vol. 1, *La Pléiade*. Paris: Gallimard.

Bowman, A.K., R.A. Coles, N. Gonis, D. Obbink, and P.J. Parsons, eds. 2007. *Oxyrhynchus: A City and Its Texts*. London: Egypt Exploration Society.

Britain, D., and J. Cheshire, eds. 2003. *Social Dialectology: In Honour of Peter Trudgill*. Amsterdam: Benjamins.

British Museum. 2013. "Wadi Sarga at the British Museum." https://www.britishmuseum.org/research/research_projects/all_current_projects/wadi_sarga.aspx.

Brown Tkacz, C. 1991. "Commendatio animae." In A.P. Kazhdan, ed., *The Oxford Dictionary of Byzantium*, p. 488. New York and Oxford: Oxford University Press.

Bruggeman, J. 2008. *Social Networks: An Introduction*. London: Routledge.

Bucking, S. 2006. "A Sahidic Coptic Manuscript in the Private Collection of Lloyd E. Cotsen (*P.Cotsen* 1) and the Limits of Papyrological Interpretation." *JCS* 8, pp. 55–78.

———. 2011. *Practice Makes Perfect: P.Cotsen–Princeton 1 and the Training of Scribes in Byzantine Egypt*. Los Angeles, CA: Cotsen Occasional Press.

Budde, A. 2004. *Die ägyptische Basilios-Anaphora, Text—Kommentar—Geschichte*. Jerusalemer Theologisches Forum 7. Münster: Aschendorff Verlag.

Budge, E.A.W. 1907. *The Paradise of the Fathers*, vol. 1. London: Chatto and Windus.

———. 1913. *Coptic Apocrypha in the Dialect of Upper Egypt*. London: British Museum.

———. 1914. *Coptic Martyrdoms etc. in the Dialect of Upper Egypt*. London: British Museum.

Burmester, O.H.E. 1938. "The *Turuhat* of the Saints (Tut Babah, Hatur)." *BSAC* 4, pp. 141–94.

Burmester, O.H.E., and A. Khater, eds. 1970. *History of the Patriarchs of the Egyptian Church, Known as the History of the Holy Church*, vol. 3, part 3. Cairo: Société d'archéologie copte.

Buschhausen, H., and F.M. Khorshid. 1998. "Die Malerei zu Deir al-Genadla." In M. Krause and S. Schaten, eds., *Themelia: Spätantike und koptologische Studien: Peter Grossmann zum 65. Geburtstag*, p. 57. SKCO. Wiesbaden: Dr. Ludwig Reichert Verlag.

Butler, A.J. 1902. *The Arab Conquest of Egypt and the Last Thirty Years of the Roman Dominion*. Oxford: Clarendon Press.

Butler, C. 1898–1904. *The Lausiac History of Palladius*. Vols. 1–2. Texts and Studies 5–6. Cambridge: Cambridge University Press.

Butrus 'Abd al-Malik, B., ed. 1906. *Kitab Mukhtasar al-bayan fi tahqiq al-iman al-mawsum bi-l-Hawi ta'lif al-shaykh al-taqi Jirjis ibn al-'Amid al-mulaqqab b-Ibn al-Makin*. Cairo: n.p.

Calament, F. 1989. "Antinoë: Histoire d'une collection dispersée." *Revue du Louvre* 5–6, pp. 336–42.

———. 2005. *La révélation d'Antinoé par Albert Gayet: Histoire, archéologie, muséographie*. Bibliothèque d'Études Coptes 18.1–2. Cairo: Bibliothèque d'Études Coptes.

———. 2008. "Nouvelles inscriptions à Baouît (campagnes de 2003 et 2004)." In A. Boud'hors and C. Louis, eds., *Études coptes X: Douzième journée d'études, Lyon, 19–21 mai 2005*, pp. 23–38. Paris: de Boccard.

———. In press. "L'apport des nouvelles découvertes épigraphiques à Baouît (2006–2012)." In A. Camplani and P. Buzi, eds., *Acts of the Tenth International Congress of Coptic Studies, Rome, 17–22 September 2012*. Louvain-la-Neuve: Peeters.

Capuani, M., O.F.A. Meinardus, Marie-Hélène Rutschowscaya, and Gawdat Gabra. 1999. *Christian Egypt: Coptic Art and Monuments through Two Millennia*. Cairo: The American University in Cairo Press.

Carter, B.L. 1984. "On Spreading the Gospel to Egyptians Sitting in Darkness: The Political Problem of Missionaries in Egypt in the 1930s." *MES* 20, no. 4, pp. 18–36.

Cat. Florence. 1998. *Antinoe cent'anni dopo*, ed. F. del Francia-Barocas. Exhibition catalogue, Palazzo Medici Riccardi, Florence. Florence: Istituto papirologico G. Vitelli.

Cat. Lyon. 2013. *Antinoé à la vie, à la mode: Visions d'élégance dans les solitudes*, ed. F. Calament and M. Durand. Lyon: Fage éditions.

Chaine, M. 1934. *Les dialectes coptes assioutiques A2: Les charactéristiques de leur phonétique, de leur morphologie, de leur syntaxe*. Paris: Geuthner.

Charles, R.H. 1916. *The Chronicle of John (c. 690 A.D.) Coptic Bishop of Nikiu*. Text and Translation Society series 3. Reprinted Amsterdam: APA–Philo, 1981.

Chassinat, É. 1911. *Fouilles à Baouît*. MIFAO 13. Cairo: IFAO.

Chitty, D.J. 1977. *The Desert a City: An Introduction to the Study of Egyptian and Palestinian Monasticism under the Christian Empire*. Crestwood, NY: St. Vladimir's Seminary Press.

Choat, M. 2007. "The Archive of Apa Johannes: Notes on a Proposed New Edition." In J. Frösén, T. Purola, and E. Salmenkivi, eds., *Proceedings of the 24th International Congress of Papyrology, Helsinki, 1–7 August, 2004*. Commentationes Humanarum Litterarum 122, vol. 1, pp. 175–83. Helsinki: Societas Scientiarum Fennica.

Choat, M., and I. Gardner. 2006. "*P. Lond. Copt.* I 1123: Another Letter to Apa Johannes?" *ZPE* 156, pp. 157–64.

Cipriano, G. 2008. *El-Bagawat: Un cimitero paleocristiano nell'alto Egitto*. Todi: Tau Editrice.

Clackson, S.J. 2000. *Coptic and Greek Texts relating to the Hermopolite Monastery of Apa Apollo*. Oxford: Griffith Institute, Ashmolean Museum.

———. 2008. *It Is Our Father Who Writes: Orders from the Monastery of Apollo at Bawit*. Cincinnati, OH: American Society of Papyrologists.

Clarke, S. 1912. *Christian Antiquities in the Nile Valley: A Contribution towards the Study of the Ancient Churches*. Oxford: Clarendon Press.

Clédat, J. 1902. "Recherches sur le Kôm de Baouît." *Comptes-rendus des séances de l'Académie des Inscriptions et Belles-Lettres* 46, no. 5, pp. 525–46.

———. 1904–1906. *Le monastère et la nécropole de Baouît*. MIFAO 12. Cairo: IFAO.

———. 1916. *Le monastère et la nécropole de Baouît: Saison de fouilles avril–mai 1903*. MIFAO 39. Cairo: IFAO.

———. 1999. *Le monastère et la nécropole de Baouît, notes mises en œuvre et éditées par Dominique Bénazeth et Marie-Hélène Rutschowscaya, avec des contributions de Anne Boud'hors, René-Georges Coquin, Éliane Gaillard*. MIFAO 111. Cairo: IFAO.

Colin, G. 1985. "La profession de foi christologique du 'Talmid.'" In C. Robin, ed., *Mélanges linguistiques offerts à Maxime Rodinson*, pp. 163–65. Paris: P. Geuthner.

———, trans. 2001. *L'homélie sur l'église du Rocher attribuée à Timothée Aelure*. Patrologia Orientalis 49, fascicule 2, no. 218. Rome: Pontifico Istituto Orientale.

———. 2010. "Tälmid." In S. Uhlig and A. Bausi, eds., *Encyclopaedia Aethiopica*, vol. 4, pp. 849–50. Wiesbaden: Harrassowitz.

Collar, A. 2013. *Religious Networks in the Roman Empire: The Spread of New Ideas*. Cambridge, UK: Cambridge University Press.

Combe, Ét., J. Sauvaget, and G. Wiet, eds. 1932. *Répertoire chronologique d'épigraphie arabe*, vol. 3. Cairo: IFAO.

Coquin, R.-G. 1975a. "Le catalogue de la bibliothèque du couvent de Saint-Élie 'du rocher' (ostracon IFAO 13315)." *BIFAO* 75, pp. 207–39.

———. 1975b. *Le livre de la consécration du sanctuaire de Benjamin*. Bibliothèque d'Études Coptes 13. Cairo: IFAO.

———. 1978. "Le Synaxaire des Coptes: Un nouveau témoin de la recension de Haute Égypte." *Analecta Bollandiana* 96, pp. 351–65.

———. 1981. "Saint Constantin, Evêque d'Assyut." *SOCC* 16, pp. 151–70.

———. 1991a. "Dayr Abu Maqrufah and Dayr al-Janadlah." In A.S. Atiya, ed., *The Coptic Encyclopedia*, vol. 3, pp. 705–706. New York: Macmillan.

———. 1991b. "Harmina, Saint." In A.S. Atiya, ed., *The Coptic Encyclopedia*, p. 1209. New York: Macmillan.

———. 1993a. "Un nouveau témoin de la 'lettre (apocryphe) de Jésus à Abgar' (recension copte)." *BIFAO* 93, pp. 173–78.

———. 1993b. "Le panégyrique d'Ammonios." *BSAC* 32, pp. 11–54.

Coquin, R.-G., and M. Martin. 1991a. "Dayr al-Bala'yzah: History." In A.S. Atiya, ed., *The Coptic Encyclopedia*, vol. 3, pp. 786–87. New York: Macmillan.

———. 1991b. "Dayr Durunkah." In A.S. Atiya, ed., *The Coptic Encyclopedia*, vol. 3, pp. 799a–800a. New York: Macmillan.

———. 1991c. "Dayr al-Izam." In A.S. Atiya, ed., *The Coptic Encyclopedia,* vol. 3, p. 809. New York: Macmillan.

———. 1991d. "Dayr al-Muharraqah." In A.S. Atiya, ed., *The Coptic Encyclopedia,* vol. 3, pp. 840–41. New York: Macmillan.

———. 1991e. "Dayr al-Qurqas." In A.S. Atiya, ed., *The Coptic Encyclopedia,* vol 3, pp. 852–53. New York: Macmillan.

———. 1991f. "Shaikh Sa'id, al-." In A.S. Atiya, ed., *The Coptic Encyclopedia,* vol. 7, p. 2130. New York: Macmillan.

———. 1991g. "Wadi Sarjah." In A.S. Atiya, ed., *The Coptic Encyclopedia,* vol. 7, p. 2312. New York: Macmillan.

Coquin, R.-G., M. Martin, and P. Grossmann. 1991a. "Dayr al-'Izam (Asyut)." In A.S. Atiya, ed., *The Coptic Encyclopedia,* vol. 3, pp. 809–10. New York: Macmillan.

———. 1991b. "Dayr al-Jabrawi (Asyut)." In A.S. Atiya, ed., *The Coptic Encyclopedia,* vol. 3, pp. 810–13. New York: Macmillan.

Coudert, M., R. Cortopassi, and F. Médard. 2013. "Textiles." In Y. Lintz and M. Coudert, eds., *Antinoé: Momies, textiles, céramiques et autre antiques: Envois de l'État et dépôts du musée du Louvre de 1901 à nos jours,* pp. 254–377. Paris: Somogy Editions d'Art.

Coudert, M., S. Mérigeaud, P.-L. Thillaud, and L. Dussarps. 2013. "Momies." In Y. Lintz and M. Coudert, eds., *Antinoé: Momies, textiles, céramiques et autre antiques: Envois de l'État et dépôts du musée du Louvre de 1901 à nos jours,* pp. 174–253. Paris: Somogy Editions d'Art.

Cramer, M., and M. Krause. 2008. *Das koptische Antiphonar (M. 575, P. 11967).* Jerusalemer Theologische Forum 12. Münster: Aschendorff.

Crippa, M.A., and M. Zibawi. 1998. *L'art paléochrétien.* Paris: Desclée de Brouwer.

Croft, W. 2003. "Mixed Languages and the Acts of Identity: An Evolutionary Approach." In Y. Matras and P. Bakker, eds., *The Mixed Language Debate: Theoretical and Empirical Advances,* pp. 41–72. Berlin: Mouton de Gruyter.

Cromwell, J. 2013. "A Coptic Epistolary Exercise from Wadi Sarga." *JEA* 99, pp. 272–75.

Crum, W.E. 1902. *Coptic Monuments.* Catalogue général des antiquités égyptiennes du Musée du Caire, nos. 8001–8741. Cairo: Service des antiquités de l'Égypte. Reprinted Osnabrück: Otto Zeller Verlag, 1975.

———. 1905. *Catalogue of the Coptic Manuscripts in the Collection in the British Museum.* London: British Museum.

———. 1907a. "Barsauma the Naked." *Proceedings of the Society of Biblical Archaeology* 29, pp. 135–49, 187–206.

———. 1907b. "The Coptic Manuscripts." In W.M.F. Petrie, *Gizeh and Rifeh*, pp. 39–43 and plates 38–39. British School of Archaeology in Egypt 13. London: School of Archaeology in Egypt.

———. 1909. *Catalogue of the Coptic Manuscripts in the Collection of the John Rylands Library*. Manchester: Manchester University Press.

———. 1921. *Short Texts from Coptic Ostraca and Papyri*. London: Oxford University Press/Humphrey Milford.

———. 1939. *A Coptic Dictionary*. Oxford: Clarendon Press.

———. 1943. "Coptic Anecdota: I. A Gnostic Fragment." *JTS* 44, pp. 176–79.

Crum, W.E., and H.I. Bell. 1922. *Wadi Sarga: Coptic and Greek Texts from the Excavations Undertaken by the Byzantine Research Account*. Coptica 3. Copenhagen: Gyldendalske Boghandel-Nordisk Forlag.

Cruz-Uribe, E. 2004. "Middle Egypt Quarries Project, 2004 Field Season." *Journal of the Society for the Study of Egyptian Antiquities* 31, pp. 1–36.

Dafnâr: Kul Ayyâm al-Sana. 1985. Beni Sweif: Bishopric of Beni Sweif.

Dal Fiore, F. 2007. "Communities versus Networks: The Implications on Innovation and Social Change." *American Behavioral Scientist* 50, pp. 857–66.

Daly, M.W., ed. 2008. *The Cambridge History of Egypt*. Vol. 2, *Modern Egypt: From 1517 to the End of the Twentieth Century*. Cambridge, UK: Cambridge University Press.

D'Amicone, E. 2009. "Assiut e gli scavi del Museo Egizio di Torino." In E. D'Amicone and M. Pozzi Battaglia, eds., *Egitto mai visto: La montagna dei morti: Assiut quattromila anni fa*, pp. 40–61. Trento: Castello del Buonconsiglio. Monumenti e collezioni proviciali.

Daoud, M. 1959. *The Liturgy of the Ethiopian Church*. Revised by B.M. Hazen. Cairo: The Egyptian Book Press.

Daoud, N.K., and A. Fakhry. 2011. *Tarikh al-masyhiyya wa al-rahbana wa atharehema fi ibarshiyat al-Giza*. Cairo: St. Mark Foundation for Coptic History Studies.

Davies, N. de G. 1901. *The Rock Tombs of Sheikh Saïd*. Archaeological Survey of Egypt, 10th Memoir. London: Egypt Exploration Fund.

———. 1902. *The Rock Tombs of Deir al Gebrâwi*. Archaeological Survey of Egypt, 11th–12th Memoirs. London: Egypt Exploration Fund.

———. 1905. *The Rock Tombs of El Amarna. Part II: The Tombs of Panehsy and Meryra II*. Archaeological Survey of Egypt, 14th Memoir. London: Egypt Exploration Fund.

Davis, S. 2004. *The Early Coptic Papacy: The Egyptian Church and Its Leadership in Late Antiquity*. Cairo: The American University in Cairo Press.

Dayr al-Muharraq. 1990. *Gabal Qusqam, Quds-Turath.* Cairo: Dayr al-Muharraq.

———. 1992. *Gabal Qusqam: Quds-Turath.* Asyut: Dayr al-Muharraq.

———. 1999–2001. *al-Mawsu'ah al-lahutiyyah al-shahirah bi-l-Hawi l-Ibn al-Makin.* 4 vols. Cairo: Dayr al-Muharraq.

———. 2002. *I'tirafat al-aba'.* Cairo: Dayr al-Muharraq.

———. 2003. *Mayamir al-qiddis Ighrighuriyus al-natiq bi-l-ilahiyyat.* 2 vols. Cairo: Dayr al-Muharraq.

———. 2012. *The Monastery of the Holy Virgin at al-Muharraq, Assiut.* Special edition for the 6th International Symposium of Christianity and Monasticism at the Monastery of al-Muharraq. Asyut: al-Muharraq Monastery.

Defremery, C., and B.R. Sanguinetti. 1969. *Voyages d'Ibn Battuta,* vol. 1, ed. V. Monteil. Reprint of the 1854 edition. Paris: Éditions Anthropos.

Delattre, A. 2007. *Papyrus coptes et grecs du monastère d'apa Apollô de Baouît conservés aux musées royaux d'art et d'histoire de Bruxelles.* Brussels: Académie royale de Belgique.

———. 2008. "Remarques sur quelques inscriptions du monastère de Baouît." *BIFAO* 108, pp. 69–81.

———. 2010a. "L'administration de Baouît au VIIIe siècle: À propos des documents peneiôt petshai." *Chronique d'Égypte* 85, pp. 391–95.

———. 2010b. "Des linteaux et des noms: Une enquête prosopographique à Baouît." In A. Boud'hors and C. Louis, eds., *Études coptes XI: Treizième journée d'études, Marseille, 7–9 juin 2007,* pp. 25–30. Paris: De Boccard.

———. 2010c. "Une curieuse table d'ombres au monastère de Baouît." *Le Muséon* 123, pp. 273–86.

———. 2012a. *Banque de données des textes coptes documentaires.* Brussels: Université libre de Bruxelles, Centre de papyrologie et d'épigraphie grecque, http://dev.ulb.ac.be/philo/bad/copte/base.php

———. 2012b. "Review of S. Bucking, 'Practice Makes Perfect: P.Cotsen–Princeton 1 and the Training of Scribes in Byzantine Egypt.'" *Chronique d'Égypte* 87, pp. 393–94.

———. In press. "La traduction des institutions administratives dans les monastères égyptiens (VIIe–VIIIe siècles)." In Fr. Colin, O. Huck, and S. Vanseveren, eds., *Interpretatio: La traduction de notions étrangères dans les civilisations de l'Antiquité.* Strasbourg: Université de Strasbourg.

Demaria, S. 2005. "Die griechischen Entlehnungen in den koptischen manichäischen Texten: Methoden und Ergebnisse." In A. Van Tongerloo and L. Cirillo, eds., *Il manicheismo: Nuove prospettive della ricerca: Quinto congresso internazionale di studi sul Manicheismo, atti: Dipartimento di Studi Asiatici, Università degli Studi di Napoli "L'Orientale," Napoli, 2–8 Settembre 2001,* pp. 95–114. Turnhout: Brepols.

De Moor, A., and C. Fluck, eds. 2011. *Dress Accessories of the First Millennium AD from Egypt*. Proceedings of the 6th Conference of the Research Group "Textiles from the Nile Valley," Antwerp, 2–3 October 2009. Tielt: Lannoo.

den Heijer, J. 1989. *Mawhub ibn Mansur ibn Mufarrig et l'historiographie Copto-Arabe*. CSCO 513. Louvain: Peeters.

———. 1994. "Apologetic Elements in Coptic–Arabic Historiography: The Life of Abraham ibn Zur'ah, 62nd Patriarch of Alexandria." In S.K. Samir and J.S. Nielsen, eds., *Christian Arabic Apologetics during the Abbasid Period (750–1258)*, pp. 192–202. Leiden: E.J. Brill.

De Nie, H. 1941. "Een Koptisch-christelijke orakelvraag." *Jaarbericht Ex Oriente Lux* 8, pp. 615–18.

Derda, T., and E. Wipszycka. 1994. "L'emploi des titres *apa* et *papas* dans l'Égypte byzantine." *JJP* 24, pp. 23–56.

Description de l'Égypte ou Recueil des observations et des recherches qui ont été faites en Égypte pendant l'expédition de l'armée française. 1822. 2nd ed., vol. 4. Paris: Imprimerie de C.L.F. Panckoucke.

Description de l'Égypte ou Recueil des observations et des recherches qui ont été faites en Égypte pendant l'expédition de l'armée française. 1826. 2nd ed., vol. 18. Paris: Imprimerie de C.L.F. Panckoucke.

de Vogüé, A. 1996. *Histoire littéraire du mouvement monastique dans l'antiquité*, vol. 1, part 3. Paris: Éditions du Cerf.

Devos, P. 1965. "Une passion grecque inédite de S. Pierre d'Alexandrie et sa traduction par Anastase le Bibliothécaire." *Analecta Bollandiana* 83, pp. 157–87.

———. 1969a. "Fragments Coptes de l'*Historia Monachorum in Aegypto*: S. Jean de Lyco et la Tentatrice." *Analecta Bollandiana* 87, pp. 417–41.

———. 1969b. "La 'servante de Dieu.' Poemenia d'après Pallade, la tradition Copte et Jean Rufus." In *Analecta Bollandiana* 87, pp. 189–212.

———. 1970. "Feuillets coptes nouveaux et anciens . . ." *Analecta Bollandiana* 88, pp. 153–87.

———. 1976. "S. Jean de Lycopolis et l'empereur Marcien." *Analecta Bollandiana* 94, pp. 303–16.

———. 1991. "John of Lycopolis, Saint." In A.S. Atiya, ed., *The Coptic Encyclopedia*, vol. 5, pp. 1363b–1366a. New York: Macmillan.

———. 1995. "De Saint Jean de Lycopolos aux règlements de vie chrétienne." *Christianismes d'Égypte*. Paris and Louvain: Peeters.

Dîb, P. 1910. "Deux discours de Cyriaque, évêque de Behnésâ, sur la fuite en Egypte." *Revue de l'Orient Chrétien* 15, pp. 157–61.

Dick, I., ed. n.d. *Théodore Abuqurra: Traité de l'existence du Créateur et de la vraie religion.* Jounieh, Lebanon: Patrimoine Arabe Chrétien.

Dodson, A. 1991. *Egyptian Rock Cut Tombs.* Shire Egyptology, 14. Princes Risborough: Shire.

Donadoni, S., A. Spallanzani Zimmermann, and L. Bongrani Fanfoni. 1974. *Antinoe 1965–1968: Missione archeologica in Egitto dell'Università di Roma.* Rome: University of Rome.

Doresse, J. 2000. *Les anciens monastères coptes de Moyenne-Égypte (du Gebel-et-Teir à Kôm-Ishgaou) d'après l'archéologie et l'hagiographie.* Vols. 1–3 = Neges Ebrix 4, 5, 6. Yverdon-les-Bains: Institut d'archéologie yverdonnoise.

Dorigo, W. 1971. *Late Roman Painting.* London: J.M. Dent & Sons Limited.

Drescher, J. 1942. "Apa Claudius and the Thieves." *BSAC* 8, pp. 63–87.

Edwards, V., and Th. J. Sienkewicz, eds. 1990. *Oral Cultures Past and Present: Rappin' and Homer.* Oxford: Blackwell.

Eichner, I., and Th. Beckh. 2010. "The Late Antique and Medieval Monuments of the Gebel Asyut al-Gharbi." *SAK* 39, pp. 207–10.

Elanskaya, A.I. 1969. *The Coptic Manuscripts of the State Public Library M.E. Saltykov-Shchedrin.* Palestinskij Sbornik 20 (83). Leningrad: Nauka (in Russian).

Elm, S. 1994. *"Virgins of God": The Making of Asceticism in Late Antiquity.* Oxford: Clarendon Press.

Emmel, S. 2004. *Shenoute's Literary Corpus.* 2 vols. Louvain: Peeters.

———. 2008. "The Coptic Gnostic Texts as Witnesses to the Production and Transmission of Gnostic (and Other) Traditions." In J. Frey, E.E. Popkes, and J. Schröter, eds., *Das Thomasevangelium: Entstehung—Rezeption—Theologie*, pp. 33–39 [with bibliography on pp. 461–503]. Berlin: Walter de Gruyter.

Emmenegger, G. 2007. *Der Text des koptischen Psalters aus al-Mudil: Ein Beitrag zur Textgeschichte der Septuaginta und zur Textkritik koptischer Bibelhandschriften, mit der kritischen Neuausgabe des Papyrus 37 der British Library London (U) und des Papyrus 39 der Leipziger Universitätsbibliothek (2013).* Texte und Untersuchungen zur Geschichte der altchristlichen Literatur 159. Berlin: De Gruyter.

Emmett, A.M. 1984. "An Early Fourth-century Female Monastic Community in Egypt?" In A. Moffatt, ed., *Maistor: Classical, Byzantine and Renaissance Studies for Robert Browning.* Byzantina Australiensia 5, pp. 77–83. Canberra: Australian Association for Byzantine Studies.

Epp, E.J. 2005. "Coptic Manuscript G67 and the Role of Codex Bezae as a Western Witness." In E.J. Epp, ed., *Perspectives on the New Testament Textual Criticism: Collected Essays 1962–2004.* NT–Suppl. 116, pp. 15–39. Leiden: Brill.

———. 2006. "The Jews and the Jewish Community in Oxyrhynchus: Socio-Religious Context for the New Testament Papyri." In T.J. Kraus and T. Nicklas, eds., *New Testament Manuscripts: Their Texts and Their World.* Texts and Editions for New Testament Study 2, pp. 13–52. Leiden: Brill.

Evelyn-White, H.G. 1933. *The Monasteries of Wadi 'n Natrun.* The Metropolitan Museum of Art Egyptian Expedition, part 3. New York: The Metropolitan Museum of Art. Reprinted by Arno Press, 1973.

Evetts, B.T.A. 1904. *History of the Patriarchs of the Coptic Church of Alexandria,* vol. 2, *Peter I to Benjamin I (661).* Patrologia Orientalis 1, fasc. 4. Paris: Firmin-Didot.

Evetts, B.T.A., and A.J. Butler, eds. and trans. 1895. *Churches and Monasteries of Egypt and Some Neighbouring Countries, Attributed to Abu Salih, the Armenian.* Oxford: Clarendon Press.

———. 1969. (Original date of publication 1895.) *The Churches and Monasteries of Egypt and Some Neighbouring Countries, Attributed to Abu Salih, the Armenian.* London: Butler and Tanner.

Fahmy, A.M. 1966. *Muslim Sea-power in the Eastern Mediterranean: From the Seventh to the Tenth Century* AD. Cairo: National Publication & Printing House.

Faltas, J.M. 2010. "Mas'alat 'al-tajdif 'ala l-Ruh al-Qudus' fi l-turath al-masihi li-l-aqbat." *Dirasat Aba'iya wa-Lahutiya* 13, no. 26, pp. 20–31.

———. 2011. "'Wahdat al-Ab wa-l-Ibn wa-wahdatuna nahnu' hasab tafsir' al-qiddis Kirillus 'amud al-din wa-Jirjis ibn al-Makin (q. 13)." *Dirasat Aba'iya wa-Lahutiya* 14, no. 28, pp. 43–54.

———. 2012–13. "Tafsir mathal al-Ibn al-Shatir l-Ibn al-Makin." *Mawdu'at Ruhiya Aba'iya wa-Lahutiy* 15, no. 30, pp. 55–68; 16, no. 31, pp. 47–54.

Fayd Allah, U. 1940. *Madinat Asyut: bahth fi bi'atiha bayn al-madi wa-l-hadir.* Cairo: al-Hay'a al-'Amma li-Qusur al-Thaqafa.

Ferrua, A. 1960. *Le pitture della nuova catacomba di via Latina.* Città del Vaticano: Pontificio Istituto di Archeologia Cristiana.

———. 1991. *The Unknown Catacomb: A Unique Discovery of Early Christian Art.* New Lanark: Geddes & Grosset.

Festugière, A.-J. 1961. *Historia monachorum in Aegypto: Édition critique du texte grec.* Subsidia Hagiographica 34. Brussels: Société des Bollandistes.

———, trans. 1964. *Les moines d'Orient,* vol. 4.1, *Enquête sur les moines d'Égypte (Historia Monachorum in Aegypto).* Paris: Les Éditions du Cerf.

———. 1971. *A History of the Monks in Egypt.* Brussels: Société des Bollandistes.

Filotheus al-Macari. 1913. *Kitab al-absaliyat wal-Turuhat Watos wa-l-Adam.* Cairo: Saint Macarius Press.

Fleisch, H. 1935–36. "Une homélie de Théophile d'Alexandrie en l'honneur de St Pierre et de St Paul: Texte arabe publié pour la première fois et traduit." *Revue de l'Orient Chrétien* 30, pp. 371–419.

Fluck, C. 2000. "Die Textilien von Carl Schmidt." In C. Fluck, P. Linscheid, and S. Merz, *Textilien aus Ägypten: Staatliche Museen zu Berlin—Preußischer Kulturbesitz, Skulpturensammlung und Museum für Byzantinische Kunst Bestandskataloge*, vol. 1, pp. 175–97. Wiesbaden: Dr. Ludwig Reichert Verlag.

———. 2004. "Zwei Reitermäntel aus Antinoopolis im Museum für Byzantinische Kunst, Berlin." In C. Fluck and G.M. Vogelsang-Eastwood, eds., *Riding Costume in Egypt: Origin and Appearance*, pp. 137–52. Studies in Textile and Costume History 3. Leiden: Brill.

———. 2010. "Kinderkleidung im römischen und spätantiken Ägypten: Ein Projekt der DressID Studien Gruppe C: 'Gender and Age.'" In *Mitteilungen der Anthropologischen Gesellschaft in Wien* 140, pp. 177–87.

———. 2013. "Textiles from Antinoupolis: Recent Finds from the So-called Peristyle Complex in the Northern Necropolis." In *Itinerari mediterranei fra IV e IX secolo.* Torino: Accademia University Press.

Fluck, C., and H. Froschauer. 2011. "Dress Accessories from Antinoupolis: Finds from the Northern Necropolis." In A. De Moor and C. Fluck, eds., *Dress Accessories of the First Millennium AD from Egypt: Proceedings of the 6th Conference of the Research Group 'Textiles from the Nile Valley,' Antwerp, 2–3 October 2009*, pp. 54–69. Tielt: Lannoo.

Fluck, C., and G.M. Vogelsang-Eastwood, eds. 2004. *Riding Costume in Egypt: Origin and Appearance.* Studies in Textile and Costume History 3. Leiden: Brill.

Forget, I. 1963. *Synaxarium Alexandrium.* CSCO 47, 48, 49, Arabici 3, 4, 5. Louvain: Peeters.

Förster, H. 2001. "'Heilung meiner Leiden': Edition von Papiro Vaticano Copto Doresse 7." *Analecta Papyrologica* 13, pp. 63–67.

———. 2002. *Wörterbuch der griechischen Wörter in den koptischen dokumentarischen Texten.* Berlin and New York: W. De Gruyter.

Fournet, J.-L. 2009. "The Multilingual Environment of Late Antique Egypt: Greek, Latin, Coptic and Persian Documentation." In R.S. Bagnall, ed., *The Oxford Handbook of Papyrology*, pp. 418–51. Oxford: Oxford University Press.

Frend, W.H.C. 1982. "Nationalism as a Factor in Anti-Chalcedonian Feeling in Egypt." In S. Mews, ed., *Religion and National Identity: Papers Read at the Nineteenth Summer Meeting and the Twentieth Winter Meeting of the Ecclesiastical History Society*, pp. 21–38. Studies in Church History 18. Oxford: Blackwell.

Funk, W.-P. 1980. "Eine frühkoptische Ausgleichsorthographie für Unter- und Mittelägypten?" *Bulletin de la Société d'Égyptologie Genève* 4, pp. 33–38.

———. 1981. "Beiträge des mittelägyptischen Dialekts zum koptischen Konjugationssystem." In D.W. Young, ed., *Studies Presented to Hans Jakob Polotsky (Bacon Hill, East Gloucester, Massachussetts 1981)*, pp. 177–210. Bacon Hill, East Gloucester, MA: Pirtle and Polson Publishers.

———. 1985. "How Closely Related are the Subachmimic Dialects?" *ZÄSA* 112, pp. 124–39.

———. 1993. *Concordance to Short Texts and Fragments in the Middle Egyptian Dialect of Coptic*. Quebec: private distribution.

Funk, W.-P., and R. Smith. 1990. "John 10:7–13:38 in Subachmimic." In W. Brashear, W.-F. Funk, J.M. Robinson, and R. Smith, eds., *The Chester Beatty Codex AC. 1390: Mathematical School Exercises in Greek and John 10:7–13:38 in Subachmimic,* pp. 57–123. Louvain: Peeters.

Gabra, G. 1990. "Zur vita des Bane (Abu Fana), eines Heiligen des 4./5. Jahrhunderts." *BSAC* 29, pp. 27–42.

———, ed. 2001. *Be Thou There: The Holy Family's Journey in Egypt*. Cairo: The American University in Cairo Press.

———. 2002. "Perspectives on the Monastery of St. Antony: Medieval and Later Inhabitants and Visitors." In E. Bolman, ed., *Monastic Visions: Wall Paintings in the Monastery of St. Antony at the Red Sea*, pp. 173–83. New Haven, CT: Yale University Press.

———. 2006. *The Treasures of Coptic Art in the Coptic Museum and Churches of Old Cairo.* Cairo: The American University in Cairo Press.

———. 2008. *Historical Dictionary of the Coptic Church*, with contributions by B.A. Pearson, M.N. Swanson, and Y.N. Youssef. Cairo: The American University in Cairo Press.

———, ed. Forthcoming. *Tarikh al-masihiya wa-l-rahbana fi Asyut.* Cairo: St. Mark Foundation for Coptic History Studies.

Gabra, G., G. van Loon, and S. Sonbol. 2012. *The Churches of Egypt: From the Journey of the Holy Family to the Present Day.* Los Angeles and Cairo: Ludwig Publishing/The American University in Cairo Press.

Galal, A. 1986. "The Continuity of the Ancient Egyptian Style in the Coptic Architecture and Art." PhD diss., Cairo University.

Gardner, I., ed. 1996–2007. *Kellis Literary Texts*, parts 1–2. Oxford: Oxbow.

Gardner, I., A. Alcock, and W.-P. Funk, eds., 1999. *Coptic Documentary Texts from Kellis*, part 1. Oxford: Oxbow.

Garitte, G. 1943. "Panégyrique de saint Antoine par Jean, évêque d'Hermopolis." *Orientalia Christiana Periodica* 9, pp. 100–34, 330–65.

———. 1950. "Constantin, évêque d'Assiout." In *Coptic Studies in Honor of Walter Ewing Crum*, pp. 287–304. Boston: The Byzantine Institute.

Gauthier, H. 1925. *Dictionnaire des noms géographiques contenus dans les textes hiéroglyphiques*. Cairo: Société royale de géographie d'Égypte.

Gee, J.P. 1996. *Social Linguistics and Literacies: Ideology in Discourses*. 2nd ed. London: Taylor and Francis.

Geoltrain, P., and J.D. Kaestli, eds. 2005. *Ecrits apocryphes chrétiens*, vol. 2, *La Pléiade*. Paris: Gallimard.

Ghali, M.B. 1991. "Coptic Press." In A.S. Atiya, ed., *The Coptic Encyclopedia*, vol. 6, pp. 2010–13. New York: Macmillan.

Giamberardini, G. 1969. *Saint Joseph dans la tradition copte*. Cahiers de Joséphologie 17. Montréal: Centre de Recherche et de Documentation.

———. 1974. *Il culto mariano in Egitto*, vol. 2, sec. 7–10. Pubblicazioni dello studium biblicum franciscanum, Analecta 7. Jerusalem: Studium Biblicum Franciscanum.

———. 1975. *Il culto mariano in Egitto*, vol. 1, sec. 1–6, 2nd ed. Pubblicazioni dello studium biblicum franciscanum, Analecta 6. Jerusalem: Studium Biblicum Franciscanum.

Giorda, M. 2011. "Does the Cowl Make the Monk? A Monastic Accessory during the First Centuries of Egyptian Monasticism." In A. De Moor and C. Fluck, eds., *Dress Accessories of the First Millennium* AD *from Egypt: Proceedings of the 6th Conference of the Research Group 'Textiles from the Nile Valley,' Antwerp, 2–3 October 2009*, pp. 182–87. Tielt: Lannoo.

Girgis, G.D. 1988. "Abba Benjamin: The Coptic Patriarch in the 7th Century." In P.O. Scholz, ed., *Nubia et Oriens Christianus: Festschrift für C. Detlef G. Müller zum 60 Geburtstag* (=*Bibliotheca Nubica* 1), pp. 17–27. Cologne: Verlag Jürgen Dinter.

Girgis, M. 2002. "The Financial Resources of Coptic Priests in Nineteenth-century Egypt." In N. Hanna, ed., *Money, Land and Trade: An Economic History of the Muslim Mediterranean*, pp. 223–42. London and New York: I.B. Tauris.

Godron, G. 1970. *Textes coptes relatifs à saint Claude d'Antioche*. Patrologia Orientalis 35, vol. 4, no. 166. Turnhout: Brepols.

Goehring, J.E. 2006. "Remembering Abraham of Farshut: History, Hagiography, and the Fate of the Pachomian Tradition." *Journal of Early Christian Studies* 14, pp. 1–26.

———. 2007. "Monasticism in Byzantine Egypt: Continuity and Memory." In R.S. Bagnall, ed., *Egypt in the Byzantine World, 300–700*, pp. 390–407. Cambridge, UK: Cambridge University Press.

———. 2012. *Politics, Monasticism, and Miracles in Sixth Century Upper Egypt: A Critical Edition and Translation of the Coptic Texts on Abraham of Farshut*. Studien und Texte zu Antike und Christentum 69. Tübingen: Mohr Siebeck.

Gonis, N. 2008. "Further Letters from the Archive of Apa Ioannes." *BASP* 45, pp. 69–85.

Goody, J. 1968. "Introduction." In J. Goody, ed., *Literacy in Traditional Societies*, pp. 1–26. Cambridge, UK: Cambridge University Press.

Graf, G. 1937. "Zwei dogmatische Florilegien der Kopten. B. Das Bekenntnis der Väter." *Orientalia Christiana Periodica* 3, pp. 345–402.

———. 1939. *Catalogue de Manuscrits Arabes Chrétiens conservés au Caire*. Studi e Testi 63. Vatican City: Biblioteca Apostolica Vaticana.

———. 1944–53. *Geschichte der christlichen arabischen Literatur*. 5 vols. Vatican City: Biblioteca Apostolica Vaticana.

Grand'Henry, J. 1981. "Les discours de Saint Grégoire de Nazianze dans le manuscript arabe du Sinaï 274." *Le Muséon* 94, pp. 153–76.

Grenfell, B.P., and A.S. Hunt. 1898. *The Oxyrhynchus Papyri*, vol. 1. Graeco-Roman Memoirs. London: Egypt Exploration Society.

Griffel, F. 2003. "Moderation." In J.D. McAuliffe, ed., *Encyclopaedia of the Qur'an*, vol. 3, pp. 401–403. Leiden: Brill.

Griffith, F.L. 1907. *Archeological Report, 1906–1907: Comprising the Work of the Egypt Exploration Fund and the Progress of Egyptology during the Year 1906–1907*. London: Egypt Exploration Fund.

Griffith, S.H. 1979. "Comparative Religion in the Apologetics of the First Christian Arabic Theologians." *Proceedings of the PMR Conference* 4, pp. 63–87. Reprinted in Griffith 2002, Essay I.

———. 1994. "Faith and Reason in Christian Kalam: Theodore Abu Qurrah on Discerning the True Religion." In S.K. Samir and J.S. Nielsen, eds., *Christian Arabic Apologetics during the Abbasid Period (750–1258)*, pp. 1–43. Leiden: E.J. Brill.

———. 2002. *The Beginnings of Christian Theology in Arabic: Muslim–Christian Encounters in the Early Islamic Period*. Aldershot, Hampshire and Burlington VT: Ashgate Variorum.

Grossmann, P. 1986. "Die Unterkunftsbauten des Koinobitenklosters 'Dair al-Balāyza' im Vergleich mit den Eremitagen der Mönche von Kellia." In P. Bridel, ed., *Le site monastique copte des Kellia: Sources historiques et explorations archéologiques: Actes du Colloque Genève 13 au 15 août 1984*, pp. 33–39. Geneva: Mission suisse d'archéologie copte de l'Université de Genève.

———. 1991a. "Dayr al-Bala'yzah: Architecture." In A.S. Atiya, ed., *The Coptic Encyclopedia*, vol. 3, p. 787. New York: Macmillan.

———. 1991b. "Spätantike Baudenkmäler im Gebiet von Dair al-Ğabrawî." *Tesserae: Festschrift Josef Engemann. JAC*, Supplement 18, pp. 170–80. Münster: Aschendorffsche Verlagsbuchhandlung.

———. 1993. "Ruinen des Klosters Dair al-Balaiza in Oberägypten: Eine Surveyaufnahme." *JAC* 36, pp. 171–205.

———. 2002. *Christliche Architektur in Ägypten*. Handbook of Oriental Studies, Section 1: The Near and Middle East 62. Leiden, Boston, and Cologne: Brill.

———. 2008. "Antinoopolis—Der Komplex des 'Peristylbaus.'" In G. Bastianini and R. Pintaudi, eds., *Antinoupolis I. Scavi e materiali*, pp. 41–44. Florence: Istituto papirologico G. Vitelli.

Guirguis, F.M. 2010. *The Vision of Theophilus: Resistance through Orality among the Persecuted Copts*. Boca Raton, FL: Florida Atlantic University.

Guy, J.-Cl. 1974. "Jean de Lycopolis." In *Dictionnaire de spiritualité ascétique et mystique*, 8, pp. 619–20. Paris: Beauchesne.

Haddad, G.A. 1970. "A Project for the Independence of Egypt, 1801." *Journal of the American Oriental Society* 90, no. 2, pp. 169–83.

Hadji-Minaglou, G. 2008. "Baouît." In L. Pantalacci and S. Denoix, "Travaux de l'Institut français d'archéologie orientale en 2007–2008." *BIFAO* 108, pp. 407–11.

———. 2009. "Baouît." In L. Pantalacci and S. Denoix, "Travaux de l'Institut français d'archéologie orientale en 2008–2009." *BIFAO* 109, pp. 560–64.

———. 2010. "Baouît." In B. Midant-Reynes and S. Denoix, "Travaux de l'Institut français d'archéologie orientale en 2007–2008." *BIFAO* 110, pp. 370–73.

———. 2012. "Baouît." In *Rapport d'activité 2011–2012: Institut français d'archéologie orientale*, pp. 132–37. Cairo: IFAO.

———. In press a. "Découvertes récentes à Baouît." In A. Camplani and P. Buzi, eds., *Acts of the Tenth International Congress of Coptic Studies, Rome, 17–22 September 2012*. Louvain-la-Neuve: Peeters.

———. In press b. "L'église principale de Baouît: États des lieux à l'issue de la campagne de fouilles 2013." In N. Bosson and A. Boud'hors, eds., *Études coptes XIV: Seizième journée d'études coptes, Geneva, 19–24 June 2013*. Paris: De Boccard.

Hamed, R.A. 1991. "Muhammad 'Ali Dynasty." In A.S. Atiya, ed., *The Coptic Encyclopedia*, vol. 6, pp. 1691–95. New York: Macmillan.

Hamilton, A. 2006. *The Copts and the West, 1439–1822: The European Discovery of the Egyptian Church*. Oxford: Warburg Studies.

Hamilton, W. 1809. *Remarks on Several Parts of Turkey. Part I: Ægyptiaca, or some account on the ancient and modern state of Egypt as obtained in the years 1801, 1802*. London: T. Payne.

Hardy, E.R. 1952. *Christian Egypt: Church and People—Christianity and Nationalism in the Patriarchate of Alexandria*. New York: Oxford University Press.

Harrell, J.A. 2012. "Building Stones." In W. Wendrich, ed., *UCLA Encyclopedia of Egyptology*. Los Angeles: UCLA. http://digital2.library.ucla.edu/viewItem.do?ark=21198/zz002c10gb

Harrell, J.A., and P. Storemyr. 2009. "Ancient Egyptian Quarries: An Illustrated Overview." In N. Abu-Jaber, E.G. Bloxam, P. Degryse, and T. Heldal, eds., *QuarryScapes: Ancient Stone Quarry Landscapes in the Eastern Mediterranean*. Geological Survey of Norway, Special Publication, 12, pp. 7–50.

Hasitzka, M.R.M. 1993. *Koptisches Sammelbuch* I. Mitteilungen aus der Papyrussammlung der Österreichischen Nationalbibliothek, n.s. vol. 23. Vienna: Hollinek.

Haslam, M.W. 1976. "P.Oxy. 3203." In A.K. Bowman, M.W. Haslam, J.C. Shelton, and J.D. Thomas, eds., *The Oxyrhynchus Papyri XLIV. Nos. 3151–208*. Graeco-Roman Memoirs 62. London: Egypt Exploration Society.

Heffernan, T.J. 1988. *Sacred Biography: Saints and Their Biographers in the Middle Ages*. New York: Oxford University Press.

Heikal, Mohamed. 1984. *Autumn of Fury: The Assassination of Sadat*. London: Corgi Books.

Henein, N.H. 1988. *Mari Girgis: Village de Haute-Egypte*. Cairo: IFAO.

Hermann, A. 1962. "Ägyptologische Marginalien zur spätantiken Ikonographie." In *JAC* 5, pp. 60–92.

Hernández-Campoy, J.M., and J.C. Conde-Silvestre, eds. 2012. *The Handbook of Historical Sociolinguistics*. Chichester: Wiley-Blackwell.

Hogendorn, J. 1999. "The Hideous Trade: Economic Aspects of the 'Manufacture' and Sale of Eunuchs." *Paideuma* 45, pp. 137–60.

Horn, J. 1988. "Untersuchungen zu Frömmigkeit und Literatur des christlichen Ägypten: Das Martyrium des Viktor, Sohnes des Romanos (Einleitung in das koptische Literaturwerk/Kommentar zum 'Ersten Martyrium')." PhD diss., Georg-August-Universität Göttingen.

———. 1992. *Studien zu den Märtyrern des nördlichen Oberägypten* II. *Märtyrer und Heilige des XI. bis XIV. oberägyptischen Gaues. Ein Beitrag zur Topographia christiana Ägyptens*. Göttinger Orientforschungen, series 4, vol. 15. Wiesbaden: Harrassowitz.

Hornberger, N.H. 2003. "Introduction." In N.H. Hornberger, ed., *Continua of Biliteracy: An Ecological Framework for Educational Policy, Research, and Practice in Multilingual Settings*, pp. i–xxix. Clevedon: Multilingual Matters.

Howell, B.P. 1960. *Lady on a Donkey*. New York: E.P. Dutton & Company, Inc.

Hunter, F.R. 2004. "Tourism and Empire: The Thomas Cook & Son Enterprise on the Nile, 1868–1914." *MES* 40, no. 5, pp. 28–54.

Husselman, E.M. 1951. "Some Coptic Documents Dealing with the Poll-tax." *Aegyptus* 31, pp. 332–38.

Hyvernat, M. 1886. *Les Actes des Martyrs de l'Egypte tirés des manuscrits coptes de la Bibliothèque Vaticane et du Musée Borgia: Texte copte et traduction française avec introduction et commentaires*, vol. 1. Paris: Ernest Leroux.

———. 1888. *Album de paléographie copte pour servir à l'introduction paléographique des Actes des martyrs de l'Égypte*. Paris: Leroux.

———. 1977. *Les Actes des Martyrs de l'Égypte*, 4 parts in 1 vol. Hildesheim and New York: Georg Olms.

Ibn al-Ji'an. 1898. *al-Tuhfa al-suniya bi-'asma' al-bilad al-misriya*. Cairo: Imprimerie nationale.

Ibn Duqmaq. 1893. *Kitab al-Intisar liwasitat 'aqd al-amsar*, vol. 5. Cairo: Imprimerie nationale.

Ibn Hawqal. 1938. *Kitab surat al-ard (Configuration de la terre/Opus Geographicum)*, vol. 2. Leiden: Brill.

———. 1965. *Kitab surat al-ard (Configuration de la terre/Opus Geographicum)*, vol. 1, 2nd ed., ed. J.H. Kramers and G. Wiet. Leiden: Brill.

Ibn Khirdadhabah. 1955. *Kitab al-Masalik wa-l-mamalik*. Leiden: Brill.

Ibn Mammati. 1943. *Kitab qawanin al-dawawin*, ed. A.S. Atiya. Cairo: Royal Agricultural Society.

Innemée, K., and L. Van Rompay. 2002. "Deir al-Surian (Egypt): New Discoveries of 2001–2002." *Hugoye, Journal of Syriac Studies* 5, no. 2, pp. 245–63.

Innemée, K., L. Van Rompay, and E. Sobczynski. 1999. "Deir al-Surian (Egypt): Its Wall-paintings, Wall-texts and Manuscripts." *Hugoye, Journal of Syriac Studies* 2, no. 2, pp. 167–207.

Irwin, R. 1986. *The Middle East in the Middle Ages: The Early Mamluk Sultanate 1250–1382*. London: Croom Helm.

Isambert, É. 1881. *Itinéraire de l'Orient*, vol. 2, *Égypte*. Paris: Librairie de L. Hachette et Cie.

Iskandar, M.M. 1999. *al-Massih fi Misr*. Cairo: Trikromi.

———, ed. 2003. *Mawsu'at 'Ulum al-din li-l-'alamah al-qibti Ibn al-Makin (1205–1273): al-arba'atu ajza' fi mujallad wahid*. Cairo: Maktabat al-Mahabbah.

Ismail, S. 2000. "The Popular Movement Dimensions of Contemporary Militant Islamism: Socio-spatial Determinants in the Cairo Urban Setting." *Comparative Studies in Society and History* 42, no. 2, pp. 363–93.

Issawi, B., M. el Hinnawi, and A. Mazhar. 1999. *The Phanerozoic Geology of Egypt: A Geodynamic Approach*. The Egyptian Geological Survey, Special Publication 76. Cairo: Egyptian Geological Survey.

Jacotin, M. 1876. *Atlas géographique*. Paris: C.L.F. Panckoucke.

Johanson, L. 2013. "Written Language Intertwining." In P. Bakker and Y. Matras, eds., *Contact Languages: A Comprehensive Guide*, pp. 273–331. Boston: De Gruyter Mouton.

John of Nikiou. 1916. *The Chronicle of John, Bishop of Nikiou*, trans. R.H. Charles. London and Oxford: Williams and Norgate.

Johnson, D. 1980. *Panegyric on Macarius Bishop of Tkôw Attributed to Dioscorus of Alexandria*. CSCO 415–16, Scriptores Coptici 41–42. Louvain: Secrétariat du CSCO.

Jones, M. 1991. "The Earliest Christian Sites at Tell el-Amarna and Sheikh Said." *JEA* 77, pp. 129–44.

Jullien, M. 1901. "Travers les Ruines de la Haute Egypte à la Recherche de la Grotte de l'Abbé Jean." *Etudes* 88, pp. 205–17.

Kadushin, C. 2012. *Understanding Social Networks: Theories, Concepts, and Findings*. Oxford: Oxford University Press.

Kahl, J. 1999. *Siut-Theben: Zur Wertschätzung von Traditionen im alten Ägypten*. Leiden, Boston, and Cologne: Brill.

———. 2007a. *Ancient Asyut: The First Synthesis after 300 Years of Research*. The Asyut Project, vol. 1. Wiesbaden: Harrassowitz.

———. 2007b. "Corridor Connecting Tomb III and IV." *SAK* 36, pp. 82–83.

———. 2012. "Regionale Milieus und die Macht des Staates im Alten Ägypten: Die Vergöttlichung der Gaufürsten von Assiut." *SAK* 41, pp. 163–88.

———. 2013. *Die Zeit selbst lag nun tod darnieder: Die Stadt Assiut und ihre Nekropolen nach westlichen Reiseberichten des 17. bis 19. Jahrhunderts: Konstruktion, Destruktion und Rekonstruktion*. The Asyut Project, vol. 5. Wiesbaden: Harrassowitz.

Kahl, J., M. El-Khadragy, and U. Verhoeven. 2006. "The Asyut Project: Third Season of Fieldwork." *SAK* 34, pp. 241–49.

Kahl, J., and J. Malur. 2011. "Tomb V (M11.1)." *SAK* 40, pp. 182–83.

Kahle, P.E. 1954. *Bala'izah: Coptic Texts from Deir el-Bala'izah in Upper Egypt*. 2 vols. London: Oxford University Press for the Griffith Institute, Ashmolean Museum, Oxford.

Kamal, A. 1916. "Fouilles à Deir Dronka et à Assiut." *ASAE* 16, pp. 64–66.

Kamil, J. 2002. *Christianity in the Land of the Pharaohs: The Coptic Orthodox Church*. London and New York: Routledge.

Kanawati, N. 2005–13. *Deir el-Gebrawi*. Vols. 1–3. The Australian Centre for Egyptology, Reports 23, 25, and 32. Oxford: Aris and Phillips.

Kasher, A. 1981. "The Jewish Community of Oxyrhynchus in the Roman Period." *JJS* 32, pp. 151–57.

Kasser, R. 1981. "'Djinkim' ou 'surligne' dans les textes en dialecte copte moyen-égyptien." *BSAC* 23, pp. 115–57.

———. 1987. "Subdialects en mésokémique?" In Sebastià Janéras, ed., *Miscellània papirològica Ramon Roca-Puig en el seu vuitantè aniversari*, pp. 159–70. Barcelona: Fundació Salvador Vives Casajuana.

———. 1990. "A Standard System of Sigla for Referring to the Dialects of Coptic." *JCS* 1, pp. 141–51.

———. 1991. "Vocabulary, Copto-Greek, Autochthonous Coptic." In A.S. Atiya and W.Y. Adams, eds., *The Coptic Encyclopedia*, vol. 8, pp. 215–22. New York: Macmillan. http://ccdl.libraries.claremont.edu/cdm/singleitem/collection/cce/id/2033/rec/2

———. 1992–93. "Le dialecte copte *V*, fayoumique sans lambdacisme, illustré par quelques extraits de son témoin principal, le P. Mich. Inv. 3520." *Enchoria* 19/20, pp. 87–124.

———. 2004. "Protodialectes coptes à systèmes alphabétiques de type vieux-copte." *ICCoptS* 7 *Leiden 2000*, pp. 77–123. Louvain: Peeters.

———. 2006. "Kat'Aspe Aspe: Constellations d'idiomes coptes plus ou moins bien connus et scientifiquement reçus, aperçus, pressentis, enregistrés en une terminologie jugée utile, scintillant dans le firmament égyptien à l'aube de notre troisième millénaire." In L. Painchaud and P.-H. Poirier, eds., *Coptica—Gnostica—Manichaica: Mélanges offerts à Wolf-Peter Funk*. BCNH, Section "Études" 7, pp. 389–492. Quebec: Les Presses de l'Université Laval Québec; Louvain and Paris: Editions Peeters.

Katos, D.S. 2011. *Palladius of Helenopolis: The Origenist Advocate*. Oxford: Oxford University Press.

Kemp, B. 2005. "Settlement and Landscape in the Amarna Area in the Late Roman Period." In J. Faiers, ed., *Late Roman Pottery at Amarna and Related Studies*, pp. 11–56. London: Egypt Exploration Society.

El-Khadragy, M. 2006. "New Discoveries in the Tomb of Khety II at Asyut." *Bulletin of the Australian Centre for Egyptology* 17, pp. 79–95.

Khalifa, M.A., M.S. Abu El Ghar, S. Helal, and A.W. Hussein. 2004. "Depositional History of the Lower Eocene Drowned Carbonate Platform (Drunka Formation), West of Assiut–Minia Stretch, Western Desert, Egypt." In

Proceedings of the Seventh International Conference on the Geology of the Arab World, Cairo University, Feb. 2004, pp. 233–54. Cairo: Cairo University.

Khalil, S. 1993. "Un texte de la philocalie sur la 'prière à Jésus' dans un manuscrit arabo-copte médiéval." *Proche-Orient chrétien* 43, pp. 5–38.

Khater, A., and O.H.E. Burmester. 1970. *History of the Patriarchs of the Egyptian Church*. Textes et documents 13. Cairo: Société d'archéologie copte.

Kheir, Q., ed. 1969. *Synaxar*. Cairo: Dayr al-Muharraq.

Kitab al-ibsalmudiya al-muqaddasa al-sanawiya: hasab tartib aba' al-kanisa al-qibtiya al-urthudhuksiya. Cairo: n.p., n.d.

Kitchen, K.A. 1977. *The Bible in Its World*. London: Exeter.

Klemm, D.D., and R. Klemm. 2001. "The Building Stones of Ancient Egypt: A Gift of Its Geology." *African Earth Sciences* 33, pp. 631–42.

Klemm, R., and D.D. Klemm. 2008. *Stones and Quarries in Ancient Egypt*. Eng. trans. London: The British Museum Press.

Klitzsch, E., F.K. List, and G. Pöhlmann, eds. 1987. *Geological Map of Egypt, 1:500,000*. Sheets NH 35 SE, NG 35 NE, NG 35 SE, NG 35 SW, NG 36 SW. Cairo: The Egyptian General Petroleum Corporation.

Koch, G., and H. Sichtermann. 1982. *Römische Sarkophage*. Munich: C.H. Beck'sche Verlagbuchhandlung.

Kramer, J. 1990. "Pfau." In E. Kirschbaum, ed., *Lexikon der christlichen Ikonographie*, vol. 3, col. 409–11. Rome, Freiburg, Basel, and Vienna: Herder.

Kuhn, K.H. 1978. *A Panegyric on Apollo Archimandrite of the Monastery of Isaac by Stephen Bishop of Heracleopolis Magna*. CSCO 394–95. Scriptores Coptici 39–40. Louvain: Secrétariat du CSCO.

Kupferschmidt, M. 1987. "Reformist and Militant Islam in Urban and Rural Egypt." *MES* 23, no. 4, pp. 403–18.

Kurth, D., and U. Rößler-Köhler, eds. 1987. *Zur Archäologie des 12. oberägyptischen Gaues: Bericht über zwei Surveys der Jahre 1980 und 1981*. Göttinger Orientforschungen, series 4, vol. 16. Wiesbaden: Harrassowitz.

Łajtar, A. 1997. "Τὸ κάστρον τῶν Μαύρων τὸ πλησίον Φίλων: Der dritte Adam über *P.Haun*. II 26." *JJP* 27, pp. 43–54.

Lamoreaux, J., trans. 2005. *Theodore Abu Qurrah*. Provo, UT: Brigham Young University Press.

Lapidus, I.M. 2002. *A History of Islamic Societies*. 2nd ed. Cambridge, UK: Cambridge University Press.

La Rue, G.M. 1984. "Khabir 'Ali at Home in Kubayh: A Brief Biography of a Darfur Caravan Leader." *AEH* 13, pp. 56–83.

———. 2002. "The Capture of a Slave Caravan: The Incident at Asyut (Egypt) in 1880." *AEH* 30, pp. 81–106.

Laurentin, R. 1982. *Les évangiles de l'enfance du Christ: Vérité de Noël au-delà des mythes*. Paris: Desclée et Desclée de Brower.

Layton, B. 1987. *The Gnostic Scriptures*. New York: Doubleday & Company.

Lee, G.M. 1982. "Coptic Christianity in a Changing World." In S. Mews, ed., *Religion and National Identity: Papers Read at the Nineteenth Summer Meeting and the Twentieth Winter Meeting of the Ecclesiastical History Society*, pp. 39–45. Studies in Church History 18. Oxford: Blackwell.

Leeder, S.H. 1918. *Modern Sons of the Pharaohs: A Study of the Manners and Customs of the Copts of Egypt*. London: Hodder and Stoughton.

Lefebvre, G. 1915. "Nouvelle Série d'Inscriptions Coptes et Grecques." *ASAE* 15, pp. 113–39.

Lefort, L.Th. 1950. "Un martyr inconnu, S. Olympios." *Le Muséon* 63, pp. 1–23.

———. 1952. *S. Pachomii Vitae sahidice scriptae*. CSCO 99–100, Scriptores Coptici 9–10. Louvain: Imprimerie Orientaliste.

Leipoldt, J. 1906. *Sinuthii Vita Bohairice*. CSCO 41, Scriptores Coptici 1. Paris: Imprimerie nationale.

el-Leithy, T. 2005. "Coptic Culture and Conversion in Medieval Cairo: 1293–1524 A.D." PhD diss., Princeton University.

L'Hôte, N. 1840. *Lettres écrites d'Égypte en 1838 et 1839*. Paris: Firmin Didot.

Lia, B. 1998. *The Society of the Muslim Brothers in Egypt: The Rise of an Islamic Mass Movement, 1928–1942*. Reading: Ithaca Press.

"Life of Ibrahim al-Fani." Dayr Anba Antuni, MS tarikh 69 (formerly 75) (1700), fols. 3b–31b.

Ling, R. 1991. *Roman Painting*. Cambridge, UK: Cambridge University Press.

Linscheid, P. 2004. "Gaiters from Antinoopolis in the Museum für Byzantinische Kunst, Berlin." In C. Fluck and G.M. Vogelsang-Eastwood, eds., *Riding Costume in Egypt: Origin and Appearance*, pp. 153–61. Studies in Textile and Costume History 3. Leiden: Brill.

Lintz, Y., and M. Coudert, eds. 2013. *Antinoé: Momies, textiles, céramiques et autres antiques: Envois de l'État et dépôts du musée du Louvre de 1901 à nos jours*. Paris: Somogy Editions d'Art.

Little, D.P. 1976. "Coptic Conversion to Islam under the Bahri Mamluks: 692–755/1293–1354." *BSOAS* 39, pp. 552–69.

Livingstone, R., T. Chandler, and D. Martin. 2008. "Reconstructing Ancient Kellis Part III: Clothing." *Buried History: The Journal of the Australian Institute of Archaeology* 44, pp. 35–38.

Loeben, C.E., ed. 2008. *L'expédition en Égypte de Karl Richard Lepsius (1842–1845) et la naissance des études égyptologiques sur la période dite "amarnienne."* Elsa Rickal, trans. Paris: Kheops Centre Vauclusien d'Egyptologie.

Loret, V. 1903. "Carnet de notes égyptologiques." *Sphinx* 6, pp. 97–112.

Louca, A. 1991. "Ya'qub, General (1745–1801)." In A.S. Atiya, ed., *The Coptic Encyclopedia*, vol. 7, pp. 2349–53. New York: Macmillan.

Lucchesi, E. 2008. "'Nachtrag' à l'édition du 'P.Vat. Copt. Doresse 7.'" *Aegyptus* 88, pp. 203–206.

Lucchesi-Palli, E. 1988. "Jagdszenen und dekorative Tierdarstellungen in den Wandmalereien von Bawit: Untersuchungen zu ihrer Herkunft." *Boreas* 11, pp. 165–76.

———. 1990. "Geometrisch und florale Ornamente in den Wandmalereien von Bawit: Untersuchungen zu ihrer Herkunft." *Boreas* 13, pp. 113–33.

Lucot, A., ed. and trans. 1912. *Histoire Lausiaque (Vies d'ascètes et de pères du désert)*. Texte grec. Paris: Librairie Alphonse Picard et Fils.

Luijendijk, A.M. 2008. *Greetings in the Lord: Early Christians and the Oxyrhynchus Papyri.* Harvard Theological Studies 60. Cambridge, MA: Harvard University Press.

Lyon-Caen, C. 2010. "Les lampes du monastère de Baouît." In *Études coptes XI: treizième journée d'études, Marseille 7–9 juin 2007*, pp. 31–44. CBC 17.

MacCoull, L. 1995. "Holy Family Pilgrimage in Late Antique Egypt: The Case of Qosqam." Akten des XII Internationalen Kongresses für Christliche Archäologie. *JAC* 20, pp. 987–92.

MacLennan, H. 1968. *Oxyrhynchus: An Economic and Social Study*. Amsterdam: A.M. Hakkert.

Maehler, H. 1983. In *Festschrift zum 100-jährigen Bestehen der Papyrussammlung der österreichischen Nationalbibliothek. Papyrus Erzherzog Rainer (P. Rainer cent.)*, pp. 384–85 (Nr. 79). Vienna: Brüder Hollinek.

Magdi, M. 2011. "Les Monuments en rapport avec le trajet de la Sainte Famille en Égypte avec tout ce qu'ils renferment d'icônes et de peintures murales." PhD diss., Alexandria University.

Makaryous, Bishop. 2013. *al-Usquf al-'amm: rahiq al-istishhad, ahdath yawm al-arbi'a' al-dami, 14 Ughustus 2013*. Minya: Eparchy of Minya and Abu Qurqas.

Mälck, K. 2004. "Technische Analyse der Berliner Reitermäntel und Beinlinge." In C. Fluck and G.M. Vogelsang-Eastwood, eds., *Riding Costume in Egypt. Origin and Appearance*, pp. 163–73. Studies in Textile and Costume History 3. Leiden: Brill.

Mallon, A. 1914. "Copte (épigraphie)." In F. Cabrol and H. Leclercq, eds., *Dictionnaire d'archéologie chrétienne et de liturgie* III/2, col. 2819–86. Paris: Letouzey et Ané.

Manfredi, M. 1998. "Gli scavi italiani ad Antinoe (1935–1993)." In Cat. Florence, F. Del Francia-Barocas, ed., *Antinoe cent'anni dopo* (Exhibition catalogue Palazzo Medici Riccardi, Florence), pp. 23–29. Florence: Istituto papirologico G. Vitelli.

al-Maqrizi. 1835. *Kitab al-Mawa'iz wa-l-i'tibar bidikr al-khitat wa-l-atar.* Vol. 1. Bulaq edition. Cairo: Dar al-Fikr al-'Arabi.

———. 1995. *al-Mawa'iz wa-l-i'tibar fi dhikr al-khitat wa-l-athar.* Vol. 16. London: al-Furqan Islamic Heritage Foundation.

———. 1998. *Tarikh al-aqbat al-ma'ruf bi-l-qawl al-ibrizi li-l-'allama al-Maqrizi.* Ed. 'Abd al-Ma'ud Diyab. Cairo: Dar al-Fadila.

———. 2003. *Kitab al-mawa'iz wa-l-i'tibar fi dhikr al-khitat wa-l-athar.* Vol. 4, part 2, ed. A.F. Sayyid. London: al-Furqan Islamic Heritage Foundation.

Maraval, P. 1985. *Lieux saints et pèlerinages d'Orient: Histoire et géographie des origines à la conquête arabe.* Paris: Éditions du Cerf.

———. 1996. *Récits des premiers pèlerins chrétiens au Proche-Orient (IV–VIIe siècle).* Sagesses chrétiennes. Paris: Éditions du Cerf.

Marchand, S., G. Marouard, M. Mossakowska-Gaubert, F. Calament, and C. Meurice. Forthcoming. "Survey du monastère d'Apa Apollô de Baouît: Premières données archéologiques et analyses préliminaires de la céramique et du verre des ermitages dits 'de la montagne.'" In V. Ghica, ed., *Actes du colloque international Ermitages d'Égypte, Cairo, 24–26 January 2009.* Cairo: IFAO.

Marinova, E., G.J.M. van Loon, M. De Meyer, and H. Willems. 2011. "Plant Economy and Land Use in Middle Egypt during the Late Antique/Early Islamic Period: Archaeobotanical Analysis of Mud Bricks and Mud Plasters from the Area of Dayr al-Barsha." In A.G. Fahmy, S. Kahlheber, and A.C. D'Andrea, eds., *Windows of the African Past: Current Approaches to African Archaeobotany: Proceedings of the 6th International Workshop on African Archaeobotany, Cairo, 13–15 June 2009*, pp. 119–36. Reports in African Archaeology 3. Frankfurt am Main: Africa Magna Verlag.

Markiewicz, T. 2009. "The Church, Clerics, Monks and Credit in Papyri." In A. Boud'hors, J. Clackson, L. Louis, and P. Sijpesteijn, eds., *Monastic Estates in Late Antique and Early Islamic Egypt: Ostraca, Papyri, and Essays in Memory of Sarah Clackson (P.Clackson)*, pp. 178–204. Cincinnati, OH: American Society of Papyrologists.

Martin, M. 1971. *La laure de Dêr al Dîk à Antinoë.* Cairo: IFAO.

al-Maskin, Fr. M. 1984. *Al-rahbana al-qibtiyia fi 'asr al-qiddis Anba Maqar.* 2nd ed. Wadi al-Natrun: St. Maqar Monastery Press.

Maspero, G. 1900. "Les fouilles de Deir el Aizam (Septembre 1897)." *ASAE* 1, pp. 109–19.

Maspero, J. 1912. *Organisation militaire de l'Égypte byzantine*. Paris: Librairie Honoré Champion.

———. 1923. *Histoire des patriarches d'Alexandrie: Depuis la mort de l'Empereur Anastase jusqu'à la réconciliation des églises Jacobites (518–616)*. Paris: Librairie Ancienne Édouard Champion.

———. 1932–43. *Fouilles exécutées à Baouît par Jean Maspero, notes mises en œuvre et éditées par E. Drioton*. MIFAO 59. Cairo: IFAO.

Maspero, J., and G. Wiet. 1919. *Matériaux pour servir à la géographie de l'Égypte*. First series, 39. Paris: IFAO.

al-Masry, I.H. 1984. *Qissat al-Kanissa al-Qibtiya*. Vol. 5. Cairo: Maktabat al-Mahaba.

———. 1992. *Qissat al-Kanissa al-Qibtiya*. Vol. 4. Alexandria: El Karnak Printing House.

Matras, Y. 2009. *Language Contact*. Cambridge, UK: Cambridge University Press.

McNaugher, J. 1931. *The History of Theological Education in the United Presbyterian Church and Its Ancestries*. Pittsburgh, PA: United Presbyterian Board of Publication and Bible School Work.

Meinardus, O.F.A. 1963. *In the Steps of the Holy Family: From Bethlehem to Upper Egypt*. Cairo: Dar al-Maaref.

———. 1969. *Christian Egypt, Ancient and Modern*. Cairo: IFAO.

———. 1977. *Christian Egypt, Ancient and Modern*. 2nd rev. ed. Cairo: The American University in Cairo Press.

———. 1985. "Die Sigmaform als Altarplatte, Grabstele und Klostertisch." *Collectanea*, pp. 153–64.

———. 1988. *Monks and Monasteries of the Egyptian Deserts*. Rev. ed. Cairo: The American University in Cairo Press.

———. 1992. *The Holy Family in Egypt*. 3rd ed. Cairo: The American University in Cairo Press.

———. 2001. *Monks and Monasteries of the Egyptian Deserts*. 2nd rev. ed. Cairo: The American University in Cairo Press.

———. 2002. *Two Thousand Years of Coptic Christianity*. Cairo: The American University in Cairo Press.

———. 2003. *Coptic Saints and Pilgrimages*. 2nd ed. Cairo: The American University in Cairo Press.

Menken, M.J.J. 2005. "Out of Egypt Have I Called My Son." In A. Hilhorst and G.H. Van Kooten, eds., *The Wisdom of Egypt: Jewish, Early Christian and Gnostic Essays in Honour of Gerald P. Luttikhuizen*, pp. 143–52. Leiden and Boston: Brill.

Menzies, A. 1912. *The Ante-Nicene Fathers: Translations of the Writing of the Fathers down to* A.D. *325*. Vol. 9. New York: Charles Scribner's Sons.

Meurer, H. 1971. "Lazarus von Bethanien." In E. Kirschbaum, ed., *Lexikon der christlichen Ikonographie*. 8 vols. Vol. 3, pp. 33–38. Freiburg: Herder.

Middleton-Jones, H. 1997. "The Akhmim Project: The Analytical Catalogue of Material from the Late-Period Cemeteries of Akhmim in Upper Egypt." MPhil thesis, Swansea University.

———. 2010. "The Coptic Monasteries Multi-Media Database Project." In G. Gabra and H.N. Takla, eds., *Christianity and Monasticism in Upper Egypt*, Vol. 2, Nag Hammadi–Esna, pp. 245–51. Cairo: The American University in Cairo Press.

———. 2011. "A Proposal for a National Register for Coptic Monuments and Sites in Egypt." Symposium at the Coptic Patriarchate, Cairo, January.

Middleton-Jones, H., and R. Dekker. 2010. "Qubbat el-Hawa: The Second Photographic Survey Using High-Resolution Imagery." Unpublished.

Mikhail, M.S.A. 2004. "Egypt from Late Antiquity to Early Islam: Copts, Melkites, and Muslims Shaping a New Society." PhD diss., University of California, Los Angeles.

Milad, M.N. 2000. *Min Misr da'awt ibni*. Cairo: Dar Vinus.

Milroy, J. 1992. *Linguistic Variation and Change: On the Historical Sociolinguistics of English*. Oxford: Blackwell.

Milroy, J., and L. Milroy. 1985. "Linguistic Change, Social Network and Speaker Innovation." *Journal of Linguistics* 21, pp. 339–84.

Milroy, L. 1987. *Language and Social Networks*. 2nd ed. Oxford: Blackwell.

———. 2002. "Social Networks." In J.K. Chambers, P. Trudgill, and N. Schilling-Estes, eds., *The Handbook of Language Variation and Change*, pp. 549–72. Malden, MA: Blackwell.

Mingana, A. 1928. "Timothy's Apology for Christianity." *Woodbrooke Studies*, vol. 2, pp. 1–162. Cambridge, UK: W. Heffer.

———. 1931. "Vision of Theophilus." *Woodbrooke Studies*, vol. 3, pp. 1–92. Cambridge, UK: Cambridge University Press.

Minutoli, D. 2008. "Antinoe, necropoli nord 2007: La tomba di Tgol: Prime informazioni." In G. Bastianini and R. Pintaudi, eds., *Antinoupolis I: Scavi e materiali*, pp. 61–73. Florence: Istituto papirologico G. Vitelli.

Mistrih, V. 1966. *Juhanna ibn Abi Zakaria ibn Siba': Pretiosa Margarita de Scientiis Ecclesiasticis*. Studia Orientalia Christiana Aegyptiaca. Cairo: Edizioni del centro francescano di studi orientali cristiani.

Moawad, S. 2010. *Untersuchungen zum Panegyrikos auf Makarios von Tkōou und zu seiner Überlieferung*. SKCO 18. Wiesbaden: L. Reichert.

———. 2011. "Die arabische Version der Vita Dioscori." *Le Muséon* 124, pp. 149–80.

———. 2012. "Al-Makin Jirjis ibn al-'Amid (the Elder)." In D. Thomas and A. Mallett, eds., *Christian–Muslim Relations: A Bibliographical History*, vol. 4, pp. 566–71. Leiden: Brill.

———. 2013. *Itlalat 'ala turath al-adab al-qibti*. Cairo: Alexandria School.

Moftah, R., M. Robertson, and M. Roy. 1991. "Musical Instruments." In A.S. Atiya, ed., *The Coptic Encyclopedia,* vol. 6, pp. 1715–45. New York: Macmillan.

Mommsen, Th. 1873. *Inscriptiones Asiae, provinciarum Europae graecarum, Illyrici latinae*, part 1. Corpus Inscriptionum Latinarum III/1. Berlin: Georg Reimer.

Monneret de Villard, U. 1928. *Deyr el-Muharraqah: Note archeologiche*. Milano: Tipografia e liberia pontificia e arcivescovile San Giuseppe.

Moreno García, J.C. 2012. "Deir el-Gabrawi." In W. Wendrich, ed., *UCLA Encyclopedia of Egyptology*. Los Angeles: UCLA. http://escholarship.org/uc/item/99j1g8zh#page-1

Mostafa, A. 2013. "Paleokarst Shafts in the Western Desert of Egypt: A Unique Landscape." *Acta Carsologica* 42, no. 1, pp. 49–60.

Müller, C.D.G. 1964. "Die koptische Kirche zwischen Chalkedon und dem Arabereinmarsch." *Zeitschrift für Kirchengeschichte* 75, pp. 271–308.

al-Muqaddasi. 1980. *La meilleure répartition pour la connaissance des provinces*. Ed. G. Tulaimat. Damascus: Institut Français d'Etudes Arabes de Damas.

Murre-van den Berg, H. 2006. "'I the Weak Scribe': Scribes in the Church of the East in the Ottoman Period." *JECS* 58, no. 1–2, pp. 9–26.

Muyser, J. 1943. "Ermite pérégrinant et pèlerin infatigable." *BSAC* 9, pp. 159–236.

Muysken, P. 2000. *Bilingual Speech: A Typology of Code-mixing*. Cambridge, UK: Cambridge University Press.

———. 2007. "Mixed Codes." In P. Auer and L. Wei, eds., *Handbook of Multilingualism and Multilingual Communication*, pp. 325–40. Berlin: Mouton de Gruyter.

———. 2010. "Scenarios for Language Contact." In R. Hickey, ed., *The Handbook of Language Contact*, pp. 265–81. Malden, MA: Wiley-Blackwell.

Myers-Scotton, C. 2006. *Multiple Voices: An Introduction to Bilingualism*. Malden, MA: Blackwell.

Nagel, P. 1991. "Lycopolitan (or Lyco-Diospolitan or Subakhmimic)." In A.S. Atiya and W.Y. Adams, eds., *The Coptic Encyclopedia*, vol. 8, pp. 151–59. New York: Macmillan. http://ccdl.libraries.claremont.edu/cdm/singleitem/collection/cce/id/2026/rec/1

El-Naggar, Z.R. 1970. *On a Proposed Lithostratigraphic Subdivision for the Cretaceous Early Paleogene Succession in the Nile Valley, Egypt*. 64 (B-3). Kuwait: Seventh Arab Petroleum Congress.

Nasir-i Khusraw 'Ulwi. 1993. *Shafar nama*. Trans. Y. al-Hashab. Cairo: al-Hay'a al-Misriya al-'Ama li-l-Kitab.

Nau, F. 1903. "Histoire de Dioscore patriarche d'Alexandrie, écrite par son disciple Théopiste." *Journal Asiatique*, 10th series, 1, pp. 5–108, 241–310.

———. 1910. "La version syriaque de la 'Vision de Théophile' sur le séjour de la Vierge en Egypte." *Revue de l'Orient chrétien*, 2nd series, 5, no. 15, pp. 125–32.

Neira Faleiro, C. 2005. *La Notitia Dignitatum: Nueva edición crítica y comentario histórico*. Nueva Roma 25. Madrid: Consejo superior de investigaciones científicas.

O'Connell, E.R., ed. 2014. "Catalogue of British Museum Objects from the Egypt Exploration Fund's 1913/14 Excavation at Antinoupolis (Antinoë)," with contributions by A.J. Dowler, F. Pritchard, St. J. Simpson, R.I. Thomas, and A.J. Veldmeijer. In R. Pintaudi, ed., *Antinoupolis III: Scavi e materiali*, pp. 467–504. Florence: Istituto papirologico G. Vitelli.

O'Leary, De L. 1937. *Saints of Egypt in the Coptic Calendar*. London and New York: Church Historical Society.

Orlandi, T. 1968. *Studi Copti. 1. Un encomio di Marco Evangelista. 2. Le fonti copte della Storia dei Patriarchi di Alessandria. 3. La leggenda di S. Mercurio*. Testi e documenti per lo studio dell'antichità 22. Milan: Istituto Editoriale Cisalpino.

———. 1981. *Omelie Copte*. Corona Patrum 7. Turin: Società Editrice Internazionale.

———. 1985. *Shenute, Contra Origanistas*. Rome: CIM.

———. 2006. "Patristic Texts in Coptic." In A. di Berardino, ed., *Patrology: The Eastern Fathers from the Council of Chalcedon (451) to John of Damascus (750)*, trans. A. Walford, pp. 491–570. Cambridge: James Clark.

Osing, J. 1978. "The Dialect of Oxyrhynchus." *Enchoria* 8, pp. 29*(75)–36*(82).

———. 1998. "PSI inv. I 3 + pCarlsberg 305 + pTebt. Tait Add. 2 e PSI inv. I 4 + pCarlsberg 306 + pTebt. Tait Add. 3. Copie delle iscrizioni nelle tombe di Assiut." In J. Osing and G. Rosati, eds., *Papiri geroglifici e ieratici da Tebtynis*, 55–100. Florence: Istituto Papirologico G. Vitelli.

Pagels, Elaine. 2005. *The Gnostic Gospels: Adam, Eve, and the Serpent: The Origin of Satan*. New York: Quality Paperback Book Club.

Palanque, C. 1906. "Rapport sur les recherches effectuées à Baouit en 1903." *BIFAO* 5, pp. 1–21 and pl. I–XVII.

Palladius. 1991. *The Lausiac History*, trans. and annotated by Robert T. Meyer. Ancient Christian Writers 34. New York and Mahwah: Paulist Press.

Pantalacci, L. 2005. "Baouît." In *Travaux de l'Institut français d'archéologie orientale en 2004–2005, BIFAO* 105, pp. 440–43.

Papaconstantinou, A. 2001. *Le culte des saints en Égypte des Byzantins aux Abbasides: L'apport des inscriptions et des papyrus grecs et coptes.* Paris: CNRS Éditions.

———. 2006. "Historiography, Hagiography, and the Making of the Coptic 'Church of the Martyrs' in Early Islamic Egypt." *Dumbarton Oaks Papers* 60, pp. 65–86.

———. 2007. "'They Shall Speak the Arabic Language and Take Pride in It': Reconsidering the Fate of Coptic after the Arab Conquest." *Le Muséon* 120, pp. 273–99.

———. 2011. "Hagiography in Coptic." In S. Efthymiadis, ed., *Ashgate Research Companion to Byzantine Hagiography: Literature, Social History and Cult.* Variorum Collected Studies Series, pp. 323–43. Surrey: Ashgate Variorum.

Papiri greci e latini. 1912–. Pubblicazioni della Società Italiana per la ricerca dei papiri greci e latini in Egitto. Edited by G. Vitelli, M. Norsa, et al. Florence: Società Italiana per la ricerca dei papiri greci e latini in Egitto.

Parthey, G., and M. Pinder, eds. 1848. *Itinerarium Antonini Augusti et Hierosolymitanum: Ex libris manu scriptis.* Berolini: Fridericus Nicolaus.

Peeters, P., trans. 1914. "Evangile arménien de l'enfance." *Evangiles apocryphes* 2: 171.

———. 1936. "Une Vie copte de S. Jean de Lycopolis." *Analecta Bollandiana* 54, pp. 359–81.

Pensabene, P. 1993. *Elementi architettonici di Alessandria e di altri siti egiziani.* Repertorio d'Arte dell'Egitto Greco-Romano Serie C, vol. 3. Rome: L'Erma di Bretschneider.

Perrier, P. 2000. *Evangiles de l'oral à l'écrit.* Vol. 1. Paris: Le Sarment-Fayard.

———. 2003. *Evangiles de l'oral à l'écrit.* Vol. 2, *Les colliers évangéliques.* Paris: Le Sarment-Fayard.

Petrie, W.M.F. 1907. *Gizeh and Rifeh.* British School of Archaeology in Egypt 13. London: School of Archaeology in Egypt, Bernard Quaritch. http://www.ancientegypt.co.uk/manchester/pages/excavation_by_w_m_flinders_petri.htm

———. 1909. *Memphis I.* British School of Archaeology in Egypt 14. London: School of Archaeology in Egypt.

Pintaudi, R. 2008. "Gli scavi dell'Istituto Pàpirologico 'G. Vitelli' di Firenze ad Antinoe (2000–2007): Prime notizie." In G. Bastianini and R. Pintaudi, eds., *Antinoupolis I: Scavi e materiali,* pp. 1–40. Florence: Istituto papirologico G. Vitelli.

Plisch, U.-K. 2001. "Die Perikopen über Johannes den Täufer in der neuentdeckten mittelägyptischen Version des Matthäus-Evangeliums (Codex Schøyen)." *Novum Testamentum* 43, pp. 368–92.

Pococke, R. 1743. *A Description of the East and Some Other Countries.* Vol. 1. *Observations on Egypt.* London: W. Bowyer.

Poethke, G. 1991. "Oxyrhynchus Papyri." In A.S. Atiya, ed., *The Coptic Encyclopedia,* vol. 6, pp. 1857b–1858b. New York: Macmillan.

Powell, E.M.T. 1999. "From Odyssey to Empire: Mapping Sudan through Egyptian Literature in the Mid-nineteenth Century." *IJMES* 31, no. 3, pp. 401–27.

Pritchard, F. 2013. "A Survey of Textiles in the UK from the 1913–14 Egypt Exploration Fund Season at Antinoe." In A. De Moor, C. Fluck, and P. Linscheid, eds., *Drawing the Threads Together: Textiles and Footwear of the First Millennium AD from Egypt*, pp. 34–55. Tielt: Lannoo.

Pseudo-Athanasius. 1904. *The Canons of Athanasius of Alexandria: The Arabic and Coptic Versions*, ed. and trans. W. Riedel and W.E. Crum. London: Williams and Norgate.

Pyke, G. 2008. "A Christian Conversion: The Tomb of Panehsy at Amarna." *Egyptian Archaeology* 32, pp. 8–10.

al-Qalqashandi. 1963. *Kitab subh al-a'sha fi sina'at al-insha*. Vol. 3. Cairo: al-Hay'a al-Misriya al-'Ama li-l-Kitab.

Quibell, J.E. 1908. *Excavations at Saqqara (1906–1907)*. Cairo: IFAO.

Quispel, G. 1991. "Gnosticism." In A.S. Atiya, ed., *The Coptic Encyclopedia*, vol. 4, pp. 1148–51. New York: Macmillan.

Ramzi, M. 1960. *al-Qamus al-jughrafi li-l-bilad al-misriya min 'ahd qudama' al-misriyin ila sanat 1945*. Vol. 3. Cairo: Dar al-Kutub al-Misriya.

Rassart-Debergh, M. 1997. *Textiles d'Antinoé (Égypte) en Haute Alsace, Donation E. Guimet*. Colmar: Muséum d'Histoire Naturelle de Colmar.

Raven, M.J. 1982. *Papyrus, van bies tot boekrol: Met een bloemlezing uit de Leidse papyrusverzameling*, pp. 80–81. Zutphen: Terra.

Reintges, C.H. 2001. "Code-mixing Strategies in Coptic Egyptian." *Lingua Aegyptia* 9, pp. 193–237.

———. 2004a. *Coptic Egyptian (Sahidic Dialect): A Learner's Grammar*. Cologne: Köppe.

———. 2004b. "Coptic Egyptian as a Bilingual Language Variety." In P. Bádenas de la Peña, S. Torallas Tovar, E.R. Luján, and M.Á. Gallego, eds., *Lenguas en contacto: El testimonio escrito,* pp. 69–86. Madrid: Consejo superiores de investigaciones científicas.

Riad, E. 1988. *Studies in the Syriac Preface*. Acta Universitatis Upsaliensis, Studia Semitica Upsaliensia 11. Uppsala: [Uppsala University].

Richard, M. 1939. "Les écrits de Théophile d'Alexandrie." *Le Muséon* 52, p. 43s.

Roberts, A., and J. Donaldson, eds. 1885. *The Ante-Nicene Fathers: Translations of the Writings of the Fathers down to A.D. 324*. Vol. 2. Buffalo, NY: The Christian Literature Pub. Co.

Robinson, J.M., ed. 1990. *The Nag Hammadi Library in English*. 3rd ed. San Francisco, CA: HarperCollins.

Römer, C. 2009. "Manichaeism and Gnosticism in the Papyri." In R.S. Bagnall, ed., *The Oxford Handbook of Papyrology*, pp. 623–43. Oxford and New York: Oxford University Press.

Rostovtzeff, M. 1919. "Ancient Decorative Wall-Painting." *Journal of Hellenic Studies* 39, pp. 144–63.

Rousseau, Ph. 1985. *Pachomius: The Making of a Community in Fourth-century Egypt*. Berkeley, Los Angeles, and London: University of California Press.

Roussillon, A. 2008. "Republican Egypt Interpreted: Revolution and Beyond." In M.W. Daly, ed., *Modern Egypt, from 1517 to the End of the Twentieth Century*, pp. 334–93. Cambridge History of Egypt, vol. 2. Cambridge, UK: Cambridge University Press.

Rubenson, S. 1995. *The Letters of St. Antony: Monasticism and the Making of a Saint*. Studies in Antiquity and Christianity. Minneapolis, MN: Fortress Press.

———. 1996. "Translating the Tradition: Some Remarks on the Arabization of the Patristic Heritage in Egypt." *Medieval Encounters* 2, pp. 4–14.

Ruffini, G.R. 2008. *Social Networks in Byzantine Egypt*. Cambridge, UK: Cambridge University Press.

Russell, J.C. 1966. "The Population of Medieval Egypt." *JARCE* 5, pp. 69–82.

Russell, N. 1981. *The Lives of the Desert Fathers: Historia Monachorum in Aegypto*. Cistercian Studies 34. London: Mowbray; Kalamazoo, MI: Cistercian Publications.

Rutschowscaya, M.-H., 1998. *Le Christ et l'abbé Ména*. Paris: RMN-Louvre.

———. 2009. "Le matériel en bois provenant du monastère de Baouît (fouilles 2003–2009)." Paper presented at Études coptes XII: Quatorzième journée d'études, Rome, 11–13 juin 2009. Unpublished.

———. 2010a. "Nouvelles peintures découvertes dans le monastère de Baouît." In A. Boud'hors and C. Louis, eds., *Études coptes XI: Treizième journée d'études (Marseille, 7–9 juin 2007)*, pp. 45–51. CBC 17. Paris: De Boccard.

———. 2010b. "Recent Discoveries from Bawit." In P. Whitfield, N. Tomoum, and S. Marei, eds., *Coptic Art Revealed*, Supreme Council of Antiquities Exhibition. Cairo: Ministry of State for Antiquities.

———. 2013. "Gabriel et Michel, les deux archanges à Baouit." In A. Boud'hors and C. Louis, eds., *Études coptes XII: Quatorzième journée d'études (Rome, 11–13 juin 2009)*, pp. 215–20. CBC 18. Paris: De Boccard.

Rzeuska, T. 2012. "The Pottery, Asyut 2011." *SAK* 41, pp. 209–33.

Sadek, A., and B. Sadek, eds. 1976–2009. *Le Monde Copte*. Collection encyclopédique de culture égyptienne. Vols. 1–11. Paris and Limoges.

———. 2000. "L'Incarnation de la Lumière: Le renouveau iconographique copte à travers l'œuvre d'Isaac Fanous." *Le Monde Copte* 29–31.

———. 2011. "Un fleuve d'eau vive, trilogie sur l'Entrée du Christ en Egypte, vol. 1: les sources." *Le Monde Copte* 34.

Said, R. 1960. "Planktonic Foraminifera from the Thebes Formation, Luxor, Egypt." *Micropaleontology* 6, pp. 277–86.

———. 1961. "Tectonic Framework of Egypt: Its Influence on Distribution of Foraminifera." *American Association of Petroleum Geologists Bulletin* 45, pp. 198–218.

Salomons, R.P., P.J. Sijpesteijn, and K.A. Worp. 1980. *Die Amsterdamer Papyri.* Vol. 1. Zutphen: Terra.

Sarkis, Nached, ed. 1936. *Al-alel' al-saneya fi al-mayamer wa al-adja'eb al-mariameya.* 1st ed. Cairo: n.p.

Sauget, J.-M. 1983. "Trois recueils de Discours de Grégoire de Nazianze en traduction arabe: Simples réflexions sur leur structure." *Augustinianum* 23, pp. 487–515.

Sawirus Ibn al-Muqaffa'. 1959. *History of the Patriarchs of the Egyptian Church Known as the History of the Holy Church.* Texts and documents, vol. 2, part 3, Christodoulus–Michael (1046–1102 A.D.), trans. and ed. Y. 'Abd Al-Masih and O.H.E. Burmester. Cairo: [Société d'archéologie copte].

———. 1970. *Ta'rikh batarikat al-kanisa al-misriya: al-ma'ruf bi-siyar al-bi'a al-muqaddasa.* Vol. 3, part 2, ed. and trans. A. Khater and O.H.E. Khs-Burmester. Cairo: Société d'archéologie copte.

Schaff, Ph., and H. Wace. 1995. *Nicene and Post-Nicene Fathers.* Vol. 11. *Sulpitius Severus, Vincent of Lerins, John Cassian.* Second Series, 2nd ed., reprint. Peabody, MA: Hendrickson.

Schenke, G. 1997. "Über Ägyptens Sonderstatus vor allen anderen Ländern." *Kölner Papyri: (P. Köln),* vol. 8, pp. 183–200. Opladen: Westdeutscher Verlag.

———. 2004. "Der koptische Papyrus P. Köln VIII 354: Zum Sonderstatus Ägyptens vor allen anderen Ländern." In Wolfgang Boochs, ed., *Geschichte und Geist der koptischen Kirche,* pp. 151–55. Grevenbroich: Bernardus-Verlag Langwaden.

Schenke, H.-M. 1978. "On the Middle Egyptian Dialect of the Coptic Language." *Enchoria* 8, pp. 43*(89)–58*(104).

———. 1989. "Mittelägyptische Nachlese I: Bemerkungen zum Adverb ϩⲓⲧⲣⲟⲩⲣ 'schnell' anlässlich der Edition von Restfragmenten der Mailänder mittelägyptischen Handschrift der Paulusbriefe mit einem neuen Beleg." *ZÄSA* 116, pp. 160–74.

———. 1991. "Mesokemic (or Middle Egyptian)." In A.S. Atiya, ed., *The Coptic Encyclopedia,* vol. 8, pp. 162a–164b. New York: Macmillan.

———. 1996. "Die Psalmen im mittelägyptischen Dialekt des Koptischen (der Mudil-Codex)." *Enchoria* 23, pp. 86–144.

———. 2000. "Das Matthäus-Evangelium in einer Variante des mittelägyptischen Koptisch auf Papyrus (Codex Schøyen)." *Enchoria* 26, pp. 88–107.

———. 2004a. "Ein anderes Matthäus-Evangelium im Dialekt *M*: Bemerkungen zum Codex Schøyen." *ICCoptS* 7 *Leiden 2000*, pp. 209–20. Louvain: Peeters.

———. 2004b. "Mittelägyptische 'Nachlese' IV: Die koptischen Bestände der Sammlung Schøyen und ihr Text eines 'Zweiten Matthäus.'" *ZÄSA* 131, pp. 83–92.

Schor, A.M. 2011. *Theodoret's People: Social Networks and Religious Conflict in Late Roman Syria*. Berkeley, CA: University of California Press.

Schulz-Flügel, E., ed. 1990. *Tyrannius Rufinus, Historia Monachorum sive de Vita Sanctorum Patrum*. Berlin and New York: Walter de Gruyter.

Scopello, M. 2007. *Les évangiles apocryphes*. Petite bibliothèque des spiritualités. Paris: Plon.

Scott, J. 2013. *Social Network Analysis*. 3rd ed. Los Angeles and London: SAGE.

Sedra, P. 2007. "Missionaries, Peasants, and the Protection Problem: Negotiating Coptic Reform in Nineteenth-century Egypt." In A. Amanat and M.T. Bernhardsson, eds., *US–Middle East Historical Encounters: A Critical Survey*, pp. 290–314. Gainesville, FL: University Press of Florida.

Seikaly, S. 1970. "Coptic Communal Reform: 1860–1914." *MES* 6, no. 3, pp. 247–75.

Severin, H.-G. 1991. "Bawit, Archaeology, Architecture, and Sculpture." In A.S. Atiya, ed., *The Coptic Encyclopedia*, vol. 1, pp. 363–67. New York: Macmillan.

Seybold, C.F. 1912. *Severus ibn al Muqaffa': Alexandrinische Patriarchengeschichte von S. Marcus bis Michael I 61–767 nach der ältesten 1266 geschriebenen Hamburger Handschrift*. Veröffentlichungen aus der Hamburger Stadtbibliothek 3. Hamburg: Lucas Gräfe.

Sheridan, M. 2011. "The Encomium in the Coptic Literature of the Late Sixth Century." In P. Buzi and A. Camplani, eds., *Christianity in Egypt: Literary Production and Intellectual Trends: Studies in Honor of Tito Orlandi*, pp. 443–64. Studia Ephemeridis Augustinianum 125. Rome: Institutum Patristicum Augustinianum.

Shisha-Halevy, A. 1983. "Middle Egyptian Gleanings: Grammatical Notes on the 'Middle Egyptian' Text of Matthew." *Chronique d'Égypte* 58, pp. 311–29.

———. 2002a. "An Emerging New Dialect of Coptic." *Orientalia* 71, no. 3, pp. 298–308.

———. 2002b. "The Focalizing Conversion: Structural Preliminaries to a Chapter in the Grammar of Oxyrhynchite Coptic." In H.-G. Bethge, S. Emmel, K.L. King, and I. Schletterer, eds., *For the Children, Perfect Instruction: Studies in Honour of Hans-Martin Schenke*, pp. 309–40. NHMS 54. Leiden and Boston: Brill.

———. 2003. "Future, Present, Narrative Past: A Triple Note on Oxyrhynchite *Tempuslehre*." In W. Beltz, U. Pietruschka, and J. Tubach, eds., *Sprache und Geist: Peter Nagel zum 65. Geburtstag*, pp. 249–309. Hallesche Beiträge zur Orientwissenschaft 35. Halle (Saale): Druckerei der Martin-Luther-Universität Halle-Wittenberg.

Shoucri, M. 1991. "Demetrius II." In A.S. Atiya, ed., *The Coptic Encyclopedia*, vol. 3, p. 893. New York: Macmillan.

Sicard, Cl. 1982a. *Œuvres.* Vol. 1. *Lettres et relations inédites*, ed. M. Martin. Bibliothèque d'étude 83. Cairo: IFAO.

———. 1982b. *Œuvres.* Vol. 3. *Parallèle géographique de l'ancienne Égypte et de l'Égypte moderne*. Cairo: IFAO.

Sidarus, A.Y. 2013. "Families of Coptic Dignitaries *(buyūtāt)* under the Ayyubids and the Golden Age of Coptic Arabic Literature (13th Cent.)." *JCS* 15, pp. 189–208.

Sidarus, A., and M.N. Swanson. 2013. "Al-Makin Jirjis ibn al-Amid." In D. Thomas and A. Mallett, eds., *Christian–Muslim Relations: A Bibliographical History*, vol. 5, pp. 254–61. Leiden: Brill.

Sijpesteijn, P.J. 1982. *Michigan Papyri.* Vol. 15. Zutphen: Terra.

Sijpesteijn, P.M. 2010. "Multilingual Archives and Documents in Post-Conquest Egypt." In A. Papaconstantinou, ed., *The Multilingual Experience in Egypt, from the Ptolemies to the Abbasids*, pp. 105–24. Farnham: Ashgate.

———. 2011. "Building an Egyptian Identity." In A.Q. Ahmed, M. Bonner, and B. Sadeghi, eds., *Studies in History, Law, and Thought in Honor of Professor Michael Allan Cook*, pp. 85–105. Islamic History and Civilization 83. Leiden: Brill.

Silsselat tarikh wa hadarat al-Fayyum. 2002. Vol. 1. *al-Fayoum*. N.p.: Dar Antoun Printing House.

Simaika, M., and Y. 'Abd al-Masih. 1939. *Catalogue of the Coptic and Arabic Manuscripts in the Coptic Museum, the Patriarchate, the Principal Churches of Cairo and Alexandria and the Monasteries of Egypt*. Cairo: Government Press.

Sourial, R. 1984. *Al-mugtama al-qibti fi Misr fi al-qarn al-tasse 'ashar.* Cairo: Maktabat al-Mahaba.

Sozomèn, J.B., and G.C. Hansen. 1960. *Church History.* GCS 5. London: GCS Editions.

Stählin, O. 1960. *Clemens Alexandrinus, zweiter Band: Stromata Buch I–VI.* 3rd ed. Ed. Ludwig Früchtel. Die griechischen christlichen Schriftsteller der ersten Jahrhunderte 52. Berlin: Akademie-Verlag.

Steindorff, G. 1892. "Eine koptische Bannbulle und andere Briefe." In *ZÄSA* 30, pp. 37–43.

———. 1950. "Bemerkungen über die Anfänge der koptischen Sprache und Literatur." In *Coptic Studies in Honor of Walter Ewing Crum*, pp. 189–213. Boston, MA: The Byzantine Institute.

Stewart, R. 1991. "Bahnasa, al-." In A.S. Atiya, ed., *The Coptic Encyclopedia,* vol. 2, p. 330b. New York: Macmillan.

St. Mark Foundation. 2011. *El Ganadla Monastery*. Shaker Heights, OH: The St. Mark Foundation. http://stmarkfoundation.com/test/cms/files/ganadla_monastery/files/el%20ganadla%20monastery%20pdf.pdf

Street, B.V. 2000. "Literacy Events and Literacy Practices: Theory and Practice in the New Literacy Studies." In M. Martin-Jones and K. Jones, eds., *Multilingual Literacies: Reading and Writing Different Worlds*, pp. 17–29. Amsterdam: Benjamins.

al-Suriani, A. 2002. *Qiddesso Dayr al-Surian al-'ame*. 2nd ed. Cairo: Dream Printing House.

al-Suriani, Samuel. 1968. *Al-adyra al-misreya al-'amera.* Cairo: The Modern Commercial Printing House.

al-Suriani, Samuel, and N.K. Daoud. 1987. *Tarikh al-Aba' al-Batarika li-l-Anba Yusab Usquf Fuwwa*. Cairo: n.p.

al-Suriani, Samuel, and B. Habib. 1990. *Guide to the Ancient Coptic Churches and Monasteries in Upper Egypt*. Cairo: Institute of Coptic Studies, Dept. of Coptic Architecture.

———. 2002. *Dalil al-kanais wa al-adyra fi Misr*. Cairo: Matba'a al-Na'am.

Swanson, M.N. 2007. "'Our Father Abba Mark': Marqus al-Antuni and the Construction of Sainthood in Fourteenth-Century Egypt." In J.P. Monferrer-Sala, ed., *Eastern Crossroads: Essays on Medieval Christian Legacy,* pp. 217–28. Piscataway, NJ: Gorgias Press.

———. 2010a. "Apology or Its Evasion? Some Ninth-century Arabic Christian Texts on Discerning the True Religion." *Currents in Theology and Mission* 37, pp. 389–99.

———. 2010b. *The Coptic Papacy in Islamic Egypt (641–1517)*. Cairo: The American University in Cairo Press.

———. 2013a. "The Life and the Miracles of Barsawma al-'Uryan," "The Life and Miracles of Marqus al-Antuni," "The Life of the Hegumenos Abra'am al-Fani," "The Life and the Miracles of Anba Ruways." In D. Thomas and A. Mallett, eds., *Christian–Muslim Relations: A Bibliographical History, vol. 5: 1350–1500*, pp. 114–18, 203–206, 226–28, 287–90. Leiden: Brill.

———. 2013b. "The Saint and the Muslim Copts: Episodes from the Life of Abba Mark of the Monastery of St. Antony (1296–1386)." In Y.N. Youssef and S. Moawad, eds., *Old Cairo to the New World: Coptic Studies Presented to Gawdat Gabra on the Occasion of His Sixty-fifth Birthday*, pp. 157–71. Louvain: Peeters.

———. 2014. "Christian Engagement with Islamic *kalam* in Late Fourteenth-Century Egypt: The Case of *al-Hawi* by al-Makin Jirjis Ibn al-'Amid 'the Younger.'" *Intellectual History of the Islamicate World* 2, pp. 214–26.

Tadmor, U. 2009. "Loanwords in the World's Languages: Findings and Results." In M. Haspelmath and U. Tadmor, eds., *Loanwords in the World's Languages: A Comparative Handbook*, pp. 55–75. Berlin: De Gruyter Mouton.

al-Tamagid al-Mouqadassa, li-l-Adhra wal mala'eka wal rossol wal shohada wal qedessine. 1972. Ordered and revised by Hegumen Atallah Arsanios, pp. 86–90. Asyut: Dayr al-Muharraq.

Tawadrus Shahhat and Fu'ad Basili. n.d. *Kitab Mukhtasar al-bayan fi tahqiq al-iman al-mawsum bi-l-Hawi ta'lif al-shaykh al-taqi Jirjis ibn al-'Amid al-mulaqqab b-Ibn al-Makin*. [Cairo: n.p.].

Telfer, W. 1937. "The Trustworthiness of Palladius." *JTS* 38, pp. 379–83.

Ten Kate, A. 2007. "À la recherche de la parenté textuelle du Codex Schøye." *ICCoptS 8,2 Paris 2004*, pp. 591–624. Louvain: Peeters.

Thomas, A. 1990. "Weintraube." In E. Kirschbaum, ed., *Lexikon der christlichen Ikonographie*, vol. 4, col. 494–96. Rome, Freiburg, Basel, and Vienna: Herder.

Thompson, H. 1911. *A Coptic Palimpsest Containing Joshua, Judges, Ruth, Judith and Esther in the Sahidic Dialect*. London: H. Frowde, Oxford University Press.

———. 1932. *The Coptic Version of the Acts of the Apostles and the Pauline Epistles in the Sahidic Dialect*. Cambridge, UK: Cambridge University Press.

Thompson, J. 1992. *Sir Gardner Wilkinson and His Circle*. Austin, TX: University of Texas Press.

Thompson, R.C. 1914. "Byzantine Research Funds: Excavations at Wadi Sarga." *JEA* 1, pp. 187–88, pl. 30.

Till, W. 1935. *Koptische Heiligen- und Martyrerlegenden*. Orientalia Christiana Analecta 102. Rome: Pontificium Institutum Orientalium Studiorum.

Tillemont, S.L. de. 1732. *Mémoires pour servir à l'histoire ecclésiastique des six premiers siècles*. Venice: François Pitteri.

Timbie, J. 1991. "Melitian Schism." In A.S. Atiya, ed., *The Coptic Encyclopedia*, vol. 5, pp. 1584–85. New York: Macmillan.

Timm, S. 1984–92. *Das christlich-koptische Ägypten in arabischer Zeit*. 6 vols. Beihefte zum Tübinger Atlas des Vorderen Orients, series B (Geisteswissenschaften), 41, nos. 1–6. Wiesbaden: Ludwig Reichert.

Toledano, E.R. 1984. "The Imperial Eunuchs of Istanbul: From Africa to the Heart of Islam." *MES* 20, no. 3, pp. 379–90.

Torp, H. 1957. "Some Aspects of Early Monastic Architecture." *Byzantion* 25–26–27, pp. 513–38.

Tosson, O. 1935. *Wadi al-Natrun, adyorato wa rohbano wa mukhtassar tarikh al-batareka*. Alexandria: al-Safir Printing House.

Troupeau, G. 1974. *Catalogue des manuscrits arabes*. Vol. 2. *Manuscrits chrétiens*. Paris: Bibliothèque nationale de Paris.

Tudor, B. 2011. *Christian Funerary Stelae of the Byzantine and Arab Periods from Egypt*. Marburg: Tectum Verlag.

Tuerlinckx, L. 2001. "Introduction." *Sancti Gregorii Nazianzeni Opera: Versio arabica antiqua II: Orationes I, XLV, LXIV (arab. 9, 10, 11)*, pp. v–xliii. Turnhout: Brepols; Louvain: University Press.

Turner, E.G. 1952. "Roman Oxyrhynchus." *JEA* 38, pp. 78–93.

Valensi, L. 2002. *La Fuite en Egypte*. Histoires d'Orient et d'Occident. Paris: Éditions du Seuil.

van Berchem, D. 1952. *L'armée de Dioclétien et la réforme constantinienne*. Institut français d'archéologie de Beyrouth. Bibliothèque archéologique et historique 65. Paris: Librairie orientaliste Paul Geuthner.

van Cauwenbergh, P. 1914. *Étude sur les moines d'Égypte depuis le Concile de Chalcédoine (451) jusqu'à l'invasion arabe (640)*. Paris: P. Geuthner.

van der Vliet, J. 2009. "The Copts: 'Modern Sons of the Pharaohs'?" *Church History and Religious Culture* 89, pp. 279–99.

———. 2013. "Ancient Egyptian Christianity." In M.R. Salzman and W. Adler, eds., *The Cambridge History of Religions in the Ancient World*, vol. 2, pp. 211–34. Cambridge, UK: Cambridge University Press.

van Loon, G.J.M. 2004. "The Meeting of Abraham and Melchizedek and the Communion of the Apostles." In M. Immerzeel and J. van der Vliet, eds., *Coptic Studies on the Threshold of a New Millennium*, vol. 1, *Proceedings of the Seventh International Congress of Coptic Studies, Leiden 2000*, pp. 1373–92. Leiden: Peeters.

———. 2008. "Dans les pas du Père Maurice Martin S.J.: Deir al-Dik." In A. Boud'hors and C. Louis, eds., *Études Coptes X: Douzième journée d'études (Lyon 18–22 mai 2005)*. CBC 15, pp. 179–98. Paris: De Boccard.

———. 2010. "La laure de Shaikh Sa'id." In A. Boud'hors and C. Louis, eds., *Études Coptes XI: Treizième journée d'études (Marseille 7–9 juin 2007)*. CBC 17, pp. 161–79 and pl. 9. Paris: de Boccard.

———. In press. "Etablissements chrétiens au Spéos Artémidos." In N. Bosson and C. Louis, eds., *Études Coptes XI: Seizième journée d'études (Genève 19–21 juin 2013)*. CBC 19. Paris: De Boccard.

van Loon, G.J.M., and V. De Laet. 2014. "Monastic Settlements in Dayr Abu Hinnis (Middle Egypt): The Spatial Perspective." In E.R. O'Connell, ed., *Egypt in the First Millennium AD: Perspectives from New Fieldwork*. British Museum Publications on Egypt and Sudan 2. Louvain: Peeters.

van Loon, G.J.M., and A. Delattre. 2014. "Patterns of Monastic Habitation on the East Bank of the Nile in Middle Egypt: Dayr al-Dik, Dayr Abu Hinnis, and al-Shaykh Sa'id." *JCS* 16, pp. 235–78.

van Minnen, P. 1994. "The Roots of Egyptian Christianity." *Archiv für Papyrusforschung* 40, pp. 71–85.

Vansleb, J.M. 1678. *Nouvelle relation en forme de journal d'un voyage fait en Egypte en 1672 et 1673*. Translated as *The Present State of Egypt*. London: Printed by R.E. for John Starke.

Veilleux, A. 1980–82. *Pachomian Koinonia*. 3 vols. Cistercian Studies Series 45–47. Kalamazoo, MI: Cistercian Publications.

———. 1991. "Pachomius, Saint." In A.S. Atiya, ed., *The Coptic Encyclopedia*, vol. 6, pp. 1859–64. New York: Macmillan.

Vergote, J. 1973–83. *Grammaire copte*. Louvain: Peeters.

Viaud, G. 1967–68. "La procession des deux fêtes de la croix et du dimanche des rameaux dans l'Église Copte d'après un manuscrit du monastère al-Baramus et du monastère al-Muharraq." *BSAC* 19, pp. 211–26.

Vivian, T. 1988. *St. Peter of Alexandria: Bishop and Martyr*. Studies in Antiquity and Christianity. Philadelphia, PA: Fortress Press.

Vivian, T., A. Athanassakis, and R. Greer. 2003. *The Life of Antony by Athanasius of Alexandria*. Cistercian Studies 202. Kalamazoo, MI: Cistercian Publications.

Vogt, H. 1920. *Griechische Kalender*. V: *Der Kalender des Claudius Ptolemäus*. Heidelberg: Carl Winters Universitätsbuchhandlung.

Vycichl, W. 1983. *Dictionnaire étymologique de la langue Copte*. Peeters: Louvain.

Wadi, A. 1996–97. "Introduzione alla letteratura arabo-cristiana dei Copti" = "Muqaddimah fi-l-adab al-'arabi al-masihi li-l-aqbat." *SOCC* 29–30, pp. 441–92.

———. 1997. *Studio su al-Mu'taman Ibn al-'Assal*. Cairo: Franciscan Centre of Christian Oriental Studies; Jerusalem: Franciscan Printing Press.

———, ed. 1998–99. *Al-Mu'taman ibn al-'Assal: Summa dei principi della Religione = Majmu' usul al-din wa-masmu' mahsul al-yaqin*. 4 vols. (2 text, 2 apparatus). Cairo: Franciscan Centre of Christian Oriental Studies; Jerusalem: Franciscan Printing Press.

———. 1999. "al-Makin Jirjis ibn al-'Amid wa-Tarikhuhu (al-juz' al-awwal: al-masadir wa-l-maraji' wa-l-sirah). In A. Wadi, ed., *Actes de la Septième Rencontre des Amis du Patrimoine Arabe-Chrétien, al-Faggalah, Le Caire, Jeudi–Vendredi 25–26 Février 1999*, pp. 5–24. Cairo: Franciscan Centre of Christian Oriental Studies.

———. 2006. "Al-Asa'ad Ibn al-'Assâl: Introduzioni alla tradizione dei quattro Vangeli—presentazione, edizione e commeto." *SOCC* 39, pp. 47–120.

Wagner, E.M., B. Outhwaite, and B. Beinhoff, eds. 2013. *Scribes as Agents of Language Change*. Boston: De Gruyter Mouton.

Walz, T. 1972. "Notes on the Organization of the African Trade in Cairo, 1800–1850." *AI* 11, pp. 263–86.

———. 1978. "Asyut in the 1260s (1844–53)." *JARCE* 15, pp. 113–26.

———. 1979. "Trading into the Sudan in the Sixteenth Century." *AI* 15, pp. 211–33.

———. 1985. "Black Slavery in Egypt during the Nineteenth Century as Reflected in the Mahkama Archives of Cairo." In J.R. Willis, ed., *Slaves and Slavery in Muslim Africa*, vol. 2, *The Servile Estate*, pp. 137–60. London: Frank Cass.

Ward, B. 1975. *The Desert Christian, Sayings of the Desert Fathers: The Alphabetical Collection*. New York: Macmillan.

Watson, A. 1904. *The American Mission in Egypt, 1854 to 1896*. 2nd ed. Pittsburgh, PA: United Presbyterian Board of Publication.

Watson, J.H. 2000. *Among the Copts*. Brighton and Portland, OR: Sussex Academic Press.

Wiet, G. 1960. "al-Bahnasa." *Encyclopédie de l'Islam*, vol. 1, new ed., p. 926. Leiden and New York: Brill.

Wilkinson, J. Gardner. 1843. *Modern Egypt and Thebes: Being a Description of Egypt*. 2 vols. London: J. Murray.

Willems, H., S. Vereecken, L. Kuijper, B. Vanthuyne, E. Marinova, V. Linseele, G. Verstraeten, S. Hendrickx, M. Eyckerman, A. van den Broeck, W. van Neer, J. Bourriau, P. French, C. Peeters, V. de Laet, S. Mortier, and Z. de Kooning. 2009. "An Industrial Site at al-Shaykh Sa'id/Wadi Zabayda." *Ägypten & Levante* 19, pp. 293–331.

Winlock, H.E., and W.E. Crum. 1926. *The Monastery of Epiphanius at Thebes*. Vol. 1. New York: [Metropolitan Museum of Art].

Wipszycka, E. 1992. "Le nationalisme a-t-il existé dans l'Egypte byzantine?" *JJP* 22, pp. 83–128.

———. 1996. "Le monachisme égyptien et les villes." In *Études sur le christianisme dans l'Égypte de l'Antiquité tardive*, pp. 281–336. Studia Ephemeridis Augustinianum 52. Rome: Institutum Patristicum Augustinianum. First published in *Travaux et mémoires* 12 (1994): 1–44.

———. 2002a. "Del buon uso delle lettere private: Commento a *SB* III, 7243 e *P. Oxy.* XIV, 1774." In J.-M. Carrié and R.L. Testa, eds., *"Humana sapit." Études d'antiquité tardive offertes à Lellia Cracco Ruggini*, 469–73. Bibliothèque de l'antiquité tardive 3. Turnhout: Brepols.

———. 2002b. "L'ascétisme féminin dans l'Égypte Tardive: *Topoi* littéraires et formes d'ascèse." In H. Melaerts and L. Mooren, eds., *Le rôle et le statut de la femme en Égypte hellénistique, romaine et byzantine: Actes du Colloque International, Bruxelles, Leuven 24–29 Novembre 1997*, pp. 355–96. Sterling, VA: Peeters.

———. 2007. "Les formes institutionelles et les formes d'activité économique du monachisme égyptien." In A. Camplani and G. Filoramo, eds., *Foundations of Power and Conflicts of Authority in Late-Antique Monasticism: Proceedings of the International Seminar, Turin, December 2–4, 2004*, pp. 109–54. Louvain: Peeters.

———. 2009. *Moines et communautés monastiques en Égypte (IVe–VIIIe siècles). JJP*, Supplement 11. Warsaw: The Raphael Taubenschlag Foundation, Warsaw University.

———. 2013a. "L'ascétisme féminin dans l'Égypte de l'antiquité tardive: un sujet difficile: Sur un livre de María Jesús Albarrán Martínez." *JJP* 42, pp. 337–52.

———. 2013b. "A Look at the Origins of Monasticism in Egypt from a Geographic Point of View." *Przegląd Humanistyczny* 2, pp. 109–26.

Wissa, H. 1994. *Assiout: The Saga of an Egyptian Family*. Lewes and Sussex: Book Guild.

Wortley, J. 2013. *The Anonymous Sayings of the Desert Fathers*. Cambridge, UK: Cambridge University Press.

Wüstenfeld, F. 1845. *Macrizi's Geschichte der Copten*. Göttingen: Dieterichschen Buchhandlung.

Yaqut al-Hamawi. 1955. *Mu'gham al-buldan*. Vol. 1. Beirut: Dar Sader.

Young, D.W. 1981. "A Monastic Invective against Egyptian Hieroglyphs." In D.W. Young, ed., *Studies Presented to Hans Jakob Polotsky*, pp. 348–60. East Gloucester, MA: Pirtle & Polson.

Youssef, Y.N. 1998–99. "Romanos Melodus in the Coptic Church." *Bulletin of Saint Shenouda the Archmandrite Coptic Society* 5, pp. 41–44.

———. 1999. "Notes on the Traditions concerning the Flight of the Holy Family into Egypt." *Coptic Church Review* 20, no. 2, pp. 48–55.

———. 2003. "Jean, évêque d'Assiut, de Manfalut et d'Abu Tig et ses activités littéraires." *Études Coptes VIII*, ed. C. Cannuyer and G.R. Delahaye, pp. 311–19. CBC 13. Paris: Association francophone de coptologie.

———. 2008. "John, Bishop of Assiut, Manfalut and Abu Tig." *Collectanea Christiana Orientalia* 5, pp. 183–200.

———. 2009a. "Consecration of the Myron at Saint Macarius Monastery." In M.S.A. Mikhail and M. Moussa, eds., *Christianity and Monasticism in Wadi al-Natrun: Essays from the 2002 International Symposium of the Saint Mark Foundation and the Saint Shenouda the Archimandrite Coptic Society*, pp. 106–18. Cairo: The American University in Cairo Press.

———. 2009b. "The Rite of the Consecration of the Church of Koskam." *Ancient Near Eastern Studies* 46, pp. 72–92.

———. 2012. "A New Witness of a Copto-Greek Hymn—Poiekon." *Ancient Near Eastern Studies* 49, pp. 184–201.

———. 2013. "A Graeco-Coptic Ode." *Ephemerides Liturgicae* 127, pp. 226–37.

Youssef, Y.N., and U. Zanetti. 2014. *La consécration du myron par Gabriel IV, 86e patriarche d'Alexandrie, en 1374*. Jerusalemer Theologisches Forum 20. Münster: Aschendorff Verlag.

Zakrzewska, E.D. Forthcoming a. "A 'Bilingual Language Variety' or 'The Language of the Pharaohs'? Coptic from the Perspective of Contact Linguistics." In P. Dils, E. Grossman, T.S. Richter, and W. Schenkel, eds., *Language Contact and Bilingualism in Antiquity: What Linguistic Borrowing into Coptic Can Tell Us about It: Papers Read at the Inaugural Conference of the DDGLC Project, Sächsische Akademie der Wissenschaften zu Leipzig, April 2010*. Lingua Aegyptia Studia Monographica. Hamburg: Widmaier Verlag.

———. Forthcoming b. "Why Did Egyptians Write Coptic? The Rise of Coptic as a Literary Language." In A. Mansour, ed., *Copts and Society: Documentary-historical Studies: Proceedings of the First International Coptic Studies Conference, "Life in Egypt during the Coptic Period: Towns and Villages, Laymen and Clergy, Bishops and Dioceses," Alexandria, 21–23 September 2010*, pp. 227–36. Alexandria: Bibliotheca Alexandrina.

Zanetti, U. 1995. "Bohairic Liturgical Manuscripts." *Orientalia Christiana Periodica* 61, pp. 65–94.

Zeghal, M. 1999. "Religion and Politics in Egypt: The Ulema of al-Azhar, Radical Islam, and the State (1952–94)." *IJMES* 31, no. 3, pp. 371–99.

Zibawi, M. 2003. *Koptische Kunst, das christliche Ägypten von der Spätantike bis zur Gegenwart*. Munich: Schnell & Steiner.

Zoega, G.D. 1810. *Catalogus codicum copticorum manu scriptorum qui in Museo Borgiano velitris adservantur.* Rome: Sacra Congregatio de Propaganda Fide.

Zuckerman, C. 1995. "The Hapless Recruit Psois and the Mighty Anchorite, Apa John." *BASP* 32, pp. 183–94.